A MINOR APOCALYPSE

A MINOR APOCALYPSE

Warsaw during the
First World War

Robert Blobaum

CORNELL UNIVERSITY PRESS   **ITHACA AND LONDON**

This book was published with the generous support of West Virginia University.

First published 2017 by Cornell University Press
Printed in the United States of America

Library of Congress Cataloging-in-Publication Data

Names: Blobaum, Robert, author.
Title: A minor apocalypse : Warsaw during the First World War /
    Robert Blobaum.
Description: Ithaca : Cornell University Press, 2017. | Includes bibliographical
    references and index.
Identifiers: LCCN 2016035605 | ISBN 9781501705236 (cloth : alk. paper) |
    ISBN 9781501707889 (pdf) | ISBN 9781501707872 (epub/mobi)
Subjects: LCSH: Warsaw (Poland)—History—20th century. | World War,
    1914–1918—Social aspects—Poland—Warsaw.
Classification: LCC DK4632 .B55 2017 | DDC 940.3/43841—dc23
LC record available at https://lccn.loc.gov/2016035605

Cornell University Press strives to use environmentally responsible suppliers and materials to the fullest extent possible in the publishing of its books. Such materials include vegetable-based, low-VOC inks and acid-free papers that are recycled, totally chlorine-free, or partly composed of nonwood fibers. For further information, visit our website at www.cornellpress.cornell.edu.

Contents

Preface

"Do books write themselves?" I ask my students every time we begin a discussion of a new monograph. The purpose of this question, now repeated over thirty years of teaching, is to have students explore the personal and professional baggage authors bring to their writing, but the truth of the matter is that every piece of scholarship is a collective, collaborative enterprise. The single author of a monograph is at best a principal investigator who may take both responsibility and credit for the work and certain decisions associated with it, but would never have been in a position to do so without the assistance of many others, including those who have paved the historiographical highway.

The idea for this book was conceived some ten years ago as a much-needed update to the only existing social history of Warsaw during the First World War, Krzysztof Dunin-Wąsowicz's *Warszawa w czasie pierwszej wojny światowej* (1974), which contained valuable data but otherwise lacked any kind of comparative perspective, ignored issues of gender and ethnicity, and was based solely on Polish sources. The original plan was for this study's publication to coincide with the centenary of the outbreak of the Great War. Unfortunately, books do not write themselves, and a series of unplanned yet eventful circumstances led to one postponement after another. When I began my research, literature on the social history of the "Eastern Front" of the First World War was still in its infancy, less than a decade old, though emerging in cutting-edge fashion through the work of Vejas Gabriel Liulevicius on the German-occupied "Ober Ost" (2000), Peter Gatrell on refugees and the socio-economic history of the war in imperial Russia (1999, 2005), and Eric Lohr on the Russian Empire's "enemy aliens" (2003). The same could be said for a new focus on the social and cultural history of the war in major urban centers, particularly for Berlin by Belinda Davis (2000), Vienna by Maureen Healy (2004), Freiburg by Roger Chickering (2008), perhaps inspired—as I was—by the *Capital Cities at War* volumes on London, Paris, and Berlin edited by Jay Winter and Jean-Louis Robert (1997, 2007). Since then, Christoph Mick's book on the experience of war in Lwów (2010), Joshua Sanborn's *Imperial Apocalypse* (2014) on the wartime "decolonization" of the Russian Empire, Jesse Kauffman's *Elusive Alliance* (2015) on the German occupation regime headquartered in Warsaw, and Katarzyna Sierakowska's book on Poland's Great War in personal documents (2015) have appeared, each with direct bearing on my own, despite differing perspectives and frameworks of analysis. They have recently been joined by Marta Polsakiewicz's published dissertation devoted to the policies of the German occupation regime in Warsaw itself.

This and other scholarship on the Great War in the east, not to mention the valuable comments of the two anonymous peer reviewers of the prepublication version of this book for Cornell University Press, have compelled me to link my analysis of everyday life in Warsaw to larger issues. As I have argued in these pages and elsewhere, public if not private memory of the lived experience of the Great War in Warsaw was initially obscured and displaced by its end-point, the achievement of Polish independence in 1918, and then buried under the surfeit of memory connected to the terror, violence, genocide, and physical destruction of the city during the Second World War. My goal to recover and interpret this otherwise diminished suffering of Varsovians from 1914 to 1918 led to the adoption of the ironic title of Tadeusz Konwicki's 1979 psychological novel about the intended self-immolation of a "dissident" writer in communist Poland, *Mała apokalypsa* (*A Minor Apocalypse*), as the most appropriate one for this book.

It soon became clear, however, that in order to justify this study, it was simply not enough to claim that in many respects measures of human suffering in Warsaw during the two wars were broadly comparable. I have had to actually juxtapose the two historical moments according to those areas in which everyday experience was similar, supported by the best available data, and to be clear about where it was not. In turn, comparison of living conditions during the two wars inevitably invited some level of comparison of the two German occupations and my entry into the broader and heated debate about Germany's twentieth-century wars and their relationship to each other. When viewed from the perspective of Warsaw, do Imperial German policies and practices in the occupied east during the first war, as well as interactions with their diverse populations, tell us anything about those of the Nazi occupation regime in the second war? And what about the German relationship to *Ostjuden*, the religious, Yiddish-speaking, unassimilated majority of Warsaw's Jews? Does the road to Auschwitz somehow lead through Warsaw during the Great War in the perceptions and attitudes of the German occupiers toward the metropole's Jewish community?

Even as these concerns became increasingly central, they joined others with which I began my study. Why did so many Varsovians support the Russian cause at the beginning of the war, and what does this say about historians' privileging of nationalism in the conventional understanding of Polish history? How politically and socially destabilizing were the mass migrations in and out of Warsaw during the war years? What were the social and political effects of the inequality of suffering brought on by the collapse of living standards? What institutions emerged to attempt to manage the crisis, and why did they fail to do so? How did the impact of the war contribute to the downward spiral of relations between

Poles and Jews? What role did the war play in women's acquisition of political rights despite no appreciable feminization of Warsaw's labor force? And what can be said about cultural expressions and their sites in wartime Warsaw? Did Warsaw follow European cultural patterns of tacking toward the traditional and the modern simultaneously?

I hope that the attempted answers to these and other questions can begin to fill a yawning historiographical gap, inspire new studies of other cities in central Europe and on the war's Eastern Front, and appeal to both specialist and non-specialist enthusiasts of the First World War. Some may question the November 1918 end date for this book, since Warsaw remained a "city at war" beyond the armistice that formally closed the Great War, as the Polish-Soviet conflict came to its northeastern approaches in the summer of 1920, and basic food and other shortages remained prevalent until 1921. Warsaw's experience was not unique in this regard; the same could be said of other urban centers in the multiple conflicts of postcolonial Central and Eastern Europe. However, the end of the total war between the European Great Powers and the change in state actors had important effects on the kinds, sources, and levels of assistance to Warsaw's still—if slightly less—distressed Polish and Jewish communities. Regime change in the now internationally recognized Polish capital, the end of the British blockade, and the subsequent arrival of food and other aid from the United States were all important factors in this regard, and if they did not fulfill the promise of significant relief from the ongoing ravages of war, then at least they held out greater hope for human endurance. There were continuities from the years of the Great War, of course, which go forward into and beyond 1919 and which deserve our attention. Nonetheless, the discontinuities, not only political but also social, economic, and cultural, are sufficient in number and substance to require years of additional archival research in new locations and are best left to a future study.

As for the archival sources employed in the present work, a brief word is necessary. I have used documents from three collections of German-language source materials but have referred to them according to how they are inventoried in the Warsaw archive that houses them, the Archiwum Główne Akt Dawnych (the Main Archive of Old Documents). For example, the collection "Kaiserlich Deutsches Generalgouvernement Warschau" ("The Imperial German Warsaw General-Government") is rendered in this book in its Polish translation as "Cesarsko-Niemieckie Generał-Gubernatorstwo w Warszawie," which is how those attempting to use it in the future will be able to locate it. I have done the same with the collections of Russian-language documents featured in this study, using the Polish title under which they can be found in the Archiwum Państwowe m. st. Warszawy (State Archive of the Capital City of Warsaw, essentially the Warsaw city archive). Thus, I use "Zarząd Oberpolicmajstra Warszawskiego" instead of "Upravlenie Varshavskogo Politsmastera" ("The Administration of the War-saw Superintendent of Police"). When I cite correspondence between German or Russian officials and other documents from these collections in my text, I will assume that the discerning reader understands that they were composed in German and Russian, not in Polish. The Polish-language documents, on the other hand, come primarily from two locations, the Warsaw municipal archives just mentioned and the Archiwum Akt Nowych (Archive of New Documents).

Ideally, competency in yet a fourth language—Yiddish—would serve well in any analysis of Warsaw and its inhabitants during the Great War. Alas and to my deep regret, it is not one that I possess. However, the Jewish experience in Warsaw can be partially reconstructed on the basis of Polish sources, and in fact, to a certain extent, there is no other choice. The recent festschrift devoted to Antony Polonsky, *Warsaw: The Jewish Metropolis* (2015), to which I contributed, indicates the extent to which those who DO read Yiddish (and Hebrew) use Polish sources to reconstruct that experience, especially before the interwar period. There are several reasons for this. First, although Yiddish was indeed the language of the Jewish street, it was still in the early phase of development as a literary language at the outbreak of the Great War. Legal publications in that language in the Russian Empire became possible only after the Revolution of 1905. When war broke out in 1914, Yiddish-language daily newspapers in Warsaw had just come into existence. At the same time, Jewish secular education employing Yiddish as the language of instruction (as opposed to its use for teaching Hebrew in the *cheder*) did not exist in Warsaw or elsewhere in the Russian Empire before the war. Bernard Singer, whose *Moje Nalewki* (1959) is the best evocation of the sights and sounds of the Jewish street on the eve of the war, could only speak what he called "kitchen Yiddish," and thus he penned his famous memoir in Polish. I will deal with the tremendous obstacles faced by Yiddish-language publications and schools during the war years later in this book. Suffice it to say that the flowering of Yiddish as a literary language and of Yiddish-based Jewish culture more generally occurred after 1918, though the championing of their cause among ordinary Jews owes much to developments during the war years.

In the course of research visits, panel presentations, the submission of chapters and articles, and invited lectures on themes related to this book, I have benefited from many conversations in a community of scholars, many whom I can also count as friends. I am particularly grateful for the questions, insights, comments, and words of encouragement from Laura Engelstein, Katarzyna Sierakowska, Jerzy Jedlicki, Jan Molenda, Seymour Becker, Serge Pukas, Dariusz Stola, Padraic Kenney, Nathaniel Wood, Troy Paddock, Keely Stauter-Halsted, Katherine Jolluck, Małgorzata Fidelis, Brian Porter-Szücs, Beth Holmgren, Edward Wynot,

Neal Pease, Glenn Dynner, François Guesnot, Antony Polonsky, Szymon Rud-nicki, Stefan Lehnstaedt, Jesse Kauffman, Marta Polsakiewicz, Jay Winter, Joshua Sanborn, Dorothee Wierling, Richard Bessel, Alexander Watson, Piotr Szlanta, John Horne, Leonard Smith, Andrew Kier Wise, and Tomasz Pudłocki. To the two anonymous reviewers for Cornell University Press I wish to express my deep appreciation for your considerable efforts to help make this a better book than it otherwise might have been. Some years ago, I was fortunate enough to be awarded a distinguished professorship from the Eberly College of Arts and Sciences at West Virginia University, for which I thank the Eberly family, not only for creating the professorship but for providing the generous annual research funding that comes along with it. I also wish to acknowledge my History Department colleagues Matthew Vester and Joshua Arthurs for organizing and participating in workshops to discuss preliminary products of my research. Special thanks goes to Danuta Jackiewicz, curator of the Iconograph and Photograph Collection of the National Museum in Warsaw, for her extraordinary efforts to help locate images for illustrating this book.

Finally, I have been blessed with the best research assistant in the world, one capable of finding needles in haystacks, especially when those haystacks happen to be Polish libraries and archives. A fellow historian, though of a later war and occupation, Donata came into my life through a stroke of good fortune in the microfilm reading room of the Polish National Library at the very beginning of this project. This history of everyday life in Warsaw during the Great War in its current shape and form is unimaginable without the many contributions of the woman who would become my wife and who adopted my name as her own. Donata Blobaum's touch is particularly evident in the chapters on Polish-Jewish relations, women, and wartime culture. Her willingness to sacrifice her own time and work for the benefit of mine deserves much more than a dedication can hope to impart.

A MINOR APOCALYPSE

Introduction

Some would take it as an omen. On the night of 26–27 July 1914, lightning from a violent thunderstorm struck an ammunition depot at the Warsaw Citadel, igniting a tremendous explosion that awakened many of the city's inhabitants. Journalist and pro-Austrian sympathizer Stanisław Dzikowski, who had been waiting out the storm from the shelter of a midtown café veranda, was reminded of "the beginning of a Sienkiewicz epic."[1] As the storm subsided, several Russian artillery regiments marched through the area, the first manifestations of the coming war witnessed in Warsaw. Dzikowski, for one, hoped that the reality of war would arouse Warsaw from its "impotence" and "passivity," and particularly its cultivation of theater, a "deity" to which all political, social, and cultural life had become subordinate. Of all the major European cities, Dzikowski claimed, Warsaw was the least prepared for war. As the rest of world had been riveted to the unfolding of the Austro-Serbian conflict, "carefree Varsovians had gone on summer vacations."[2]

However we evaluate this depiction of a somnolent and contented Warsaw on the eve of the war from a less-than-neutral observer, the city was stirred to great commotion during the last days of July. The storm contributed to an atmosphere that soon bordered on panic, fed by rumors of an imminent Russian evacuation. Indeed, just two weeks earlier a contingency plan had been distributed within the ranks of the Warsaw police to guide their actions in the event of the approach of the German enemy and the evacuation of Russian troops.[3] The mere prospect of a Russian evacuation was sufficient to promote a run on local commercial banks on 30 July, as city residents began to withdraw their savings and deposits in the wake of Germany's rejection of a British offer of mediation following the partial Russian mobilization of the previous day.[4] In response, the banks closed, leading to a suspension of credit transactions, a shortage of money in circulation, the interruption of wage payments, and a general disruption of commerce. Large crowds filled Warsaw's train stations as families of Russian officials began to flee, while Dzikowski's would-be vacationers returned, many on the Warsaw-Vienna line. The city's hotels quickly filled with individuals and families whose places of residence were in close proximity to the German border and who now sought refuge in the metropolis. En route to their temporary lodgings, they passed by storefronts pasted with red-colored, Russian-language announcements of mobilization.[5] Warsaw's "peace" had most definitely been disturbed, and the war had not even begun.

Did the outbreak of the Great War look and feel different in Warsaw than in London, Paris, Berlin, Vienna, and St. Petersburg? I would argue that it did, for a number of reasons. First, unlike these metropolises, Warsaw entered the war not as a capital city but as the third city of the Russian Empire (after St. Petersburg and Moscow) and as the administrative center of ten Polish provinces under Russian imperial rule, provinces that had originally comprised the autonomous Polish Kingdom following the Congress of Vienna. It was also a city that would immediately come under direct military jurisdiction, which replaced the existing restrictions of emergency rule, themselves a softer version of the martial law imposed at the end of 1905 when Russian imperial authority nearly came unraveled during the peak of that year's revolutionary ferment. Finally, Warsaw was a deeply divided city, especially between its slight Polish majority and substantial Jewish minority.[6] Nonetheless, the city's Polish and Jewish elites, the mainstream press, and the Polish National Democrats, the largest political organization in Warsaw, would support the cause of Russian arms in August 1914 and would remain loyal to the empire until the Russian evacuation of the city a year later. Whether that loyalty was calculated or genuine is debatable. Even if Warsaw did show some of the features of a typical home front over the next weeks and months, it would come to exhibit even more those of a frontline city, one whose distance from the East Prussian border to the north was less than 160 kilometers at the outset of the war. Warsaw would immediately feel this exposure and vulnerability to German forces from the north and west as well as Austro-Hungarian forces from the south, as witnessed in the events that accompanied the war's outbreak.

Warsaw's role as a frontline city ended exactly one year into the war as the front passed through and the city came under German occupation in the first days of August 1915. As the front quickly moved east into the Russian Empire's

Baltic provinces and deep into contemporary Belarus, Warsaw's removal from it soon stretched to four hundred kilometers. For a short time, wounded and convalescing German soldiers in Warsaw's hospitals and parks would have served as visible reminders of the front, as had their Russian counterparts before them, but those sites were made temporarily off-limits to civilian noncombatants until it became more convenient for German troops to recuperate in East Prussia from the fighting in Lithuania. The front may have moved on, but the experiences of the previous August in Warsaw foreshadowed much of what was to come, not only during the war's first year but over the next several years—the crisis and collapse of the urban economy; the creation, expansion, and ultimately failure of institutions involved in the provision of public assistance; the escalation of social and ethnic conflict; the erosion and resetting of gender boundaries; intense cultural debates and conflicts over propriety in wartime—all of which accompanied the larger processes of imperial disintegration and decolonization in East–Central Europe.

Especially in the war's first year, Warsaw was also a city in tremendous flux, one that witnessed massive shifts in population as a consequence of mobilization, evacuations, deportations, and male labor out-migration on the one hand, and the arrival of refugees and wounded soldiers on the other. The situation would settle down somewhat following the establishment of a German occupation regime, particularly after the city had been cleared of its refugees, only to be disturbed again following the Treaty of Brest-Litovsk of March 1918, which formally ended the war on the Eastern Front and led to the return to the city of tens of thousands who, both voluntarily and involuntarily, had been part of the wartime migration to the east.[7] In the meantime, Warsaw's demography had been dramatically if not permanently altered—between men and women, and between Poles and Jews—and these changes had their own consequences for gender and ethnic relations.

After August 1915, Warsaw became first the headquarters of a German General-Government that shared in the occupation of the Polish Kingdom with Austria-Hungary, and then the "capital" of quasi-state entities sponsored by the Central Powers but devoid of real authority and quickly drained of political legitimacy. Preceded by concessions to Polish national sentiment and gestures toward self-government, including the holding of Warsaw's first modern municipal elections in the middle of 1916, these experiments in state-building promoted by General-Governor Hans von Beseler and centered in Warsaw have been favorably contrasted by Jesse Kauffman, Robert Spät, and Marta Polsakiewicz with the ferocity of the Nazi German occupation of Warsaw during the Second World War.[8] However, the abysmal living standards of Warsaw's population during the Great War—mainly the consequence of the German seizure and diversion of resources—differed little from those prevailing among the city's Poles during the second German occupation, nullifying any potential political benefit to be derived from a conciliatory strategy designed to bring central Poland into the imperial German orbit once it lost value as a potential bargaining chip in initiating separate peace negotiations with the Russian Empire in 1916. By the formal end of the war and the handing over of power by the German occupation authorities to forces loyal to Józef Piłsudski on 11 November 1918, the old-new capital city of "Poland" featured scenes more of tragedy than triumph, of incredible hunger and rampant disease suffered in cold homes on streets long vacated by electric power, public transportation, and effective law enforcement. Meanwhile, class and ethnic tensions in the city had reached a boiling point, which the new authorities would struggle to contain.

By the second winter of the war many Varsovians already looked nostalgically on what seemed to be an irretrievably lost past, as their city experienced rapidly escalating incidences of starvation, disease, death, and conflict over the increasingly scarce resources necessary to sustain human life. The title of Tadeusz Konwicki's famous novel from 1979, *Mała apokalipsa* (*A Minor Apocalypse*), serves as an apt if borrowed heading for a study of the impact of the world's first total war on the daily lives of the inhabitants of one of Central Europe's great cities. Overshadowed by the greater horrors of a war yet to come, the *major apocalypse* of devastation and destruction that characterized Warsaw's amply documented experience of the Second World War, the deprivation and desperation marking the existential crisis of Varsovians during the Great War has been largely forgotten. In Warsaw today, one is hard pressed to find any sign or site of public memory that might recall or reflect on the suffering of its citizens during the Great War, even as *minor apocalypse*. This is in stark contrast to the innumerable commemorative plaques, memorials, and monuments devoted to Warsaw's experience of the Second World War that dominate the city's memory culture.

Not surprisingly, the historiography on Warsaw during the Great War is extremely limited, while that devoted more generally to Poland in the First World War occupies little more than a shelf in the stacks of the Warsaw University library. Again, the contrast with the ever-expanding literature on the city's experience of the Second World War couldn't be more striking. Moreover, in the traditional Polish national narrative that has dominated the sparse scholarship on the First World War that does exist, Warsaw figures as little more than the major urban political setting in the larger story of the recovery of an independent Polish state.[9] One glance at the existing Polish-language secondary literature reveals an overwhelming preponderance of outdated titles on the military history of the war, devoted primarily to battles in which Polish Legions participated, along with accounts tracing the activities of political parties and personalities during that period, especially those identified with the struggle for Polish independence.[10] This has been supplemented in recent years by important German- and English-language scholarship on the German occupation regime that established its seat in Warsaw following the Russian evacuation of the city in August 1915.[11] However, inasmuch as Warsaw appears in these studies, it does so mainly as a setting or target of German occupation policy, rather than as a subject worthy of study in its own right.

The only real scholarly treatment of the experience of Warsaw's inhabitants during the Great War is that of Krzysztof Dunin-Wąsowicz published nearly forty years ago.[12] While Dunin-Wąsowicz's focus was directed partly at the material condition of the population and the demographic consequences of the war, his short monograph was descriptive rather than analytical or interpretive and lacked any kind of comparative perspective. Given the time and political context in which it was written, Dunin-Wąsowicz's book also ignored important issues related to class, ethnicity, gender, and culture that have inspired the best recent scholarship of the wartime experience of other capital and major cities. Three years earlier, Dunin-Wąsowicz was also responsible for the publication of the only significant anthology of memoirs on the First World War in Warsaw, which informed and shaped his later study. As the anthology's editor, Dunin-Wąsowicz was able to track down only 132 diaries and memoirs in Warsaw's libraries and archives at the time (from which he selected twenty for inclusion), admitting in his introduction that "Warsaw memoir and diary-writing of the period of the First World War is not as rich and varied" as it is for other historical periods. Particularly in comparison with the Second World War, for which historians by the early 1980s had identified approximately two thousand extant Warsaw memoirs and diaries, this was a dramatic understatement indeed.[13]

The dwarfing of Warsaw's experience during the First World War by the story of recovered independence and to a far greater extent by that of the Second World War is even more visible in the city's monuments. One example here will have to suffice. In 1923, a group of anonymous citizens, inspired by state-sponsored monuments and commemorations originating in Britain and France, placed before the Saxon Palace, then the seat of the Ministry of War, a stone tablet commemorating the unknown Polish soldiers who had fallen during the years 1914–20. This effort at commemoration already conflated two wars, the Great War of 1914–18 and the Polish-Soviet War, not to mention the border wars and armed conflicts with Ukraine, Lithuania, and Germany. Soon enough, the war minister, General Władysław Sikorski, took up the initiative for an official tomb, and of some forty battlefields considered by the ministry for removing and transporting to Warsaw the remains of an unknown soldier, that of Lwów during the Polish-Ukrainian War in eastern Galicja was selected. On 2 November 1925 a twenty-one-gun salute and the lighting of the eternal flame by President Stanisław Wojciechowski accompanied the ceremonial reburial.[14]

The burying of the memory of the Great War, by heaping on it more recent memory, had clearly begun. Moreover, the ministry's decision to use the site of the tomb to honor those who had died fighting for an independent Poland since 1794 contained within it a silence about the majority of Poles who had died fighting in the Great War in the service of the imperial Russian, German, and Austro-Hungarian armies. Of the thirteen battles of the years 1914–18 currently inscribed on tablets at the site in what is now Piłsudski Square, all of them involve Polish legions and brigades that fought—presumably for the idea of an independent Poland—under their own banner but as part of other armies, particularly the Austro-Hungarian and French. If the reality of Pole fighting Pole for the greater part of the First World War, rather than for independence, contradicted the emerging narrative, so too did the collaboration of the Polish political elites with the ruling regimes and occupation authorities, even if those elites were divided in their support of the Entente and Central Powers. This includes those rival political figures now credited through their combined efforts with the restoration and defense of an independent Poland, Józef Piłsudski and Roman Dmowski, to whom statues, squares, and roundabouts have been dedicated in Warsaw.[15]

The thirteen battles featured in Piłsudski Square, therefore, are not representative of Polish fighting during the First World War. However, they are overshadowed by twenty-four battles from late 1918 to 1920, the years of the Soviet-Polish war and of Poland's border wars with its Ukrainian, German, and Lithuanian neighbors, when Polish soldiers were mobilized and fought for a Polish state. The Battle for Lwów, as mentioned, fits this category, and the selection of one of its battlefields, Gródek Jagielloński, over dozens of others for the removal of the remains of an unknown soldier was not accidental. General Sikorski had commanded troops there in fending off a bloody Ukrainian siege in January 1919.[16] The wars of 1918–20, too, would be subsequently dwarfed after 1945 by the seventy-three inscriptions commemorating the land, naval, and air battles of the Second World War in which Polish forces participated, along with the sites where Polish prisoners of war were murdered in Soviet captivity. They would also be bracketed by fifty-two "battles" prior to 1914, including terrorist attacks on Russian soldiers and officials during the revolutionary years of 1904–8. Thus, of the 162 battles featured at Poland's Tomb of the Unknown Soldier, approximately 45% are dedicated to the Second World War, 32% to the period 972–1914, 15% to the wars of 1918–20, and only 8% to the years of the Great War—again, none of which commemorate the thousands of Polish soldiers who died in the service of imperial armies. Ironically, Poland's amnesia about the First World War is shared by Russia, where it has been treated as backdrop to revolution and civil war and is overshadowed by the Great Patriotic War of 1941–45.[17]

"Commemorations," according to Michel Rolph-Trouillot, "impose a silence on events they ignore and fill that silence with narratives of power about the event they celebrate."[18] Whatever the intentions of the Warsaw citizens and their homemade tablet in 1923, the state-driven narrative at the Tomb of the Unknown Soldier is about the state, and those who fought and died for it for nearly a millennium. The tomb embraces accompanying themes of victimization and martyrdom while excluding and trivializing what ill fits the conceptual framework shaping its creation and evolution. The effective silencing of Polish military casualties during the Great War is not the result of conspiracy or even political consensus. Instead, its roots are structural. This memory structure is also reflected in Warsaw's larger monumental landscape, which in its few references to the First World War emphasizes its outcome—namely, independent Poland—at the expense of its actual course.

One can hardly expect military cemeteries, even symbolic ones like the Tomb of the Unknown Soldier, to commemorate noncombatants of any era, yet as Katrin Van Cant has shown in her analysis of the nearly eighty open-air monuments erected in Warsaw between 1989 and 2009, the emphasis on the heroes of recent Polish military history and particularly those of the Second World War is similarly pronounced in the city's streets.[19] Thirty percent of these monuments are directly related to the Second World War, the majority of which commemorate the Home Army and the Warsaw Uprising. By comparison, only 6.5% of the new statues refer to the First World War, and all of these are in reference to the restoration of an independent Polish state. "The most natural explanation for this," according to Van Cant, "is that in Polish national memory, this war, despite the terrific human and material losses on the Polish side between 1914 and 1918, mainly has a positive connotation, because of its outcome."[20] In other words, the Great War does not easily fit the dominant narrative told by Warsaw's monuments (any more than it did the Tomb of the Unknown Soldier) "of Poland and the Polish people as victims of their history, nevertheless always displaying an indestructible will to fight for the existence and freedom of the nation."[21] As Van Cant explains, "Warsaw as the capital fulfills the role of visiting card to the entire country," and the narrative delivered by its monuments is firmly focused on the history of the middle of the twentieth century "because it was extremely traumatic and [because] the scars inflicted by those events are still very fresh in the national consciousness."[22]

If we compare the two wars outside of the framework of public commemoration and memorialization, however, we begin to see greater symmetry between them in terms of suffering, at least for the city's Polish population prior to the outbreak of the Warsaw Uprising in the summer of 1944. Official daily food rations, for example, were relatively similar if we omit those assigned to the inhabitants of the Warsaw Ghetto during the second war. As we shall see, during the First World War those rations steadily declined, dipping below 900 calories for adults by the spring of 1918. During the Nazi German occupation they fluctuated wildly, particularly in 1941 when they ranged between 385 calories for Polish adults in May as mass numbers of German troops were transferred to central Poland in anticipation of Operation Barbarossa, and 981 calories at the end of that year when most of these troops were deep inside Soviet territory. By that time Jews received far less than half the daily rations assigned to Poles. From there the trend, if anything, was upward for the latter, reaching a high of 1,377 daily calories in October 1943 before falling again to 807–959 calories during the first six months of 1944.[23]

During the period of Nazi rule in the city, the actual caloric content available through ration cards was at least 20% less than the official allotment. Regardless, if people were forced to rely on ration cards alone, according to Tomasz Szarota, it "would have led to general death by starvation in the occupied city," as indeed it did in the Warsaw Ghetto before the great deportations of the second half of 1942.[24] The same could be said for Warsaw during the Great War, when rationed bread was also baked with as much sawdust as flour. In both global conflicts, black markets, smuggling, and the corruption of the German occupying forces— soldiers and civilians—allowed Varsovians access to food not otherwise available, even at rapidly inflating prices. As a consequence, the average daily caloric intake for the Christian population in mid-1943 actually may have ranged from 2,300 to 2,650 calories, or double the official rations, while smuggling and the black market may have satisfied 70–80% of the nutritional needs of the city's Poles during the Nazi occupation. Most revealing, however, is that Polish boys' weights and heights in Warsaw remained relatively constant between 1930 and 1943, evidence that of the many travails of the Nazi occupation, severe malnutrition may not have been chief among them.[25]

In many Polish narratives of the Second World War, food smugglers are portrayed as practically heroic figures and are regarded with respect and gratitude for preventing hunger from turning into starvation.[26] However, the very word "szmugler" first appeared and became widespread in the Polish language during the Great War, and while the role of the smuggler in bringing food from the countryside into the city at a profit was basically the same during the two wars, the smuggler's reputation was far more negative in the first.[27] There are several reasons for this difference. First, the smuggler was less effective in meeting the food needs of Warsaw's population during the Great War and proved unable to make up the difference between the rationed calories and those calories needed to fend off malnutrition for a far greater percentage of Varsovians. Significantly, children's weights and heights did not remain constant but fell during the years of the Great War. The role of the German occupier is significant here. Corruption among the Germans during the Great War was certainly widespread, but there was at least some effort to combat smuggling and to disrupt black-market trading. Supplies of basic foodstuffs coming into Warsaw also appear to have been far more tightly controlled during the first war. During the Second World War, German corruption and participation in the black market were far more fundamental to their operation than during the Great War. "Corruption permeated the whole administrative hierarchy" of the Nazi occupation regime from the very beginning, according to Jan Tomasz Gross, and became "the single most characteristic social phenomenon" of the occupation whereby "everyone undertaking an economic initiative had to become a speculator."[28]

If speculation was ubiquitous enough to become a morally justifiable feature of Polish society during the Second World War, both speculation and smuggling during the Great War were associated in the Polish imagination almost exclusively with Jews. Cast as yet another exploitative speculator, the Jewish smuggler of the First World War could only become an object of scorn rather than of gratitude, even if the food made available through that smuggler's activities, in spite of what appears to have been greater obstacles, also saved lives. During the Great War, there are many tales of Germans boarding trains and seizing food brought in from the countryside on commuter and suburban lines. A generation later, smugglers used those same lines with far less interference.

There was yet another reason why the Germans turned a blind eye toward smuggling and black marketeering of food during the Second World War, namely, their need for a relatively healthy Polish labor force *inside the city*. During the first year of the Great War, when the Russians still controlled the city, factory employment collapsed in Warsaw, and it never recovered. For their part, the Germans placed far greater emphasis on recruiting labor for employment in the Reich than on restoring and developing local industry following their takeover of the city in 1915. During the Second World War, factory production was severely crippled at the outset as well, mainly as a result of the German bombing campaign, and in December 1939 employment in Warsaw's industrial sector stood at 24% of the prewar level, a percentage roughly equal to that which prevailed in the middle of the Great War. However, industrial employment in Warsaw recovered to 78% of the prewar level by October 1941, and increased employment also translated into greater access to food, whether through a factory canteen or through "unofficial income" derived from the sale of pilfered items from the factory.[29] In both wars, the rate of inflation of living costs far outstripped any increases in nominal wages; however, at least during the Second World War, a far greater proportion of Varsovians were paid wages, even if their purchasing power continued to erode.

Thus, in these two significant areas—access to food and paid employment—Christian Poles in Warsaw may well have been better off during the Second World War than during the Great War. Other comparisons are possible as well. Warsaw's population losses between 1914 and 1918 and again between the end of 1939 and the end of 1943 (before the Warsaw Uprising) are roughly similar, which means that despite the round-up of over eighty-six thousand city residents for labor in the Reich during the Second World War,[30] the Polish population of the city remained relatively stable. The main factors in the city's demographic decline during the Second World War up to the Warsaw Uprising in the summer of 1944 were the deaths and deportations of hundreds of thousands of Jews in 1942. During the First World War, labor out-migration of Polish males, first to Russia and then to Germany, was the principal cause of Warsaw's population loss. In sharp contrast to the Second World War, the Jewish population of Warsaw remained much more stable than and actually grew in proportion to the Christian population during the First World War.[31]

Between 1938 and 1942, the marriage rate among Warsaw's Poles fell by one-third and the birth rate by 20–30% (by 50% for Jews). For the years of the Great War, the decline in marriage and birthrates was even steeper, both at around 50% for the population as a whole.[32] During the Second World War, infant mortality among Poles in Warsaw increased by 20% (33% for Jews by the first half of 1941); during the Great War, infant mortality more than doubled among the general population. The death rate among Poles due to "natural causes" nearly doubled between 1938 and 1942 (and was ten times higher for Jews); during the Great War the non-infant-mortality rate tripled.[33] During both wars mortality caused by tuberculosis tripled, constituting approximately 30% of all Polish deaths by 1942 and a similar proportion among Warsaw's general population by the end of 1917.[34] During the Nazi occupation, deaths exceeded births four times over in 1941 and even more in 1942, primarily because of rapidly deteriorating conditions in the Warsaw Ghetto.[35] Yet among Poles during the Great War, deaths exceeded births by a factor of three by the middle of 1917.

It was also easier to get around Warsaw during the Second World War, even if one risked capture in a round-up and shipment off to Germany or elsewhere for forced labor. Buses, taxis, and automobiles quickly disappeared due to military requisitioning and the shortage of gasoline. By 1944 the rickshaw had become the chief mode of private transportation. However, trolleys remained the chief mode of public transportation, and service was restored quickly after the considerable damages caused by the September 1939 bombing campaign. Trolley cars may have been overcrowded in the absence of buses and the reservation of front sections for Germans, but at least they moved Varsovians through their city. One trolley even ran in the Ghetto.[36] During the Great War, Warsaw became a city on foot as both private and public vehicular transportation had ceased entirely by the middle of 1917, while its residents were less likely to have shoes—even wooden—to traverse their streets.

The one aspect of daily life where Varsovians in the Great War appear to have had a clear advantage over their counterparts of the Second World War was in the area of housing. During the Second World War, destruction of housing stock during the September campaign, evictions of tens of thousands from their apartments to make way for Germans, and the removal of entire Jewish communities into Warsaw before their deportation to the death camps created an acute housing crunch. In the Ghetto, per-room density increased from 2.9 people at the end of 1940 to 5.5 by the middle of 1942, according to reports of the Warsaw Judenrat. Reliable housing data for the Polish population is more difficult to come by, but three people living in a one-room apartment appears to have been the norm.[37] During the Great War, the Russian evacuation and labor out-migration depressed the housing market. Per-room occupancy throughout the city actually declined from 2.25 at the beginning of the war (then among the highest in Europe) to 1.83 in January 1917, and rents fell by a similar degree.[38] In both wars, shortages of electricity and gas occurred periodically, though they were more severe and longer-lasting during the first and last years of the Great War. Again, the Warsaw Ghetto constitutes a case of its own as supplies of gas and electricity were first reduced and diverted to the "Aryan" (i.e., Christian) side before being cut off entirely in October 1941.

The purpose of these comparisons (and more will appear throughout this book) is not to downplay the suffering of Poles, and most especially Jews, during the Nazi occupation. The savagery and violence that characterized everyday life in Warsaw during the Second World War was unprecedented. Dunin-Wąsowicz attributes 700,000 deaths in the city (this from a prewar population of 1.3 million) from 1939 to 1945 to the direct consequences of war and occupation: 160,000 to military activities, 430,000 to murder and extermination, 45,000 to prisons and camps, 52,000 to forced labor, and 13,000 to "other causes." These do not include the 180,000 "natural" deaths, 92,000 of which occurred in the Warsaw ghetto and were premeditated. All comparisons, moreover, crumble into irrelevance after the outbreak of the Warsaw Uprising in August 1944 and the leveling of the city. Nonetheless, what I have attempted to demonstrate is that up to the Warsaw Uprising, one's chances of avoiding a "natural" death in Warsaw's "Aryan" side during the Nazi occupation may actually have been slightly better than during the imperial German occupation of the entire city during the First World War.

This suffering, too, deserves to be remembered, but first it must be retrieved from the available sources before it can be reconstructed. That in itself is a problem.

The recording of history, as Jan Assmann has argued, is accompanied by forgetting and suppression "by way of manipulation, censorship, destruction, circumspection, and substitution."[39] According to Trouillot, "[Sources] privilege some events over others, not always the ones privileged by the actors. . . . Silences are inherent in the creation of sources, the first moment of historical production."[40] If, as Trouillot claims, "history is the fruit of power" and "in history, power begins at the source,"[41] what can be said of the sources available for an examination of the everyday lives of ordinary Varsovians during the First World War?

Let us begin with the archival evidence. Working with spotty and incomplete evidence is familiar to all historians working on Poland before the Second World War, making it difficult to recover the voices of the poor and marginalized without teasing out people's experiences by reading between the lines. However, this problem and its challenges are even more pronounced for the period of the First World War. As noted, Warsaw was under Russian rule during the first year of the war until early August 1915, after which the city came under German occupation. The documents written and compiled by these political authorities, whether Russian or German, obviously reflect a certain perspective, if not always from the top, then from various ranks of administrations concerned primarily with the preservation of order and control. Seldom do we hear from those who are the subjects of these documents, except when they offer resistance to or come under suspicion of the authorities. The most significant archival collection of Russian administration for the first year of the war, the files of the Warsaw Superintendent of Police, demonstrates a preoccupation with requisitioning and evacuation, along with ungrounded fears of Jewish espionage on behalf of the Central Powers. No attention is paid to the steady deterioration of living standards caused by the war and requisitioning, at least in the documents available to us. And what is available to us represents only a small fraction of the written record, since many documents were deliberately destroyed during the Russian evacuation, while others were transported from Warsaw, never to return. Thus, what have survived are fragments, such as the files of the requisitions commission for Warsaw's fourth precinct,[42] which historians may take as representative—at least for a particular process.

The documents of the German occupation authorities in Warsaw fared no better—in fact, even worse. Again, there was purposeful destruction. The majority of the most important and secret documents from the Warsaw governor-general's office were burned in November 1918, as described in the memoirs of Bogdan Hutten-Czapski, the principal "Polish expert" of Governor-General Hans von Beseler.[43] Nevertheless, some 980 volumes were preserved, as were those of the chief of administration, and deposited in the Archiwum Akt Nowych (AAN), newly founded in 1919. Following the German invasion of 1939, these documents were packed off in their entirety to the Potsdam Reichsarchiv, where they also went up in flames in 1945 as a consequence of Allied bombing. Meanwhile, fragments from Beseler's personal collection had been preserved by his family and were transferred after the Second World War to the German federal archive in Koblenz. Some were reproduced on microfilm and in photocopies and returned to Poland. Today, some thirty-six files as well as fragments from fifteen others, only a tiny fraction of what had once existed, are available to researchers at the Archiwum Główny Akt Dawnych (AGAD).[44] These consist primarily of Beseler's reports to the kaiser, the quarterly reports of the chief of administration, and a small number of announcements, declarations, orders, and petitions. The collection of the Imperial German Presidium of Police in Warsaw contains only a few random documents that are practically useless, since it is difficult to place them in larger contexts.

Nonetheless, the available German documents, taken as a whole, reveal something more about living conditions in Warsaw during the war than do the Russian documents, perhaps because the political implications of those conditions grew as the war continued. Official quarterly reports, for example, discuss the refugee crisis the Germans encountered upon entering Warsaw, high inflation and unemployment, threats to public health, tensions in Polish-Jewish relations, fraternization of German troops with Polish women, and especially issues related to the food supply—its control and distribution and associated activities such as smuggling. Appendices to the reports of the chief of administration contain particularly valuable statistical data on various diseases and levels of employment. What is striking, however, is the absence of references in these documents to the political situation in Warsaw, perhaps because those were precisely the kinds of documents that were purposefully burned in November 1918.

In an early report from the fall of 1915, Beseler claimed that one of his main tasks was "to contain or deflect political propaganda" for independence.[45] To do so, the German occupation regime first permitted cultural expressions of Polish (and Jewish) national sentiment and, as the war continued and the Russians failed to sue for peace, political expressions as well, some of which became institutionalized in the course of 1916 and 1917. Among them was the Provisional State Council (Tymczasowy Rada Stanu—TRS), a consultative body formed to work with German and Austrian authorities to design state institutions in the occupied Polish Kingdom. Before it was replaced by one of those institutions, the Regency Council, the TRS lasted some seven and a half months, from 14 January to 31 August 1917. It is estimated that more than 25% of its archive survived the Second World War, a far higher percentage than that of its successor. Both of these collections then, as now, were located in Warsaw's AAN, which itself lost 97% of its archive by the end of the Nazi occupation.[46] Whereas one is hard-pressed to find references to the political situation in the German documentary collections housed in Warsaw-based repositories, politics appears to have been a primary concern of the TRS, whose files reveal a careful monitoring of the Warsaw press, both legal and underground, thanks to which we have some evidence of incidents of unrest—food riots and student strikes in May 1917, demonstrations and political vandalism following the arrest of Józef Piłsudski in July 1917. However, such documents afford us only fleeting and fragmentary glimpses into the daily struggles of ordinary Varsovians to endure and survive the First World War, and these through lenses trained on other objects.

The best view of those struggles from the archives, at least for the first twenty-one months of the war, is contained in the minutes of the meetings of the Warsaw Citizens Committee, originally a nongovernmental organization (NGO) formed at the beginning of the war with imperial Russian approval in order to assist the Russian authorities in dealing with the war's economic and social side-effects on the Warsaw home front. As the war continued and the needs of Warsaw's inhabitants mounted, the committee became the main welfare organization in the city. Following the Russian evacuation, the committee's executive branch was transformed into the Warsaw City Administration and, nine months later, the committee was dissolved in anticipation of elections for a new municipal council.

The protocols of the meetings of the committee and its presidium are available in the Warsaw city archive.[47] Even though the municipal archive was completely destroyed during the Second World War, copies of the minutes of the Warsaw Citizens Committee were preserved by individuals to whom they had been distributed, which enabled the reconstitution of this collection after 1945. These minutes are quite detailed and demonstrate how the committee's responsibilities expanded in conjunction with the needs of the city and its population. From concerns about the city's unemployed, waves of refugees, energy supplies, and price ceilings in the early months of the war to the provisioning of public kitchens, food rationing, preventing the spread of infectious diseases, and drafting an electoral ordinance during the first year of the German occupation, the challenges facing the committee are well documented. However, while the committee's discussions of the reports of its sections and subsections appear in the minutes, they are abbreviated, while the reports themselves—which would provide an even closer view of everyday life on the ground—are not available. Thus, what we often see is in the aggregate—the number of refugees sheltered or meals served in public kitchens over a particular period—instead of the specific. Far less complete are the archives of the committee's successor organizations, the Warsaw City Administration and the Warsaw City Council, although what is available provides evidence of financially strapped city institutions trying to make ends meet while dealing with an implacable occupier and growing urban unrest, including a strike of municipal employees.[48] Basically, the documentary evidence is far more robust for the first year of the war, when Warsaw remained under Russian rule and before the Warsaw Citizens Committee and its sections were transformed into organs of self-government, than in the last three-plus years when the general economic crisis experienced by the city's inhabitants gradually became an existential catastrophe.

Indeed, a similar imbalance can be noted in a reading of the mass-circulation press, the principal chronicler of everyday life. The difference can be explained by censorship, whose constraints were fewer under the Russians than the Germans. In part, this was because Warsaw's Polish-language daily press, by and large, was emphatically pro-Russian, as were the city's elites. Greater press freedom was also a consequence of the Russian Revolution of 1905, which led to a veritable explosion of newspapers and periodicals in Warsaw, including those in Yiddish and Hebrew. Compared to its Polish counterpart, the Jewish-language(s) press in Warsaw was viewed with far greater suspicion by the Russian government during the first year of the war, which led to a great deal of self-censorship. All publishing in Yiddish and Hebrew was then banned entirely as the Russians prepared their evacuation from the city in the summer of 1915.[49] While reporting on the situation at the front, especially as it drew closer to Warsaw in the fall of 1914 and again in the summer of 1915, was largely taboo, the Polish-language press in Warsaw remained free to express itself on practically everything else, including the now perennial "Jewish question." Through featured sections titled "Z miasta" ("From the City"), dailies such as the long-standing and conservative *Kurjer Warszawski*, with its close ties to the city's political and cultural elites,[50] as well as the more liberal *Nowa Gazeta*, representative of Warsaw's assimilated Jewish community, were able to offer relatively clear snapshots of how the city's residents sought to negotiate the hardships of the war's first year, although the accompanying commentary reflected the biases of the journalists and editors.

This situation was reversed under the Germans, who were well aware of the politically destabilizing effects of the ever-deteriorating living conditions in the city, to which their policies of requisitioning and control of resources were the main contributing factors. Thus, reporting on those conditions and their consequences became increasingly taboo, particularly following the establishment of preventive censorship on 25 September 1915, which specifically targeted "all rumors, news and commentaries about the decisions of the occupation authorities, whether civil or military" and "all articles about incidents, accidents, epidemics and poverty."[51] While some circumvention of the censor was possible, the issues had to appear politically innocuous to avoid scrutiny. One will, therefore, find no mention of Warsaw's major food riots of June 1916 and May 1917 in the officially registered Warsaw daily press—a most dramatic instance of silencing. What we know about these riots comes from other sources—a list of ransacked grocery stories subsidized and administered by the city that *Nowa Gazeta* and other legal dailies intended but were never able to publish, as well as accounts published in the clandestine press. Interestingly, even in a media outlet whose self-proclaimed goal was "to provide information that could not otherwise appear in the Warsaw press," news about the May 1917 riots appeared in its back pages, this despite the fact that looting had lasted an entire day.[52]

As if in compensation, the German occupation authorities were more than willing to permit public expressions of Polish national pride in commemorations, the most significant being the 1916 celebrations of the 125th anniversary of the Constitution of 3 May 1791, and in the press commentary leading up to them. Particularly welcome were discussions of events in Polish history that had an anti-Russian flavor, such as the 1794, 1830, and 1863 uprisings. There was another form of venting, however, that proved even more valuable to the Germans. After an initial attempt to put a lid on public expressions of Polish-Jewish hostility in order to prevent disturbances in the rear of their armies, as the war continued the German authorities gradually began to lift the ban in order to release steam from frustrations built up by their own policies. By the end of the war, the vitriol in Polish-Jewish press polemics in Warsaw matched that of the last years of Russian rule.[53]

The point here is that over the course of the war, as everyday struggles in Warsaw literally became a matter of life and death, the Warsaw press moved away from those struggles in its coverage. One might blame the German censor in the case of the legal press, but the issues of malnutrition and starvation were not a priority of the uncensored "independent" press, even when the result of the collapse of living standards was food rioting. Similarly, starvation did not make it to the front pages of the Polish underground press during the Second World War, perhaps because Jews rather than Poles were its principal victims.[54] During the Great War the Warsaw press, whether Polish or Jewish, legal or illegal, was likewise preoccupied by other issues, and frequently with one another.

This leaves us with personal correspondence, memoirs, diaries, and travelers' accounts, often categorized by contemporary historians as "ego-documents." Does autobiographical writing, in which the "I" is always present in the text as the describing subject, bring us any closer than other source materials to the "authentic" experiences of ordinary Varsovians during the years of the Great War? Widespread illiteracy and semiliteracy among Warsaw's lower classes before the Great War made it difficult if not impossible for their members to express themselves in writing, and thus it is necessary to seek out and find other evidence of their concerns and frustrations, which may have been given voice by others but were often politicized in the process. Do the ego-documents that survived the flames of 1944 and 1945 or were composed thereafter tell us a story different from that told by other sources, reflecting the perspective of those whose main concern was their next meal rather than the politics of nation- and state-building?

Let us take the example of the personal accounts compiled and edited by Krzysztof Dunin-Wąsowicz for his previously mentioned anthology, especially since it has remained from the time of its publication in 1971 the first place students and scholars turn for an initiation into these kinds of ego-documents. From a total of 132 diaries and memoirs then located in Warsaw's archives and libraries, three-quarters of which had already been previously published, the editor selected twenty to excerpt for his anthology and only three from previously unpublished manuscripts. Despite its claim to represent a cross-section of perspectives, Dunin-Wąsowicz's selection of the twenty authors displays a clear bias in favor of political activists and journalists from the male Polish intelligentsia. According to Dunin-Wąsowicz, of the then-known published and unpublished diaries and memoirs from which he made his selections, only twenty were written by women, or 14% of the total.[55] By taking excerpts from only two women for his anthology, Dunin-Wąsowicz further reduced their proportion to 10%, despite Warsaw's pronounced demographic feminization during the war. Even here, however, the editor appears to have been begging rather than choosing to include women who are represented by authors with ties to the radical-left ancestors of the communist regime that ruled Poland at the time of the anthology's publication in 1971.

It is also important to note that Dunin-Wąsowicz's anthology appeared a mere three years after the Polish communist regime's 1968 "anti-Zionist" campaign, a purging of Jews from the state bureaucracy, party apparatus, and the larger Polish society. Excerpts from the memoirs of two assimilated Jews—those of Maria Kamińska (whose actual name was Maria Eiger) and the journalist Aleksander Kraushar—do make an appearance, but their authors' ancestry remains unacknowledged. Wartime Warsaw thus appears in the anthology as ethno-religiously homogeneous and without a single mention of Polish-Jewish relations, the defining issue of local politics, especially following the Warsaw municipal council elections in 1916. In any case, neither individual can be taken as a representative of Jewish Warsaw, one of whose tribunes, later the co-founder and director of the YIVO Institute for Jewish Research, Dunin-Wąsowicz chose to ignore. I am referring to Noah Prylucki (1882–1941) and his speeches delivered as an elected delegate to the Warsaw City Council.[56] Editor of the Yiddish-language daily newspaper *Der moment* and, following the Russian evacuation in 1915, founder and leader of the Jewish "Folkist" party, Prylucki was also an experienced and talented attorney who published his speeches in the Polish language of their delivery in 1920. These speeches contain valuable ego-documents in the form of depositions and personal testimonies that Prylucki read verbatim at city council sessions in support of his many motions and countermotions, and to document the growing impoverishment of the Jewish community in the face of discrimination from Polish municipal officials and institutions.

The absence of women and Jews from Dunin-Wąsowicz's anthology is mirrored in the city's larger memory culture. Both groups, as Van Cant shows in her study, are considerably underrepresented in Warsaw's public monuments. At late as 2009 and before the opening of the POLIN Museum of the History of Polish Jews, only three of Warsaw's standing monuments commemorated Jews, all of them directly related to the Second World War and the Holocaust, of which only one was erected after 1989 in the distant suburb of Falenica. Women came off slightly better, with four new monuments since 1989, raising the total to seven, which honor "the fighting (and caring) woman and first-class patriot."[57] Primarily viewed as noncombatants during the First World War, no Jews or women are remembered for that period.

The two most important wartime diaries published since Dunin-Wąsowicz's anthology, both of them edited by Jerzy Pajewski, have done little to rectify this imbalance. The first belongs to Stanisław Dzierzbicki, published in 1983.[58] A civil engineer by training, Dzierzbicki was a dedicated public servant who during the war years became involved in the provision of relief and assistance to noncombatants, most significantly as the president of the Supervisory Council of the Main Welfare Organization, or Rada Główna Opiekuńcza, after which he became a member of the Provisional State Council in January 1917. However, little of the mundane is featured in his diary, which instead narrates its author's political involvements, despite its editor's claim that Dzierzbicki's observations of the mood of "Polish society" (essentially, landowners and different circles of the Polish intelligentsia) comprised the most interesting and valuable part of the journal.

Pajewski was also responsible for bringing out the diary of Princess Maria Lubomirska, wife of Zdzisław Lubomirski, arguably the most important Polish political figure in Warsaw during the war. There is no question that Lubomirska's wartime diary makes for fascinating reading, with its recording of rumors, its repetition of stereotypes, its reports from a Red Cross hospital, and its empathy for the travails of her husband, who began the war as the respected head of the Warsaw Citizens Committee and ended it as a perceived and compromised collaborator of the occupying Central Powers because of his key role in the ill-fated Regency Council.[59] Yet Lubomirska's perspective came from the salon and, though rendered in the feminine voice, was focused primarily on the "important" men who frequented it. When she encountered the street it was literally from above, as she observed soldiers, refugees, and crowds (or, as she was apt to put it, "waves," "hordes," and "wild people") below the window of the couple's palatial urban residence. By the end of the war, she feared entering the street entirely and became something of a shut-in, anticipating imminent attacks from revolutionaries and Jews.

Finally, there are the travelers' accounts, three of which appear in Dunin-Wąsowicz's anthology, and one of which is conspicuous by its absence. All three of Dunin-Wąsowicz's travelers are Polish dignitaries and intellectuals from Krakow. The keenest eyes and ears belong to the historian Stanisław Kutrzeba, after the war rector of Jagiellonian University and president of the Polish Academy of Science, who came to Warsaw in 1916 to participate in the celebration of the 125th anniversary of Poland's Constitution of 3 May, the most symbolic of the German concessions to Polish national sentiment.[60] A different traveler's account altogether is that of S. Ansky, the penname of the assimilated Russian Jewish writer, politician, and folklorist Solomon Zanvel Rappoport, whose account of the war on the Eastern Front was not translated from Yiddish until this century.[61] Best known for his classic play *The Dybbuk*, Ansky spent a month at the end of 1914 in Warsaw en route to Russian-occupied territory in Austrian Galicja. Though Ansky's time in Warsaw was also limited, he was an acute and vividly articulate observer of the city's feverish state as thousands of wounded soldiers and predominantly Jewish refugees, forcibly removed from their homes by the Russian Army, poured into the city. Awaiting a means to reach his ultimate destination, Ansky was temporarily thrust into the role of assisting in the setting up of emergency medical and food-distribution centers. For all of the light it throws on a metropolis that was breathing "with the hot gasping of a man with a deadly disease," Ansky's record of his brief encounter with wartime Warsaw suffers from some of the same problems as those of other travelers in that it offers a snapshot rather than a panorama, of a particular moment in time, with limited knowledge of local conditions. Like Kutrzeba, Ansky resided at the Hotel Europejski, the most exclusive in Warsaw, which also limited his field of vision.

Unfortunately, there has not been a concerted effort at the Polish national or state level—as has occurred in Germany, France, the United Kingdom, and elsewhere—to solicit, recover, and collect ego-documents related to the experience of the First World War. This is in stark contrast to the public campaign that accompanied the launching of the Museum of the Warsaw Uprising in 2004 to retrieve ego-documents and other personal and family memorabilia. Thus, few jewels remain to be discovered in the archives, and one of them has already been excerpted at length in Dunin-Wąsowicz's anthology, that of Franciszek Herbst, who served as secretary of the Labor Section of the Warsaw Citizens Committee and continued his employment in the Warsaw City Administration following the committee's dissolution in 1916. The entirety of Herbst's unpublished memoir is located in the Warsaw City Archives and is unique in the immediacy, breadth, and detail of its observations. Herbst also covered the entire war, didn't have any visible political ax to grind, and viewed social conditions in Warsaw from a variety of different vantage points. The reporting and accounting functions that Herbst performed in his various posts, as well as his contacts with counterparts in other sections and departments of the Warsaw Citizens Committee and city administration, are evident in the quantitative particulars contained in his manuscript. Herbst's eye for detail also embraced the social and political side-effects of the collapse of living standards, which are reported in a matter-of-fact fashion with little embellishment. Herbst's perspective on the war comes from the middle ranks of the municipal bureaucracy and reveals much about the experiences of ordinary Varsovians, but almost entirely in the aggregate.

The list of ego-documents discussed here is far from exhaustive, but it is sufficiently representative for us to address their value as registers of everyday life in Warsaw during the First World War. Can they, more than police documents or reports in the daily press, come any closer to relating the quotidian reality of wartime as experienced by the majority of Varsovians, whether Polish or Jewish? I think that the answer to this question is no, because unfortunately ordinary Varsovians did not leave behind ego-documents from which we can hear their voices. They did not spend the war in a residence on Krakowskie Przedmieście, in a room at the Hotel Europejski, in a newspaper editor's office, in a lecture hall at Warsaw University, in an underground political cell, or as a department head in the city administration. The authors of ego-documents that do exist, just like those of other source materials, at best may offer themselves as mediators of those voices, but that is all. In the case of ordinary Varsovians, their actions do speak louder than their words, which remain silent, but those actions also come down to us through mediated channels, interpreted, misinterpreted, and reinterpreted. The challenge for historians in dealing with ego-documents, as with all documents, is to take them for what they are, sources that are useful but inevitably flawed, and sources that have contributed to a narrative and memorialization of the Great War in Warsaw that largely exclude women, Jews, children, the elderly, and most ironically, Varsovians themselves.

Professional historians, of course, are also mediators between the past and the present, ones who nonetheless enjoy the benefit of hindsight and access to a broader range of source materials, previous scholarship, and comparative perspectives. However, even with these advantages, historians are also more than capable of participating in myth-making and sanitization, of shaping and reshaping conceptual frameworks that determine what is important to prospective consumers of their work and what is effectively silenced, despite their belief in scientific inquiry and their ability to set aside their own preferences and stakes.[62] To tell the story of the wartime experiences of ordinary Varsovians who lack their own voice in the public record and archives, I have necessarily been forced to read between the lines and to interpret actions reported by others while trying to remain conscious of my own possible participation in the distortion of history and in the neglect of alternative narratives, particularly those rendered in Yiddish, for which I have attempted to compensate, for example, by using the Polish-language versions of *Der moment* (published by the Folkists under the title *Głos Żydowski—The Jewish Voice*) and *Dos yidishe vort* (published by the Orthodox Union as *Słowo Żydowskie—The Jewish Word*).[63] In the existing literature, the war's impact on Warsaw's noncombatants has served, at best, as backdrop to the recovery of Polish state independence or to the failure of the policies and strategies of imperial actors. In bringing the story of ordinary Varsovians to the forefront, I have tried to remain mindful of the role of these "external" actors and the local elites with whom they dealt, but mainly as they affected and responded to street-level concerns.

To do so, I have divided this work into six chapters. While most of these chapters explore themes that transcend the periods of Russian rule and German occupation in Warsaw, the first chapter deals solely with the war's first year and the last year of Russia's imperial presence in the city. During this year, Warsaw was a frontline city and the setting for experiences that were not repeated following the Russian evacuation, although they indeed had long-term impacts. Artillery bombardment in and from the city suburbs, aerial bombing, scorched-earth demolitions and explosions, and exchanges of fire across the Vistula between departing Russians and entering Germans were loud and visible reminders of Warsaw's exposure to the fighting. So, too, was the constant movement of people and things: reserves and conscripts passing through the city for the front, thousands of wounded soldiers returning from the front for treatment in the city's hospitals and infirmaries, more thousands of refugees who arrived faster than they could be resettled, trains full of enemy subjects rounded up and deported to the east, tens of thousands migrating from the city in search of work, also to the east. These occurred amidst rumors of various kinds, spy scares, and reports of miracles typical of a state of siege mentality, even though the city was actually spared a siege. The trials and tribulations of Warsaw's inhabitants would only worsen, but those suffered during the first year were, often enough, sufficiently distinct and different to justify separate treatment.

The second chapter discusses the disastrous state of Warsaw's wartime economy. An almost complete disruption in the supply of coal in the war's first months dealt a crippling blow to industrial production in the city, reducing output by 70–75% by the end of 1914. The impact on employment was equally devastating, and no recovery was possible as long as the war continued, thanks to the requisitioning of raw materials, machines, industrial equipment, and even entire factories first by the Russians and then more systematically by the Germans. Shortages of basic goods and commodities, particularly food, were prevalent from the very beginning and became ever more acute during the German occupation, as reflected in the official price inflation of more than 800%. Meanwhile, German efforts to strictly control the consumption of food and other basic goods in Warsaw led to widespread smuggling and thriving black markets, which advantaged those who could pay even higher prices in order to access vital resources. While disruptions in the food supply constituted the most important wartime issue, shortages of coal and other sources of energy and heat were not far behind and, in the war's first year, were even more important. By comparing data on production, employment, inflation, rations, and consumption, this chapter will demonstrate that Warsaw's economic crisis of the First World War dwarfed those of Berlin, Vienna, and Petrograd, to which the fall of empires have been attributed. Since the collapse of living standards in Warsaw occurred during the years of the German General-Government, I will also have something to say about the debate between those who argue that imperial German policies and practices in the east during the Great War paved the way for Nazi plans of conquest, colonization, and exploitation, and those who claim that there is little evidence they served as a harbinger of German intentions during the Second World War.

The third chapter looks at transfer payments and social policy, which were not determined by the Russian or German imperial governments but left to local actors, including a network of philanthropic associations. However, the major part of this chapter will focus on the Warsaw Citizens Committee, which emerged in August 1914 to assist in the basic provisioning of the city, finding work for the unemployed, assisting the families of military reservists called up to the Russian Army, and mobilizing financial resources to deal with the war's expected hardships. Those hardships, however, would be far greater than anticipated, which would lead to a rapid expansion of the committee's activities. Soon enough, the committee would find itself involved in the organization of public kitchens, the sheltering of refugees, the setting of price controls, the monitoring of public health, and the protection of children (especially those orphaned by wartime circumstances). By virtue of its indispensable social-welfare activities, the Warsaw Citizens Committee acquired quasi-governmental status by the time of the Russian evacuation and would provide the basis, first for a new municipal administration and then for Warsaw's first elected city council in 1916. Nonetheless, with so many of Warsaw's inhabitants relying partially or completely on public support, escalating needs outstripped the city's financial resources by a factor of ten to one, and by the end of the war a bankrupted city administration was unable to pay its own employees, let alone feed some two hundred thousand people in the public kitchens inherited from the Warsaw Citizens Committee.

The fourth chapter addresses the impact of the war on relations between Warsaw's two principal and competing national groups, Poles and Jews, by exploring themes that take into account the dramatically different attitudes of the Russian and German regimes toward the Jewish population, but are also part of a much longer story. The existential crisis of wartime, however, would do more than the presence of either Russians or Germans to define the political, socio-economic, and cultural expressions of Polish-Jewish relations, which reached the breaking point on two occasions—at the time of the Russian evacuation in the summer of 1915, and as Polish forces took control of the city from the Germans in November 1918. Exceptional intercommunal violence was nonetheless avoided, even though Polish-Jewish relations in the city had never been so strained. Such an outcome also requires our attention, in part by shifting the frame of reference from "relations" shaped by modern and competing nationalisms to those Poles and Jews, perhaps even the majority, for whom identity politics were likely a secondary or even tertiary concern.

The fifth chapter will focus on the intersection of war and gender in Warsaw. The resurrection of an independent Polish state in the aftermath of the First World War was accompanied by the establishment of equal political rights and suffrage for women, a cause that had minimal support before the war but was accepted after the war with little public debate or dissent. That the war itself had something to do with this important development in Polish political culture, however, is assumed rather than established in the historiography of modern Poland and the emerging scholarship about women and gender. Moreover, in the scant literature on the role of women in wartime Poland, the focus had been placed—or misplaced—on a small minority of women who served as volunteers in auxiliary military organizations, particularly those in support of the Polish legions. The purpose of this chapter is not to refute the significance of the war in fostering and accelerating political change, but actually to define and analyze it by examining the peculiarities of women's experiences on the Warsaw "home front," the principal location of women's visibility, voice, protest, and power during the war. Consideration of these experiences in comparative context, moreover, will demonstrate how the resetting of gender boundaries in Warsaw as a result of the war fits into a larger European story.

The sixth chapter will look at Warsaw's wartime culture wars. Before the war, Warsaw was a busy metropolis, a city in a hurry with coach traffic comparable to that of the largest of European urban centers, proud of its high culture dominated by the classical performing arts and boasting a lively nightlife revolving around its many cafes and restaurants. This Warsaw was assaulted almost immediately by the exigencies of war, as disruptions of public transportation, the imposition of curfews, and a ban on alcohol sales undermined the efforts of the city's cultural elites to maintain "business as usual." At the same time, the exacerbation of existing social, ethnic, and gender tensions found expression in the public discourse on culture and propriety during wartime, reflected in heated debates about horseracing and legalized gambling, temperance and prohibition, the emerging new venues of cinema and cabaret, and radical changes in (particularly women's) fashion. The chapter will conclude with an analysis of the "Barefoot Movement" in Warsaw that emerged among students in the summer of 1917 and returned again the following summer to promote a populist cultural agenda against the "cosmopolitanism" of the big city and its elites.

The final and concluding chapter begins with an attempt to capture Warsaw in November 1918 in imagery that is in stark contrast with the standard narrative of the city as the scene of recovered Polish statehood. This imagery will be drawn from scenes set in cold and unlit streets that featured ubiquitous begging, long lines for foul-tasting "bread" containing more surrogates than flour, riots and the looting of public stores, everyday theft and banditry, widespread prostitution, and mounting incidents of personal, intercommunal, and political violence. Then, by looking more precisely at the prevalence of certain kinds of disease, mortality and fertility rates, and the war's larger demographic consequences, and by comparing these data with those obtained for other European cities, we will be able to better appreciate and evaluate the "minor apocalypse" that occurred in Warsaw during the First World War. We will also come to a better understanding of the problems confronting the establishment and consolidation of a functioning parliamentary democracy in Poland's "old-new" capital city.

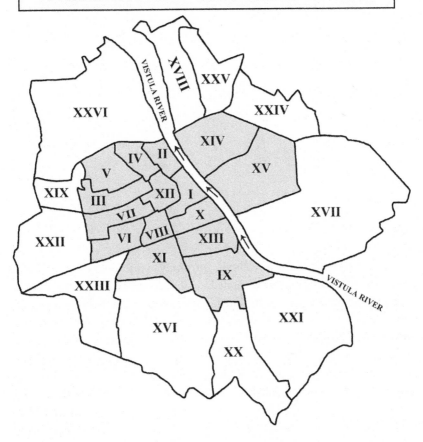

Precincts I-XV: Warsaw in 1914
Precincts XVI-XXVI: Suburbs annexed in 1916

MAP 1. Warsaw and Its Precincts in the First World War

THE FRONTLINE CITY

During the first year of the war Warsaw's proximity to the front, which in October 1914 approached its suburbs, generated an atmosphere characterized above all by recurring uncertainty. The bank panic at the end of July, fed by rumors of a Russian evacuation, immediately destabilized the urban economy. The suspension of normal banking operations resulted in a cash shortage, as factories were able to pay employees only 25–50% of their wages. Consequently, on 1 August— the day officially marking the outbreak of war between the Russian and German Empires—workers at a number of Warsaw factories and brickyards left their worksites.[1] As they returned to their homes, most likely on foot since they lacked small denominations necessary to pay the conductors of Warsaw's new electric streetcars, they may have witnessed any number of quarrels in stores, shops, and cafeterias throughout the city over the issuing of spare change, some of which required police intervention.[2] Such conflicts often involved women whose panic-driven food purchases immediately drove up prices, leading to the hoarding of coin as a hedge against the inflation of paper banknotes while further exacerbating the currency shortage. Until the banks reopened and the money supply could be replenished,[3] cash surrogates—coupons, vouchers, and stamps—would have to suffice for legal tender. Before their printing and accepted use, by which time the shortage of coin had eased, commerce in Warsaw essentially came to a standstill.[4] Meanwhile, the reduction of all forms of vehicular traffic, not only trolleys but also automobiles and horse-drawn carriages, as a consequence of military restrictions on their movement and the requisitioning of horsepower, contributed to a visible depopulation of street life in the city center less than a week into the war.[5]

According to Jon Lawrence, all major capital cities experienced a sharp decline in economic activity with the outbreak of the war. In this regard, Warsaw was no exception. However, like Paris, it remained in the grip of economic crisis due to the city's proximity to the front and the loss of productive capacity to the Germans.[6] In Warsaw's case, despite observable shortages of basic goods from the very beginning of the war, of far greater concern was the disruption of Warsaw's supply of coal. Electricity generation in Warsaw was almost entirely dependent on supplies from Zagłębie Dąbrowskie, a coal-rich basin neighboring German Upper Silesia, which came under German occupation in the first days of the war. Factory production, yet to recover from the bank panic, was crippled permanently by the coal shortage.

Despite the economic shock effects that accompanied the outbreak of the war in Warsaw, public order was not seriously disturbed. As the conservative writer and politician Czesław Jankowski later observed, "The machine of the city of 800,000 still functioned efficiently."[7] Aside from the disputes over spare change, a remarkable calm prevailed. Expressions of genuine enthusiasm for the cause of Russian arms, which crossed boundaries of class and ethnicity, surprised the tsar's Polish detractors like Stanisław Dzikowski who had come to the city from Lwów (today the Ukrainian city of Lviv) in 1909 and attributed the behavior of his compatriots to "helplessness, and the lack of political experience and national solidarity."[8] Even supporters of Polish-Russian reconciliation like Princess Lubomirska thought the displays of pro-Russian sympathies in Warsaw "strange" and "exaggerated":

> The Russian authorities have been received with model behavior in Warsaw—there is general calm, etc. The rush of recruits to the colors is completely unexpected. But will we be repaid for our sacrifice?
>
> In the evening a long line of troops march below our window accompanied by a large enthusiastic crowd, crying "Hurrah! Long live the Army!" The whole street was in fervor. This was a shocking sight on this starlit night—a new sight, completely unexpected. Where are the ghosts of the past? Is Kościuszko [hero of the 1794 anti-Russian insurrection] turning in his grave?[9]

The mobilization of some 4,500 reservists in the city had likewise gone off without a hitch and seemed to have had little impact on the normal course of daily life, although the presence of fewer male industrial workers in the city was noticeable. These workers were the most conspicuous social group subject to mobilization, and they reported to some sixteen points in the city, accompanied by family and friends.[10] With the end of mobilization, the points where reservists reported for service, such as the university, were returned to civilian use.[11]

Dzikowski witnessed the mustering of the reservists in the east-bank suburb of Praga. As they departed for the battlefield, weeping women ran after them at length with children in tow. A similar scene, which Dzikowski described as "unbearably depressing," occurred on Krakowskie Przedmieście, the boulevard filled by crowds of Jewish workers and women who stopped traffic as they waited for their brothers, sons, and husbands to be led from the university area.[12] Wives and families of reservists immediately became objects of public empathy. Support for these families was one of the originally cited reasons for the formation of the Warsaw Citizens Committee on 3 August, but this reason became moot when the Russian military authorities announced that military families would receive state assistance for food purchases.[13] A few weeks into the war, the Russian government also enacted special regulations to protect reservists' wives, popularly known as *rezerwistki*, from eviction for failing to pay rents, a move strongly endorsed in the Warsaw press.[14]

Even prior to the publication on 14 August of the proclamation of Grand Duke Nikolai Nikolaevich, the tsar's uncle and commander-in-chief of the Russian Army who promised the reunification of an autonomous Poland under the scepter of the Romanovs, support for the Russian side among Warsaw's population was especially visible against the nearly complete absence of pro-German or pro-Austrian sympathies. Even as it became clear that Poles would be fighting Poles, divided as they were among the three empires, the Warsaw press launched what an angered Dzikowski referred to as an "unprecedented campaign" against the Polish press in Austrian Galicja, which responded in kind.[15] Large crowds cheered the long lines of Russian troops as they marched through the city on the way to the front. Meanwhile, several hundred volunteers, the majority of whom were Polish workers and students, began to enlist at the Russian Army's main staff building on Saxon Square. By 12 August they already numbered three thousand.[16]

While pro-Austrian supporters like Dzikowski preferred to believe that over the next weeks and months hostility toward and distrust of Russia "grew by the day, spontaneously and unstoppable,"[17] almost all of the evidence points to the contrary. As physician Walenty Miklaszewski observed in his diary entry of 24 September, even a company of mounted Cossacks—the face of the tsarist suppression of the 1905 revolution in Warsaw—was greeted by families and friends of their former victims with flowers and cries of "God be with you! Defend Warsaw!" as it marched through the city to meet the approaching Germans outside of Skierniewice, some sixty-five kilometers to the west.[18] To be sure, voluntary enlistment may have subsided after the first weeks, but six call-ups of approximately twelve thousand new conscripts over the next year went as smoothly as had the initial mobilization. When those already serving tours of duty before the summer of 1914 are included, approximately twenty-one thousand Varsovians filled the ranks of the Russian Army during the first year of the war, many of them in the defense of their own city in the fall.[19] If official statistics published in the press are to be believed, draft evasion in Warsaw remained incredibly low: a mere 69 in the second half of 1914, rising only slightly to 113 in the first three months of 1915.[20]

Just as Warsaw's males of military age loyally reported for duty, so too did many young women. On 9 August, in anticipation of the arrival of wounded soldiers from the front, the Women's Section of the Warsaw Citizens Committee received permission directly from the Russian authorities to organize nursing courses.[21] Shortly thereafter, the Red Cross began to receive offers from private individuals, primarily women, to serve as nurses and nurses' aides, while others offered to care for the wounded in their homes.[22] Over the next weeks, hundreds of women from all social classes but especially the Polish intelligentsia would subsequently respond to the appeal of the Women's Section for volunteers after attending lectures on emergency care.[23]

Indeed, nothing better characterizes the public mood in Warsaw at the beginning of the war than the first encounters of its residents with wounded soldiers returning from the front and the moving scenes of public solidarity with them. The streets along which the wounded were conveyed became lined by tens of thousands of people who offered the soldiers flowers, cigarettes, and other tokens of empathy. Men removed their hats as a sign of respect as the wounded passed by. Włodzimierz Perzyński, a columnist for *Tygodnik Illustrowany*, was particularly moved by the behavior of these ordinary Varsovians, recording his belief that "Warsaw has never been as calm as it is now." When someone asked him if Warsaw had become a "nicer" place since the war began, Perzyński replied that based on all of his observations, "Warsaw has found itself."[24] Meanwhile, crowds also formed at hospitals to see if husbands, sons, and brothers were among the wounded. As local hospitals posted lists of all wounded soldiers, the press began to publish the names of those from Warsaw who had been admitted for treatment.[25]

One other sign of the "model behavior" prevailing in the city, which Princess Lubomirska attributed at the time to the "very clever" decision of the Russian government to ban vodka sales but which obviously had deeper roots,[26] can be found in the crime statistics. Although the Warsaw Citizens Committee worried about the shortage of police in some of the city's peripheral working-class precincts, the rate of registered crime as measured by police protocols, and particularly the cases of reported theft, declined by the day during the war's first weeks.[27] Indeed, despite the inactivity of a number of factories because of the coal shortage and the resulting layoffs and reduced hours, the "unusual peace and quiet" in Warsaw's industrial suburbs would continue in the war's early phase as their working-class residents concentrated on making ends meet. According to a report published in *Nowa Gazeta*, in Warsaw's suburban and factory districts "all regulations are being strictly observed and even domestic disputes are being temporarily arbitrated."[28]

The fact of the matter is that, at least as far as Warsaw's Polish population was concerned, civil-military relations in the frontline city were good during the first eight months of the war, even as conditions steadily deteriorated and circumstances became more difficult. In fact, one could almost think of Warsaw in the same terms as the capitals of the major belligerents when it came to early Polish enthusiasm and support for the cause of an army that many in the city treated as their own. In exchange, the Russian military authorities behaved "correctly," as Jan Molenda and Jerzy Holzer put it fifty years ago.[29] They guaranteed the security of private property, paid those who worked for the army, limited and made compensation for requisitions, supported the families of reservists and conscripts, and approved initiatives coming from civil society to bolster the home front. As we shall see, these relations would be tested in October 1914 when the city was threatened with a direct attack, but they would survive that test.

Meanwhile, the behavior of the Russian authorities toward Warsaw's other residents, especially Jews but also enemy subjects, could hardly be described as "correct," even in the war's first weeks. The government's decision to expel all German and Austro-Hungarian subjects from Warsaw would lead on 13 August to the police extraction of hundreds of people from their homes and apartments for transport to points farther east.[30] For Warsaw's Jews, the first weeks of the war were fraught with fears of a pogrom brought on by the attitudes and behaviors of Russian Army commanders who both believed and encouraged rumors of wholesale Jewish espionage on behalf of the Central Powers. Consequently, in the middle of August drunken soldiers from the 86th Infantry Regiment began to beat Jews whom they encountered at random in the city's fourth police precinct.[31] The Russian Army's perception and treatment of Jews as "enemy aliens," despite Jewish professions and acts of loyalty toward the Russian cause, would also have negative implications for Polish-Jewish relations in the city, which became particularly evident in the aftermath of the October crisis.

The "Battle of Warsaw"

Following initial Russian military successes in East Prussia and especially in Galicja against Austro-Hungarian forces, major defeats at Tannenberg and the Mazurian Lakes suffered at the hands of the German Eighth Army under the command of General Paul von Hindenburg at the end of August and early September would lead to German occupation of the western part of Suwałki province, to Warsaw's northeast. To the west, the Russian Army had already abandoned Kalisz and Częstochowa to the Germans in early August, but this withdrawal did not prevent their inhabitants from being subjected to extraordinary violence by the invading forces. While German atrocities in western Poland and especially the wholesale destruction of Kalisz, the Polish equivalent of Leuven, became fuel for both Russian and Entente propaganda,[32] they did not affect the optimism expressed in the Warsaw press in August for an easy Russian victory, an attitude that began to dissipate only in September.

The heavy censorship of news from the front, along with an abundance of mixed signals from the authorities, contributed to the confusion. The discernible return of Russian officials who had left the city at the war's outbreak and official statements that Warsaw was out of any immediate danger of enemy incursion toward the end of August may have calmed some nerves. However, others may have been rattled by the Warsaw military governor-general Aleksandr Turbin's announcement on 5 September that any Zeppelins appearing over the city would be shot down by artillery and machine guns. Some residents even preferred to rely on prognostications based on readings of a late-summer solar eclipse, or on the latest rumor in circulation—for example, that the Russians were preparing to announce the conscription of 14–17-year-olds.[33]

By the end of September there were signs of growing fears of a German occupation, which pro-Russian forces in Warsaw tried hard to dispel. "From the beginning of war," wrote Ignacy Grabowski in *Kurjer Warszawski*, "Warsaw has been the terrain of alarms and rumors, almost all of them unjustified by common sense." He cited two examples: 1) when the lights went out for a moment, citizens believed that the Germans had captured the electric power plant; 2) that the #18 east-west trolley would go only as far as Krakowskie Przedmieście because the enemy had been seen in Praga on the Vistula's east bank.[34] The spotting of a Zeppelin in the city's western approaches along the Warsaw-Vienna railroad was no hoax, however, and the craft had to be diverted to the north by artillery and machine-gun fire.[35] This harbinger of the enemy's advance on the city was enough to reinvigorate the panic-buying of food that had characterized the war's first weeks and to cause a renewed and rapid inflation of food prices, leading to calls for intervention against "profiteering" from either the magistrate or the Warsaw Citizens Committee, as the latter was already beginning to assume quasi-governmental status.[36]

As a joint German-Austrian offensive from the south and west in early October brought enemy forces to the very gates of Warsaw, General Turbin issued a public denial of rumors that a German occupation of the city was imminent. Indeed, following the loss of Łódź, Piotrków, and Skierniewice to German forces, the Russian high command announced that it would make every effort to defend

Warsaw. Despite the German advance to the city's outskirts, many Varsovians could not admit to themselves that the metropolis might fall prey to the enemy, an attitude that Wincenty Miklaszewski recorded in his diary: "Let the Germans come to Pruszków, Czersk, Grójec, even a few versts farther. But they will never take Warsaw!"[37]

Others weren't so sure. Despite previous assurances, during the second week of October the Russian military authorities ordered a partial evacuation of state institutions and personnel based on a contingency plan developed the previous July. The closing of the State Bank and post office, the departure of officials, and the mustering of a local militia to preserve order in the event of a full evacuation certainly alarmed those with something to lose. According to Krzysztof Dunin-Wąsowicz, who based his information on contemporary press accounts, some 260,000 people left Warsaw as the city came under the threat of siege in October 1914.[38] Since the Russian population of the city constituted no more than 5%, or 40,000–45,000, of the city's total prewar inhabitants, and since Jews had more to fear from Russian forces outside of the city than from the potential German occupiers, we can only assume that the vast majority of those who left were Polish residents. These Poles fled for political reasons (namely, they were prominent pro-Russian conservatives and National Democrats), or because they were Russian state employees and were evacuated with their institutions, or because they simply desired and had the means to get out of harm's way.

Those who stayed, however, displayed remarkable calm and resilience in the face of renewed anxiety. One can only imagine scenes from the height of the crisis, which began on 10 October. "In the city there is real panic," Princess Lubomirska noted in her entry of 11 October, as wounded soldiers and officers continually poured into a metropolis whose capacity to treat them had been overwhelmed.[39] As Joshua Sanborn has noted, Russian military authorities "had made preparations for a war on the scale of the Russo-Japanese war rather than the war they fought in 1914" with casualty rates that were more than twice as high as expected.[40] Refugees from the surrounding countryside, some with livestock tied to carts and wagons, mixed with larger crowds, one of which had gathered to watch and then cheer the striking of a German airplane by Russian fire. Meanwhile, the booming sound of enemy artillery in the city became "ever louder, more unpleasant and surprisingly close" as rumors spread that the Germans would enter Warsaw the next day. Then just as suddenly, the panic subsided by the evening of 12 October, at least to Lubomirska's mind: "It's hard to define, but palpable. . . . It appears that large numbers of troops have arrived."[41]

Indeed, Russian confidence that Warsaw could be defended and the tide turned would lead to a suspension of the evacuation of the city administration and police and the arrival of fresh troops from the east. As they marched through

FIGURE 1.1. Postcard by Hans Rudolf Schulze of a Zeppelin dropping bombs on Warsaw.

FIGURE 1.2. "The Bombardment of Warsaw," *The Graphic* (2 January 1915). Muzeum Narodowe w Warszawie.

the city, according to Lubomirska, they were treated like saviors: "The sympathy for the soldiers here is unbelievable, groups of women gather in the streets and give them what they can—a cup of hot tea, cigarettes, fruit. The soldiers stop for a moment, they collect these items, sometimes taking a loaf of bread on their bayonets, and then they move on, a grey anonymous mass."[42]

Memoirists like Czesław Jankowski would recall "more than one sleepless night," whether caused by the rumbling of Russian artillery on Aleje Jerozolimskie (Jerusalem Boulevard) on its way to the front only kilometers away in Pruszków, Raszyn, and Piaseczno, or the explosion of bombs dropped from German aircraft on "the defenseless streets of Warsaw."[43] Only now did the war impinge on the consciousness of many, including the fifteen-year-old Irena Krzywicka, who was awakened from her self-described "fog" as a relatively privileged youth by the blasts of approaching German artillery.[44] Others observed the battle as a spectator sport and not always from a safe distance. According to Stanisław Dzikowski, Warsaw's residents calmly watched the German airplanes over the city, as well as the Russian attempts to bring them down with rifles and machine guns. Only once in a while would people scramble to safety behind a wall. "If it were not for the sounds of artillery fire," Dzikowski added, "these days in October would remind one of any fall day, as streets quickly returned to normal, without a care in the world." Hearing the artillery, Varsovians would wager with one another, "Is it closer today, or farther away?"[45] "It would have been hard to tell," Zdzisław Dębicki observed after the fact, "that the fate of a city of a million was at stake."[46] Not surprisingly, dozens of people were injured or killed that autumn as a result of exploding projectiles and bombs.[47]

Although Dzikowski found in this "business as usual" approach yet another sign of Warsaw's political passivity, *Kurjer Warszawski* led a far more general chorus in singing the praises of the "good city" and applauding "Polish society" for doing everything to maintain all possible appearances of a normal life during the emergency. In its estimation, Warsaw's ability to rise to the occasion demanded by the war in the specific circumstances of October 1914—which it defined as "work for a slice of bread, nursing the wounded, providing meals to the poor, sheltering refugees, the food problem, the fuels problem, a whole multitude of preoccupations and difficulties"—was a matter of civic pride.[48] *Nowa Gazeta*, the Polish-language daily of the assimilated Jewish elite, concurred, adding that the public had been able to overcome its fears "and adjust its mood to the circumstances of this important historical moment."[49] Once again, according to Dębicki, Warsaw "gave proof of a high level of maturity" and was "prepared for everything that the historic hour demanded of it."[50]

By 19 October the sounds of artillery fire coming from the south and west of Warsaw, to which its citizens had become accustomed over the course of more than a week, could no longer be heard. Fearing that their flanks could become exposed, the German forces had begun to withdraw from the neighborhood of Warsaw. Three days later, big bold headlines in the city's dailies announced the repulsion and retreat of the Germans from the approaches to the city, which had been saved from what *Kurjer Warszawski*, for its part, termed a "Teutonic invasion."[51] On 23 October Archbishop Kakowski celebrated a thanksgiving mass for the victory of Russian forces in St. John's Cathedral in Warsaw's Old Town. A similar thanksgiving service was held the following day at the great Tłomackie Street Synagogue to accompany Saturday morning prayers.[52] "Today the streets are alive!" exclaimed Lubomirska on 29 October as captured trophies of war were paraded and German POWs, including several dozen on stretchers, were marched down Warsaw's main thoroughfares of Nowy Świat and Krakowskie Przedmieście en route to camps in the east-bank suburb of Praga.[53] The Russian state agencies and their personnel that had earlier been evacuated were now instructed to return, soon to be followed by the majority of those who had fled with them.

If Warsaw experienced a moment of triumph during the First World War, this was it. Indeed, the mood and experience of the home front in Warsaw once the immediate danger had passed were not unlike those that characterized Paris. In singing the city's praises in *Tygodnik Illustrowany*, Zdzisław Dębicki took obvious pride in the comparison with the French capital, which had also been threatened by the advancing German enemy and had held firm that fall: "There is only one other similar kind of public community in the world—Paris . . . Warsaw extends its hand to you over a sea of blood."[54] That "sea of blood," however, was very close to home, in the towns and countryside of the city's immediate environs, which would bring on Warsaw's next wartime crisis.

Forced Evacuations and Refugees

Although the October assault on Warsaw had done little actual damage to the city's core, its surrounding suburbs—having taken the brunt of the attack—had been devastated. According to Czesław Jankowski, the psychological effect of these aftershocks so close to home constituted Warsaw's "worst moments" since the outbreak of the war.[55] The even greater destruction of outlying villages and small towns left a lasting impression on Dzikowski, then a Red Cross volunteer who brought wounded soldiers from the front back to Warsaw in the wake of retreating German armies. "The fields were empty, the villages dead, the manors abandoned, and the small towns gave the impression of living corpses, in which the spirit of life barely circulated," he recalled shortly thereafter.[56] Amidst such scenes of ruin and despair, Warsaw itself would function as a relative oasis and would soon play host to tens of thousands of new refugees from the war zone and small towns like Skierniewice and Rawa, where according to Dzikowski it appeared that the line of battle had crossed through their Jewish districts.[57] They were not the first, nor the last, refugees to appear in Warsaw during the war's first year.

Weeks before the first wounded soldiers from the Russian Army began to appear in Warsaw, the recently formed Warsaw Citizens Committee at its session of 11 August 1914 noted the arrival of refugees, people "without means" and frequently without passports, from Kalisz, which had been heavily bombarded, as well as from Konin and Koło. By the next day, the committee realized that it would need to become involved in their care while it sought free rail passage for refugees to points farther east. Finally, at its second of two meetings on 14 August 1914, the committee resolved to establish a separate Commission for Refugees, with the immediate task of finding night shelters.[58] By that time, according to committee social activist Franciszek Herbst, the number of refugees in Warsaw already reached into the thousands, many of whom had made their way to Dolina Szwajcarska, whose recreational facilities were converted into the committee's main refugee shelter, while others found temporary lodging with families and friends or, if they could afford it, in Warsaw's hotels.[59] Slightly more than three weeks later, the committee had offered shelter to some twelve thousand people, only a fraction of the total of those seeking refuge in Warsaw from the fighting.[60]

Over the course of the next ten months, Warsaw would experience an unprecedented refugee crisis, with effects extending well into 1916 and even beyond, particularly for Polish-Jewish relations. However, it is difficult to estimate the refugee numbers in any precise terms, for several reasons. First, accurate figures are available only for those refugees who received public assistance in the form of meals and shelter, the burden of which fell almost entirely on local nongovernmental organizations, especially the Warsaw Citizens Committee and Jewish community institutions. Independent Polish and Jewish estimates from early February 1915 noted that barely one-tenth of the city's refugee population at the time, which was estimated at between fifty and sixty thousand, were actually living in public shelters.[61] By my own reckoning, between one-fourth and one-third of all refugees who came to Warsaw during the war received some form of public assistance, if not temporary lodging, then free or subsidized meals, clothing, and part-time employment. Thus the Christian refugee section under the Warsaw Citizens Committee served a total of sixty thousand people during the first year of the war. A separate section for Jewish refugees, which was created in mid-October 1914 and reported to and was partially subsidized by the committee, sheltered some twenty thousand people during the same period and provided meals to many more.[62] However, it must be reiterated that the majority of Warsaw's refugees did not receive public assistance, which was also true in other central European cities during the war. For example, refugee camps in Vienna, which sheltered primarily Jews who had fled the ravages of war and the Russian Army in Galicja, at no point held more than 20% of the one hundred thousand Jewish refugees who came to the city.[63]

This still leaves us with the question: How many refugees came to Warsaw during the war and especially during its first year? We do have some time-specific snapshot estimates. According to historian Peter Gatrell, Warsaw had become home to one hundred thousand refugees at the end of 1914, approximately one-eighth of Warsaw's total population at the time, a figure corroborated in contemporary Russian and Polish press accounts.[64] However, this is a peak rather than static number. In fact, Warsaw's refugee population was in a constant state of flux as one contingent replaced another, often on a daily basis. Already in August 1914, dozens of refugees began to return to their homes in the Łowicz and Kutno areas, and in early September the number of meals served at the Dolina Szwajcarska facility dropped from three thousand to one thousand. However, a week later that number rose again to three thousand with the arrival of new refugees from Kalisz and Mława. As the front moved ever closer to Warsaw in October, thousands more came from various locations in the Polish Kingdom and from the city's own suburban reaches. According to Witold Żukowski, head of the Warsaw Citizens Committee's Refugee Section, some sixty-five thousand refugees had sought shelter in Warsaw during the October crisis alone.[65] However, once that crisis had passed with the retreat of German forces from the city's gates, the majority of refugees from Warsaw's immediate vicinity sought to return to their homes and properties, only to find them in total ruin.

During the October crisis the Warsaw Citizens Committee, with its shelters overflowing, began to make plans for sending the refugees farther east in the direction of Siedlce.[66] As various plans of relocation, resettlement, and evacuation of Warsaw's refugees succeeded one another, a change in public attitudes toward the refugees also became discernible. The original sympathy toward the plight of refugees expressed in Warsaw's Polish press before the October crisis gave way to concerns about the spread of contagious diseases and "freeloading" among the refugees.[67] Wincenty Kosiakiewicz, in a lead article published in *Kurjer Warszawski*, argued that evacuation of the refugees should be placed at the forefront of the city's agenda and should target those who had reportedly refused offers of employment, preferring instead to live off of private and public philanthropy. Kosiakiewicz fell short of calling for coercive methods to remove these refugees from Warsaw's shelters, but he did call on the exertion of "moral pressure" to get them to leave.[68] Another means of containing the number of refugees receiving public support was to restrict their categories. In mid-February 1915, for example, the Refugee Section of the Warsaw Citizens Committee announced it would no longer accept unwed males of working age.[69]

It should be noted that the change in attitudes toward refugees expressed in Warsaw's mainstream Polish press corresponded to a change in the refugees' ethnic composition. In the early phase of the war, as refugees began to arrive in Warsaw from the western provinces of the Polish Kingdom, little public heed was paid to their religion or ethnicity, although many of them were Jewish.[70] However, the turning back of the German attack on Warsaw in October 1914 proved devastating for the Jews. As German forces were temporarily rolled back through the small towns (or shtetls) surrounding Warsaw later that fall, the Russian Army began to expel entire populations, forcing tens of thousands to seek refuge in the city. "More than any other place," S. Ansky observed, "Warsaw bore the evidence of the calamity that had struck the Jews of Poland. Each day brought thousands of additional refugees, most of them on foot, robbed, naked, starving, shaken and helpless. All of these wretched people headed toward Warsaw's Jewish community center, which was boiling like a kettle, overflowing with anguish."[71] Ansky was also able to visit Błonie, before the war "a rich and elegant Jewish town" some seventeen miles from Warsaw, after it had been retaken from the Germans, its population reduced to some four thousand to five thousand, one-tenth of its prewar total. The Russian Army's actions at the end of October had also reportedly led to an influx of four thousand refugees from Grodzisk, who were followed by hundreds more from Mława.[72] "It was the same story everywhere," Ansky reported. "Cossacks had ridden in with swords and sticks, driven the Jews out of their homes and ordered them to leave town."[73]

These forcible expulsions of Jews from the immediate front zone toward the interior involved a handful of communities before January 1915, after which time a more systematic policy of coordinated mass expulsions of Jews began in earnest, as "all Jews and suspicious people" joined German colonists over the age of fifteen on lists of those scheduled for deportation across the Vistula.[74] In the spring of 1915, Russian Army headquarters and the Warsaw governor-general coordinated the mass expulsion of Jews from some forty towns in the vicinity of Warsaw, affecting roughly one hundred thousand individuals, eighty thousand of whom appeared in the city shortly thereafter.[75]

Such was the context when in April 1915, in response to directives from the Warsaw governor-general to accelerate the evacuation of Warsaw's overwhelmingly Jewish refugee population to the east bank of the Vistula, the Warsaw Citizens Committee developed a plan that divided the refugees into four categories, with those residing outside of public shelters—the vast majority—the last on the list for resettlement.[76] When an Evacuation Commission implemented the plan in mid-May 1915, it immediately encountered resistance among part of the refugee population. Thus, "moral pressure" quickly gave way to measures executed "energetically" to force the departure of those who "qualified."[77] By the end of June, the numbers of "homeless" served by the Warsaw Citizens Committee's Refugee Section had been reduced by more than half, and with the relocation of the refugees in full swing, hotel vacancies began to appear in Warsaw for the first time in months.[78] As the resettlement proceeded, however, the front began to close in again on Warsaw, bringing new refugees to the city's edges. While many were redirected immediately to shelters on the Vistula's east bank,[79] as the Russians began a final withdrawal from the city in the last weeks of July, a tremendous inflow of refugees from Piaseczno, Jeziorna, Wyszków, Radzymin, and Nasielsk forced the committee, which had already repurposed some of its existing shelters, to approve the creation of a new facility at the freight station of the Warsaw-Vienna railroad.[80] As for those refugees transferred to the east-bank towns and settlements of Otwock, Falenica, Józefów, Świder, and Płudy in May, Stanisław Dzikowski would later observe them "living like wild animals," struggling to survive by stealing produce from the gardens of local residents.[81]

Deportations

As noted above, Warsaw's refugee crisis, particularly at the end of 1914 and during the first half of 1915, was exacerbated by the Russian Army's mass expulsions of Jews in a broad zone behind the front line, some of whom were subsequently deported to the Russian interior as "enemy aliens," that is, a category of Russian subjects that conflated ethnic Germans, Muslims, Jews, and other non-Slavic groups.[82] While Jewish subjects of the tsar residing in Warsaw before the war were left in relative peace, the widespread belief among Russian Army commanders that Jews constituted an "unreliable element" who posed a security risk to Russian troops and were engaged in wholesale espionage on behalf of the Central Powers certainly made them anxious.[83]

Even though Jewish behavior in Warsaw remained loyal and beyond political reproach, many Warsaw Jews sought additional insurance by changing their German-sounding names to Slavic ones.[84] Jewish leaders also became justifiably alarmed, first by the idea and then by the reality of state confiscations of property from Warsaw's ethnic Germans toward the end of 1914, viewing the violation of property rights on the basis of ethnicity as a slippery slope that could easily extend to the Jewish community.[85] The steep nature of that slope was revealed in

January 1915 when the Warsaw governor-general ordered the closing of all German sporting, cultural, and philanthropic associations in the city.[86]

However, the Russian Army's actions against persons and property were initially aimed at citizens and subjects of enemy states. Starting on 26 December 1914, commanders of the Northwestern Front coordinated the deportation to the east of all Austro-Hungarian, German, and Ottoman subjects from the Polish Kingdom, allowing exceptions for Slavs—mainly ethnic Poles from Galicja or Prussia—who "were in no way suspected of spying."[87] Following the decision of the authorities to deport subjects of enemy states from Warsaw by 14 February 1915, the Warsaw and Central (that is, countrywide) Citizens Committees, as well as the chancery of the Warsaw Superintendent of Police, would be besieged by thousands of people attempting to confirm their identity, their Polishness, and their loyalty to the Russian state. The citizens committees were especially busy as people, many of them Poles with German surnames, stood in line for hours.[88] A reported twenty thousand subjects of belligerent states, officially classified as "civilian prisoners of war," filed petitions in Warsaw to stay in the city; those of German or Hungarian descent, however, became subject to unconditional deportation.[89] As the committees handed out thousands of "guarantees" to people threatened with expulsion from the city, news of the extension of the deadline and the initiation of a more orderly process had a temporarily calming effect.[90]

Thereafter, subjects of foreign states who remained on the deportation lists, upon receiving proper documentation from the Warsaw superintendent of police, proceeded to the U.S. consulate for a visa before being directed to Petrograd or to Bucharest. At this time, the neutral United States served as a caretaker of German and Austrian subjects in Entente states. On the evening of 23 February 1915, the first 560 German subjects departed from Warsaw.[91] For the expelled foreign subjects directed to Bucharest in converted freight cars, the American consulate provided up to eighteen rubles per person in support.[92] On the other hand, for those hoping to remain in Warsaw on the basis of a "guarantee" from the citizens committees, recommendations from three imperial Russian subjects were required.[93] In the last three weeks of February, the Warsaw Citizens Committee alone gave guarantees to 3,281 persons of Polish ancestry who were subjects of foreign states, while rejecting 89 other requests.[94] The Central Citizens Committee, the Warsaw Provincial Citizens Committee, the Land Credit Society, the Czech "Beseda" organization, and the Slavic Literary Society issued thousands of other guarantees.[95] By June 1915, as the Russians prepared their own evacuation of the city, some 14,890 enemy subjects had been deported from Warsaw, while 7,199 were allowed to stay, nearly all of whom were Polish.[96] As we shall see, they too would also be swept up in the movement of population to the east just a few weeks later.

While we have fairly precise figures on enemy subjects expelled from Warsaw, the data available for Russian subjects classified as "enemy aliens" are less certain. Wartime persecution of minority populations was not unique to the Russian Empire. However, feverish anti-German popular hysteria and press propaganda certainly contributed to the violent measures against Russia's ethnic Germans.[97] Before the war, some 420,000 Germans resided in rural areas of the Polish Kingdom, with another 100,000 in urban locations, all of whom were threatened with the prospect of deportation after February 1915.[98] According to Peter Gatrell, some two hundred thousand Germans were deported from the Polish Kingdom to Siberia, which was followed by the expropriation of their property.[99] As with their Jewish counterparts, the ethnic Germans' forced removal was originally based on security arguments, but the subsequent transfer of their property to Russians and other "reliable elements" suggested an agenda more akin to ethnic cleansing. In any event, the number of the tsar's German subjects removed from Warsaw can only be guessed. Like Warsaw's Jews, they were much more secure if they had been residents of the city before the war than if they had come to Warsaw from the surrounding region after August 1914. We know that shortly after the majority of Warsaw's enemy German subjects had been expelled, hundreds of ethnic German families from Żyrardów and its surrounding area suddenly appeared in Warsaw, where they were temporarily lodged in refugee shelters until they could be removed farther east.[100]

Male Labor Out-Migration

The migrations of population to and from Warsaw caused by the war and imperial Russia's war planners during the first year of the conflict on the Eastern Front involved more than twenty thousand reservists and conscripts, an approximately equal number of enemy subjects deported from the city, far greater numbers of wounded soldiers, refugees, and "enemy aliens" in transit to locations farther east, and those Russian and Polish subjects of the tsar who fled in the panics and partial evacuations of August and October, many of whom returned in November only to leave yet again the following summer.[101] Yet another significant factor affecting the city's demography, one that may have had even greater long-term effects, was the out-migration of working-class males, mostly "voluntary," at least until the summer of 1915.

As mentioned at the beginning of this chapter, electricity generation in Warsaw before August 1914 was almost entirely dependent on supplies from

Zagłębie Dąbrowskie, which was immediately invaded and then occupied by German forces. The disruption of Warsaw's supplies of coal crippled factory production in the city, which forced municipal authorities to look toward the distant Don Basin (Donbas) as a potential long-term supplier.[102] Satisfaction of Warsaw's energy needs proved impossible, even as the city became completely dependent on supplies from the east Ukrainian coalfields, which quickly became subject to transportation difficulties. The rail system of the Russian Empire matched the river system by having a north-south emphasis and was simply not set up for east-west traffic. When large-scale troop movements took place, the transportation system simply failed to cope.[103] The first consignment of fifty wagons of Donbas coal arrived only on 23 September, and even then it took the combined efforts of the Warsaw Citizens Committee and the Magistrate's Office to secure it.[104] In 1913, Warsaw had consumed approximately 160 freight cars of coal on a daily basis; by the end of September 1914 it was receiving only half that amount from the Donbas. By that time the Distribution Commission of the committee expected supplies to increase eventually to 110 freight cars,[105] but this optimistic estimate never came close to being realized.

As a consequence of the energy shortfall, factory production declined precipitously, leading to mass unemployment. By early October it was estimated that more than half of the city's labor force had been deprived of work and wages, which matched the decline of electricity generation. In thirty-one larger factories for which data are available, working hours for those who remained employed had been reduced to 35% of the norm.[106] As the war progressed, so did massive unemployment. According to data collected by German occupation authorities in early 1916, 77,809 industrial workers had been employed in Warsaw's factories before the war, about half of Warsaw's working-class labor force. By early 1916, the total number of industrial workers in Warsaw had dropped to 14,632, less than 19% of the prewar total.[107] Many of these workers, as we shall see, had left Warsaw before the German occupation. Unemployment outside of Warsaw's industrial sector among domestic servants, construction workers, artisans and craftsmen, office personnel, and the salaried intelligentsia also rose to unimaginably alarming proportions.

Thus unemployment was recognized as the most serious and painful social problem confronting the city in the war's first weeks. In response the Warsaw Citizens Committee opened employment agencies (giełdy pracy), which immediately received hundreds and then thousands of workers. As a result of the conscription of adult males from the rural labor force into the army, the giełdy pracy were initially successful in finding work for Warsaw's unemployed as seasonal field workers, where they toiled digging potatoes outside of the city.[108] While demand for farm laborers remained high throughout the early fall, especially in the Russian interior, low wages and uncertain conditions of employment hindered recruitment. Although the Warsaw Citizens Committee's rural employment agency had sent more than eight hundred workers to Kursk province by the end of September, with plans to send hundreds more, it was unable to satisfy the Russian demand for field labor.[109] By early October the farm workers employment office of the committee had found work for more than 2,500 individuals in the Polish Kingdom and the Russian Empire in practically equal proportions,[110] after which demand for rural labor dropped off with the end of the harvest season.

Before the first month of the war was out, the Warsaw Citizens Committee and the Magistrate's Office collaborated in the creation of new public-works projects initially designed to employ 1,250 people.[111] Those numbers would continue to rise, and in early 1916, after the city had come under German occupation, some twelve thousand were employed by the city in public works,[112] only slightly fewer than the number employed in industry. Otherwise, Warsaw's unemployment crisis, which affected hundreds of thousands in working-class families, could only be alleviated by labor migration from the city.

Figures reported on a regular basis by the *giełdy pracy* of the Warsaw Citizens Committee reveal the scale of that migration. By mid-September 1914, the committee's agencies had found employment for 918 people as farm workers and for 1,079 factory workers and 929 skilled craftsmen, mostly outside of the increasingly war ravaged Polish Kingdom.[113] Approximately three weeks later, the *giełdy pracy* had found work for 5,505 individuals who had sought their assistance—791 in the city, 2,249 in the Polish provinces, and 2,466 in the Russian Empire. Actual demand from Russia was then estimated at being more than eighteen thousand workers, but rail fares presented the main obstacle to labor migration from Warsaw to points farther east, an issue that wasn't resolved until the following spring.[114] Nonetheless, the numbers of labor migrants continued to rise, from more than 10,000 in mid-November, to 17,729 at the beginning of the New Year, to 24,412 by the last week of February 1915, by which time the greatest demand was for coal miners due to the labor shortage in the Donbas.[115] According to Franciszek Herbst, secretary of the Warsaw Citizens Committee's Labor Section, which coordinated the work of the *giełdy pracy*, during their first year of existence the employment agencies found work for fifty-seven thousand candidates, mainly in Russia proper.[116] Dunin-Wąsowicz estimates that seventy to eighty thousand workers left Warsaw during the first year of the war, including the thousands of skilled workers swept up in the Russian evacuation during the summer of 1915,[117] a matter to which we will now turn.

The End of Empire

Up until that summer, support in Warsaw for the cause of Russian arms remained firm, particularly among the city's Poles. Following the October "Battle of Warsaw," Polish women continued to nurse wounded Russian soldiers, some of them sharing the patronizing attitude of Princess Lubomirska, recorded after her visit to a large Red Cross hospital in November 1914:

> The Russian soldier is generally amazing—his martyrdom on the battlefield, his persistence, his simple, childlike behavior and his resignation to fate. The nurses prefer the Russians to the Poles—they are more grateful, they will gladly share their bread or cigarettes with their brothers and are less calculating than our countrymen.[118]

Moreover, such expressions of sympathy and support continued to cross boundaries of class, if not ethnicity. To be sure, the Russian police remained alert to any sign of opposition, which included a whiff of Polish Socialist Party (PPS) agitation to observe the eighty-fourth anniversary of the November 1830 Insurrection, by gathering students and workers in Catholic churches from where they were expected to mount street demonstrations. However, the detention of twenty individuals and police patrols outside of five churches were enough to keep things quiet, aside from a minor incident of vandalism to a Russian monument and the breaking of windows in the surrounding square caused by a homemade explosive device.[119]

To counter such opposition, limited though it was, Russia's Polish supporters in Warsaw loudly praised even the most minor of concessions, such as the permitted use of Polish as the instructional language for the teaching of general history and geography in private schools, even though in these same schools Russian and Church Slavonic as well as Russian history and geography continued to be offered in Russian by teachers of Russian ancestry.[120] Following a three-day fundraiser in Petrograd for the victims of the war in Poland, the literary critic and director Adam Grzymała Siedlecki went so far as to argue in *Tygodnik Illustrowany* that a major turning point had been reached in Russians' view of Poles, who by their actions had belied stereotypical expectations of treason.[121] More cultural, educational, and religious concessions were forthcoming in the spring. In March 1915 the long-promised Russian statute on urban self-government was finally introduced to the Polish Kingdom. Radical groups condemned the announcement of this more significant conciliatory measure as antidemocratic because of a weighted franchise for projected municipal elections, the expected absence of lower-class representation in the future self-governing institutions, and the limited jurisdiction of these institutions over urban social policy.[122] Such protests, however, had little impact on the pro-Russian opinion that continued to dominate in the city among its Polish population.

For its part, the imperial administration continued to cultivate Polish support in a number of ways, first and foremost by providing subventions to social and charitable institutions, and particularly to the Warsaw Citizens Committee. Such assistance was crucial to the provision of relief to growing numbers of the resident urban population affected by the economic crisis, and to thousands upon thousands of refugees who had fled to the city from various parts of the nearby and fluctuating war zone. Warsaw, moreover, depended on the Russian Empire for shipments of almost all items of primary need because so much of the Polish Kingdom had been devastated by war-related damages.[123] At the same time, the requisitioning of horses for military use hampered the transport of agricultural produce from nearby areas to the east of Warsaw not physically devastated by the recent battles. Perhaps for these very reasons, Russian administrative officials and military officers continued to treat the noncombatant Polish population of Warsaw with uncharacteristic tact and did what they could to guarantee the security of private property. Acts of malfeasance among Russian officers and officials were punished, and as the Christmas holidays approached toward the end of December 1914, special measures were taken to ensure that Russian troops remained confined to barracks to avoid any possible conflicts with Catholic Poles.[124]

This is not to suggest that there were no signs of strain in Russo-Polish relations in Warsaw before the evacuation, in part because Russian authorities feared ceding too much autonomy to the Poles at the local level. For example, the otherwise pro-Russian Warsaw Citizens Committee found itself contesting government recalcitrance toward the expansion of its activities, including the full public emergence, if not the organization and training, of a citizen militia. In this regard, the best the committee could achieve was permission to form a "Warsaw Honor Guard," the name and function of which were carefully chosen so as not to be construed as belonging to a Polish police force.[125] The Warsaw Citizens Committee also chafed at similar state obstructions in approving its educational initiatives, including the holding of private adult literacy courses conducted in the Polish language, a project rejected by the curator of the Warsaw Educational Region in the early spring of 1915.[126] Finally, the committee criticized the Russian government's inability to enforce price controls on its own as well as its refusal to grant to the committee such powers of enforcement.[127]

Civil-military and Russo-Polish relations in Warsaw would be most severely tested, however, by requisitioning. According to the Military Statute of July 1914, all requisitions effected within the borders of the Russian Empire were to be paid for, and although plundering was widespread among both combat and supply units dealing with the Polish Kingdom's Jewish and German populations, up until the spring of 1915 the Russian Army had largely adhered to this rule in its interactions with Poles.[128] At the beginning of the New Year, all still seemed to be in order as the Warsaw Governor-General announced the planned establishment of requisitioning commissions to determine bills on all items taken by the army for military use and to square accounts that had not been paid by the state treasury.[129] Then in February, owners of shops and stores in Warsaw were ordered to provide inventories of basic goods, and police commissars were instructed to conduct periodic inspections to ensure that the lists reflected reality.[130] However, it was the army's seizure of one of the warehouses holding provisions secured by the Warsaw Citizens Committee toward the end of April 1915 that marked the beginning of more arbitrary and desperate measures.[131]

Up to that point, there had been no clear indication of a turn in the tide of the war on the Eastern Front, at least not in Warsaw. To be sure, isolated German aircraft had dropped a few dozen bombs on Warsaw since the end of February, but they had caused little serious damage and only a few casualties.[132] On the other hand, Austrian forces had been forced to surrender Przemyśl in central Galicja to the Russians on 22 March, leading to a street celebration of a substantial crowd of mainly Russian students who carried portraits of Tsar Nicholas II as they made stops in front of the British and French consulates.[133] Otherwise, Warsaw's residents seemed more disturbed by rising incidents of theft, frequent blackouts caused by the coal shortage, and the ongoing ban on sales of beer and alcohol than by the particularly heavy-handed censorship of the city's press, which began in mid-April.[134]

Within days, German bombing raids on the city were renewed, marking the beginning of a massive German-Austrian counteroffensive that began on 2 May 1915 and resulted in a major breakthrough in the Gorlice-Tarnów area southeast of Krakow. This devastating blow to Russian forces in Galicja would force the Russian general staff to initiate what became known as the Great Retreat, not only from Galicja but also from the Polish Kingdom, in order to limit further casualties and establish a strategic line of defense farther east, one less exposed from the north and south. None of this, however, was immediately apparent in Warsaw, whose residents were purposefully kept in the dark as enemy forces again closed in on the city. In the absence of verifiable news from the front, rumors, conjectures, and official denials filled the vacuum as they had during the war's first weeks and months. For example, one hopeful rumor, fed undoubtedly by Warsaw's acute energy shortage, held that coal deposits had been discovered near Warsaw. Meanwhile, darker rumors that the city itself was in danger were dismissed as "senseless" by *Warszawska Myśl*, a press organ close to the government.[135]

According to Stanisław Dzikowski, for much of the spring and early summer of 1915, "Warsaw lived in a surrounding desert, where death circled only a few versts from its noisy and busy streets." In those streets, troops heading for the front passed parallel to the wounded returning from it, while several eastbound trains of wounded men waited at the station for evacuation. Anyone who had spoken to these soldiers, Dzikowski wrote, knew that "this army is tired and has lost its spirit. . . ." Defeat was already in the air, "a matter of two or three months." As a consequence, Dzikowski detected "a slow but steady dissipation of all pro-Russian sympathies" as Russians became the primary butts of a local and increasingly morbid humor.[136]

Far less humorous was the destruction of supplies, the expulsion of populations, and the burning of villages that accompanied the Russian Army's retreat to and across the Vistula. In an effort to implement the scorched-earth policy in more orderly fashion in Warsaw itself, the requisitioning commissions that had been announced the previous January were now activated in altered form in the middle of June. Shortly thereafter the Warsaw Citizens Committee, following a long debate and believing that the commissions would be based on the more innocuous January criteria, acceded to government requests for its participation in a survey of the city's reserves "by accepting and checking declarations of owners of their stores of food and provisions in the aim of establishing the existing amounts of products in the city and of considering the best means for their distribution among the population."[137] The committee reversed itself, however, once its agents discovered that the purpose of the commissions was to take inventories of metals, raw materials, and industrial machinery as well as reserves of fodder, food, kerosene, and other nonindustrial goods. The Warsaw governor-general responded by exerting pressure on the committee to delegate five representatives to each of five precinct commissions established in the city. While recognizing that most of the goods would be requisitioned and the remainder redistributed, the committee did succeed in exercising a moderating influence on the commissions and did ensure that receipts were left with factory- and store-owners for intended compensation after the war.[138] Judging from surviving documents for Warsaw's 4th precinct, the commissions concentrated mainly on industrial machinery, metals, and strategic raw materials, particularly copper.[139] According to the Warsaw superintendent of police, in a report from early October 1915 following the Russian evacuation of the city, the commission carried out no less than 180 separate requisitions of factories, plants, and shops. Some 300,000 puds (over a million pounds) of various metals valued at more than 1.2 million rubles were subsequently transported to the east.[140]

If requisitioning at least retained a semblance of order in the last several weeks of imperial rule, other kinds of Russian behavior contributed to an atmosphere bordering on chaos. This was particularly the case with several botched attempts at creating labor battalions. In early February 1915, the Russian Army began to advertise its need for large numbers of workers to dig trenches, to be paid in both cash and kind.[141] Herbst later recalled that the army approached the committee at the end of June 1915 for twenty thousand people to work on field fortifications in anticipation of the final German assault on Warsaw. After two days, only two hundred workers had been recruited, despite the fact that the Russians were now willing to pay twice what they had offered in previous months. However, even these workers were turned away from the forts where no defense work was in progress. Two weeks later the committee was approached yet again about the formation of auxiliary labor battalions for emergency defense work in the rear of the army, a scheme that also came to nothing, proof of the confusion then at work in the Russian military command structure.[142] Consequently, the committee distanced itself from all calls for the formation of labor brigades to dig trenches for the army, and by 19 July it had received assurances that there would be no mass labor drafts for such purposes.[143]

Anticipating retreat across the Vistula, the Russian Army and police began to take special security measures in mid-June to defend Warsaw's bridges from (presumably Jewish) spies and saboteurs in German pay. Within weeks, boat traffic was banned within one hundred paces of the bridges, all normal repair work on them was suspended, and all foot and vehicular traffic—even of people in uniform—was carefully controlled. The documents of all pedestrians who attempted to cross the Vistula were examined, while automobiles and trucks were stopped before entering as orders were given to sentries to fire on all rapidly approaching vehicles.[144] At approximately the same time, the police began to conduct political background checks on workers and employees in war-related factories and enterprises in Warsaw and its suburbs in preparation for their evacuation to Russia's Central Industrial Region. Amazingly, police discovered little of political concern in its examination of this component of Warsaw's labor force, which had been a hotbed of working-class radicalism during the Revolution of 1905. For example, a list of workers at K. Rudzki and Company, a machine-building firm, provides data on the age, hiring date, and residence for 791 workers as well as 183 engineers, technicians, sales agents, office workers, and managers. Of the Rudzki employees, only five—all workers—had police records connected to illegal strike participation or membership in an antigovernmental political party.[145]

In the meantime, such developments prompted *Tygodnik Illustrowany* to publish a lead editorial on 3 July 1915 in an attempt to calm public opinion. Over the previous days, the influential weekly claimed, Warsaw had been in a state of panic, the population's nerves frayed by months of danger and the front's movement toward the city. "Let's not forget, however, that in October [the front line] was ten times closer and it didn't reach the edges of the city's corners." Although the weekly's editors had to admit that Warsaw might indeed again come under siege and even fall to the enemy, the city still needed to "stand firm." Warsaw had been the center and source of the country's life in peace; "let it be the same in the days of cataclysm." The editors closed with a reference to the trying times as "a test of citizenship" that "will decide our existence for entire centuries."[146]

While the police prepared for the evacuation of state monetary instruments, sensitive documents, arms and ammunition, and other state property,[147] the Russian authorities continued to insist in public as late as 19 July that the government's recent actions were of a preparatory nature, that the departure of only a few institutions had been initiated, and even in these cases that evacuation had been suspended. Rumors of the impending forced removal of factories to the Russian interior were also denied, and the government claimed instead that all factories currently functioning in Warsaw would continue their operations without interruption.[148] The simultaneous announcement that the planned elections to institutions of municipal self-government had been suspended indefinitely, however, could hardly have helped to restore public confidence.[149] Thus the rumors continued to proliferate: that the electricity would be shut off, the trolleys would stop running, and the water pumps would cease to function.[150] In the east-bank suburb of Praga on 19 July, crowds of people gathered at the intersection of Ząbkowska and Radzymińska Streets, where reportedly a miracle had occurred at a chapel bearing the image of the Black Madonna of Częstochowa.[151]

The next couple of days were characterized by extraordinary street traffic, including evacuees and refugees with their livestock from surrounding villages, seemingly swept up in the flotsam and jetsam of horses, wagons, and automobiles evacuated to the right bank of the Vistula, where they would be subject to requisitioning.[152] The Russian military authorities at this time issued a communiqué to reassure their "Slavic kinsmen," whom they were defending from the "cruel enemy," that the scorched-earth and requisitioning measures were not actions of ill will toward the Poles but were required by strict military necessity.[153] A German bombing raid on 23 July, resulting in two dozen casualties, only added to a "fraying of nerves" and the "plague of rumors" that had beset the city.[154] On the same day, the government announced—despite its assurances of less than a week before—that industrial firms and factories involved in military production would be evacuated, but that all others would continue to operate normally so long as they had the necessary fuel and raw materials.[155]

Despite all official statements to the contrary, the evacuation had actually begun two months before the government and the army finally quit Warsaw for good, and was accompanied by the removal of various segments of the city's population. In early June, the Grand Duke Nikolai Nikolaevich decreed that all those who were not permanent residents of the city, employed in public service, or without specified occupations would be resettled. In the middle of June an order was issued to police to register all persons regardless of sex and age who had come to Warsaw since 1 July 1914. This registration was to be carried out in every home, every hotel, all "furnished rooms," and inns. Those without employment in state service or the private sector or in connection with the army, who were not refugees from the war zone, or who were not family members of soldiers at the front were required to leave the city's borders immediately. Consequently, some seventy thousand nonpermanent residents were forced to leave Warsaw within the month.[156] Among their number were the "Prussian" and "Austrian" Poles who just a couple of months earlier had been allowed to remain in the city. They were soon joined by the vast majority of the city's prison population, which was not inconsiderable. Since the outbreak of the war, Warsaw had become a repository for prisoners from other evacuated cities, and some five thousand had already been dispatched to the Russian Empire's interior provinces. Now, as the Russians began to evacuate Warsaw, the departure of prisoners was accelerated, beginning with another two thousand at the beginning of July.[157] They would soon be joined by three thousand political prisoners, many of whom had been arrested as a precautionary measure on the eve of the evacuation and who were now deported to the Russian interior. The Warsaw district prosecutor had recommended the release of the less important prisoners under investigation, but the Warsaw governor-general rejected this recommendation, agreeing with the special deputy for police affairs that such prisoners could be released only after they had been evacuated to the empire's interior. Indeed, some five hundred were subsequently released later that autumn, most of them students and members of scouting organizations.[158]

The families of Russian officials also began to depart at this time, leaving a number of domestic servants in the city without employment.[159] They were followed soon enough by husbands and fathers in Russian service. According to the evacuation plan worked out a year earlier and partially implemented in October 1914, Russian state institutions and their personnel were evacuated over the course of three days at the end of July on twenty-one trains that carried some 14,700 passengers eastward across the Vistula.[160] Meanwhile, some sixteen individuals were assigned to oversee the evacuation of valuable objects of art from the St. Aleksandr Nevskii Cathedral on Saxon Square, which were loaded onto ten train cars.[161] Among the last to leave, aside from rearguard units consisting of mounted police and Cossacks covering the army's retreat, were four thousand police employees, including members of the Warsaw County Land Guard, the Okhrana, the gendarmes, and the city police.[162]

As already noted, the evacuation included not only administrative offices and state officials but also industrial plant, their technical personnel, and at times entire factory crews with their families. On 1 August General Turbin issued a proclamation informing the population that the evacuation of machines and factories engaged in military production was solely designed to keep them in operation for the purposes of state defense and to prevent them from falling into enemy hands. Turbin promised that all affected workers would be able to continue their employment, if they wished, and would be transported to their new places of employment at state expense. There they would receive the same wages they had received in Warsaw and would be paid for wages lost from the time that their factory or plant had been dismantled. Moreover, the families of these workers were promised transfer payments similar to those received by families of reservists called up to active duty.[163] A sum of 500,000 rubles was assigned to the Warsaw governor-general to cover various expenses connected with the evacuation of Warsaw's industrial enterprises to the interior provinces of the empire.[164] In mid-July 1915 the Warsaw superintendent of police received lists detailing demands for 7,320 workers from six branches of industry in the Moscow industrial region.[165] Evacuated managerial personnel and technical personnel received 200-ruble stipends, and evacuated workers 100-ruble payments to cover the costs of their relocation.[166] In addition, owners of sixty-two industrial enterprises voluntarily sought to transport their most expensive machinery and parts, with the assistance of the requisitioning commissions, to the empire, although a shortage of freight cars hindered implementation of their plans.[167] Other factories, particularly those of potential military use, were destroyed entirely as part of the scorched-earth policy.[168]

In the last days of the Russian withdrawal from Warsaw, the Magistrate's Office was evacuated together with all city funds, including cash on hand, leaving the Warsaw Citizens Committee with only 500,000 rubles against an estimated need of 3.5 million rubles for the remainder of the year.[169] The evacuation did not spare the city's cultural resources—paintings, furniture, bronze doors, and public documents—"the remnants of our former splendor," according to Stanisław Dzikowski.[170] Another observer and member of the "independence camp," Stanisław Thugutt, summed up the Russian evacuation in the following words: "They took everything that was theirs and much that was ours."[171] Meanwhile, the Russian Army's implementation of scorched earth on the Vistula's west bank led to the joining of "evacuated peasants" with the previously expelled small-town Jewish inhabitants in the city's refugee population, whose numbers created a difficult atmosphere in the city in August 1915. Some refugees had been hurriedly dispatched to the east-bank forest settlements of Jabłonna and Łochów, where Dzikowski observed them engaged in conflicts with local residents in a common struggle for survival. "Behind us are only ashes," the refugees told Dzikowski, justifying their theft of edible produce as Warsaw became "surrounded by a ring of fire."[172]

On the morning of 5 August, the retreating Russians blew up the city's three bridges over the Vistula. Both Thugutt and Aleksander de Rosset would later recall being shaken from their sleep at 6:00 a.m. by the tremendous blasts.[173] Despite the Warsaw Citizens Committee's efforts to save them, some of the city's new electric trolley lines had been dismantled the day before and transported out of the city.[174] At the last minute, the retreating Russians also dynamited train stations and a number of factories. The first German vehicles entered the city at 7:00 a.m., followed by cavalry patrols, then infantry. Around 10:00 a.m., the Germans answered strong Russian machine-gun fire from Praga. Dozens of civilian spectators died as victims in this and similar exchanges until 7 August, when the Russians abandoned the east-bank suburb, which had become deprived of both water and electricity, was the target of artillery shelling from the west bank, had been looted by demoralized Russian soldiers, and was the scene of fires and explosions.[175]

The calm determination and sense of common purpose among Russian officials and "Polish society" in Warsaw that characterized the previous autumn had certainly degenerated by the summer of 1915 into a proclivity toward arbitrary

FIGURE 2.   The Russian evacuation of Warsaw with requisitioned livestock, 4 August 1915. The Polish Institute and Sikorski Museum, London.

and deceitful actions among the former and a sense of betrayal among the latter. However, it had not eroded entirely. The story of Warsaw's experience of the end of Russian imperial presence is hardly complete without recognition of the ties that continued to bind the city and particularly its elites to the empire, part of a longer history of co-optation and cooperation that has found only sparse recognition in the existing scholarship on Polish-Russian relations under the tsars. The main narrative, driven by an overstated focus on nationalism, emphasizes instead moments of breakdown in those relations, Russian persecution, and Polish victimization. Readers accustomed to a conventional understanding of that history may, therefore, find it implausible that by and large Poles in Warsaw, led by and dependent upon their elites, supported the Russian cause during the Great War. In fact, however, Russian rule in the Polish Kingdom and the empire's western provinces could not have lasted as long as it did without Russian reliance on local elites and the participation of those elites in various aspects of imperial governance at the local level. It is high time to bring the Polish-Russian story in Warsaw out of the monotone confines of "conflict history" by adopting the more nuanced perspectives of the "new imperial history," for which the journal *Ab Imperio* has been the torchbearer in studies of the Russian Empire, even as it has focused more on that empire's non-European periphery than on its western territories.[176]

In Warsaw and the Polish Kingdom more broadly, the links between the imperial state and "society" had already been strengthened on the eve of the war. In part, the social unrest and violence of the 1905 revolution had sufficiently frightened local elites toward greater support of the state in defense of their interests, but the state itself had, after suppressing the social and political unrest of 1905, also moved toward improving relations with strategic Polish groups, first and foremost in the countryside but also in the cities. The most significant Polish political party that emerged from the revolution, the National Democrats, backed the restoration of state order, voted in favor of Russian military budgets in the imperial Duma, and by 1908 and the appearance of Roman Dmowski's *Niemcy, Rosja i kwestia polska (Germany, Russia and the Polish Question)* had thrown in its lot with the Russians at the time of the Bosnian crisis. The National Democrats, increasingly supported by the Catholic clergy, were joined by traditional conservatives and even progressives in prewar electoral coalitions in support of a "national list" of candidates to the Russian State Duma and in shared hostility toward Jews, something that also gave them common cause with the imperial state once the war began. They were opposed by the socialist Left, but with diminishing effect as its key constituency among industrial workers tired of radical politics. During the first year of the war, the Left had basically become a nonfactor, as had opposition to Russian rule. Indeed, the convergence of Polish "nationalism" with "imperial patriotism" was cemented in 1914 and held together well into 1915 and even beyond. Prince Lubomirski continued to think of himself as a Russian subject for yet another year following the Russian evacuation. So did many other Varsovians. If decolonization was at hand in the war's first year, as Joshua Sanborn argues, it was not evident to those who experienced it, however recognizable the pattern may be to us, particularly in the summer of 1915.

Thus, as Warsaw nervously awaited the entrance of German troops into the city in early August 1915, the representatives of an evaporating imperial regime successfully negotiated a transfer of authority in the city with the Warsaw Citizens Committee in a final replay of the "good' civil-military relationship that had characterized the war's first months. This handoff of power was based first and foremost on a shared interest in the maintenance of public order in the period between the Russian departure from and the German entrance into the city. While the Russians were obviously concerned about security in their rear, from the committee's perspective the new occupier would be confronted with already functioning Polish institutions headed by local officials invested with political and moral authority.[177]

With the evacuation of the Russian courts in mid-July, the Warsaw Citizens Committee developed a plan to maintain the legal order by reorganizing the courts and by nominating new judges from the ranks of sworn attorneys. At the same time, the committee opposed more radical calls for a purge of the lower judiciary on the basis of its members' ties to the Russians. On 26 July it took over from the Russian government the building housing the Warsaw Prosecutor's Office, one among many important signs that the transfer of power was under way.[178] Earlier, the security of the Warsaw Polytechnic had been turned over to three assistant professors who appealed to the committee to relieve them of this responsibility.[179] Shortly thereafter, the Russian president of the city assigned 500,000 rubles in cash to the committee to assist in its assumption of city administration and security for other public buildings and institutions. Thus on 25 July, the committee took over the municipal prison at the Arsenal with its remaining seventy inmates and, on 26 July, the building housing the quasi-governmental Russian Philanthropic Society.[180] There followed the state-run theaters on the last day of the month, the Customs House on 3 August, and on the same day the recently constructed Aleksandr Nevskii Orthodox Cathedral on Saxon Square, a monumental symbol of Russian imperial rule.[181] On 4 August, the day it officially took over administration of the city, the committee transferred its operations to the building that had housed the Warsaw Magistrate.

Meanwhile, members of the committee's long-prepared militia, officially the Citizens Guard (Straż Obywatelska), came out into the open and assumed their posts. The militia's commissars and deputy commissars had already been selected and formally approved as part of a preconceived plan that had been worked out

with the Russians.[182] Distinguished by their blue caps and red and white armbands (the armbands were soon replaced by insignia bearing the image of Syrena,
the historical emblem of the city), the members of the Citizens Guard constituted
the only real police authority in many areas orphaned by the Russians in the first
five days of August 1915.[183] Through the Citizens Guard the committee not only
maintained order in the city but also provided essential fire services. In the course
of the Russian evacuation the city's firemen had been called up into the ranks,
leaving only 82 in service by mid-July from a force that had originally numbered
460. By August, they had been replenished by new cadres from among the candidates for the militia, which even assisted in making some postal deliveries during
the evacuation.[184]

The emergency fundamentally transformed the Warsaw Citizens Committee.
On 3 August it co-opted six new members, including Michał Bergson, president
of the Jewish community board, to replace the National Democrats who had
served on the committee and had fled with the Russians. The committee's Presidium, which consisted of a president (Prince Lubomirski), two vice presidents
(one of whom was the chair of a newly created Department of City Affairs), and
two secretaries (one for City Affairs and the other for the committee's General
Section), maintained an "Emergency Office" daily from 8:00 a.m. to 8:00 p.m.,
while the Presidium itself met in twice-daily sessions.[185] When Prince Lubomirski took over authority from Aleksandr Müller, the Russian president of the city,
he headed what was essentially an already functioning executive institution and
skeletal administration, while the General Section had begun to function as an
unelected city council. As organs of Russian state power ceased to exist, the remnants taken over by the Warsaw Citizens Committee functioned with an efficacy that Aleksander de Rosset, for one, could only describe as "amazing" under
the dire circumstances.[186] Similarly, from the perspective of the Warsaw Superintendent of Police, in a report summarizing the course of the evacuation two
months later, public order in the city had been maintained practically without
incident during the Russian withdrawal. Only on 4 August, the last day of the
evacuation, were there several instances of crowds dismantling wooden buildings
belonging to the railroads, which required the sending of police and Cossacks
to the scene.[187] Otherwise, an amazing calm prevailed. "There is only duty, service, doing what we ought to do," proclaimed *Tygodnik Illustrowany*, which called
upon Warsaw's residents to be guided by "the highest regulator of a fruitful life:
public conscience."[188]

More physical damage was done to Warsaw in the evacuation of 1915 than
from German bombing and artillery shelling the previous October. By the
beginning of July 1915, the city numbered 190,000 fewer inhabitants than it had
at the onset of the war, a decline of more than 20%.[189] Yet to the utter dismay

of those like Dzikowski, who had eagerly awaited the end of the Russian rule, Warsaw had "remained loyal, loyal to the end," as he recorded disparagingly.[190] Others, like Citizens Guard member Mieczysław Jankowski, recalled greater tension and anxiety at the prospect of regime change than ongoing support for the Russians.[191] Perhaps Czesław Jankowski was closer to the truth, however, when he noted that all politics during the two months of the Russian evacuation had become subordinate to thoughts of maintaining life and limb, and of securing personal property.[192] In any case, there is no evidence to support Bogdan Hutten-Czapski's later claim that upon their entrance into Warsaw, German troops were greeted as liberators, except perhaps by a Jewish population fearing the outbreak of a pogrom.[193] Instead, the Warsaw Citizens Committee and its offspring would prove subsequently less cooperative and more confrontational with the German occupation authorities than they had been with the Russians, at least until the 1917 revolutions brought an end to Imperial Russia and destroyed any lingering expectations of ultimate Russian victory and a Russian return to Warsaw. Tellingly, no serious public discussion of removing the remaining symbols of Russian rule in the city, or at least those left untouched by the Germans, would occur until October 1916, some sixteen months after the evacuation.[194]

FIGURE 3. Damaged Vistula Railway Bridge and the Building of a Temporary Bridge. Muzeum Narodowe w Warszawie.

Finally, as damaging as the last weeks and days of the Russian Empire were, they could also have been much worse. Police and Cossacks were often successfully bribed to ignore orders for carrying out the more draconian of the scorched-earth policies in the city.[195] Thus, Warsaw was largely spared the physical destruction suffered by villages and small towns, whose wooden structures and thatched roofs "went up like fireworks," in the words of Holzer and Molenda.[196] Moreover, agriculture suffered to a far greater extent than did industry in the Russian implementation of scorched earth in retreat. And although factories and train stations had been dismantled and damaged in Warsaw, rolling stock, the water supply, gas, electricity, and telephones were all left unscathed by the evacuation.

The city's inhabitants had also remained relatively calm, in part because they had experienced similar events the previous October. Amid the hectic nature of the Russian evacuation and the explosions of sporadic German bombs, the city's theaters, cinemas, and cafés had remained open, and people had continued to take afternoon and evening strolls as they had ten months earlier.[197] Perhaps this was not enough to inspire any immediate longing for the "good old days" of Russian rule in Warsaw. However, as ubiquitous rationing, hyperinflation, wholesale requisitioning, mounting social divisions, increasingly bitter ethnic tensions, devastating epidemics, and starvation became the reality of everyday life over the next three years of the war, there were certainly some who would have traded the many and not insignificant German political and cultural concessions to Polish national conceits in exchange for the relative stability and sense of social solidarity that had characterized, at least in part, the last year of the imperial Russian presence in the once and future Polish capital.

LIVING ON THE EDGE

In their initial encounters on 5 August 1915, the entering German Army and residents of Warsaw greeted each other with a great deal of mutual suspicion. Early that morning, around 6:30 a.m., the Germans had entered Warsaw through its southern (Mokotów) and western (Jerozolimskie and Wola) gates and by 9:00 a.m. could already be seen in the city's midtown district of Śródmieście, where Stanisław Thugutt observed them "staring with particular relish at displays of freshly baked bread."[1] Crowds had already begun to appear in the streets at 5:00 a.m., followed by a number of taxis an hour later. By the time the Germans reached the city center, stores and shops had opened on Krakowskie Przedmieście and Nowy Świat and on Ujazdowskie and Jerozolimskie Boulevards, traversed by trolleys as were other thoroughfares, save for those heading east to and across the Vistula, which had been suspended the previous afternoon and would remain so for some time.[2] According to Aleksander Kraushar, these visibly hungry German soldiers were hardly an attractive sight. Spectators kept their distance from these first representatives of the coming occupation, their faces covered in grime and their boots in mud.[3] Some of these same spectators, like Franciszek Herbst, may have been on hand on Królewska Street to observe the arrest of a few stranded Russian officers who, after the demolition of the Vistula bridges, had made one last visit to an illegal drinking hole or to "the apartment of a Warsaw daughter of Corinth," a reference to the temple of prostitutes in ancient Greece.[4]

The first announcements of the Germans also began to appear that day, almost entirely proscriptive in nature. At a meeting with leading representatives of the Warsaw Citizens Committee, the Germans informed their Polish counterparts of their intention to take twelve hostages from among the city's most important dignitaries.[5] For Kraushar, these early draconian measures were based on common German prejudices and stereotypes about a semi-Asiatic people living in conditions deprived of civilization, and only when the Germans were confronted with the reality of a European city did the early aggressiveness of the occupying forces abate.[6] That may have been so, but we must also remember that Warsaw and especially its Polish elite had supported the Russian side before August 1915 and that the Germans were then still militarily engaged with Russian forces, who continued to fire upon them from Praga on the east bank. Thus, while the Germans provisionally recognized Prince Lubomirski, the chairman of the Warsaw Citizens Committee, as president of the city and entrusted public safety to the committee's Citizens Guard, these "concessions" should be considered in the light of immediate security measures, which also included the suspension of all telephone communications and instructions to the Citizens Guard to treat all acts of disobedience as resistance to the German military authorities and punishable as such.[7]

FIGURE 4. Postcard "Warsaw under German Occupation 1915. The Entrance of German Infantry." Muzeum Narodowe w Warszawie.

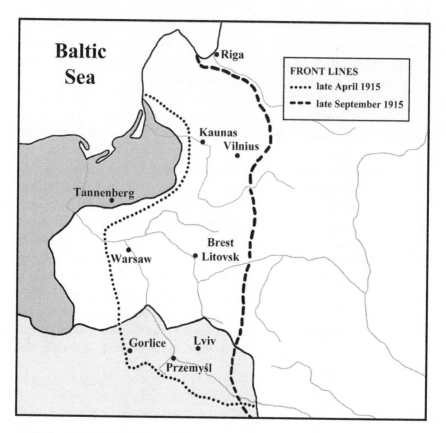

MAP 2.   The Eastern Front in 1915

Within a few days, the Russians abandoned Praga, and the Germans followed up their capture of Warsaw with the taking of the fortresses of Modlin on 20 August and Brest-Litovsk on 26 August. Success in the east, coinciding with the repulsion of Entente offensives in the west, marked the peak of the Central Powers' military fortunes. However, their intentions regarding the Polish Kingdom and Warsaw were not immediately clear. Apparently, General Erich Ludendorff expected Russia's Polish Kingdom to come under the military administration of the Supreme Commander of Germany's eastern armies, Field Marshal Paul von Hindenburg, in whose name the ambitious chief-of-staff planned to exercise an almost vice-regal authority. When the decision was made in Berlin to place Russia's Polish provinces under a civilian rather than military occupation authority, Ludendorff reportedly vowed that this would not happen in Russia's soon-to-be conquered Northwest Territory in Lithuania and Latvia: "Since they have taken Poland from me," Ludendorff is recorded to have said, "I must find another Kingdom for myself."[8]

MAP 3. Occupied central and eastern Europe under the Central Powers, 1915–17

Thus, the Polish Kingdom was spared the political if not economic fate of the "Ober Ost," the experiment in German empire building in the northeastern Baltic region under Ludendorff's military dictatorship. Instead, Russian Poland was divided into *two* zones of occupation, an Austro-Hungarian zone headquartered in Lublin and a larger German zone centered in Warsaw. On 23 August, General Hans von Beseler was appointed governor-general of the German zone, thus officially ending the military administration in Warsaw that had prevailed until then. Preceding Beseler on 9 August was Ernst von Glasenapp, the police chief of Cologne who now assumed that function in Warsaw, and General Ulrich von Etzdorf, who was appointed the German governor of Warsaw on 18 August. Bogdan Hutten-Czapski, destined to serve as Beseler's principal advisor, had arrived earlier with the first German troops. With the appointment of Wolfgang von Kries as chief of civilian administration in the General-Government on 1 September, the group of men who would formulate and implement occupation policies for the rest of the war was complete.

Scholars of the German occupation in the Polish Kingdom and Warsaw have focused primarily on Beseler's failed efforts to build a state economically and militarily dependent on Germany, though the original idea was to hold Russia's Polish territories as a bargaining chip in potential negotiations for a separate peace. As Beseler reported to the kaiser, the political unity of the Poles existed only in their "desire for political autonomy." His task, as he saw it, was "to contain or deflect political propaganda" for independence, rather than encourage it by gestures toward Polish statehood.[9] However, as the war continued and the Russian Empire continued its participation in it, Beseler came to consider and then to convince others that such gestures were necessary. These began with German approval and encouragement of public manifestations of anti-tsarist sentiment in national observances, anniversaries, and demonstrations, starting with the eighty-fifth anniversary of the 1830 November Insurrection in 1915 and culminating in a massive public celebration by tens of thousands of the anniversary of the 3 May 1791 Constitution the following year. The Germans quickly removed the most publicly visible Russian-language signs and replaced them with their Polish-language equivalents. In the area of education, the occupation authorities approved the renewal of the Polska Macierz Szkolna (PMS) organization, which the tsarist authorities had suspended in 1907, to function as a Polish national school board. Although the PMS and other educational institutions were assigned curators, Prussian Poles in German uniform, Mieczysław Jankowski, then a member of the PMS executive board, recalled that these curators helped rather than hindered the board's activities.[10] It was particularly in the area of education where Poles enjoyed greater freedoms than under Russian rule, symbolized above all by the reopening of Warsaw University and the Polytechnic as Polish institutions of higher education on 15 November 1915. According to Hutten-Czapski, their appointed curator, Beseler forbade any participation of representatives of the occupation authorities "in an official capacity" in the reopening ceremony.[11]

As Marta Polskakiewicz argues, from the very beginning German occupation policies displayed a strong ambivalence between cultural and eventually political concessions on the one hand, and the strict control and diversion of resources on the other. The tight grip on Warsaw's economy was at first a requirement of military necessity. Later, however, it was also meant to alleviate food shortages and contain popular opposition to the war in the Reich itself.[12] The challenge for the occupation regime of using the resources of the occupied Polish Kingdom to wage total war without bringing the population out in widespread opposition against it was one that could never be met, even with the most symbolic of political concessions, the joint proclamation in Lublin and Warsaw of the Act of 5 November 1916, in which the German and Austro-Hungarian Emperors announced the creation of a Kingdom of Poland from the occupied Russian territories. Meanwhile, the controls on the civilian population and the country's resources, if anything, became even more severe. "If he skinned us," Aleksander Kraushar wrote of Beseler, "it was in the name of an idea, of providing resources to his own country as a price for freeing Poland of the 'Russian yoke,' rather than for himself."[13]

This brings us to the debate among historians, and most recently between Jesse Kauffman and Vejas Gabriel Liulevicius, about the relationship between German occupation policy in the east during the First World War and that of the Nazis. According to Kauffman's study of Beseler's political strategies in the Warsaw General-Government from 1915 to 1918, there is no direct connection to the later policies and practices driven by Hitler's ideology of race and space overseen by another general-governor, Hans Frank. To suggest otherwise, Kauffman argues, is to indulge the largely discredited *Sonderweg* approach to German history. Indeed, when viewed from above, there is no connection between the two occupations *in Warsaw*. Beseler and others of like mind sought to encourage the Polish state idea and the prominence of Warsaw in it, albeit for their own purposes of creating a potential subordinate Polish ally. Hitler and Frank sought to eliminate the very notion of Polish statehood and to diminish the political significance of Warsaw. Moreover, the two regimes could not have differed more dramatically in their approach to and treatment of Warsaw's Jews. Liulevicius, in his study of the "Ober Ost" during the Great War and elsewhere, has argued that German plans of conquest, colonization, and exploitation of the lands comprising this occupied territory administered by Hindenburg's Tenth Army and dominated by Ludendorff, essentially paved the way for their realization and extension during the Second World War. According to Liulevicius, the interactions of Germans with the local populations in the "Ober Ost," including and especially *Ostjuden*, resulted in cultural assumptions about the east and a justification for a German civilizing mission there. Thus the German experience and then treatment of the "uncivilized" peoples of the "Ober Ost," to oversimplify a complex argument, provided the "poison" for Hitler's murderous worldview and its implementation with the launching of Operation Barbarossa.

One is tempted to refrain from entering this debate because German occupation policies, personnel, and practices during the Great War differed sufficiently from place to place so as to render such larger judgments about the occupation of the western borderlands of the Russian Empire impossible. This was as true of the Warsaw General-Government and the "Ober Ost" as it was true of two cities within fifty kilometers of each other, Warsaw and Łódź, the first to be privileged as the capital city of a quasi-state, the latter the subject of discussions for potential annexation into the Reich and perhaps even fuel for the future Litzmannstadt of the Nazi imagination. This was particularly true in regard to labor recruitment, as Christian Westerhoff has demonstrated in his comparative study of the "Ober Ost" and the Warsaw General-Government, pointing also to significant differences between Warsaw and Łódź.[14] However, what unites Kauffman and Liulevicius is their emphasis on the Germans, and although the latter attempts to give a corrective "view from below" of the structures of occupation in the "Ober Ost" by using Lithuanian sources from the era, his focus remains firmly planted on the occupier. When viewed from the vantage point of the occupied population, intention matters less than practice, and policy even less than its impacts. Policy and even practice may have differed from place to place in the east during the Great War, less so their impacts on ordinary lives.

The Central Powers declaration of 5 November 1916 may have been "one of the worst political blunders of the war," in the words of Liulevicius, in that it raised Polish expectations rather than Polish troops to fight in the east, while slamming the door to any possibility for a separate peace with Russia.[15] Kauffman here agrees, demonstrating that German efforts to recruit Polish soldiers into a new army loyal to the kaiser proved a fiasco.[16] This may have been true, but the concessions toward Polish national culture and statehood were primarily targeted at the Polish elites rather than the larger population. In any case, they were of little consequence to ordinary Varsovians, who had other, far more basic concerns that had become fundamental to their survival long before the Act of 5 November 1916. Indeed, shortly after the November declaration, the city's residents would experience even greater existential catastrophe, to whose causes and markers we now turn.

The Collapse of the Local Economy

According to Thierry Bonzon, the urban economies of London and Paris adapted far more effectively to total war than did that of Berlin; the same can also be said for St. Petersburg (or Petrograd after the outbreak of the war) and Vienna. The British and French metropolises could more easily access the resources of their colonial empires, while capturing those of Imperial Germany. Moreover, the British could effectively blockade Germany, sealing off the Second Reich, its cities, and its occupied territories from access to overseas markets. Paris and especially London simply had greater capacity to increase war production without sacrificing elements essential to the well-being of their urban populations. Labor-market instability was also greater in the capitals of the Central Powers, measured by much more pronounced female participation in the Berlin labor force and the use of some seven thousand Italian and Russian prisoners of war to fill labor shortages in Vienna.[17]

Rates of inflation offer a significant measure of wartime stress on urban economies. Up until the middle of 1916, which Jean-Louis Robert and Jay Winter view as the economic turning point of the war, rates of inflation were roughly similar for London, Paris, and Berlin, after which the German capital experienced far more rapid price increases that eroded real wages and salaries and effected a significant decline in living standards.[18] Berlin's plight is comparable to that of other German cities. In Freiburg, inflation eroded the income of all but a handful. The official cost of living rose at least 100% in the city over the course of the war, while wages of male workers in war-related industries (that is, the highest paid) rose only 50%.[19] In Leipzig, official prices climbed 150% during the course of the war, although the real inflation rate was more likely above 200%, which led to a 35% decline in real wages between 1914 and 1918, and this decline was even steeper for skilled workers.[20]

If wartime inflation in Germany was fueled as much by government borrowing to finance the war as by shortages of goods in high demand, this was even more the case in Russia, where the government effectively renounced 26% of its revenue by banning the sale of alcohol in August 1914.[21] Thus, in just the first two years of the war, the prices of essential goods rose more than 131% in Moscow and more than 150% in Petrograd, though it would be later wartime shortages that seriously undermined the legitimacy of the Russian state and its representatives.[22] Finally, according to Maureen Healy, inflation during the war turned traditional measures of wealth and status in Vienna upside down. In the Austrian capital, prices were 5.7 times higher in 1918 than at the beginning of the conflict.[23]

Thus far, Petrograd and Vienna, the capitals of two empires that collapsed under the strain of total war, provide our worst-case scenarios of wartime economic crisis. What about Warsaw, the center of Russian administration in the Polish Kingdom and later the capital of the quasi-state sponsored by the Central Powers? According to Krzysztof Dunin-Wąsowicz, market prices in Warsaw rose by a multiplier of 20 during the war years, although the "official" prices of rationed goods were 3–4 times lower than the black market prices. The official cost of living is estimated to have increased 6.67 times during the war years, with half of it coming in 1918. Food and clothing costs led the way, increasing by 8.65 times; the official cost of fuel increased by 4.71 times.[24] Thus, in terms of official prices, inflation was higher in Warsaw than in all of the cities mentioned above, but even more significantly, the discrepancy between the official and the black market prices was considerably larger. While the rate of inflation remained somewhat contained under the Russians, it skyrocketed under the Germans. In his report to the kaiser of October 1915, two months after assuming his position, Governor-General Beseler noted that prices for basic goods were already "very high."[25] To take but one example, the price of a pound of bathroom soap rose from 20 to 33 kopecks during the first year of the war.[26] By the time Stanisław Kutrzeba arrived in Warsaw from Kraków in May 1916 to witness the massive public anniversary celebration of the constitution of 3 May 1791, the price of a pound of soap had risen nearly another tenfold to three rubles.[27] Shortly thereafter, soap became practically impossible to obtain at any price.

The average nominal wages for those industrial workers who remained employed in Warsaw may have risen by 100%,[28] a higher increase than in German cities, but their real wages declined at well more than double the rate of those of their German counterparts, with disastrous effects on their standard of living. Consequently, the value of currency declined, gradually in the case of the Russian ruble during the first year of the war, and more rapidly and purposefully during the German occupation. The ruble remained in circulation almost two years into the German occupation, although as Mieczysław Jankowski recalled, the slightest imperfection could lead to its rejection as legal tender.[29] On 27 April 1917, following a series of manipulations of the exchange rate between the ruble and the German mark, the former was replaced by a new Polish mark, which immediately lost 27% of its value. Of the various economic deprivations of the occupation, the currency "reform" particularly inflamed attitudes toward the Germans as transactions in rubles were declared illegal and those taken in exchange for Polish marks went to Berlin. In popular opinion, the visiting Jan Hupka recorded in his diary, the currency reform was nothing else but "a new contribution, levied on Poland. . . ."[30] Aleksander Kraushar was even less charitable, calling the Polish mark with its national White Eagle a German "machination" that further impoverished the population, to the utter ruin of many.[31] The purchasing power of the Polish mark continued to decline over the next eighteen months, falling by well over 100% by August 1918, a trend that accelerated even more dramatically after the war until the Grabski currency reform of 1924 led to its replacement with the złoty.

The dramatic fall of living standards was bad enough for those fortunate enough to actually have access to wages and salaries, but their numbers paled in comparison to the ranks of Warsaw's unemployed. We have already mentioned the impact of the coal shortage on industrial production and employment at the beginning of the war. In December 1914, a survey was conducted of 139 of 500 industrial enterprises employing more than 20 workers. Among these firms, employment had been reduced to 52.5%, hours had been reduced to 40%, and the value of production had been reduced to 30% of prewar norms.[32] At the same time, it was estimated that overall industrial production in Warsaw had declined by 75%, and in the Polish Kingdom as a whole by 90%.[33] Moreover, as a consequence of first Russian and then German requisitioning of Warsaw's industrial stock, not even the slightest recovery would be possible so long as the war continued. The Russian evacuation of several dozen of the most important industrial firms in Warsaw, all of them militarily related, had a devastating enough effect. However, the German decision to requisition and sequester what remained, rather than rebuild and restore Warsaw's industry, proved even more harmful.

According to Mieczysław Jankowski, the articles subjected to initial German requisitioning included metals, fats, leather, kerosene, and petroleum.[34] Shortly thereafter, German requisitioning turned to raw materials, which forced the closure of the majority of Warsaw's remaining industrial firms and completely paralyzed commerce in the city as 70% of what was extracted went to German industry, until the middle of 1916. Then the Germans turned to machines and industrial equipment, starting around March 1916, and by the end of 1917 the Germans were demolishing entire factories. At best, their owners were compensated at a rate of 10% of the actual value of the requisitioned goods, with the remainder to be paid after the war, a promise that was never realized.[35]

Massive unemployment hardly remained confined to industry but quickly spread to practically every sector of Warsaw's economy, starting in 1914. Due to the coal shortage, the city's electric power company laid off 10% of its labor force two weeks into the war.[36] Construction projects in Warsaw also came to a standstill with the outbreak of the war and, after briefly showing some signs of recovery, stalled completely due to a lack of credit and low demand.[37] The general stagnation of construction, coupled with the credit crunch, the high cost of raw materials, and the inability of customers to pay for work completed, would force many of Warsaw's locksmiths to shut down by early 1915.[38] The milling industry in and around Warsaw was reported to be in its death throes by the end of January 1915, as the devastation of the Polish countryside had forced the Warsaw Citizens Committee to purchase already prepared flour from the east instead of from locally produced grain, resulting in layoffs of three thousand workers employed by the industry and affecting some fifteen thousand people.[39] In line with its concern for Warsaw's Christian tradesmen, *Kurjer Warszawski* also highlighted the plight of dye-makers and publicized their request for a tax break. The dye-making industry had been affected by transport difficulties, the lack of necessary materials, and a 75% increase in the costs of doing business. Soon, master furniture craftsmen joined in the appeal for a tax exemption to last to the end of the war, as 85% were forced to close their shops.[40]

The salaried intelligentsia, particularly teachers and journalists, were also immediately affected by the collapse of employment and wages. In December 1914, the Polish Teachers Union appealed to the Warsaw Citizens Committee for direct assistance to its members in critical need; teachers had been forced to accept less than half of their regular average pay in order to salvage the 1914–15 school year.[41] Even worse off, according to *Kurjer Warszawski*, were "workers of the pen." By the end of November 1914, all of Warsaw's monthlies, most of its weeklies, all of its special periodicals, and even one of its dailies had gone under due to a growing paper shortage and prohibitive transportation costs, leading to massive unemployment among journalists and printers.[42] Warsaw, the epicenter of the publishing industry in all of partitioned Poland before the war, began 1914 with some 169 press titles; by the time of the Russian evacuation in August 1915, that number had been reduced to 56.[43] As unemployment spread to Warsaw's educated class, journalists such as Ignacy Grabowski began to argue that an idled white-collar employee was worse off than his factory counterpart who "can always find work [e.g., in the countryside]" compared to the "more physically delicate" member of the intelligentsia.[44] However, employment prospects improved somewhat for the Warsaw intelligentsia during the German occupation of the city, as the Russian evacuation created a shortage of educated personnel in various administrative offices. As would occur during the Second World War, thousands found employment within the city administration, albeit at insufficient salaries.[45] The publishing industry in Warsaw also recovered somewhat, with 112 titles in print at the beginning of November 1916.[46] The same cannot be said for industrial and artisanal workers, whose options were restricted to leaving the city in search of work or finding minimal earnings locally through temporary employment in public-works projects.

Finally, a key difference between Warsaw and the major capitals and cities of the main belligerent European powers during the war years was that female employment declined in absolute terms and failed to rise in proportion to male employment. The cause of women's suffrage in the Anglophone world, if not in France, may have been bolstered by female employment in war-related industry; however, this was most certainly not the case in Warsaw, where women were simply lucky to find any kind of job. Before the war, 18,420 women were employed in industry in Warsaw, roughly 24% of the industrial labor force. In early 1916, the number of women employed in industry had declined to 3,650, just 25% of all industrial workers—despite military conscription and substantial male labor out-migration.[47] By contrast, the percentage of women in Russia's labor force rose from 26.6% to 43.2% between 1914 and 1917.[48] Moreover, employment outside of

Warsaw, especially far afield in Russia before the summer of 1915 or in Germany afterward, was not a realistic option for female factory workers, in part because of a preference for men in heavy industry but also because women could not easily abandon other family members, especially their children and parents. The absence of this option for women is reflected in Warsaw's demographic feminization. Before the war, women held a 9% advantage over men in Warsaw's total population. By January 1917, that advantage had grown to 32%.[49]

Other options for women disappeared as well. Work as domestic servants, the largest single category of women's employment before the war, practically collapsed with the evacuation of Russian officials and the general impoverishment of the Warsaw intelligentsia. According to data from the Employment Office of the Warsaw Citizens Committee's Commission for Women's Work, over a five-month period during the winter and spring of 1914–15, domestic servants comprised one of the largest single categories among its 18,277 applicants. The other, in roughly equal numbers, was comprised of women from the intelligentsia, whose employment as sales clerks was dramatically curtailed as a consequence of the general decline in the city's commerce. Only 20% of all categories of registered women seeking work received any kind of offer of employment.[50] Nor were women able to find temporary employment in public-works projects, which almost exclusively hired men.

Some occupations dominated by women before the war even became masculinized. For example, Warsaw's haberdashery industry before the war employed some 1,600 workers, 60% of whom were women. By the end of January 1915, seven hundred of these workers were unemployed, almost all of them women, as drapers, curtain-makers, and manufacturers of window blinds had almost all gone out of business.[51] For a time under Russian rule, it appeared that employment on the railroads, which had offered up more than their fair share of conscripts and volunteers to the army, would open up to women, but military developments quickly closed that door.[52] The garment industry was one area of women's employment that held relatively firm, enough so that once the city experienced a slight economic upturn in early 1918, female workers went on a successful six-week strike.[53] However, the only profession that saw both an absolute and a proportional increase in female employment was teaching, especially in the secondary schools, as a consequence of the expansion of public education during the German occupation. Indeed, as women gained increasing access to higher education in Warsaw starting in 1915, they came to comprise 56% of all secondary school teachers by the end of the war.[54]

Work in education may have alleviated unemployment among women of the Warsaw intelligentsia, just as jobs in state and municipal administration did for their male counterparts during the German occupation. Their lot, of finding and purchasing goods in tremendous shortage at inflated prices with a currency that consistently lost its value, was hard enough. For the majority of Varsovians and especially for women, children, the elderly, and those without employment or any visible means of subsistence, it is a wonder that they survived, if indeed they did survive, the First World War. By looking closely at the basic living conditions of Warsaw's residents during the war years—especially in terms of their housing, heating, food, and health—we can come to a better understanding of the existential challenges that all of them faced, but which some of them were better able to confront than others.

Housing

London, Paris, and Berlin all experienced sporadic rent increases during the war, in part due to an almost complete halt in new housing construction. The state began to emerge not only as the director and author of municipal construction, but also as a supporter of private construction, if it had the means to encourage it at all. An even more visible form of state intervention came in the form of rent control, which emerged during the war to contain the inflation of housing costs. Though briefly suspended after the war, rent control was renewed everywhere at the hyperinflationary beginning of the 1920s.[55]

As with many other things, the housing situation in Warsaw during the war stands more in contrast than it does in comparison with that in the British, French, and German capitals. Before the war there was an acute housing shortage in Warsaw, with average occupancy of 2.25 persons per room.[56] Reflecting this situation, tenants and landlords signed many new lease agreements in July 1914, which raised rents by as much as 15%.[57] The first wartime development that would lead to a dramatic reversal of these housing trends was the mobilization and conscription of male breadwinners; this left their families in a difficult situation, unable to pay their rents, whether or not those rents had been recently raised. At first, the Warsaw Building Owners Association sought to find a solution that it thought acceptable to both tenants and landlords, in the form of rescinding or postponing the recent rent increases. However, several landlords refused to make any concessions to their tenants, thus arousing the ire of public opinion against them. Such landlords, according to *Kurjer Warszawski*, "apparently don't believe that there is a war going on and that as a consequence there is an unavoidable and fatal economic crisis."[58] Soon enough, reservist and conscript families stopped paying their rents entirely, and landlords began to seek their eviction as the Warsaw dailies became flooded with letters of recrimination from both sides. As hundreds of these disputes over unpaid rents made their way into the courts, however, judges found for the tenants, refusing to have them evicted or to force them to make immediate payment.[59]

Nevertheless, as evictions continued to mount, with even larger numbers on the immediate horizon at the beginning of October 1914, the Warsaw Citizens Committee decided to take up the matter of providing housing to those who had been ousted from their apartments for nonpayment of rent.[60] However, it would take the committee nearly four months to establish a Housing Section to find free or low-cost housing for those among Warsaw's permanent residents who had been made homeless as a consequence of the war.[61] In the meantime, at the beginning of October, a recently established Landlords and Tenants Association set up an arbitration and information bureau staffed by delegates from both groups.[62]

Eventually, the Russian government would step in and declare a moratorium on rent payments for soldiers' families to the end of the war. This did not end the complaints coming from landlords, however. The Building Owners Association claimed that a number of soldiers' families who had taken advantage of the moratorium were nevertheless subleasing rooms to boarders, many of them refugees, in the process earning in excess of the rent that they would otherwise have paid their landlords. *Rezerwistki*, a term that came to embrace wives of both reservists and conscripts, were even accused of setting up small shops and workshops in the rent-free apartments.[63] Having been rebuffed in the courts, which continued to side with Warsaw *rezerwistki*, landlords refused to rent to soldiers' wives coming from the provinces, even if they offered to pay in advance, for fear that they would not pay in the future. If provincial *rezerwistki* tried to reside with relatives, landlords refused to register them, concerned that their presence would become a pretext for future nonpayment. For that reason, many soldiers' wives were housed in refugee shelters, regardless of their ability to pay rent.[64]

If the moratorium for soldiers' families deprived landlords of one source of income, an unprecedented level of vacancies deprived them of another. In the summer and fall of 1914, the departure of the families of Russian officials left a number of apartments standing empty, while the city struggled to shelter incoming refugees, an irony noted by Wincenty Miklaszewski in his diary.[65] By the end of January, some four thousand apartments had been vacated since the start of the war by the families of officials, German and Austrian subjects deported to the interior, and the families of wealthy landowners with estates to the east of Warsaw.[66] As the Russians began their final evacuation of the city in the summer of 1915, rents had already declined by 25–30%, that is, to the level that had existed a decade earlier. Reduced demand had also reduced the purchasing costs for private housing, a phenomenon hailed in the press as an end to "the golden age of speculation."[67]

Under the circumstances, it was natural that landlords themselves would hope for relief, and following the moratorium on rents for soldiers' families, rumors circulated in the press that property taxes on buildings would be suspended. However, the Russian state continued to collect taxes energetically and began to sequester the property of those delinquent in payments. By the first week of January 1915, some one hundred buildings in Warsaw had been sequestered, leading to a petition from the Building Owners Association to the Ministry of the Treasury. In it the association explained that landlords were not receiving rents or credits to pay their taxes and expressed the fear that their properties would be sold at auction.[68] In response, by mid-January 1915 tax collection on immovable property in Warsaw was temporarily suspended.[69]

In December 1914, the Warsaw Credit Society applied for an interest-free or low-interest loan from the state for 10 million rubles. The intended loan was designed to provide relief to property owners who were increasingly unable to pay taxes, installments, and mortgage interest due to arrears in rent payments from tenants, not to mention the fact that thousands of soldiers' families were not paying any rent at all. In March 1915, however, that application was rejected.[70] Instead, by the end of the month, the city administration raised the apartment tax paid by landlords by 50%, even though most landlords had been forced to lower their rents as a result of the war.[71]

The Russian evacuation may have ended the obligations of owners of rental property to the Russian state, but little else changed during the German occupation. Rents failed to recover, if they were paid at all, remaining 25% lower than the prewar level, even by the end of the war. The depressed housing market was also reflected in the decline in per room occupancy to 1.83 in January 1917,[72] which in most circumstances could be viewed as a positive development. While landlords continued to find it almost impossible to take legal action against *rezerwistki* who continued to withhold their rent, they had only a slightly freer hand in evicting others who had been even more impoverished by the war. When Stanisław Kutrzeba visited Warsaw from Krakow in May 1916, he noticed that "public opinion stridently condemned" evictions, but that the city's owners of rental property had "ceased to be objects of jealousy" as they had been before the war.[73] Thus, the conflict between landlords and tenants remained at a stalemate. However, while tenants may have been able to reduce the proportional cost of housing in their overall cost of living, the availability and affordability of practically everything else, beginning with fuel to heat their dwellings, more than obliterated this minor advantage.

The Energy Crunch

From the very beginning of the war there were observable shortages of all goods of primary need, but the most acute during the war's first year was that related to fuel. As discussed previously, the inability of coal transported from the Don Basin to make up for the shortfall caused by the German occupation of the coalfields to Warsaw's southwest had an immediately devastating effect on industrial production and employment. However, the coal shortage also affected the city's ability to feed its inhabitants, as supplies were needed to fire ovens in bakeries or to heat stoves in the Warsaw Citizens Committee's recently established public kitchens.[74] With colder weather already imminent by mid-September 1914, the coal shortage assumed even greater urgency. As an anonymous author in the weekly *Tygodnik Illustrowany* put it: "Where are we going to get it? And how are we going to pay for it, since it has already increased in price?"[75] According to a *Bluszcz* editorial from early October, "coal has become the symbol of well-being and the source of envy."[76]

With no end of the coal shortfall in sight, the city and its institutions focused on the conservation of existing supplies to meet the needs of public utilities and hospitals. In fact, by the end of September 1914, as a matter of public policy, little coal was being sold at all to individuals, prioritizing social and institutional needs.[77] With the designation of most Donbas coal for use by Warsaw's factories, it was assumed that public and administrative buildings and offices could be heated in winter with firewood, the supplies of which were then abundant, given the relatively close proximity of large tracts of state and private forest. Individuals were also encouraged to use firewood, along with coke and peat, and to convert their kitchens to gas-burning stoves.[78] Street lighting was reduced in early October and again in the middle of November, a measure that was projected to save thirty carloads of coal by the end of the year. Similarly, limitations on the use of lighting in building entrances and hallways were expected to create an additional 3% savings on the city's use of coal and a 10% savings on its use of gas.[79] To further save on coal, the electric trolleys reduced their hours of operation by cutting one hour each from their morning and evening routes.[80] Whether by *force majeure* or intentional conservation measures, the consumption of electricity in Warsaw had been cut in half and its consumption of gas reduced by 28% by the fourth week of September.[81]

In time, the coal crisis led to pressures on other fuels. The Warsaw Citizens Committee considered the idea of appealing to factories to switch from coal to coke as their principal source of energy, especially since coke was of less practical use to individual consumers, but a shortage of coke was already perceptible by the end of October, and this shortage harmed a number of the city's small industrial plants that had managed to continue some level of production.[82] At the beginning of December, Warsaw faced an extreme shortage of coke as a result of increased demand from factories filling orders for the Russian military; those factories exceeded the amounts of coke used by the Warsaw gasworks and exhausted existing stocks. As with coal, Warsaw would have no choice but to import coke from the Don Basin to try to make up the shortfall.[83]

For a time the Warsaw press saw firewood as something of a panacea for the city's emerging energy crisis. Given the uncertainties about the supply and transport of coal and other fossil fuels, Ignacy Grabowski, writing in *Kurjer Warszawski*, called for the immediate acquisition of firewood from nearby forests, so that it would have time to dry before the onset of winter. Work in the forests, moreover, was seen as a source of employment for workers made idle by the decline in factory production in the Warsaw industrial region.[84] By the end of September 1914 the Warsaw Citizens Committee itself came under Grabowski's criticism for placing too much emphasis on contracting supplies of Donbas coal instead of cutting and drying firewood in suburban forests.[85] Indeed, the Russian government in mid-September had set aside parcels of state forest and parkland in the vicinity of Warsaw for the committee's exclusive use, which the committee began to discuss seriously only two weeks later.[86]

Nonetheless, transportation difficulties in supplying a frontline city in close proximity to armies engaged in intense combat led to a shortage of firewood for distribution. By 26 October 1914, the committee's stores reported that they hadn't received any new supplies of firewood for nine days.[87] Shortly thereafter, the committee resolved to post members of sporting organizations—the anticipated members of its planned militia—permanently at its stores to preserve order.[88] In early November, firewood was still not making its way to the committee's distribution sites. Soon thereafter, the unanticipated shortage of firewood, the unresolved problems of its transport, and conflicts with the committee's Distribution Commission would lead to the resignation of the director of the committee's Fuels Section, Stanisław Norblin.[89]

At times sheer rumor could spark a shortage. For example, an imagined disruption in supplies of kerosene due to the outbreak of war between Russia and the Ottoman Empire in November 1914 never materialized but still caused hoarding in Warsaw in anticipation of winter shortages, thus driving prices up by 50%.[90] As early as mid-September, there had been concerns that the city's supply of kerosene was enough to last for only six to seven weeks.[91] By December, those local suppliers that continued to sell kerosene did so in limited amounts at restricted hours, and in Praga, with police present to maintain order. Elsewhere, owners were forced to close stores against "attacking crowds."[92] As rail freight transportation difficulties mounted, ever-larger crowds were reported in front of factories and stores, queuing for several hours to purchase kerosene in even the smallest amounts.[93]

While the kerosene shortage would temporarily subside by the end of the year, the coal shortage became ever more pronounced. By early December, the amount of coal being shipped to Warsaw from the Donbas amounted to only 25% of the city's prewar supply.[94] On 10 December 1914, *Kurjer Warszawski* announced that Warsaw stood on the "brink of catastrophe" as even a minor interruption of coal shipments from a single source, the Donbas, would leave the city without fuel, light, and water. The gasworks were reportedly down to just several days of supply, the city trolley system down to three to four weeks, the waterworks down to a month's supply for the operation of its filters and pumps, and the electric power station down to supplies sufficient only to the end of February. Even with the reduction of demand caused by the city's major industrial slowdown, needs were said to be double the available supply.[95]

Warsaw's energy shortage led to acts of desperation, particularly among the urban poor, that would later characterize the food crisis during the German occupation. In the second half of September 1914, Warsaw's working-class suburbs reported an increasing number of thefts of coal, firewood, and "anything that burns" from enclosed storage sites. Given the complicity of local residents, the apprehension of thieves proved nearly impossible.[96] In December, the poor from Praga and other outlying suburbs began to rob those few coal trains actually destined for the city as they waited to be unloaded. Both adults and children were involved in these incidents, the railroad guards helpless against them.[97]

Fuels and especially coal also became the object of speculation, corruption, and controversy, not to mention organized crime. By early December the courts became increasingly flooded with complaints from purchasers of coal and firewood who claimed they had been short-changed; in February 1915 there were reports of coal being mixed with soil or sand before being sold at the controlled price.[98] Private warehouses were accused of engaging in "unconscionable acts of profiteering" as a result of the "coal hunger."[99] At the height of the winter crisis in January 1915, suspicion fell on the Warsaw Citizens Committee's Fuels Section, which had become responsible for the procurement and purchase of coal and whose "instructors" were accused of collusion in profiteering schemes with warehouses by delaying the creation of public storage units for coal distribution. Indeed, the Fuels Section came under such heavy public criticism that Prince Lubomirski sent a note to the press in which he expressed his understanding of the section's difficult position in trying to meet Warsaw's pressing energy needs and denied any lack of confidence in it on the part of the committee's leadership. For the moment, Lubomirski's action forestalled a mass of resignations from the section.[100] Nevertheless, continued accusations of corruption and mismanagement appeared in the press and would lead to the resignation of the entire membership of the Fuels Section a few weeks later.[101]

For a short time from the middle of January through February 1915, it appeared as if the situation might improve, to the point that the committee believed that supplies of coal from the Donbas could satisfy demand by spring, as shipments that had taken four weeks or more to reach their destination in Warsaw in December were arriving in as few as ten days.[102] Indeed, toward the end of February, the committee felt confident enough in future supplies to actually lower the price ceiling for coal.[103] To enforce adherence to the ceiling and to regain public confidence in its monitoring of warehouses, the committee's Fuels Section claimed to have uncovered eighty-one violations leading to state or committee sanctions.[104] Nonetheless, the city continued its sparing use of street lighting. Before the war, Warsaw had been lit by 820 electric lights. This was reduced to 534 at the end of September, and by the end of January 1915 only 250 electric lamps remained in use.[105] Shortly thereafter, experiments in reducing the city's lighting resulted in blackouts, something that the city had experienced in 1905, only now without "the danger that accompanied one's steps around every corner" in that revolutionary year, according to *Tygodnik Illustrowany*.[106]

Whatever relief seemed to be on the horizon in February proved short-lived, and by the middle of March, shipments of Donbas coal to Warsaw were reduced to a mere trickle. To maintain the functioning of the electrical grid, the gasworks, the trolley system, the sewers and the water pumps, and the heating of hospitals, the city's Russian president Aleksandr Müller called for the creation of a special commission to ensure the efficient distribution of coal among public institutions.[107] The problem by that time was not simply one of transportation from eastern Ukraine but also of production, which had declined from 160 million puds of coal extracted in October to 135 million puds in January, the main cause of which was a labor shortage caused by the conscription of Donbas miners. By 23 March, the electric power station in Warsaw had supplies for only the next several days, the gasworks for little more than a week, and the trolley system for a month, while private use of coal had been reduced to a minimum. In response the state agreed to pay for the passage of contracted workers to the Donbas mines, lifted restrictions on the employment of women, minor children, and POWS in the mines, and exempted the existing male mining labor force from military service.[108] A proposal of the Russian authorities to convert industrial furnaces in what still remained of Warsaw industry to firewood could not be realized, since it would have required a guaranteed six-month supply, which, in the face of requisitioning from both the state-owned railroads and the army, proved impossible.[109] Of the 2,200 wagons per month of firewood requested by the Warsaw City Magistrate, only one-third of that amount was actually making its way to Warsaw in April.[110]

By the beginning of May, Warsaw's fuel supply had reached a "critical" state, as the Warsaw Citizens Committee received word from the Warsaw Governor-General that only the city's gasworks, which was down to four days of supplies and in danger of closing even after reducing pressure in the lines, had any hope of receiving future shipments of coal. At the same time, the Russian authorities promised to do everything to enhance the delivery of firewood and to exempt all firewood purchased by the committee from military requisitioning.[111] However, the shipment of firewood to Warsaw by rail remained doubtful at best, leaving only the possibility of river transport. During the week of 15–22 May 1915, the committee's Fuels Section purchased some 2,000 freight car loads of firewood, adding to its previous purchases of 8,656 car loads. However, not a single one had reached Warsaw, while a plan to ship 150,000–200,000 cords of wood to Warsaw by boat in the coming months was also never realized, at which point the Russian evacuation overwhelmed all other considerations.[112]

During that evacuation, both the Warsaw Citizens Committee as well as local residents sought to secure what remained of Russian government stocks. As the committee prepared to assume control of the city in August 1915, it received the permission of the Russian military authorities to take over the kerosene reserves of the Nobel firm in Warsaw.[113] Meanwhile, according to a police report, the railroad authorities' decision to give the remaining stocks of coal and firewood to the population free of charge caused the only incidents or evidence of disorders at the time of the evacuation. The crowds, armed with tools to demolish the wooden buildings along the rail lines, formed in large numbers on 29 July 1915, and police and Cossacks had to be called in to restore order.[114] A few days later, on 4 August, the Russian military authorities allowed local residents to gather wood for heating from fences and rail stations in Praga, as well as from the Kovel station, thus legalizing what had earlier been prohibited. Those who managed to carry their haul away in carts would now finally have wood for fuel for several months.[115]

Such acts of desperation proved unnecessary, at least for the short term, as the German occupation would effectively restore supplies to the city from the coal mines of Zagłębie Dąbrowskie, the southwestern part of the Polish Kingdom, which had come under German control at the beginning of the war. For at least the next year, energy would cease to be a cause of everyday concern and even more so of commentary in the legal press, whose reporting on such matters the German occupation authorities strictly prohibited in any case. Nonetheless, by the summer of 1916, energy pressures again began to mount, although they would never reach the level of the war's first year. The first signs of a renewed energy crunch came in the form of the Warsaw City Administration's effort to tighten control over available resources in July of that year, at the time of the dissolution of the Warsaw Citizens Committee. In a pointed memorandum, it reminded its officials that all fuels, and particularly coal, purchased by the Fuels Section and supplied to other sections, city stores, and any other institutions were intended for the exclusive use of the sections, offices, administrations, and stores. The sections under the Department of Assistance to the Population were authorized to supply small amounts of fuel to the poorest of Warsaw's inhabitants free of charge, but no department, section, or any other city institution had the right to sell even the smallest amounts of fuel to any individual, institution, or association. Only those individuals who were assigned apartments at city stores in connection with their service to or employment by the city were to be provided fuel within well-defined limits and timeframes.[116]

In any event, the ration system did not spread to coal and other fuels until October 1917 and was soon accompanied by a sharp reduction of electric power and the return of severe shortages of heating materials for Warsaw's population. As a consequence, long lines immediately formed at coal warehouses, lasting day and night, as a brisk business developed in the buying and selling of queuing places.[117] As had occurred during the first year of war under the Russians, the city once again became mainly illuminated by gas lanterns, which themselves were extinguished early to effect savings. By 1918, the city was fortunate to be illuminated at all, as the gas supply too declined dramatically as a result of the renewed coal shortage.[118] Firewood, too, proved to be an unavailable alternative. In the forests proximate to Warsaw, the Germans clear-cut 70% of the existing stands of trees—compared to an average annual felling norm of 5% then considered appropriate to proper forest management—which in turn had an obvious impact on local supplies.[119] Indeed, German control over and exploitation of the forests led to a 400% increase in the cost of firewood less than two months into the occupation, leading to the auctioning of farm buildings on the outskirts of Warsaw, which were then demolished and their wood used for heat.[120]

In many ways, by the end of the war Warsaw's coal and energy crisis was comparable to that of other major cities. London, too, was forced to ration coal in 1917, and Paris experienced even more severe shortages than did the British metropolis. In Berlin, failure to meet the needs of noncombatants was primarily a matter of distribution rather than supply, as coal became subject to illicit trading and rampant inflation, not unlike the situation in Warsaw.[121] What distinguished Warsaw from these other cities was that its energy crisis at the end of the war, though bad enough, paled in comparison to what had been experienced in 1914–15, which perhaps is one reason why the later crisis left little register in public memory of the war after that point. More importantly, however, the shortage of coal and other fuels had long since become secondary to malnutrition as the most basic feature of everyday suffering.

The Food Catastrophe

At the end of September 1914, in commenting in his diary on the sale of "entire galleries" of art to afford food purchases at prices 30–50% higher than at the beginning of the war, Wincenty Miklaszewski claimed that even "the most spiritual of impulses" had become "subordinate to the stomach."[122] Less than two years later, as food riots swept through Warsaw in the summer of 1916, everything indeed—including life itself—came to depend not on merely securing food at an affordable price as in the fall of 1914, but on securing it at any price and in whatever quality was available.

All major European urban centers in the belligerent countries faced food crises of varying severity, less so in London and Paris, which managed to avoid catastrophic shortages and serious declines in average caloric intakes, than in the cities of Imperial Germany, Austria-Hungary, and their occupied territories.[123] During the war's second half, the daily caloric intake of the average German male was well under half that of the 3,400 calories consumed by his average British counterpart. In Vienna, a theoretical 830 calories per day were allotted urban residents by 1917, but the level was likely well lower in practice as 91% of all school-aged children were reportedly malnourished by the end of the war.[124] In both wartime Vienna and Berlin—where, as Bonzon and Davis put it, "only the rich and corrupt could obtain what everyone else had to go without"[125]—food became *the* main arena of political conflict. In both imperial capitals, food shortages were central to the deterioration of popular support for the war and faith in the existing regimes.

However, popular discontent had as much to do with expectations as with actual shortages, whether because of shared sacrifice and the state's responsibility to ensure it, or because of diets that had become more varied in the years before the war. Food prices in Berlin may have increased by 250% during the war, but such a level of inflation paled in comparison with the situation that prevailed in Vienna, not to mention Vilnius and other cities of the German-occupied "Ober Ost," which were gripped by famine and where thousands died of starvation in the winter of 1916–17.[126] In the cities of the Russian Empire, food riots broke out mainly over the cost and availability of sugar during the first two years of the war, an indication of how the market had raised lower-class aspirations "to live by more than bread alone," in the words of Barbara Engel.[127] In fact, despite the stimulus provided by military purchases, grain prices in Russia did not accelerate rapidly until 1916 as exporters initially unloaded their goods on the domestic market.[128] By contrast, Imperial Germany imported more than one-third of its food supply before the war; therefore, Germans in cities like Berlin immediately felt the impact on prices, beginning with the cost of bread, in the fall and winter of 1914–15.[129]

Against this larger perspective, Warsaw's wartime food catastrophe can be best compared to that of Vienna and the cities of the "Ober Ost," fitting somewhere in between these two poles. However, during the first year of the war, as a frontline city of the Russian Empire, Warsaw's food shortages were more sporadic than chronic and varied from product to product, their prices fluctuating—sometimes wildly—depending on the proximity of the fighting and the availability of road and rail transport. Hunger among the general population appeared but was held in check. Starvation remained a specter, which only later during the German occupation became a horrific reality for the underprivileged part of the population.

Before the war, Warsaw's food supply was almost entirely dependent on rail transport; only fruit was shipped to the city by river.[130] This became a concern for two reasons: 1) the previously mentioned north-south emphasis of the Russian railway system, and 2) its division into independent military and civil networks at the outbreak of the war. Large-scale troop movements, in particular, put enormous strain on the transport system throughout the empire, but particularly in the western provinces and the Polish Kingdom.[131] Government policy concentrated on feeding the army, leaving noncombatants to fend for themselves. However, a ban on food exports from provinces closest to the front helped to control food prices in the regions under greatest stress, including Warsaw.[132]

The first shortages in the city resulted from the panic buying and hoarding of food in the war's first days, leading to immediate price increases. According to the Warsaw Citizens Committee, the largest price increases in this early period were for meat, followed by flour, milk, and peas.[133] Emotions would eventually calm down, however, and there was a relatively rapid restoration of normal food supplies. By 10 August, prices in the area around Warsaw were falling quickly, and by the next day in the city itself, beginning with a 25% decline in the price of potatoes.[134] On the other hand, the press attributed a 20% increase in the price of bread since the start of the war to profiteering by four Warsaw mills, a charge subsequently refuted by local millers who blamed a severe shortage in supplies of bran, which before the war had been imported.[135] A survey conducted toward the end of August 1914 showed that food prices, with the exception of meat, had returned to levels that were prevalent in the spring. Even with meat, particularly beef and veal, the main problem influencing prices at this stage was one of transport from distant

Ukrainian and Podolian markets, but by mid-September the meat shortage had also eased.[136]

Even though the metropolis had effectively weathered the immediate crisis, the Warsaw Citizens Committee believed the city to be the most poorly provisioned in the Polish Kingdom.[137] Nonetheless, Warsaw's supply of butter was apparently sufficient to contemplate the sending of a wagonload in support of Łódź, which was closer to the front and under even more duress. By the end of September, the Warsaw Citizens Committee's main concern focused on the city's grain supplies, especially as transports were being immediately consumed.[138] At approximately the same time came the first reports of food-related fraud. In one scam, young men dressed in military uniform delivered news to relatives from soldiers at the front, and then claimed that they needed to get back quickly to their "comrades" who were under aerial bombardment. The alarmed relatives would then quickly put together food parcels, which the con artists then consumed or sold.[139]

A far more serious disruption in Warsaw's food supply, accompanied by rapidly escalating prices, occurred during the "Battle of Warsaw." With the Germans at the gates of the city during the first half of October 1914, panic purchases of bread and other foods led to a citywide shortage. Crowds of women and children also began to appear at military barracks and camps and at rail stations to meet arriving military trains, hoping to get the army's leftovers.[140] Meanwhile, the inability to transport milk to Warsaw because of the fighting created a situation described as "fatal," with supplies sufficient only for hospitals and philanthropic organizations caring for the ill and infant children. There had been concerns about a milk shortage for infants in lower-class families the previous August, but they paled in comparison to the situation during and after the October battle.[141]

As the German Army temporarily retreated to the west, the persistence of high prices for bread and flour was attributed in part to the increase in Warsaw's population by "tens of thousands" of refugees, in part to the fatal state of the country's agricultural sector, particularly in areas recently occupied by the Germans.[142] The milk shortage in Warsaw continued after the battle as well, with no end in sight. With the front still relatively close, both rail shipment and horse-drawn transport were nearly impossible, and a fairly high proportion of dairy cattle had been taken out of production by the fighting armies of both sides and by German requisitioning. Meanwhile, consumers were warned of watered-down milk and the addition of false ingredients by unscrupulous storeowners to stretch existing supplies.[143] However, it soon became clear that the Germans had requisitioned horses, milk and other dairy products, not to mention entire fall harvests, during the fighting on the Mokotów, Grójec and Kalisz sides of the city.[144] For the first time, hunger now struck the more distant Warsaw suburbs, scenes of recent fighting, which had also suffered deprivations caused by the retreating German

Army. In several locations within a fairly significant radius of the city, it was impossible to find bread. Only supplies from a hardly abundant Warsaw helped to prevent catastrophe, which required the lifting of a ban on shipments.[145]

Fortunately, the supply of rural products from the east bank of the Vistula began to compensate for the losses on the west bank, and by the first week of November 1914, renewed shipments on suburban roads and the end of requisitioning of supplies destined for Warsaw would lead to a drop in prices for potatoes, cabbage, vegetables, and poultry.[146] As in the case of coal, the major problem in provisioning Warsaw with food beyond the city's vicinity was the shortage of freight cars. Thus, there was only a slight improvement in grain shipments, while arrivals of cattle and hogs from Ukraine and Bessarabia were treated as major events.[147]

With the onset of the war's first winter and the near exhaustion of the city's flour reserves, there were reports of hungry children "of the street" who had been reduced to begging.[148] As the holiday season approached, dates, almonds, candies, marmalades, coffee, and herring were all reported in short supply. In the last weeks of 1914, among the more basic goods only sugar was being loaded and transported to Warsaw, and the city faced the real danger of a food emergency.[149] In reference to the growing shortage of dairy products in the city, *Kurjer Warszawski* commented, "Every step along the way one encounters the fatal economy on the railroads, leading to shortages and inflation of the most necessary food provisions, despite their availability in areas not far from Warsaw."[150]

Varsovians survived the war's first winter, but shortfalls remained, the most persistent of which affected supplies of beef and milk, although relatively normal availability of veal, pork, and kielbasa was restored. Disease among livestock shipped on the Polesie and Northwest lines into the city, the now customary transport irregularities and holding up of railcars at branch stations, the Russian Army's requisitioning of cattle, the wholesalers' withholding of the remaining cattle from the market in protest of the city's price controls, and the exhaustion of pasture and fodder on the Vistula's east bank all contributed to growing inflationary pressures on beef and dairy products.[151] These problems, along with a petition from local butchers, forced the Warsaw Citizens Committee to accept a 30% increase in the price ceiling for beef in the early spring and then to lift it altogether in May.[152]

By that time, the supply and sale of beef in Warsaw had become "a real Gordian knot," in the words of *Kurjer Warszawski*, not only because of the usual transportation problems but also because of a newly imposed government ban on the shipping of livestock out of Podolia and Ukraine.[153] Moreover, Russian military requisitions took an even greater toll, from approximately one-third of the cattle that had been transported to Warsaw since January 1915 to up to 60% by the second half of May. Under the circumstances of acute shortage, the city administration and the Warsaw Citizens Committee decided that price controls on beef would be impossible to maintain.[154] *Kurjer Warszawski*, however, strongly

FIGURE 5.   A food line on Koszykowa Street, 1915. Muzeum Narodowe w Warszawie.

criticized this decision, fearing that if the ceiling on beef were lifted, others would certainly follow. The newspaper argued that thanks to the introduction of price controls six months earlier, the "mad orgy of speculation" had been tamed. Instead, the newspaper called for the imposition of controls at the wholesale level to accompany those on retail prices and for the Warsaw Citizens Committee to serve as a middleman between producers and consumers.[155]

As Lars Lih has shown for the Russian Empire as a whole, such a level of market intervention would have required statewide enforcement, as merchants diverted shipments elsewhere when confronted with the attempts of municipal authorities to regulate wholesale prices. Indeed, the tsarist government restricted its intervention in the market to the diversion of supplies to the army. Thus, there would be no resort to food rationing in cities like Petrograd to the bitter end of the tsarist regime.[156] However, while more stringent controls on prices and the imposition of rationing may have provided a temporary sense of food security, they did little to contain the real cost of living, which regulated market prices could no longer measure accurately in any case. What contained food prices in Warsaw during the first year of the war was not controls but the relatively greater availability of food on the market, despite the spot shortages of particular items, such as beef, that vexed the Warsaw press at the time.

To take but another example: on the eve of the Christian (Catholic and Ortho-dox) Easter and Passover holidays, which all coincided in the 1915 calendar year, *Kurjer Warszawski* exclaimed, "Future generations reading about the European war of 1914–1915" will be amazed that "in our times of increasing inflation and unhampered profiteering, we are being asked to pay 18 Polish groszy for a sin-gle Easter egg."[157] While the newspaper recognized there was greater than usual seasonal demand, caused in part by the influx of tens of thousands of visitors registered by the police who came to the city to take advantage of its relative abundance, it was more eager to target the "enormous profit-taking by Warsaw hucksters." Needless to say, one year later, Varsovians would have been thrilled to find an egg at eighteen groszy, if they could find one at all, as what essentially was a problem under Russian rule was transformed into a catastrophe during the German occupation, despite and even because of state intervention in local markets through price controls and rationing.

Thus, with the Russian evacuation of Warsaw already in full swing, the Provi-sions Section of the Warsaw Citizens Committee reported on 23 July 1915 that the city had abundant supplies, despite panic buying and speculation. The sec-tion was then currently stocking some seventy public stores in the city serving the poor population but was forced temporarily to cease its sales of goods to owners of private stores and bakeries.[158] It was only a week later that the city entered into a situation that could be described as a food emergency, one that the committee feared could lead to "complete starvation" if the evacuating Russians continued to take provisions out of Warsaw while holding up new transports into the city.[159] In the days of transition between Russian and German control of the city, entire wagonloads of unripened fruit were being sold, to the indigestion of many, while the prices of potatoes and cabbage doubled.[160] In the face of renewed calls for a general freeze on prices, the committee requested requisitioning power from the Russian military authorities, which it would execute with all necessary means if private individuals did not sell to the Provisions Section what it presumed they had been hoarding. In the meantime, the section limited its sales to public stores and philanthropic organizations and suspended all of its wholesale purchases.[161]

The Russian authorities shortly thereafter authorized the Provisions Section to requisition articles of primary need from private stocks. All requisitioned goods became the property of the Warsaw Citizens Committee and were sold to the population under the strictest possible controls. Goods subjected to requisitioning included flour, grain, oats, sugar, salt, grits, lard, peas, fat, rice, beans, bran, as well as soap and candles. The Provisions Section also possessed a list of "several hundred" private stores where "violations" had occurred and whose stocks would be requisi-tioned. If necessary, the requisitions would also be executed in private apartments if there were evidence of the possession of goods beyond normal family requirements.[162] On 5 August, with the Russians having withdrawn to the east bank of the Vistula, the committee called upon residents to declare their stocks or large supplies of flour, sugar, and salt by 6:00 p.m. of 6 August, which it would purchase at the fixed maximum price. Only goods voluntarily declared would be purchased at the controlled prices set by the committee, otherwise they would be requisitioned. Such draconian pronouncements must have created alarm, and with German forces already in the city, the committee sought to reassure citizens that it did not intend to seize goods intended for private use, just those intended for resale, and that it would discontinue its forced purchases and requisitioning once normal prices had been restored, a development it expected once the immediate crisis had passed.[163]

Strict control over Warsaw's food supply—characterized first by the setting of maximum prices on particular items under Russian rule, followed by the far more universal price regulations, forced sales, and confiscations carried out on an ad hoc basis by the Warsaw Citizens Committee in the first days of August 1915—would not disappear following the change in regime. Instead, even tighter controls came to characterize German occupation policy, to which it added rationing. With the departure of imperial Russian authority, Warsaw's food crisis now began in earnest as basic commodities that had still been available at inflated prices soon became rarities. In stark contrast to the Russian reluctance to ration any goods in short supply, the Germans introduced rationing to Warsaw in October 1915, beginning with bread and then matzo. Sugar followed in January 1916. Thereupon, ration cards spread quickly to meat, potatoes, and other foodstuffs, to nonfood items like soap, and finally in the fall of 1917 to coal and other fuels.[164]

Prior to the introduction of bread rations, in the districts of Powiśle and Mokotów inhabited by the poor, people lined up at 2:00 a.m. for bread to come out of bakery ovens four hours later.[165] Less than two weeks into the occupation, the new German police chief Glasenapp informed a representative of the Central Citizens Committee of the intended German solution to Warsaw's current short supply of grain and flour. In addition to rationing, the occupation authorities planned a complete takeover of the grain trade in its zone of the Polish Kingdom, with all harvested grains sent to Germany for milling, the flour from which would then be returned to the kingdom in a mixture containing potato additives.[166] According to war diarist and publicist Alexander de Rosset, the introduction of rationing, along with the import of this "war bread" from Germany, helped alleviate the immediate "bread hunger."[167] *Tygodnik Illustrowany* was of a different opinion entirely, pronouncing the sale of bread by ration cards as a failure less than two weeks after its introduction. Not only had the official ration of half a pound per person per day already become more the exception than the rule, the weekly noted, but the quality of the bread was "enormously different" from that to which Varsovians had been accustomed. Instead of alleviating hunger, the rationing of German "war bread" had helped contribute to a situation in which fainting in the streets from weakness and exhaustion had become increasingly commonplace.[168]

German censorship soon silenced such critical commentary in Warsaw's legal press, but it was hard to hide the reality on the streets. Princess Lubomirska, who had left the city at her husband's urging during the Russian evacuation, noted a visible difference upon her return at the end of November 1915 to "this poor, empty Warsaw, as if to a city of the dead . . . to poverty, grayness, growing inflation, the specter of hunger, the impression that nobody knows anything about what's going on, because it's not worth reading any of the newspapers here."[169] According to Konrad Zieliński, in 1914 not a single ambulance was sent for someone who had collapsed from hunger in Warsaw, but in 1915 an ambulance was sent on 113 occasions, and in the first six months of 1916 on 204 occasions.[170] By the spring of 1916, dozens of people had already died from starvation, with far more yet to come. Yet officially, Warsaw's food supplies in February 1916 were said to be sufficient for at least three months and even longer for certain products. Local authorities dismissed temporary shortages, then of sugar and potatoes, as "only the maneuvers of speculators" and called talk of an impending food crisis "much exaggerated."[171] Yet as Lubomirska recorded in her diary in early February 1916, "our dreams at night are being disrupted by visions of potatoes." This was followed a few days later by another entry: "People are dying like flies."[172]

Nonetheless, the control of Warsaw's food supply grew ever tighter as more items were banned from sale on the free market. In February 1916, sales of meat and meat by-products, poultry, and fish were specifically prohibited in eleven Warsaw bazaars "in the interest of public health."[173] A week later the transport of livestock and meat from Warsaw County, even to the city of Warsaw, was prohibited.[174] In the early months of the German occupation, the Provisions Section of the Warsaw Citizens Committee, unable to purchase supplies from either Germany or Austria-Hungary, contracted through a Berlin office with European neutrals such as Sweden, Denmark, and the Netherlands to purchase lard, butter, dried and salted fish, herring, and teas, although in time such shipments would be held up in Germany before they ceased altogether.[175] At the same time, the ban on shipments of meat, poultry, and fish to Warsaw from the countryside was extended to other food products, first from the Austrian zone of the occupied Polish Kingdom, and then from the German zone.

Requisitioning further aggravated the resulting shortages. Outside of Warsaw, the Germans would requisition a million horses from their occupation zone, in some counties up to 80% of the existing stock, which dealt a devastating blow to agriculture in the region.[176] However, food would be requisitioned inside Warsaw as well, as the occupation authorities resorted to the practices of the Warsaw

Citizens Committee initiated during the summer 1915 emergency. At the end of February 1916 the police issued a new regulation requiring all inhabitants of Warsaw and its suburbs to report their stocks of potatoes, vegetables, sugar, butter, lard, and soap in excess of specified amounts—ten pounds in the case of potatoes, one pound in the case of soap, for example. Those who had more than the amounts specified for per capita consumption would have their goods sequestered "in the interest of the less well-to-do part of the population."[177] This action sparked disquiet among local residents, who feared a shortage of potatoes in the city. The Provisions Section of the Warsaw Citizens Committee claimed that such alarm was based on false rumors that were without any basis.[178] Within two weeks, however, potatoes joined the list of rationed goods.[179]

These restrictions and controls on Warsaw's food supply were quickly accompanied in rapid succession by long queuing at food stores, accelerating inflation, ever-greater impoverishment of the general population, and ubiquitous begging in Warsaw's streets. By March 1916, the outstretched hands of beggars to those in military uniform had become a common sight, according to *Tygodnik Illustrowany* columnist Zdzisław Dębicki. So, too, was the appearance of rings of professional beggars who, employing small children, had taken up positions in all of the city's main and busiest streets and at trolley stops, undeterred by police action against them.[180]

Among a host of other illegal violations and criminal activities born of the general desperation, one of the earliest to appear was the counterfeiting of ration cards. In January 1916 a dozen individuals were arrested on charges of possessing counterfeit cards for bread.[181] Two months later, in an effort to eliminate what was becoming increasingly widespread, particularly with the expansion of rationed items, the authorities offered three hundred–mark rewards for information leading to the arrest of counterfeiters.[182] People also tried to cheat the system by registering "dead souls" for bread and flour rations in order to obtain extra coupons for their own use or for sale to others, for which several women were detained and questioned in June.[183]

Thus as Warsaw prepared to celebrate one of the most symbolic concessions to Polish national sentiment during the German occupation, the anniversary of the 3 May 1791 Constitution, which so captivated both German authorities and Polish elites, the lived experience of the city's food situation very much depended on one's perspective. When the historian Stanisław Kutrzeba visited Warsaw from Krakow at this time, he was struck by the discrepancy between what he had heard about "the difficult conditions in our capital" and what he saw: store and sweet-shop displays of white bread, "cakes, even with cream . . . and fruits, there is no lack of tea or coffee, which doesn't require standing in line, the stores are full of tobacco and it's sold on the streets." He quickly learned that the "difficult conditions" stemmed from the high prices of unrationed goods and in the quality and availability of rationed items. Despite being told that half of rationed potatoes were frequently rotten and had to be discarded, he concluded that "what is available for sustenance is cheap, if only available on a ration card," which he credited to "the great service of the Citizens Committee. That it is necessary to stand and wait in line to get it, this is already a reality that today surprises no one. One doesn't see these lines during the day but rather at dawn." "Beyond the coupons," however, "practically everything is available, as much as one wants. Only it's necessary to have money, lots and lots of money."[184] Kutrzeba himself didn't lack for food during his short visit, which certainly wasn't the case for ordinary Varsovians, who soon took matters into their own hands.

In early June, approximately a month after the great public celebration of 3 May, a crowd attacked a wagon in front of a bakery on Grzybowska Street and emptied it of 1,200 pounds of bread.[185] Then on 19–20 June, major food rioting erupted throughout the city, as some twenty-three of the eighty-six public stores operating under the supervision of the Provisions Section of the Warsaw City Administration, which had taken over food distribution from the Warsaw Citizens Committee earlier in the year, were partially or completely ransacked.[186] Following the June riots, even the German authorities were forced to acknowledge that the food situation in the summer of 1916 had become "very difficult." The old ration cards had lost their validity, and potatoes, rapidly becoming the only sustenance for Warsaw's poor, were being plundered on the way from Warsaw train stations to retail outlets. Indeed, police or military escorts would now accompany such transports.[187] Varsovians responded by going to outlying villages themselves to purchase potatoes rather than waiting for potatoes to come to them.[188]

With new harvests coming in the fall of 1916 from agricultural land that had not seen military combat for a year, Count Adam Ronikier, chair of the Directorate of the Main Welfare Organization (Rada Głowna Opiekuńcza—RGO) for the Polish Kingdom, pleaded with the German authorities to raise ration norms, even at prices without precedent, to feed "the starving and physically weakened population" of the cities, particularly Warsaw.[189] Instead, a new round of crackdowns and restrictions exacerbated Warsaw's food emergency. Dozens more were arrested for the production or possession of counterfeit bread rations; bakers were prosecuted for selling bread above the price ceiling, manipulating weights, loading "war bread" with sawdust, and conspiring to bribe officials; more than thirty building superintendents were arraigned on charges of exaggerating the numbers of their tenants in order to obtain and sell additional ration cards.[190] Meanwhile, the authorities announced that lost ration cards would not be replaced and prohibited the baking of special "hospital bread" from wheat flour for thousands of patients whose conditions prevented them from eating the surrogate-loaded "war bread."[191]

To enforce the ban of shipments of food to Warsaw from the Polish countryside, the Germans set up checkpoints on all roads leading into the city and also searched passengers on incoming trains for meat, fats, bread, and flour. As

Mieczysław Jankowski later recalled, "People made every kind of effort to hide and smuggle these articles." For example, Jankowski's father successfully hid kielbasa in a bouquet of flowers.[192] Many, like Aleksander Kraushar, believed that Warsaw had been purposefully starved of milk, meat, poultry, eggs, and fruits in order to feed Berlin.[193] While Berlin too experienced food riots and faced what Belinda Davis terms a "virtual famine" during the "turnip winter" of 1916–17, there is little doubt that the gap in the level of rations between Warsaw and Berlin continually widened, even as they declined in both cities.[194] When flour rations in Warsaw were cut by 25% in April 1917, from 160 to 120 grams per day, Varsovians began to receive half as much as what was officially available to their German counterparts and one-sixth of what they had consumed on average before the war.[195] Reductions in potato rations would soon follow suit.

By the beginning of May 1917, hunger protests and demonstrations became a common feature in the city. Teacher and social activist Władysława Głodowska-Sampolska, who worked among Warsaw's newspaper boys and helped them establish a club, described the atmosphere prevailing at the time of Warsaw's "sweetshop riots" of that spring:

FIGURE 6. Józef Rapacki, "Our Daily Bread," lithograph from Series *Pro Memoria: Prusak w Polsce 1915–1918* (Warsaw: Wydawnictwo "Tygodniku Ilustrowanego," 1918). Muzeum Narodowe w Warszawie.

People were exhausted from the unbelievable hunger. The children suffered most. The group which studied at the club in the morning, despite the compassionate and repeated efforts of its leadership to acquire money for its nourishment, looked miserable. [The boys'] complexions were pale and they fell asleep during lessons. Hunger demonstrations spread throughout the city at this time. When the German police dispersed them on one street, the demonstrators rapidly created a new procession on another street. Such spontaneous demonstrations created a major impression. I remember one of them. The crowd proceeded down Marszałkowska Street, beating on the windows of cafes and sweetshops filled with German officers. . . . During this explosion of strikes and demonstrations, people demanded increased food rations, above all bread. The bread at that time was very bad; people became sick from eating it. It contained a bare amount of flour and a multitude of other ingredients such as potato peels, field peas, and milled chestnuts. This bread fell apart a day after baking and had a terrible stench.[196]

According to Mieczysław Jankowski, the bad taste in his mouth left by such bread stayed with him years after the war was over, to the extent that postwar American white bread from the "Hoover committee," which was also rationed, nonetheless tasted like "the greatest delicacy" by comparison.[197]

Not surprisingly, a new round of hunger riots broke out on 11–12 May 1917, again accompanied by widespread looting of grocery stores as well as the aforementioned sweetshops—which, as a subsequent PPS appeal put it, "allowed people to eat their fill, at least for a couple of days."[198] Beginning as a demonstration of women and children in front of the city hall in protest of the potato shortage, the riots were also characterized by markedly visible anger against the occupying Germans and lasted several days before they were brought under control by two additional companies of infantry when crowds numbering in the thousands could not be contained by intensified police patrols.[199] "On the streets so many sad, lean faces next to full, even fat German soldiers," Princess Lubomirska had remarked eighteen months earlier.[200] Now that ever more obscene contrast had brought about an explosion. The riots led the Warsaw City Council to demand that food norms in Warsaw be raised to the levels prevailing in Berlin, that supplies be allowed to come freely into Warsaw, that the city be allowed to make its own purchases of potatoes on the free market, and that border restrictions be removed for goods coming from the Austro-Hungarian zone, where authorities appeared more sympathetic to Warsaw's plight. Threatening to dissolve itself in case of refusal, the council was unable to gain concessions on any of these points from the Germans.[201]

Not only the requisitioning and restrictions of the occupation regime and the privileges of its personnel relative to the local population aroused popular anger against the Germans. Smuggling and black markets had also become part of the general urban scenery and with them, the corruption of German officials, particularly at the lower levels of the occupation administration. "Any kind of product received by Warsaw must pass through several German bribes," claimed a PPS appeal in the aftermath of the sweetshop riots, which also called for "the removal from our city of German police and officials as soon as possible" and the creation of a Central Food Office under the control of "Polish society."[202] Writing immediately after the war, Kraushar referred to the "legendary" graft among German officials as they participated in the "robbery" of private and public property and in a system of bribery and corruption "on a scale far greater than anything known in Russian times."[203] During the last summer of the occupation, a number of German soldiers and officials were arrested for pilfering goods, especially food, which were then exchanged for bribes.[204] For Kraushar, it was this exploitation of local inhabitants as living conditions deteriorated that most contributed to hatred for the occupier, which "grew gradually and reached a chronic state."[205]

The Germans were not entirely insensitive to public perceptions of food privilege and inequality. For example, after the May riots, they banned the display of cakes in sweetshop windows, the baking of specific breads and cakes, the use of cream in coffee, the on-site consumption of chocolates and cakes, and the sale of more than three cakes per client at sweetshops and cafés.[206] And since the cafés and sweetshops in those days were frequented primarily by German personnel, such a measure took them somewhat out of harm's way. If the Germans couldn't have their cake and eat it too, at least *inside* public establishments, these restrictions didn't conflict with the demands of total war on the occupation administration, which were much more resounding than those of the Warsaw street or the entreaties of the city council and municipal administration.

At its session of 6 December 1917, the Warsaw City Council, realizing that all attempts to improve provisions by working with the German occupation authorities had been in vain and that their further pursuit would be aimless, determined to take the only means available to it: namely, "self-help and self-defense in close collaboration with the widest strata of the population."[207] This statement, however, seemed more an expression of the council's own impotence and despair than a resolution to take independent action. Warsaw's food situation, which had been deteriorating steadily since the beginning of the war, worsened significantly when rations were cut yet again in February 1918.[208] In the war's last winter, the majority of the city's inhabitants wore visible signs of hunger on their legs, hands, and especially ears in the form of dry red patches, swelling, and skin discoloration, the result of poor blood circulation. As for the council, it was reduced to appealing to German authorities to issue regulations banning the introduction and use of food surrogates without the permission of the city's Office of Public Health in an effort to ensure that the artificial quantities were not injurious or did not violate the minimal norms required of the primary contents of food products, particularly in milk, butter, and cheese.[209] Long before that, however, "unconscionable" Warsaw merchants had been selling egg, sugar, meat, and honey "extracts" that were not only of no nutritional value but were especially harmful to human health.[210] Apparently, what had once been considered fraud had now become a common practice, which local authorities could only hope to contain.

In the spring of 1918, official rations provided for a theoretical 891 calories compared to a prewar norm of 3,000 calories.[211] By that time, as Bronisław Fijalek recalled, long lines at public kitchens for rationed food of poor quality had become a regular feature of everyday life, as had demonstrations of desperate workers before city hall, demanding "Bread and Work" from a helpless city government, the only authority that had made every effort to provide them with both.[212] Thus, the food catastrophe discredited not only the larger experiment in German state-building, but also institutions with origins in real autonomy deprived by the German authorities of any initiative in dealing with matters of life and death. Many would have likely agreed with an anonymous letter to Beseler, most likely from May 1917, that accused the Provisions Section of corruption, unfair distribution, "prices ten times higher than under the Russians," and chastised the Warsaw City Council for spending money on anniversaries, wasting time on "various stupidities about the dead Kościuszko" and debates about street names, and in general for doing "more for the dead than for the living."[213] The writer's plea to the German authorities to take over food distribution from the "Polish bloodsuckers" may have been horribly misinformed, but the seething anger expressed in the letter, diverted from the occupation regime to the local elites, was certainly in the German interest.

The Crisis of Public Health

Throughout Europe, the peril of epidemics was a universal feature of the First World War, and the reactions of medical communities to that peril constitute a story of both successes and failures. Generally speaking, in the first half of the war, governments were able to contain the diseases of smallpox, typhus, and cholera, which were more prevalent on the Eastern than on the Western Front, to protect infant and maternal health, and to defend adult well-being. However, even in the west of Europe, those early successes were uneven, as children of the poor and elderly suffered higher-than-normal mortality rates. During the second half of the war, particularly in central Europe, the growing food and fuel crises led to a dramatic increase in mortality among the most vulnerable social and age cohorts, of which tuberculosis was the main cause.[214] Farther east, the physical weakening of Russian society was best demonstrated by typhus rates, which in 1919 were 515 times higher than before the war.[215] By 1918, however, all of Europe experienced the catastrophe of the Great Influenza pandemic, which despite regional variations affected all demographic categories. In Leipzig, for example, the mortality rate was 37% higher than for the rest of Germany due to the lethal global influenza.[216] The Great Influenza may have coincided with the peak of home-front exhaustion, particularly in central Europe, but it was largely the result of "the adaptation of the virus to man," for which the population of the United States served as the prime example.[217]

Warsaw's public health history during the First World War shared many of the features of this European narrative, including those of initial success thanks in large part to the social activism of physicians. The Medical Section of the Warsaw Citizens Committee was already active in the war's first weeks, calling for an increase in the number of ambulances, shelters for the poor, and assistance to hospitals for the mentally ill (which were overflowing with patients). It also sounded the alarm about the city's lack of preparedness to deal with the feared outbreak of epidemics.[218] Three weeks into the war, it became involved in the establishment and staffing of infirmaries for the terminally ill, elderly, and disabled and to prepare hospitals for the arrival of wounded soldiers from the front.[219]

One of the early problems of the war was a shortage of different medicines that were frequently produced in and imported from Germany.[220] The first cases of dysentery in the city were noted in early September, as doctors issued a warning about fruits and especially cucumbers shipped to Warsaw from the Lublin region.[221] Evidence of the first cases of typhus, in five separate locations in the city, followed a week later.[222] As the Warsaw Citizens Committee's Medical Section continued to make preparations for an expected epidemic, it sought to increase the number of hospital beds available to the noncombatant population.[223]

The unsuccessful effort by the Germans to capture Warsaw during the middle of October coincided with an on-going increase of those being treated for infectious diseases, which were being spread by soldiers and noncombatants alike in the city's hospitals.[224] The appearance of tens of thousands of refugees in Warsaw in October

1914 also raised fears of the spread of contagious diseases, and as a consequence, two physicians were placed permanently on staff to monitor the health of the refugee population at the shelters on a daily basis.[225] Cases of smallpox soon appeared among that population, and in early November 1914 all refugees in public shelters were given free vaccinations.[226]

Nonetheless, the association of disease with refugees had now become firmly implanted in the press as fears of the spread of scarlet fever among the refugee population led to demands for the immediate removal of infected persons from the shelters.[227] Scarlet fever, measles, and smallpox reportedly resulted in high mortality among Jewish refugee children: fifty-five funerals were scheduled for 17 January 1915, but because of the shortage of hearses, only twenty-seven could actually be arranged.[228] In January 1915 the Warsaw Citizens Committee's Christian Refugee Section again expressed fear of the spread of measles, scarlet fever, and smallpox, cases of which had appeared in its shelters. Consequently, it called for the creation of a center to isolate and treat those refugees who were carrying disease into Warsaw.[229] At the end of January 1915 the section's main shelter at the Dolina Szwajcarska facility was temporarily closed after the outbreak of a stomach disease among the refugees, so that the building could be disinfected.[230] Stomach-related illnesses also appeared within the Russian Army at this time. Consequently, all wounded and ill soldiers traveling through Warsaw had to stay in the city under quarantine for five days as doctors closely watched for any signs of stomach ailments; those who developed intestinal problems were placed in isolation wards and had their clothes and linens disinfected.[231]

In the neighborhoods surrounding Warsaw, with their own refugee shelters operated by provincial and county citizens' committees, the Medical Commission of Warsaw Province turned up numerous manifestations of stomach illnesses connected to malnutrition in its investigations. The hungry poor in the suburban shelters were eating rotten produce, and several had reportedly died in Wola after eating contaminated meat.[232] More generally, poor sanitary conditions in Warsaw's suburbs made them potential havens for the spread of infectious diseases, although Mokotów, where the Warsaw Citizens Committee had been particularly active, was a noted exception.[233] The poor quality of drinking water and the problem of waste removal were identified as the main causes of conditions favorable to the spread of infectious diseases in Warsaw's suburbs.[234] With an estimated population of 230,000, Warsaw's suburbs did not possess a sewage system, and waste disposal in them was said to violate "even the most elementary notions of hygiene." In response, medical authorities sought to create three firms to remove waste in the southern, western, and right-bank suburbs.[235]

In mid-March 1915 the citizens of Mokotów petitioned for annexation by Warsaw, claiming that they could no longer meet the needs for sanitation and disease prevention on their own.[236] Commenting on the prospect of Mokotów's incorporation into Warsaw, *Kurjer Warszawski* noted that it was long overdue and that the Russian authorities who had blocked it earlier were now pushing actively for annexation due to concerns for the health of both the local population and the army.[237] However, incorporation of Mokotów, Wola, and Praga into a greater metropolitan Warsaw was an expensive proposition. Earlier, medical authorities estimated that it would take 358,000 rubles just to connect the suburbs with the city's sanitation system.[238]

The incorporation of the suburbs would have to wait for a change of regime. In the meantime, for *Tygodnik Illustrowany* in particular, the health of Warsaw depended on the health of a surrounding area even farther afield. The fall battles on the city's left bank had left many dead, who only in the spring of 1915 were being properly buried in common graves with the assistance of fifteen sanitary units. Such work had only recently been completed in the Góra Kalwaria area and had just begun in Sochachew and Błonie counties.[239]

Long before that, the Medical Section of the Warsaw Citizens Committee began to publicize its concern about the lack of hospital space in Warsaw in the event of an epidemic or the threat of one.[240] To deal with the immediate problem, the premises of state middle schools were turned into hospitals, which forced their instructors to hold lectures in the buildings of the city's private schools during afternoon and evening hours.[241] At the end of November, the Warsaw Sanitary Committee, consisting of city medical officers and representatives of the Warsaw Citizens Committee's Medical Section, was formed and given the task of monitoring public health in Warsaw and its environs and of preventing the spread of infectious diseases. It was given an initial capital allocation of 138,146 rubles to create a large new hospital and thirty doctors' offices. Its six-month budget was projected at more than 350,000 rubles, and its jurisdiction included Warsaw's suburbs.[242] Within weeks, Warsaw's medical community faced the prospect of a major outbreak of typhus as dozens of cases were reported in December and January, which coincided with the arrival of thousands of new refugees into the city.

As the city braced itself against epidemics during the winter of 1914–15, another problem arose connected with the ban on sales of spirits, namely a growing number of cases of alcohol poisoning, first reported in the Warsaw press toward the end of November 1914. In the course of five days, between 22 and 27 November 1914, some twenty-eight people died of alcohol poisoning, and fifteen others were seriously ill after drinking rubbing alcohol and concoctions made from it.[243] The death toll continued to mount, according to a running tab kept by *Kurjer Warszawski*, a strong supporter of prohibition. In August two people had died of alcohol poisoning, and eight each in September and October. In November that number rose to forty-seven. Over the first five months of the war, some seventy-six individuals died of alcohol poisoning, and twenty-four more deaths in January brought the six-month total since the start of the war to one hundred.[244] After that time, incidents of alcohol poisoning and death by such means declined markedly, but only because the production of moonshine improved, as reported cynically by Warsaw's leading daily.[245]

Warsaw's medical community was active on other fronts as well. In December 1914 the Medical Section of the committee, faced with the shortage of dairy products, attempted to fend off an increase in the child mortality rate by proposing the establishment of four Kropli Mleka ("Drops of Milk") stations in the city for infants and their mothers.[246] Then in June 1915 it proposed to organize forty-one physicians to care for the children in homes and shelters operated by the committee.[247] Recognizing that Warsaw's hospitals were incapable of meeting current needs, the section also worked to organize new facilities for the care of individuals suffering from mental illness.[248] It also sought to educate the public about measures it could take to prevent the spread of infectious diseases through lectures, press releases, and the publication of special brochures. On the eve of the Russian evacuation, the Warsaw Sanitary Committee sponsored a successful exhibit "The Fight against Epidemic Diseases" that was visited by more than 30,000 people and raised some 4,000 rubles.[249]

As Rosset attests, the state of public health in Warsaw before 1916 was "completely satisfactory," thanks mainly to the conscientious efforts of the Warsaw Citizens Committee, which became and remained responsible for the provision of medical care to the noncombatant population. The effectiveness of the committee and its Medical Section's activities can be measured by the fact that Warsaw was able to avoid major epidemics despite the numerous challenges posed by large transient soldier and refugee populations and primitive sanitary conditions immediately beyond the city center. By the end of November 1915, according to Rosset, cholera had been contained to some thirty cases.[250] Hundreds of Varsovians had become ill with typhus, but even that disease seemed to be under control. In August 1915, as Kraushar later recalled, the incoming Germans, mainly on the basis of a cultural prejudice that associated disease with "the east," posted and published a number of proclamations and announcements containing a list of prophylactic measures to prevent horrific diseases, including some that had not even been mentioned in the Warsaw press, whose reporting on public health issues and scares had gone largely uncensored by the Russians.[251]

Thus at first the German authorities could report only separate and isolated incidents of disease, mainly of the sexually transmitted kind among their own troops, but they were already preparing "energetic measures" to contain all forms of contagious and infectious disease in Poland's cities, particularly Warsaw.[252] Less than six months into the German occupation, the occupation authorities noted that the spread of infectious diseases, especially typhus, called for immediate measures in those parts of the city that had experienced earlier incidents of the disease. Police announced that buildings and homes would be subjected to basic cleaning and inspection by representatives of an official commission.[253] Shortly thereafter, the Germans introduced compulsory smallpox vaccinations, free of charge, for every inhabitant of the city.[254] As Marta Polsakiewicz notes, the Germans made "major investments in public health," ultimately to little avail as epidemics would follow one after the other.[255] What she doesn't say is that the rapid deterioration in public health coincided with the collapse of basic living standards to which German economic exploitation was the major contributor. If German marks went down the drain in fighting disease in Warsaw, it was the Germans themselves who created the drain.

As noted previously, of special concern to the German authorities during the first year of the occupation was typhus, particularly its possible spread to soldiers stationed in the city. According to data for Warsaw cited by Konrad Zieliński, 1,809 individuals became ill with typhus in 1915, 4,598 in 1916, and 15,871 in 1917, by which time it had become a full-blown epidemic. In this last year, Jews accounted for 11,612, or 73%, of the cases, which helped feed the stereotype of the dirty, louse-carrying Jew that contemporary Polish antisemites were more than happy to indulge.[256] Zieliński attributes the higher rate of certain diseases among Jews, especially typhus but also typhoid fever (known colloquially as the "Jewish fever"), to a large transient population.[257] However, the virulence of typhus increased at the same time the Jewish refugee population was in significant decline. Indeed, the peak of the typhus epidemic in Warsaw occurred when that population had been reduced to a few thousand. Instead, as we shall see in chapter 4, a substantial deterioration of living standards among Jews relative to Poles followed U.S. entry into the war in April 1917, which cut off the Jewish community from further assistance provided by the U.S.-based Joint Distribution Committee; Polish municipal authorities' reluctance to make up the substantial difference was the most probable cause for the dramatic spike in the incidence of typhus among Warsaw's Jews. Relatively greater residential density in Jewish neighborhoods and apartments was another contributing factor, as was a more general inability to maintain daily hygiene in the absence of soap and a breakdown in public waste and garbage removal toward the end of the war. Finally, Jews experienced quarantine and disinfection as an invasion, especially when carried out by overzealous Polish sanitary police, and resisted these measures either through bribes or subterfuge.

To their credit, local authorities eventually joined the German occupation regime in its fight against typhus. In December 1917 the Warsaw City Council assigned an additional 100,000 marks to existing appropriations for covering the cost of cleaning certain districts of the city as part of the ongoing fight against the typhus epidemic.[258] However, this amount was but a drop in the bucket compared to the 2-million-mark subvention the council requested a month later from the "Polish state authorities" (the cabinet serving under the Regency Council) to support the struggle against typhus in the city.[259] In the spring of 1918 the council called upon the magistrate to demand that the German authorities turn over to the city government buildings, some of which were completely empty, for emergency use as hospitals for an estimated 1,500 to 2,000 people ill with infectious and contagious diseases who were not being currently treated. In particular, it was noted that an abandoned military barracks on Zakroczymska Street could be used as a hospital once it had been cleared of prostitutes, as the city's elected representatives combined their concern for public health with their concern for public morality.[260]

For all the official concern over typhus and typhoid fever, mortality resulting from those diseases paled in comparison with that coming as a consequence of tuberculosis, the most proficient killer in wartime Warsaw. From 1905 to 1914, the average number of deaths in Warsaw resulting from tuberculosis was 1,764 per year, accounting for some 11.62% of all deaths, or 223 per 100,000 of population. By European standards of the time, this was high. In 1915 the number of tuberculosis-related deaths rose to 2,774, in 1916 to 4,032, in 1917 to 4,748. In 1915–17, tuberculosis-related mortality accounted for 13.05%, 21.81%, and 29.45% of all deaths, or 319, 435, and 1,135 per 100,000 of population.[261]

As is evident from these figures, the calamity of tuberculosis in Warsaw, which "threatens death to those who have managed to come out of this war alive" in the words of Tygodnik Illustrowany,[262] coincided with the highest incidence of typhus, a demonstration of the physical state of a considerably weakened population. Yet tuberculosis as well as what the German occupation authorities were calling the "Spanish disease" in the summer of 1918,[263] both of which spared no one, didn't receive nearly the public attention that was accorded to typhus. Perhaps this is precisely because of the fact that the first two diseases, unlike typhus, couldn't be associated with a particular ethnic group.

Before concluding this discussion of public health in Warsaw during the First World War, let us consider some available data on reported suicides to the end of 1916. In 1915 and 1916, suicides among women averaged twice as many as among men, but some of that difference can be explained by the growing proportion of women to men in the urban population as a result of the dominance of young males in labor out-migration, not to mention military conscription. Still, the working class accounted for roughly 30% of suicides in both 1915 and 1916, despite a substantial reduction in its numbers during the war years. Before the war, it should be recalled, the working class comprised 40% of Warsaw's population. By ethnicity, Jews constituted 18.4% of the 1915 suicides, 21% in 1916, well below their 35–40% proportion of Warsaw's total population. Not surprisingly, 75% of the suicide cases came from teenagers and young adults, equally divided between the 16–20 and 21–30 age cohorts. What is most interesting, however, is the reduction of the total number of suicides by nearly two-thirds, a steep decline characteristic of all demographic categories. Before the war, the number of suicides in the city averaged slightly more than a thousand per year—1,023 in 1912 and 1,003 in 1913, to be exact. In 1914 that number declined to 671 and in 1915 to 364, with only a slight uptick to 375 in 1916.[264] One preliminary conclusion, which would need to be tested against comparative data from other cities facing similar existential challenges, is that in Warsaw the everyday struggle for physical survival took precedence over everything else, including emotional health, and that individuals when confronted with the imminent threat of death by other means, became less likely to surrender their lives voluntarily.

Falling off the Edge

The noteworthy decline in the suicide rate, however, made only a negligible dent in otherwise much higher mortality rates, which are easier to interpret as the consequence of malnutrition, starvation, and infectious disease. The death rate peaked in 1917, the most difficult year of the war due to the food and health crises. According to Dunin-Wąsowicz, the death rate increased from 18.4 per thousand in 1914 to 41.4 per thousand by the end of 1917. According to Holzer and Molenda, when infant mortality is removed from the equation, the death rate in Warsaw tripled in comparison to that of the prewar years.[265] Among other cities in central Europe and the "Ober Ost" for which comparative data is available, only Vilnius appears to have suffered mortality rates similar to those of Warsaw.[266] Interestingly, the biggest jump in mortality occurred not in 1917 but earlier, between August 1915 and April 1916, when noninfant mortality increased from 15.88 per thousand to 34.0 per thousand.[267] This suggests that the rapid decline of living standards and the deterioration of public health in the war's second year removed from life some of the more physically vulnerable members of the city's population before they affected others.

We have already noted the major contribution of tuberculosis to the increase in the mortality rate, particularly by the end of the war when incidences of the disease, having quadrupled since August 1914, were still on the rise.[268] In other European cities, young women employed in munitions and other war-related industries were particularly hard hit by tuberculosis and other respiratory infections.[269] While young women were also vulnerable to tuberculosis in Warsaw, it was not because of their industrial employment, which more or less collapsed during the war; instead, tuberculosis appears to have been an equal-opportunity killer. One cannot say the same about starvation and malnutrition, which also took their fair share of lives but were less equally distributed among demographic categories. Although no exact figures in this regard are available for Warsaw, we can get an indication from data available for Vienna, where the nature and extent of the food crisis was roughly comparable. According to Maureen Healy, 7–11% of Viennese deaths during the war were the direct result of starvation, while malnutrition was a main contributing cause of death in 20–30% of all other cases.[270]

Elsewhere, overall mortality rates during the war years, measured by life expectancy, remained unchanged in cities like Paris and London, whereas German cities experienced a significant increase. In Freiburg, mortality increased by 60%, and in Leipzig by 100%; in Berlin, life expectancy was reduced by 3.7 years.[271] This was bad enough, but the situation in Vienna was far worse, where less than 10% of the city's children could be classified as "completely healthy" in 1918.[272] It was also far worse in Warsaw, finally a capital city but one that would remain at war for another two years after November 1918. As early as September 1914, the Warsaw Citizens Committee believed Warsaw to be the most poorly provisioned city in the Polish Kingdom, if not the Russian Empire.[273] In April 1917 the president of the committee's successor, the new Warsaw City Administration recruited from its ranks, declared in a letter to Warsaw governor-general Beseler: "No German city finds itself in such a critical condition as does Warsaw, because none has been so economically ruined and burdened with providing assistance to a population deprived of the means of existence, nor has any been forced to bear a similar level of burdens to the state."[274] Such burdens only grew heavier as the war continued, contributing to the failure of these local and municipal institutions to manage the crisis and prevent catastrophe, try as they might.

WARTIME CRISIS MANAGEMENT AND ITS FAILURE

Throughout Europe the economic demands of total war strained as well as transformed existing institutional means, both public and private, to provide assistance and relief to those made destitute by the direct or indirect consequences of the fighting or by the exactions of military occupation. Maintenance of family incomes, at least at some basic level, was essential to management of the war on the home front. In some cities, like London and Paris, the war led to the development of a far more systemic and centrally determined redistributive social policy that dramatically expanded publicly funded transfer payments to a much broader proportion of the population in need. By contrast, in Berlin and other German cities where before the conflict a national system of locally administered social insurance was already in place, the much more pronounced material shortages caused by the war forced a prioritization of social payments in the direction of strategic social groups such as soldiers' wives and dependents, munitions workers, and pregnant and nursing mothers.[1] As Bonzon succinctly states in his comparative analysis of the war's effect on social policy, "German rights became privileges, whereas British and French privileges became rights."[2]

As subjects of the Russian tsar before the war, Varsovians had neither rights nor privileges when it came to relief or public assistance. Indeed, according to Adele Lindenmeyr, throughout the Russian Empire, "outside of a few large cities and a few provinces with particularly progressive *zemstva* [self-governing rural assemblies—RB], local public assistance was rudimentary or non-existent."[3]

Warsaw was not among those cities, denied as it was institutions of municipal self-government that, for example, had capably funded and administered relief for the poor in Moscow. Instead, Warsaw's nonelected city administration shared the belief of the vast majority of local governments that the existence of private charitable organizations, the major source of institutional assistance to the poor in the empire before the war, "absolved them from any responsibility for relief beyond a modest subsidy."[4]

Moreover, the development of private charitable organizations and other kinds of voluntary associations in Warsaw and in the Polish Kingdom as a whole was slow in coming. The autocracy's lenient attitude toward such associations in the era of the Great Reforms did not extend to Russia's Polish provinces and the western borderlands in the aftermath of the January 1863 Insurrection. Elsewhere in the empire, the process of registration and confirmation of mutual aid and charitable societies was simplified in the Ministry of Internal Affairs, but in the territories of the 1863 insurgency, the establishment of such organizations had to obtain imperial permission through the Council of Ministers, a much more laborious bureaucratic process. Warsaw thus missed out on the vigorous development of private charitable organizations until the Revolution of 1905, when new laws about unions and associations led to a sudden mushrooming of such organizations in both the Polish and Jewish communities. Many of these organizations had social agendas far more ambitious than the relief of widows and orphans, activities typical of the state-subsidized and elite-favored Warsaw Philanthropic Society founded in 1814.[5] Meanwhile, the autocracy's ongoing distrust of local government jurisdiction contained, and in Warsaw blocked, the growth of publically funded and administered assistance.

If in all major European cities before the war private institutions were fundamental to the provision of social assistance, they nevertheless overlapped to a greater or lesser degree with those of the state and local governments. In Warsaw and most other cities of the Russian Empire, they were the only actors, their services and assistance inadequate to the need. Thus, the assumption of war relief by voluntary associations and, where applicable, by local self-governing institutions in the Russian Empire was a logical continuation of prewar patterns. Again, in the absence of a centrally funded system of organized relief, private charities ultimately proved inadequate to the far greater wartime need. It is in this context that we will now examine the Warsaw Citizens Committee, a hybrid institution between state and society that emerged out of the network of voluntary and charitable organizations to reshape social policy in the city and distribute aid, assistance, and relief to a distressed population.

A Quasi-Official Russian Institution

The Warsaw Citizens Committee began its history on 3 August 1914 as a voluntary nongovernmental organization under the patronage of the City Magistrate, and therefore under the titular chairmanship of Russian city president Aleksandr Müller, who presided over the committee's plenary sessions. However, the committee's actual executive officer was Prince Zdzisław Lubomirski, the former vice president and then president of the Warsaw Philanthropic Society, who chaired the committee's General Section. The committee's fifteen founding members represented the cream of Warsaw society—its engineers, industrialists, financiers, economists, and lawyers, many of noble or aristocratic descent. Many had been active in professional associations before the war, others in educational and social work. The latter included Father Marceli Godlewski, founder of the Association of Christian Workers. Piotr Drzewiecki, who became the committee's vice president, had earlier served as chair of the Warsaw Association of Technicians and as director of the Society of Scientific Courses, whose most famous student was future Nobel Prize–winner Maria Skłodowska-Curie. The committee's secretary, Stefan Dziewulski, was one of the founders of the Society of Polish Economists and Statisticians. Though the committee itself was officially nonpartisan, those who claimed political affiliation belonged to the conservative Party of Realists, the National Democrats who were radical only in their antisemitism, and the right wing of the Polish Progressive movement. Three members of the committee were of Jewish descent, including the banker Józef Natanson, who served as the committee's treasurer, and the lawyer and publicist Henryk Konic, but they had little connection to Warsaw's largely Yiddish-speaking Jewish community.

As Władyław Grabski noted after the war, the committee's relationship with the Russian administration in the city endowed it with a "dualistic" and "quasi-official" character that both aided and limited its activities.[6] The committee, while it cooperated with the Russian government and was largely dependent on its funding, enjoyed far-ranging autonomy in the selection of its leadership and personnel as well as in the range of activities in which the committee decided to involve itself. However, its main task was to provide assistance to the population of Warsaw, the organization and management of which the City Administration was ill prepared to undertake. Indeed, the City Magistrate was as dependent on the Warsaw Citizens Committee to provide this assistance as the committee was on the magistrate to provide the funding for it. In its first press release, the committee announced that it would occupy itself with issues related to basic provisioning of the city, mobilizing financial resources, finding work for the unemployed, assisting the families of reservists, and ensuring public safety, an already ambitious agenda that hinted at aspirations that would take the committee beyond the organization of relief.[7]

Originally, the Warsaw Citizens Committee consisted of eight sections: Provisions, Press and Information, Assistance to Soldiers' Families, Finance, Medical, Women, Labor, and Legal. Its ninth, or General Section, served as a committee of the whole.[8] The committee's structure, as well as its functions, would undergo continual expansion during the war's first year. By its third session, the committee decided to create a Coal Commission to supply coal to the poor as well as to firms involved in food processing.[9] Two days later, the committee created a new Donations Section consisting of twelve members, representing the Christian and Jewish communities in rough proportion to their percentages of the urban population.[10] As the war entered its fourth week, the committee set up a separate Distribution Commission, which divided the city into five regions. In each region, five stores would be established for the distribution of food and other basic provisions, while in the Jewish district the commission established a special kosher store. It was also at this time that the committee agreed to the establishment of a section to manage "low cost" public kitchens, thus rescinding an earlier decision not to become directly involved in establishing institutions to feed the city's poor or to accept donations for that purpose. By the end of the month, some ten "street kitchens" were in operation.[11] Finally, the city's ongoing energy crisis led the committee to create a separate Fuels Section at the end of September.[12]

Originally, the Warsaw Citizens Committee had planned to provide basic support to the families of reservists called up at the end of July 1914. The Russian state, however, through an agency known as the Curatorium (staffed by fifteen "curators" in the same number of Warsaw precincts), quickly relieved the committee of that burden; thereafter, the Warsaw Citizens Committee played only a supporting role toward reservists' families, although it was enough to create confusion among recipients in the war's first weeks.[13] Following the July–August 1914 mobilization, some 4,500 families became entitled to receive support for food purchases at a monthly rate of 4.84 rubles for adults and children over the age of five, and 2.42 rubles for younger children.[14] In addition, some seven hundred wives and children of reservists received warm meals from leftovers at the military hospital on Ujazdowskie Boulevard.[15] By the end of 1914, the state had allocated more than a million rubles in support of soldiers' families in Warsaw.[16]

The most serious and painful social problem confronting both the committee and the Warsaw City Administration during the war's first weeks, and then beyond, was mass unemployment. Finding work for Warsaw's idled workers was the immediate task of its Labor Section, which required close cooperation with the Russian authorities. We have already discussed the role of the Warsaw Citizens Committee in male labor out-migration during the first year of the war. Inside the city, and before the first month of the war was out, the committee and the magistrate collaborated in the creation of a couple of new public-works projects designed to employ 1,250 people, a number that was only destined to rise.[17]

In the first year of the war, 439,000 of the committee's approximately 4.7 million rubles in total funding came from private donations in cash and kind.[18] Especially in the war's first weeks, donations to the committee cut across class lines, with the lower classes making contributions often in the form of pears, cigarettes, bread, lard, and beer.[19] The Warsaw Citizens Committee also joined the kingdom-wide Central Citizens Committee in a number of joint fund-raising activities aimed at individual donors, including the sponsorship of a demonstration of the new sport of basketball as well as a soccer match in Agrykola Park to support their new public-health initiatives.[20] With donations also came the issue of accountability, which was difficult enough in regard to cash donations and even more so with donations in kind. In this regard, the committee was particularly alert to opportunities for fraud because many people claimed to be working for it and even wore the committee's special ribbons but otherwise did not possess the proper documentation.[21] Bands of professional beggars also took immediate advantage of the spirit of giving and began to appear on the city's main thoroughfares to ply their trade, especially during evening hours.[22]

These "heroic" days of a voluntary and nongovernmental committee of citizens supported by the general public through private donations, one that presumably assumed the "entire burden of dealing with the consequences of the war, and especially of assistance to the population,"[23] mythical in any case, came to an end with the October crisis and its aftermath, as enemy forces advanced on and retreated from Warsaw. Instead, the City Administration and the Warsaw Citizens Committee became increasingly dependent on each other, as the latter increasingly assumed governmental functions supported by the former's funding. From 1 August 1914 to 1 July 1915, more than 64% of the committee's income came from direct subventions and separate donations of the Warsaw City Magistrate, while its largest institutional donor, the Grand Princess Tatiana Committee for Aid to War Victims, provided another 14%. With slightly less than 10% of the committee's funding derived from the donations of "Polish society," the planned but never realized establishment of a Warsaw branch of the Tatiana Committee would have spelled "the de facto extermination" of the Warsaw Citizens Committee, as Władysław Grabski explained after the war.[24] While the committee avoided that fate, more than 75% of its funding came from Russian sources.

What the committee lacked in sources of funding, it made up in organization, personnel, and moral authority as its activities began to assume a more official character. One of the first was the committee's involvement in the establishment of price ceilings. The Military Statute of July 1914 gave the Russian Army the authority to impose maximum prices in the war zone, but the actual decisions to do so were left to municipal authorities, who in turn were persuaded or dissuaded by competing local interests.[25] During the war's first month, the prominent Warsaw sociologist Ludwik Krzywicki called for price ceilings on items of primary need because the committee's stores, although they sold such items at lower cost, were too few in number to stabilize prices.[26] By 9 September, price ceilings on basic necessities had been established in provincial cities but not yet in Warsaw, and nationalists and conservatives now joined in calling for their imposition.[27] These calls were renewed at the end of September as the front seemed to be closing in on Warsaw and panic buying again drove up food prices.[28] With the price of coal driven up by shortages, transportation costs, and speculation, the committee was pressured to impose controls on energy prices as well.[29] Finally, with the enemy advancing toward the approaches of Warsaw, the committee sought and then acquired the power from the magistrate to regulate the prices of flour, grits, meat, lard, sugar, firewood, and coal.[30]

Even with violations carrying fines of up to 3,000 rubles and a month in jail, the price controls were only partially effective because, as mentioned earlier, they affected only retail prices, which themselves were inadequately enforced by an overburdened city police force. Moreover, many retail merchants treated the price controls as guidelines and suggestions rather than as strict instructions carrying heavy penalties for violations. Almost immediately, the authorities were deluged with all kinds of complaints from consumers who were being told by merchants to go to the magistrate if they wanted goods at controlled prices.[31] Consequently, two developments occurred simultaneously, reflecting the pressures of both consumers and retailers. First, the number of regulated items continued to expand to include sugar, soap, kerosene, butter, oats and hay, and even horse-drawn cab fares. At the same time, possessing only the power of regulation and not of enforcement, the committee found that it had no choice but to continually raise the price maximums. When in February 1915 the committee decided again to raise price ceilings on meat, lard, grits, soap, and potatoes, it also approved the selection of twenty-six individuals by the Citizens Guard Section to serve as price controllers, with three controllers assigned to each precinct to monitor adherence to the price ceilings. The Russian police authorities, however, sought to keep the Citizens Guard on a short leash and were reluctant to cede to it any powers of law enforcement.[32] Thus, the situation remained unchanged, and the February price increases were followed by higher ceilings for kerosene, flour, and bread in mid-March.[33]

The very idea of a citizen militia, like the Warsaw Citizens Committee's request for authority to set retail prices, emerged out of the October crisis. With Warsaw under threat of enemy attack in the first half of October 1914, the committee requested and received permission from the Russian authorities to organize a force that would be ready to act at any given moment to preserve order in the city.[34] Though the planned militia would muster on a trial basis in three different locations during the October emergency, the regular police remained at their posts, and the existence of the volunteer force remained primarily on paper. In this regard, at the end of November Stanisław Popowski, the chair of a newly established Straż Obywatelski (Citizens Guard) Section, presented the committee with a list of potential candidates for precinct commissars.[35] By the second week of December, the Citizens Guard was set to begin training exercises—with the knowledge of the Warsaw superintendent of police.[36] At the same time, Russian police authorities were reluctant to grant the Citizens Guard any kind of official recognition and even required it to call itself the "Warsaw Honor Guard," the name and function of which were carefully chosen so as not to be construed as belonging to a Polish police force.[37] The committee subsequently agreed to seek the approval of the Warsaw governor-general to maintain the Citizens Guard in a state of organization in preparation for an eventual evacuation, but to otherwise refrain from any activities of a public nature.[38] Thus, one will not find the Citizens Guard Section on any official list of the Warsaw Citizens Committee's various sections and commissions made available to the public, yet its existence was the worst-kept secret in Warsaw.

The assumption of ever-greater responsibilities on the Warsaw home front, in terms of providing relief and assistance as well as economic-social organization, would lead to fundamental changes in the size, structure, and nature of the Warsaw Citizens Committee. During the October crisis alone, the committee had created six new sections, which like the Citizens Guard Section mirrored the departments of a modern municipal government.[39] From its original nine sections, by the end of the year the Warsaw Citizens Committee had grown to twenty-nine sections and commissions.[40] Heading them was the General Section, whose membership expanded much more slowly; thus, decision-making powers remained confined to a relatively small group of individuals. Moreover, in the aftermath of the October crisis, a three-man Presidium consisting of Lubomirski, Drzewiecki, and Dziewulski was formed to expedite, screen, and organize the committee's business. In early November, Prince Lubomirski received a delegation that sought the doubling of the General Section to thirty members, which in effect would have created a surrogate city council. While the committee agreed that an expansion of its membership was inevitable, it felt that the creation of anything resembling a city council would be premature.[41] Instead, the committee decided to expand its membership by six through co-optation and internal election, a practice that would eventually lead to calls for its democratization.[42]

Expansion of the committee's activities, and the war's expected continuation into the foreseeable future, also led to the decision at the end of November 1914 to replace a certain proportion of its nearly nine thousand volunteers with paid functionaries and to establish a salary schedule.[43] Becoming a Warsaw Citizens Committee employee brought more than just a salary; it provided access to scarce goods as well as opportunities for corruption and fraud. The arrest of individuals posing as committee employees demonstrated the value of such access.[44] It is perhaps not coincidental that public accusations of corruption levied at committee sections first arose at approximately the same time the committee was being transformed from an all-volunteer organization. This was particularly true of the Fuels and Provisions Sections and the Distribution Commission. Untainted in this regard were those sections where the work of female volunteers continued to predominate, especially the Commission for Women's Work and the Commission for the Care of Children, both of which emerged from the Warsaw Citizens Committee's Women's Section once the latter was dissolved in September 1914.[45]

As early as the third week of October 1914, the Commission for the Care of Children provided assistance to some 1,600 children in its shelters and halls, where they were supervised for half a day and received a warm meal. Providing children with shoes and warm clothing soon became the organization's most crucial need as winter approached.[46] By December, the number of children served directly by the commission and its 400 volunteers had risen to 2,200 in its own 22 locales, while it provided supplementary support for 2,800 additional children served by other organizations. A mere month later and as a consequence of the mass influx of refugees, the Commission for the Care of Children was assisting more than nineteen thousand children (although only three thousand directly), which led the committee to organize a separate School Commission and to petition the authorities to register and legalize the offering of elementary instruction for children and literacy courses for adults.[47] In the first seven weeks of 1915, the commission opened up two new shelters, five recreation halls, and one home for the children of the intelligentsia, altogether serving another thousand children.[48]

By March 1915 the committee acutely felt the need to support the growing number of children orphaned as a result of the war.[49] In early April, the Commission for the Care of Children published a report that stated that it had registered 19,500 children in need. Five thousand of them were in shelters and recreation halls founded by the commission; the remainder could be found in the city's streets and courtyards, close to starving, waiting to be received in new spaces whose opening depended on donations.[50] Meanwhile, the situation in Warsaw's suburbs was even more alarming; in Bródno township, for example, of an estimated 1,300 children requiring assistance at the beginning of 1915, only 120 were actually being served.[51]

Before the war, care for orphaned and homeless children had been the primary domain of private philanthropic and charitable organizations, but their growing numbers and other mounting needs quickly overwhelmed the resources of these organizations. Consequently, by the end of 1914 they too became suppli-cants for the Warsaw Citizens Committee's direct financial support. The commit-tee initially denied these requests because of budgetary as well as administrative constraints.[52] Ultimately, particularly in the case of the urgent needs of Warsaw's children, the committee would come to find it more expedient to support exist-ing institutions served by volunteers than to continue to create its own, particu-larly after receipt of a million-ruble personal gift from the tsar in early March, which went to fund the requests of twenty different philanthropic organizations in the city.[53]

Otherwise, the pressures to expand its jurisdiction proved impossible for the committee to ignore, both from within Warsaw's existing boundaries and imme-diately beyond from the city's immediate suburbs. At the beginning of the war's fourth week, citizens committees were formed in Praga to meet the needs of the population in Warsaw's east-bank suburb and in the suburban township of Bródno, with its eighty thousand inhabitants. Both of these committees would remain in close contact and cooperation with the Warsaw Citizens Committee, on which they would become increasingly dependent as the war continued.[54] This was particularly true of the Praga committee, which by mid-November 1914 was issuing hundreds of daily coupons for purchases in the Warsaw Citizens Committee's stores.[55] Shortly thereafter, the Praga committee became an official but still nominally separate entity of the Warsaw Citizens Committee, and by the middle of February 1915 more than a thousand of Praga's residents were receiv-ing the latter's assistance on a daily basis in the form of products or coupons for use in public kitchens.[56] Praga, however, had been incorporated within Warsaw's official boundaries in 1832, a status not enjoyed by Mokotów, Wola, and Ochota on the west bank, whose citizens accelerated their efforts to be annexed by the city, motivated by the war's hardships and the acute need to improve sanitation in the three suburbs.[57] As early as December 1914, the Warsaw County Citizens Committee appealed to the Warsaw Citizens Committee to take charge of public assistance in the suburbs; this required doubling the number of its grocery stores from forty to eighty and ensuring a shipment of thirty railcars of foodstuffs daily to supply them.[58]

As the Warsaw Citizens Committee's support continued to expand to different constituencies, including lower-level state employees and artisans who sought and received access to public kitchens and small loans,[59] the committee reorganized itself at the end of March and yet again at the end of April. As a consequence, all sections and commissions became subordinate to four large departments: General Affairs, Philanthropy, Public Assistance, and Economic-Financial. As the committee's bureaucracy expanded, so too did its executive branch, which now included the chairs of the last three departments as well as the committee's treasurer.[60] As part of the reorganization, the committee also began to publish its own news information bulletin, the *Dziennik Komitetu Obywatelskiego*. Finally, as Warsaw faced multiple renewed crises in the late spring and early summer of 1915, the Presidium, led by Prince Lubomirski, made most of the decisions and then sought confirmation for those decisions from the General Affairs Department, as the former began to meet in emergency session far more frequently than the latter.

Thus, at the time of the Russian evacuation the Warsaw Citizens Committee could be described as a shadow municipal administration whose main task could be described as public assistance, but it was soon to venture into areas of justice and education usually reserved for governments. The committee was far from a democratic organization, and its self-proclaimed apolitical nature may have served as a useful fiction, but it represented more pluralism of opinion than did the kingdom-wide Central Citizens Committee dominated by the National Democratic Party, which it both preceded and outlasted. For that reason and because it had capably delivered assistance to tens of thousands of Varsovians, the Warsaw Citizens Committee enjoyed a legitimacy and moral authority that withstood the stress of the war's first year and enabled it to step successfully into the political vacuum left by the departing Russians. As it did, it completed its transformation from a nongovernmental to a governmental organization.

A New Municipal Government and the End of the Warsaw Citizens Committee

As previously noted, during the Russian evacuation of Warsaw the committee's Citizens Guard took over public-safety functions, starting with its 27 July 1915 appeal to the population, printed in ten thousand copies, to turn over all weapons, horses, and bicycles, and in general to cooperate with the militia.[61] At the same time, the committee took over postal and telegraphic services, the fire department, and the prisons. Meanwhile, its Legal Commission prepared to organize the local courts, and its School Section created three commissions to oversee the development of elementary, secondary, and higher education in the city.[62] The committee also created a new Department of City Affairs consisting of ten sections as the basis for a new city administration, which took over from the Russians on 4 August, a day before German troops entered Warsaw.

The question was whether the Germans would accept what were clearly being presented as accomplished facts, as well as those responsible for accomplishing them, especially Prince Lubomirski, who met with them on 5 August.

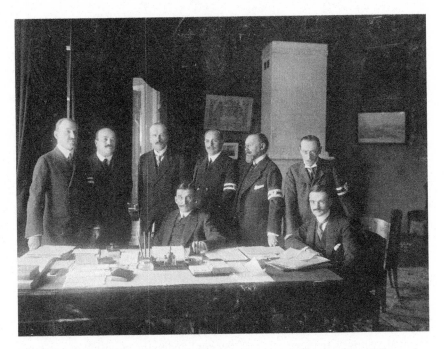

FIGURE 7. Zdzisław Lubomirski (center, seated) and officers of the Citizens Guard, 1916. Muzeum Narodowe w Warszawie.

Lubomirski's wife, Maria, like others among the urban elite, had left the city with her children nearly a month earlier when it remained unclear whether Warsaw would come under siege or be surrendered by the Russians without a fight. As the princess fretted in her diary when she learned of Lubomirski's decision to remain in Warsaw out of a sense of duty and to prevent the city from falling into the hands of "the worst elements," her husband had been "seriously compromised" by his support for the Russian side.[63] He was hardly alone in this regard as six other members of the committee, all of them National Democrats, fled with the Russians.

On 5 August 1915 fourteen members of the Warsaw Citizens Committee met twice with German military authorities in the office of the Fire Department of the defunct Russian City Magistrate, now in the committee's possession. Rather than arrest Lubomirski and other members of the committee, the Germans decided to leave the city administration provisionally in their hands, to appoint Lubomirski as its president and Drzewiecki as its vice president, and to recognize the Citizens Guard as the city's functioning police force.[64] In short order, that administration was organized, consisting originally of eleven men, four of whom were specialists drawn from the old magistrate. The committee also created a new Department of Education and a Factory Inspectorate, and for a time it appeared that the Germans would recognize the local courts established by the committee.[65]

However, following the arrival of Beseler and Kries on the scene a few weeks later, it became clear that once the Germans themselves became more organized, they would seek to limit the functions of the Polish institutions and either eliminate them entirely or subordinate them to German administration. As the Warsaw Citizens Committee sought only to establish itself as a self-governing institution in the once and future capital, it collided less with German interests than did the Central Citizens Committee, which practically considered itself a national government and established country-wide judicial and educational systems during the Russian evacuation. As Marta Polsakiewicz points out, in all other cities in its occupation zone, the German administration appointed a mayor from the Reich, whereas in Warsaw the Germans confirmed Lubomirski and others in their unelected posts.[66] Yet the dissolution of the Central Citizens Committee and all of its subordinate committees on 12 September 1915 certainly put the self-standing Warsaw Citizens Committee on notice. Shortly thereafter, the Germans approved the creation of the Rada Główna Opiekuńcza (RGO—Central Welfare Council), whose activities were thereafter confined to the provision of assistance and relief earlier conducted by the Central Citizens Committee.[67]

By contrast, the initiatives of the Warsaw Citizens Committee taken in July and August were reigned in more gradually as the new German administration sought to gain control over the court and school systems, as well as the local police. The first to be affected was the system of municipal courts created by the committee at the time of the Russian evacuation. On 10 September 1915 the German occupation authorities closed these courts and replaced them with their own, which led to the vigorous protest of the committee's Legal Department, led by Henryk Konic. A meeting of Warsaw jurists unanimously passed a resolution claiming the German action to be in violation of the Hague Convention. In protest against the relegation of Polish to a language of secondary importance in the German-organized courts, the lawyers also declared that they would not fulfill their duties in courts that were not officiated in the Polish language.[68] While the Germans subsequently conceded the use of Polish as the official language in the peace and appeals courts, the Polish bar, with the committee's support, refused to participate in the lower instances until the entire system of justice in the city was Polonized.[69] The committee's dispute with the German authorities over the courts peaked in early November 1915 when Konic was arrested and briefly interned, and the committee's open letter of protest was censored in its entirety and even removed from the committee's own official digest.[70]

The committee's educational initiatives and institutions came next. Earlier, the committee's Education Department had decided to reduce but not eliminate Russian language instruction in the secondary schools, placing it on a par with other foreign languages, to replace obligatory courses in Russian history and geography with Polish courses in these subject areas, and not to privilege the German language in any way.[71] The first sign of trouble came in early September when the occupation authorities demanded that German be taught as an obligatory foreign language in the city's secondary schools.[72] Meanwhile, the German civil administration established its own School Inspectorate, which initially confined itself to the collection of information but which on 10 October claimed authority over all educational matters in the German occupation zone. In the process, German was introduced as the primary language of instruction in Protestant and Jewish schools, with local school administrators nominated and confirmed by the School Inspectorate, which also had to approve all textbooks. In November, a new curriculum was introduced for the primary schools, with bilingual instruction in the secondary schools and higher schools. A final conflict over teachers' education helped bring tensions to a boiling point, leading to the decision of the committee's Education Department to dissolve itself on 17 February 1916, with its remaining functions transferred to a commission under the City Administration.[73]

Only slightly less contentious was the issue of jurisdictional authority over the Citizens Guard, which had swelled to a force of approximately eight thousand by the end of the Russian evacuation.[74] Street disturbances over bread shortages toward the end of August, including the looting of bakeries and vans by hungry crowds that could not be contained by the Citizens Guard, would lead to German efforts to bring this Polish police force under the control of the occupation authorities.[75] Shortly thereafter, the Citizens Guard began to receive demands to assist German police in making arrests, and on 6 September the German political police summoned all precinct commissars of the Citizens Guard, a demand that was not even communicated to the Warsaw Citizens Committee or to Prince Lubomirski.[76]

Because the dispute over the Citizens Guard did not revolve around issues of language and, by extension, national identity, the committee was more amenable to negotiation. At the end of October, on the same day it protested growing German control over the courts, the committee accepted in principle the German authorities' project of transforming the Citizens Guard into a paid, uniformed police force.[77] However, the outcome of that process again demonstrated the committee's growing political powerlessness. The Germans initially agreed that the new force would be an organ of the City Administration, which would appoint its chief, but by early December the Germans drafted statutes that clearly deprived it of real autonomy.[78] On 31 January 1916 the Citizens Guard was officially transformed into the City Militia, with a new commander (Prince Franciszek Radziwiłł) appointed by the City Administration but subordinate to Glasenapp, the German president of police. At the same time, financial responsibility for maintaining the City Militia, which fulfilled the functions of a sanitary, traffic, building, and industrial police force, was assigned to the City Administration. The numbers of this force, whose members were authorized to carry weapons only in specific instances, were also substantially reduced from those belonging to the old Citizens Guard, to 1,230 men of the ranks, 245 sergeants, and 43 commissars and deputy commissars.[79] Meanwhile, the criminal police remained in the hands of the German Police Presidium, while authority over the security police was held jointly by the Police Presidium and the German Army.[80]

Thus, having lost effective control over the courts, education, and police, and having been reduced to an organization providing assistance and relief only, the Warsaw Citizens Committee began to dissolve itself in planned stages, surrendering more and more of its functions to the City Administration and closing various sections and commissions in the process. Facing increasing demands for greater representation on the committee, it determined that the city's "state of transition" should end and that complicated issues could no longer be decided by a "provisional organization" set up for other purposes.[81] In March 1916 the committee proposed and Kries, the head of the civil administration in the German occupation zone, agreed to the establishment of an elected city council. Kries then empowered the committee to draft an electoral ordinance and set the deadline at 10 April.[82] That deadline was subsequently extended by more than a week as the committee met in four extraordinary sessions from 15 to 18 April. However, true to form, the Germans rejected the electoral ordinance passed by the Warsaw Citizens Committee as "not corresponding to the demands of a modern urban economy," though in effect it was too democratic for their tastes. They replaced it with their own City Statute based on the Prussian curial system of municipal elections. The next day the Warsaw Citizens Committee, or what was left of it, was dissolved by order of the German authorities.[83]

Thus what had begun as a philanthropic-welfare organization and been transformed into a self-governing body ended where it began, as a philanthropic-welfare organization. Deprived of autonomous power and authority, the Warsaw Citizens Committee passed any legacy on to its successor, the new municipal government formed under German auspices. Following City Council elections based on a socially and economically weighted franchise in mid-July, the new Warsaw city government officially came into being on 8 August 1916, as the makeshift city administration headed by Lubomirski over the previous year was replaced by a magistrate, which the prince continued to serve as president and Drzewiecki, who also doubled as mayor of the City Council, as vice president. Before its dissolution, the Warsaw Citizens Committee's main task had been to deal with the war's side effects of poverty, hunger, disease, and epidemics, as the City Administration occupied itself with larger issues of the urban economy, even as the committee's requisitioning authority was eliminated and its purchasing authority substantially reduced. The burden of public assistance passed on to the new municipal government and with it the responsibility to secure the tremendous resources necessary to carry it. Warsaw's new "self-governing" institutions would also inherit growing expressions of opposition to the committee's social policy, symbolized above all in the controversy over the public kitchens and in calls for democratization in the administration of social welfare.

Social Policy and Social Divisions

In later chapters I will discuss how ethnicity and gender shaped the distribution and receipt of public assistance. In this section, I will focus on the role of class. Both hardship and assistance to those dealing with it were socially conditioned in Warsaw, as they were across Europe during the First World War. Access to a broad range of goods, services, and institutions, not to mention the black market, was often based on social prejudices and biases on the one hand, and social privileges and advantages on the other. The consequences, painful for some and disastrous for others, led to social protest and labor unrest not seen in Warsaw since the Revolution of 1905, both despite the wartime development of a municipal welfare system and because of the inevitable failure of that system to alleviate hardship in the absence of sufficient resources. The growing incidence of strikes in conditions of incredibly high unemployment is an indication of the level of desperation among the more privileged members of the lower classes. What then can be said of those who had even fewer cards to play?

The Warsaw Citizens Committee, given its basis in the city's aristocratic and business elites and perhaps recalling labor unrest and violence in the city during the 1905 revolution, worried about socialist agitation spreading among the working class before the end of the war's first month. This dangerous agitation, "which could threaten peace in the city," as it turned out, revolved around the issue of representation on the committee and included a request for the creation of a separate Workers Section, both of which the committee resisted. Instead, it proposed that the workers elect three representatives each to the committee's Labor Section and Distribution Commission.[84] The issue of representation was raised again in February 1915, when delegates from twenty-four workers' organizations convened to elect two representatives to a slightly expanded Warsaw

Citizens Committee undergoing reorganization. A conflict ensued between the committee and workers' delegates over the representativeness of the workers' organizations, which members of the committee believed to be one-sided, dominated by leftist parties. For their part, the workers' delegates protested the presence of committee members at the meeting. Following the appearance of these "revolutionary sparks," which Princess Lubomirska attributed to "German or Jewish money,"[85] negotiations were then initiated to come to an understanding with a "more representative" group of workers' organizations, namely those of Christian and National Democratic persuasion who could be counted upon to be less confrontational at meetings of the committee's General Section.[86] Three working-class delegates, only one of whom came from the socialist left, were finally added to the committee's ranks in the fall of 1915 following the Russian evacuation.

The committee's main strategy for dealing with potential labor unrest was to find employment for workers idled by the economic crisis, by whatever means. For example, it was decided early in the war that winter work and the clearing of Warsaw's streets of snow and ice, which traditionally occupied peasants from villages surrounding Warsaw, would be reserved for the unemployed from Warsaw's working-class suburbs.[87] However, such offers of employment were not as graciously received as the committee and its upper-class backers expected, and committee members expressed their dismay in statements, attitudes, and policies toward the "idle poor." Following a January 1915 snowfall, the administration of the city's trolley service and the committee put out calls for workers to clear the tracks and remove snow in the city for a daily payment of 1–1.5 rubles. Only a couple of hundred day laborers responded, which *Kurjer Warszawski* considered "characteristic" of twelve thousand unemployed workers in the city who had become dependent on public support. The daily repeated that charge less than a week later, when it published information received from the committee's Labor Section, which reported that 1,089 of the 1,389 individuals for whom it found employment during the period of 4–10 January were engaged in "winter work" but that several thousand could have been employed in such jobs for "relatively high wages."[88]

Thus, when delegates with ties to socialist political parties first approached the Warsaw Citizens Committee about subsidizing the "workers' kitchens" then being organized and grouped around a Workers Economic Committee (Robotniczy Komitet Gospodarczy—RKG), the initial result was an acrimonious exchange about workers' failure to use the committee's employment agencies and their rejection of the work offered to them.[89] As early as the war's first month, the first three workers' kitchens, staffed almost entirely by women and supplied by fourteen bakeries and groceries in the Jewish quarter, opened on Miła, Gęsia, and Nowolopie Streets.[90] It took little time for the parties of the socialist Left (the Bund, PPS-Left, and Social Democracy of the Kingdom of Poland and Lithuania or SDKPiL), reduced to operating in the shadows of legality under Russian rule, to exploit the opportunities afforded by workers' kitchens for agitation and political mobilization.[91] The Warsaw Citizens Committee realized this as well, which is why in initial negotiations it questioned the very existence of workers' kitchens when the committee's own public kitchens were available to Warsaw's proletariat.[92] However, the committee was already sponsoring class-based tearooms and kitchens for Warsaw's intelligentsia. In the end, the committee's decision to subsidize the workers' kitchens organized by the RKG was most likely a political calculation; namely, to use its resources as a means of exercising leverage over the RKG and its socialist sponsors.

The result of this arrangement, as described by one of its participants, was "ceaseless struggle" between the Warsaw Citizens Committee and delegates from the RKG.[93] This struggle began on 28 November 1914, when the committee announced its willingness to support special public kitchens designated for workers in dire need, with free meals to be served only to workers who were considered to be without means, while other workers would receive meals at discounted prices. No more than 20% of the meals were to be free of charge, a ceiling that drew strong objections from the workers' delegates of the RKG.[94] On 3 December the committee gave the RKG delegation five days to accept its previously established conditions.[95] The workers' delegates had little choice but to accept these demands, and on 11 December the committee's Presidium approved a proposal to create a special department of workers' kitchens.[96] At the same time, however, the placing of the workers' kitchens under the committee's umbrella provided a new argument for representation of workers' delegates in the General Section, that is, on the committee's ultimate decision-making body.[97]

By early March 1915, two issues were said to be dividing the committee and the organizations grouped around the RKG: the financial accountability of the workers' kitchens to the committee, which the RKG viewed as an infringement on its self-government; and the question of who should represent workers before the committee, especially since the committee had just called upon Catholic and Polish nationalist working-class organizations to select their own representatives. Those who had been delegated earlier by the RKG to deal with the committee vehemently opposed this obvious attempt to circumvent the socialist parties, arguing that an independent mass meeting should select workers' representatives.[98] Meanwhile, conflict over the first issue had erupted following a dispute with the administrative committee of one of the workers' kitchens in Praga, and this conflict would lead the committee to insist that all workers' kitchens be held to the same level of financial accountability as other public kitchens supported by the committee.[99] It was subsequently agreed in negotiations with the representatives of the workers' kitchens that while their administrative boards would remain autonomous, they would present on demand records of those who were served discounted and free meals, and that the financial accountability of the kitchens would follow the rules set up by the Section for Public Kitchens. In exchange, the workers' kitchens would receive monthly subventions.[100] Thus in April 1915 the committee accepted requests for 4,450 rubles in support from nine workers' kitchens, which was followed shortly thereafter by its acceptance of the May budget of eleven workers' kitchens for 5,275 rubles.[101]

For all of the tensions surrounding the workers' kitchens in their first year of existence, when the Russian police arrested members of the kitchens' administrative boards at the end of May 1915, the Warsaw Citizens Committee did appeal to the authorities for their release.[102] However, as the Russians began their final evacuation of Warsaw in the summer of 1915, the committee suspended subventions to the workers' kitchens, ostensibly because of their failure to submit themselves to the committee's financial control.[103] Moreover, the committee was facing its own funding uncertainties during the Russian evacuation as promised loans from the central government in Petrograd failed to materialize. In any case, the relationship between the workers' kitchens and the Warsaw Citizens Committee was restored following the German takeover of the city, as were the disputes between them.

By the end of 1915, the Warsaw Citizens Committee supported thirteen workers' kitchens operated by the RKG, and an additional six kitchens organized separately by the right-wing faction of the PPS.[104] By the summer of 1916, their monthly budgets had been increased from 5,000 to 18,000 rubles, which more or less kept pace with inflation. However, with the dissolution of the committee and the transfer of all of its functions to the City Administration, the RKG balked at the subordination of its kitchens to the new municipal authorities, and on 16 July 1916 the workers' kitchens were liquidated.[105] Those whom they supported would have recourse to some but not all of the sixty-four public kitchens and twenty-five tearooms that were also transferred by the committee to the jurisdiction of the new City Magistrate and were serving some 105,000 meals on a daily basis.[106] Those numbers would only continue to rise, and by May 1917 some 150,000 people in Warsaw, approximately 17% of the population, had become completely dependent on the city's public kitchens for their sustenance.[107] To put this in perspective, at their peak in the Second World War, public kitchens served 133,000 meals daily to approximately 10% of Warsaw's population.[108]

Of the public kitchens supported by the city administration, some twenty-three were "kosher kitchens" in the Jewish community, which in October 1916 were serving some thirty-seven thousand dinners on a daily basis.[109] Although this example of the segregation of public assistance could be justified in terms of religious-based dietary restrictions, the separate kitchens and tearooms set up for the Warsaw intelligentsia could not be. The intelligentsia comprised somewhat less than 10% of Warsaw's unemployed population during the first year of the war, but the Warsaw Citizens Committee, which had argued against the need for workers' kitchens, believed that members of the more socially respectable intelligentsia who required assistance were "too proud to beg" for support. Thus, support to the intelligentsia had to be funneled more discretely; this support started as early as August 1914 through the committee's Women's Section.[110] Unlike workers, members of the intelligentsia would not be expected to take their meals in public kitchens along with everyone else, and because the unemployed among them were "more physically delicate," they would not be condemned for refusing to take up temporary jobs in snow removal or digging potatoes. Instead, to avoid the appearance of dependence on public philanthropy, they would simply be asked to pay a token amount (originally twenty-five kopecks) for nutritious three-course meals, served in settings such as the Dolina Szwajcarska recreational facility. By June 1915, such special kitchens were serving a thousand low-cost meals a day to impoverished members of the Warsaw intelligentsia.[111] During the first phase of the German occupation, the committee budgeted twenty kopecks per dinner for meals served to the intelligentsia, compared to twelve kopecks per dinner for those served in the workers' kitchens.[112]

The Warsaw Citizens Committee and its supporters never imagined that workers could be humiliated by publicly visible dependence on outside assistance or that they might also find snow removal demeaning. To give one example: in July 1915 a workers' kitchen operated by the Association of Jewish Workers' Cooperatives reported that two-thirds of its meals were eaten on site and the rest carried out to be consumed elsewhere. Slightly more than half of its meals were served free of cost, a figure that rose to 76% of those meals that were taken home, an indication that a high percentage of workers were more willing to actually dine in the kitchens if they were able to pay at least something and thereby preserve their dignity.[113] Belinda Davis reports a similar phenomenon in Berlin—namely, that public kitchens carried a certain stigma that could have been removed only through the obligatory participation of all. Berlin's factory canteens, on the other hand, removed from the public view and connected to workers' employment, were much preferred.[114]

In Warsaw only the intelligentsia's sensitivities were taken into consideration, to the extent that the Warsaw Citizens Committee and the Central Citizens Committee joined forces to create a common Section on Assistance to the Intelligentsia, the only joint body formed by the two organizations.[115] This section provided eligible members of the intelligentsia not only with dinners but also with direct cash payments, loans, assistance in exchange for work, and subventions for apartment rents, doctors' visits, and medical prescriptions.[116] The intelligentsia also had privileged access to publically dispensed preventive medicine. By the end of January 1915, the recipients of more than 1,500 cholera vaccinations and an even greater number of inoculations against smallpox came almost entirely from the intelligentsia.[117] The need to inoculate Warsaw's lower classes and especially its refugee population was clear; however, with a cost of 200 rubles per 1,000 doses for the smallpox vaccine at the time, the prohibitive expense encouraged existing tendencies toward prioritization according to class. Mass inoculations would have to wait for the German occupation of the city.

While the Warsaw intelligentsia fared somewhat better during the German occupation, at least in terms of salaried employment, the material situation only became worse for the lower classes, even for the small minority of its members who retained or found employment, as their wages failed to keep pace with inflation. Under the Russians, strikes were more of a threat than a reality and came from those whose livelihoods were connected to traditional trades and crafts. The first note of a strike action was sounded at the end of February 1915, when bakers complained about access to city supplies of flour. A strike was averted, however, when authorities agreed to release a certain amount of flour to the bakeries.[118] Then in April, Warsaw carpenters, who found themselves in a very difficult position because of a shortage of boards, appealed to the Warsaw Citizens Committee to assist in supplying them with seventy wagonloads of sawed lumber.[119] The carpenters too could be mollified, at least temporarily. Shoemakers, although certainly affected by the leather shortage, also demanded a 25% wage increase during their strike in the middle of June 1915 and employed coercive means, including violence, to enforce solidarity in their ranks. The shoemakers' strike resulted in a shooting at a work site, which *Kurjer Warszawski* was quick to denounce as "terror" in fearful remembrance of similar incidents ten years earlier.[120]

Revolution was still more of a reminder than a specter in the summer of 1915, but social unrest escalated as living standards rapidly collapsed during the German occupation. To be sure, the Germans authorities reopened the space for legal trade-union activity, which the Russians had prohibited at the beginning of the war. Thus four central trade unions with ties to the radical Left (including the Jewish Bund), the right wing of the PPS, the National Workers Union, and the Christian Democrats resurfaced in Warsaw. However, the impact of these trade unions on subsequent developments was minimal as they managed to organize only a small percentage of workers in conditions of extraordinarily high unemployment.[121] The "bread and work" demonstrations involving thousands in various parts of the city on 13 September 1915 were hardly the work of labor agitators and, for the moment, were easily dispersed.[122]

While the German occupation authorities were loath to provide bread in the desired quality and quantity, they were willing not only to provide work but also following the September demonstrations to take over labor recruitment from the Warsaw Citizens Committee's Labor Section. As Christian Westerhoff has convincingly demonstrated, German economic and food policy in the Warsaw General-Government was intimately connected to the recruitment of labor for employment in Germany. The conscious decision of the occupation regime not to rebuild Polish industry, relieve unemployment, and contain the further impoverishment of the population was purposefully designed, he argues, to incentivize "voluntary" registration for work in Germany and to a lesser extent in the mining industry and road construction projects within the occupied zone.[123] The Labor Section's ties to Russian industry and the Russian Army were, therefore, of little use in the changed circumstances, while the demands of German agriculture, German factories, and the German Army for labor would only grow. Thus, a Central Labor Office under the German Presidium of Police was created in Warsaw, modeled after a similar agency earlier established in Łódź. The early recruitment advertisements of the "Central" emphasized the higher wages to be made in Germany, two to three times more than for those employed to work on the railroads in the Polish Kingdom, along with paid travel expenses and low-cost housing.[124] In its first three months, the "Central" recruited 7,000 workers from Warsaw, and by March 1916 it had found work for 17,809 workers, 10,472 of them in Germany and 7,337 in the German occupation zone. Unlike labor recruitment under the Russians, which tended to exclude non-Christians, 4,820 Warsaw Jews accepted offers of employment from the "Central," but only 1,027 in Germany.[125]

These numbers did not live up to German expectations. By comparison, German labor recruitment in the smaller city of Łódź over a five-month period from April to September 1915 had reaped some 26,626 workers.[126] Warsaw Christians joined Jews in their reluctance to leave for the Reich as news filtered back that Polish workers were poorly treated in Germany, were given the most physically demanding work at the lowest possible wages, and were being prevented from leaving the country. When only 1,500 workers were recruited in Warsaw over the next month, the German occupation authorities hinted at applying more coercive measures if voluntary recruitment failed.[127] On the one hand, the "Central" now began offering monthly subventions of approximately ten marks per family for workers willing to depart for Germany; on the other, it issued veiled warnings that it was "in the worker's own interest" to accept the "Central's" offers of employment.[128]

Within weeks, the Germans began to publish regulations to combat "aversion to work,"[129] even though in December 1915 the German Presidium of Police had estimated that there were only twenty to thirty thousand unemployed workers in Warsaw and that one-third of the city's prewar labor force had either been conscripted for military service or evacuated to Russia. If those figures were at all accurate, or honest, then at most there would have been only a few thousand "shirkers" (*"Arbeitsscheu"*) in Warsaw by the summer of 1916 after several additional months of voluntary labor recruitment. Moreover, these figures from December 1915 had been used as part of Beseler's justification for rejecting the requests of industrialists for support of factory production inside the Polish Kingdom. Thus, Beseler had already tipped his hand. "The best way" to relieve local unemployment, he informed local entrepreneurs, was "to send workers to German industry" rather than to employ them where they lived.[130] On 3 October 1916 the General Headquarters of the German Army, in an order signed by Ludendorff, authorized the forced labor conscription of twenty-eight thousand workers to be drawn from the German occupation zone in Poland to serve on the Eastern Front in fourteen labor battalions.[131] Subject to Ludendorff's forced-labor draft were men on public assistance between the ages of eighteen and forty-five, and soon German police began to round up people on the streets of Warsaw whom they suspected of being on the dole.[132]

The introduction of forced labor in the Warsaw General-Government, Westerhoff has shown, met with Beseler's approval despite the opposition of Kries, the chief of administration, who feared that it would undermine the planned Polish quasi-state soon to be established, would have a negative impact on recruitment for a Polish Army expected to fight alongside the Central Powers, and would ultimately reduce the effectiveness of ongoing "voluntary" labor recruitment, which forced labor was never meant to replace. Beseler, for his part, thought that coercive measures would have little impact, particularly if they were introduced as part of the struggle against "shirkers" and targeted primarily at the Jewish population, which the Poles would not oppose. To win the support of Polish authorities, German occupation officials were to emphasize that the application of forced labor would be limited to those who were unemployed, but this effectively blurred the line between the Polish "unemployed" and the Jewish "shirkers." In Warsaw itself, city officials were given ten days to register "voluntarily" one thousand people for work in Germany along with hundreds of others for fortifications work in the east, and to turn over lists of all of Warsaw's unemployed. Then at the end of 1916 Police President Glasenapp declared publicly that it was up to the population to determine whether forced labor would be further implemented or could be avoided through "voluntary" registration.[133]

Coercion, however, did not increase the numbers of those who "voluntarily" left for Germany. As early as the previous April, Prince Lubomirski had protested the "single solution"—the departure of workers to Germany "where they are exploited, have their freedom of movement restricted, are under constant police surveillance, and resented by the local working class"—of the occupation authorities to massive unemployment, growing impoverishment, and acute hunger among the population in Warsaw. "Our workers," he argued, "would prefer hunger and poverty at home to leaving their native land."[134] Small wonder, then, that the City Administration failed to cooperate in the execution of Ludendorff's October order, which would lead to Beseler's reluctant change of course. Lubomirski and the City Administration's refusal to provide German police with lists of the able-bodied unemployed in Warsaw, Beseler argued, was based on erroneous assumptions and opinions about the occupation authorities' intent to forcibly transport these men to Germany. Referring to the roundups for Ludendorff's labor battalions on the Eastern Front, he claimed that Polish stubbornness had forced the Germans to take matters into their own hands. Besides, the removal of such individuals from the large numbers of those on public assistance, Beseler concluded, would serve "the city's best economic interests."[135]

Nonetheless, resistance to coercive labor-recruitment measures in Warsaw had proved effective and led Beseler to abandon them on 6 November, the day after the Central Powers' proclamation of a Polish Kingdom, though they would remain in effect elsewhere in the German occupation zone for yet another month. Fearing further alienation of the City Administration and the local population to the German state-building project, Beseler was finally coming around to the position taken earlier by Kries, but the damage had already been done in the "capital city." Forced-labor recruitment had been intended for use mainly as a threat to accelerate voluntary recruitment, but as Westerhoff argues, Beseler's strategy had backfired and turned both Poles and Jews against the German administration. Moreover, as Kries had predicted, the short-lived experiment with forced labor also ensured the failure of recruitment of soldiers into a Polish Army under German auspices.[136]

There would be one last effort by both German and Austro-Hungarian military authorities to revive coercive labor-recruitment measures in the Warsaw General-Government in the early spring of 1917. However, at a conference attended in Berlin by representatives of both of the Central Powers, Kries spoke forcefully in favor of "voluntary" labor recruitment and helped to defeat efforts at reinstituting forced labor.[137] In the meantime, street roundups may have come to an end, but new means were devised to "encourage" labor migration to Germany. On 22 March 1917 Glasenapp informed the Warsaw Magistrate that as of 15 April no new public-works projects in the city would be approved—this at a time when well over thirteen thousand individuals derived at least some means of support from such employment.[138] At the same time, Glasenapp informed the City Magistrate that access to public kitchens by the physically able unemployed males who had not registered with the German "Central" was "completely unacceptable."[139] *Godzina Polski*, the Polish-language daily closest to the German occupation authorities, was also prepared to support "draconian means" to compel labor from "the lazy" in Warsaw, who it claimed numbered in the "tens of thousands." Assistance should be confined to the "really deserving poor," whom the daily defined as the elderly and infirm, while those who didn't fit that category should be forced to work and their children placed in public shelters.[140]

The attitudes expressed in *Godzina Polski* were not confined to that newspaper but were also an expression of elite fears of mounting social unrest in the city, particularly following the February and October revolutions in Russia. In January 1916 new "bread and work" demonstrations in front of the city hall were explicitly aimed at gaining the attention of the Warsaw Citizens Committee and the City Administration's Factory Inspectorate. Strikes of bakers, shoemakers, and millers followed in March 1916, and two months later city water, sewer, and transport workers went on strike.[141] Warsaw's first hunger riots in June 1916, which resulted in widespread looting, were repeated again in the spring of 1917. Ever-declining rations, however, did not affect those who could afford to purchase food, even delicacies, of much better quality at much higher prices, causing Princess Lubomirska a rare moment of social reflection in September 1917: "I have all of the comforts, enough to eat, and peace and quiet; I think frequently about the desperate fate of the sick and the poor. The crazy inequality between the privileged classes and those who are not strikes me now like a blow to the head."[142]

Meanwhile, this "desperate fate" and "crazy inequality" continued to express itself in social and labor unrest. In March and April 1917 strikes of approximately two thousand Polish and Jewish workers broke out in the metal factories of Gerlach and Pulst and "Parawoz," among the few still in operation, thanks to contracts with the German military authorities. The Germans responded by interning the strike leaders and arresting hundreds of workers, which in turn led to street skirmishes in Wola (the location of the Gerlach and Pulst factory) and the construction of makeshift barricades.[143] The German military authorities then took over direct control of the two factories and dismissed hundreds of workers, ostensibly to cut costs. The Germans also rejected an offer of those workers who remained employed to accept lesser wages to save their colleagues' jobs. This resulted in renewed strikes on 5 July in both factories, which were then surrounded by troops whose roundup of striking workers for imprisonment at the Warsaw Citadel was met by a human barricade of workers' wives and daughters. As the women used their bodies to stop the police vans carrying their husbands and fathers from leaving factory sites, the arrested workers tried to escape from the trucks. In the ensuing chaos, a machine-gun round was fired into the crowd, and soldiers turned on the women with bayonets.[144]

The original strikes at Gerlach and Pulst and "Parawoz" the previous spring were the result of a decline of real wages among the most fortunate members of the lower classes, namely full-time employed industrial workers who now comprised only 22% of the prewar total. Real wages had already declined by 25% by September 1916, and the decline would reach 50% by May 1918—facts that were well known to the German occupation and Polish municipal authorities.[145] For unskilled workers, the decline in real wages was even worse. While the nominal wages of skilled workers would double, that for unskilled males had increased by less than 20% by mid-1916. A few months earlier, in February 1916, the Factory Inspectorate had proposed a daily minimum wage of 2 rubles for adults and of 1.25 rubles for adolescents of both sexes to keep pace with inflation. However, as of January 1917, the average wage was only 1.37 rubles for adult men, 77 kopecks for adult women, 59 kopecks for adolescent boys, and 35 kopecks for adolescent girls.[146] Finally, those employed in public-works projects, almost entirely adult males, worked in five-hour shifts for a daily wage of 70 kopecks at a time when a pound of poor-quality bread cost 45 kopecks.[147] With bread rationed at 4.5 pounds every two weeks by May 1917, such purchases alone accounted for nearly 30% of the wages of a public-works employee. Given the depression of wages, one can understand why access to public kitchens in Warsaw may have been more valuable than employment and certainly preferable to what socialists were calling "slavery" in Germany, which is why the German occupiers sought to eliminate that access.[148]

Employed or unemployed, lower-class Varsovians increasingly acted out of despair, while the successful Bolshevik coup against the Provisional Government in Russia encouraged radical labor activists. On 19 January 1918 a general strike broke out in Warsaw and then spread to other cities in the occupied Polish Kingdom. It also embraced the city's own twelve thousand full-time employees (as opposed to those employed part-time in public-works projects), including health-care workers in Warsaw's hospitals whom the city had been unable to pay. *Tygodnik Illustrowany* apparently expected the hospital employees, who were replaced by volunteers and nuns, to work without wages as it "categorically condemns strikes of this kind," actions that it found "inadmissible in a civilized society."[149] The Warsaw City Council, which also appealed to city workers to end their participation in the general strike, nevertheless called upon the occupation authorities to release all arrested workers, and especially workers' delegates who were necessary for negotiations with the City Administration.[150] Despite German repression of the January general strike, smaller strikes would become common-place by the spring of 1918, one of the largest and longest being that of female garment workers, who were among the few women outside of teachers who were employed in Warsaw at the time.[151]

The reality, however, especially for the City Administration, was that it was running out of money to support the public kitchens and other forms of public assistance and to provide employment through public-works projects—indeed, to pay its own employees. By the time of the January general strike, the city faced the prospect of bankruptcy as its appeals for any kind of relief met the deaf ears of the German occupation authorities. Ultimately, failure to manage the crisis on the Warsaw home front was the result of city's dire financial straits, to which we will now turn.

Deficit Spending, Writ Large

From the very beginning of the war and, therefore, of the existence of the War-saw Citizens Committee, government subventions, though substantial under the Russians, were insufficient to fund relief and assistance activities in the city, and no amount of private donations raised internally and externally could hope to fill the gap. During the first five months of the committee's existence, a full one-third of its expenditures went into serving its debt, while its largest source of income was 915,492 rubles from "various creditors." Not surprisingly, the committee sought a 50% increase in its 30,000-ruble monthly subvention from the City Magistrate.[152] By early March 1915, and as the need for assistance escalated, the committee began to lobby the Russian government for a monthly subvention of 100,000 rubles—this when the budget of the Warsaw City Administration itself was being cut by 6 million rubles, or approximately 30% when compared to the 1914 budget.[153]

Thus, the Warsaw Citizens Committee had little choice but to approach the Russian central government for a loan of 9 million rubles to purchase food and fuel for the city in the middle of May 1915. Earlier, it had turned down the offer of a 300,000-ruble loan from the Central Citizens Committee at 5% interest, a rate the Warsaw committee felt was exorbitant, higher than what was then available from Warsaw's private banks.[154] Subsequent developments would force the committee to take this loan, however. First, the Council of Ministers in Petrograd agreed to a loan of only 3 million rubles, well below the original sum requested.[155] Four weeks before the final Russian evacuation of the city, the committee bud-geted the 3 million rubles as the bare minimum necessary for the city to survive through the second half of 1915, and indeed the City Magistrate had this amount on deposit with the Russian State Bank in Warsaw for distribution to the committee. However, with the evacuation of the Russian State Bank's local branches, the City Administration was unable to cover its obligations, and when the magistrate too was evacuated, the committee was left with only 500,000 rubles on hand and was forced to cut the budgets of all of its sections.[156]

Not only did the Russian evacuation leave the Warsaw Citizens Committee drained of funds, it also meant that soldiers' wives and state pensioners, earlier supported by the Russian government, as well as the population of the suburbs now appealed to the committee for assistance. One of the committee's earliest measures to generate new revenue was a tax of slightly less than 17% on all income generated by the city's cinemas.[157] By these and other means, the committee and the new City Administration formed from it had 661,927 rubles on hand in mid-August 1915, while the cost of purchasing a forty-day supply of food and fuel for the city was estimated at 10 million rubles, and that of providing assistance and relief to the population another 5.7 million.[158] The difficult negotiations with a consortium of private Warsaw banks for a loan were entrusted to the City Administration, while the committee itself became dependent on the city for the majority of its funding—which restored the kind of relationship it had had with the Russian City Magistrate during the first year of the war. Thus, for the remainder of 1915, 64% of the committee's 5.5 million–ruble budget came directly from the City Administration, a percentage that increased during the first four months of 1916 even as the committee's expenditures declined significantly in the course of its gradual dissolution.[159]

Eventually, the city was offered a 5 million–ruble loan at 6% interest, higher than the committee had been willing to accept just a few months earlier. It sought to cover most of its remaining financial needs by raising 4 million rubles issued in bonds covered by future taxes, although for the moment the German occupation authorities would agree only to a one-time compulsory tax.[160] That tax, announced by the committee in December as a "contribution" (*ofiara*), was accompanied by fines for delayed payment.[161] To support soldiers' families, some of whom were already receiving free meals in the public kitchens, the committee at first proposed to the banks that they make 420,000 rubles in payments in what was essentially another loan, the principal presumably covered by the Russian government and the interest by the committee. This effort failed, and in mid-October 1915 the City Administration took over the Russian government's obligations to *rezerwistki* and state pensioners by contracting a 2 million–ruble loan at 5% interest, repayable at the end of the war, presumably by the Russians.[162] By such an arrangement, *rezerwistki* received 4.80 rubles in monthly support and their children 2.40 rubles, practically the same amounts they had been provided by the Russians.[163] Shortly thereafter, several of Warsaw's suburbs presented requests for 60,000 rubles in monthly support to assist a population of more than 133,000.[164] By the end of the year, the German authorities made approval of loans contracted by the City Administration contingent on its use of a portion of those funds to make loans of its own to Warsaw County—that is, to the city's suburbs.[165]

With all of these pressing needs, the City Administration's expenditures on public assistance increased ninefold between August 1915 and June 1916. On 5 August 1915, when the Germans captured Warsaw, some 30,573 inhabitants of the city and the suburb of Praga were receiving public assistance, a figure that rose to 111,506 by 1 July 1916. The numbers only kept growing: a month later the City Administration was supporting some 20% the population of Warsaw's First Precinct.[166] By January 1916, the city had had no choice but to contract another major loan for 10 million marks with the Disconto Gesellschaft in Berlin to finance its food purchases.[167] Having borrowed the equivalent of 15 million rubles since the beginning of the occupation, the City Administration sought in vain the assistance of the German authorities to avoid what it called "financial catastrophe."[168] Yet when the city issued its budget projections for all of 1916 in October of that year, its expenditures of more than 47 million rubles were expected to exceed its income by only 30–35%.[169] That the city's budget deficit remained relatively contained before the disastrous winter of 1916–17 was in large part due to the support of organizations abroad that delivered wartime relief to Warsaw and other parts of the occupied Polish Kingdom.

The most substantial relief came from organizations formed in neutral countries, particularly Switzerland and, until the spring of 1917, the United States. Of particular significance was the Vevey Committee, headed by honorary presidents Henryk Sienkiewicz and Ignacy Paderewski. Organized officially as the General Committee to Aid the Victims of the War in Poland in Lausanne on 9 January 1915, it subsequently moved its headquarters to Vevey. Through it, organizations such as the Polish Central Relief Committee founded in Chicago in October 1914 and the Rockefeller Foundation also provided financial and other forms of assistance to Warsaw. Indeed Prince Lubomirski, Piotr Drzewiecki, and Michał Bergson, president of the Jewish community board, were all honorary members of the Vevey Committee, whose first 100,000 Swiss francs went directly to Warsaw on 4 March 1915 to aid those in greatest need, particularly women and children. During the course of the war the Vevey Committee would funnel some 12 million Swiss francs, or approximately $4 million, to Poland from the United States, 90% of which went to the occupied Polish Kingdom.[170] How much of that went to Warsaw, however, is difficult to determine from the sources, but it must have been substantial.

The other and equally important source of funds for Warsaw from the United States was the Jewish Joint Distribution Committee, originally an ad hoc organization formed of three committees to support Jews in Palestine following the entrance of the Ottoman Empire into the war. The "Joint" became active in Poland and the Pale of Settlement following Russia's Great Retreat in the summer of 1915, and from August 1915 to December 1916 provided 1.5 million rubles to Warsaw's Jewish community. Support from the "Joint" accounted for 60% of the Jewish community's revenues available for local relief, compared to 23%, or 556,000 rubles, received from the City Administration.[171] Indeed, the influx of funds from the "Joint" provided the Warsaw Citizens Committee and City Administration with an excuse to exact savings at the expense of its own public assistance to the Jewish community, which led to the intervention of the German occupation authorities.[172] In any case, most of the "Joint's" support went into food relief, and in one month in early 1917 the "Joint" claims to have funded six hundred thousand meals in Warsaw.[173] However, with U.S. entry into the war in April 1917, the direct distribution of aid from Polish- and Jewish-American organizations to territories occupied by the Central Powers came to an end.

In 1916 it had still been possible for Lubomirski to receive 400,000 rubles, designated by the Princess Tatiana Committee to alleviate the city's wartime suffering, from a Stockholm bank and to deposit another 204,000 rubles sent by Laurence Alma-Tadema, a daughter of the famous Dutch-English painter and close acquaintance of Ignacy Paderewski, from London via Berlin.[174] In 1917, however, as it became extremely difficult to assess external sources of support, the City Administration again turned to the German authorities. In a letter of 6 February 1917, city vice president Piotr Drzewiecki noted that in the eighteen months of the German occupation, the City Administration had acquired debts of 36 million rubles, that its annual expenditures had increased from 12 to 45 million rubles, and that 5 million rubles were being used to pay the costs of the occupation. Meanwhile, income from trolleys and monopolies (such as the reestablished vodka monopoly) was going to the German authorities rather than to the city treasury. Claiming that the city was bearing the burden of obligations that should belong to the state or the entire country, Drzewiecki cited Article 52 of the Hague Convention, which set rules on what occupation authorities could demand of local communities based on the extent of their resources.[175]

The Germans, however, were unmoved. In his response, Police president Glasenapp advised the City Magistrate to cut its expenditures by one-third—this at a time when Varsovians were in greatest need. Arguing that the city was spending too much on the militia, welfare and philanthropic activities, and public works, Glasenapp also recommended cost savings by reducing both the staffs and patients in the city hospitals and by lowering the percentage of free meals served in public kitchens. To raise income, Glasenapp proposed the imposition of new taxes and the raising of existing ones, the adding of surcharges to state taxes, and the imposition of a forced loan on the city's inhabitants based on income. The city could also issue bonds, which it could then purchase at a "nominal price" three years following the end of the war. In short, Warsaw could expect no help from the German occupation authorities and no relaxation of their own exactions on the city.[176]

As if in anticipation of a negative German response, the magistrate announced budget cuts at the end of February 1917. On the one hand, the city declared that it had no choice but to close the opera house and to limit the funding of theaters to the maintenance of their property. More tellingly, the city reduced the budget of the public kitchens, the largest single line item in its expenditures, by charging half price for at least 5% of dinners previously offered free of charge and by no longer offering free bread, but charging two pfennigs per quarter pound.[177] Still the city's expenditures continued to grow, as did the numbers of those served in public kitchens, which averaged 150,000 by May 1917. In the middle of 1917, the city treasury projected a budget deficit of 40 million marks, but by the end of the year the city had generated an estimated income of 17,411,666 Polish marks against expenditures of 71,108,000 Polish marks.[178] Thereafter, as its total wartime expenditures rose to 180 million Polish marks,[179] the city had little choice but to adopt the combination of austerity and revenue-generating measures proposed earlier in the year by the Germans.

In the course of 1918, the Warsaw City Council approved budgets that declined by the month, for example, by 20% between April and May.[180] In 1917 there had already been reductions in the number of paid officials in city departments as well as in the militia. For example, paid staff in the Department of Public Philanthropy was reduced by one-third, from 117 to 76. As for the militia, before the April 1916 annexation of the suburbs, there had been 1,166 patrolmen serving in fifteen police commissariats; only 23 more members had been added to the force since then to serve in twenty-six commissariats.[181] The city hoped to affect more savings by requesting that the "Polish government" (the government created under the German-sponsored Regency Council) take over payments to soldiers' wives that by the summer of 1918 had accumulated to more than 16 million marks, and to assign 2 million marks for combatting the typhus epidemic in the city.[182] The "Polish state authorities," however, were no more forthcoming with funds than the German occupation authorities under whom they labored, despite the fact that Prince Lubomirski, an individual obviously sympathetic to and well aware of the needs of the city, was now serving as one of the three members of the Regency Council.

In the meantime, the City Administration sought to generate revenue by any means possible. In December 1917 the City Council approved regulations regarding the realization of a forced loan of 75 million marks, to be repaid at 6% interest. Owners of properties assessed between 75,000 and 85,000 marks would be forced to cough up 3% of their value, while properties with higher assessments would pay graduated rates of up to 10% for those valued at 250,000 marks or more. In addition, the City Council introduced new taxes on income and property both to meet the city's current needs and to forestall default on its debts.[183] At the beginning of March 1918 the City Council approved a lottery designed to raise slightly less than 450,000 marks in profit to support institutions involved in child welfare.[184] The resort to lotteries is more significant when one considers the long-standing opposition of many among the city's political elites to any form of gambling during wartime. However, in this as in much else, the city had little choice if it was to avoid bankruptcy and its social consequences. For the strapped Warsaw City Administration, exigency had become the ordinary, and deep deficit spending would remain standard practice well after November 1918.

Ultimately, management of Warsaw's wartime social and economic crisis was bound to fail, as the Warsaw Citizens Committee and its successors lost the race against impending catastrophe. Reasons for that failure are not difficult to determine, though certainly the consequences may have been less socially divisive. The administration of public assistance could have been more democratic, its organization more efficient, its distribution less prejudicial, its corruption better contained. Funds could have been diverted from political and cultural projects of "national" significance to those of far more immediate and crucial social need. Yet even under these imagined circumstances, Warsaw's wartime crisis was beyond manageable due to other more important factors.

The first has to do with the scale of the crisis itself. The collapse of industrial production in Warsaw and the destruction of the surrounding countryside in the war's first year set the tone for the twin crises of mass unemployment and acute food shortages and for unprecedented expenditures on public assistance, particularly in the form of public works and public kitchens, which together ate up half of the Warsaw Citizens Committee's and then the City Administration's budgets. The city also subsidized food, fuel, and other basic purchases sold at discount through its chain of stores, issued small loans to artisan shops and businesses to keep them afloat, and fed and sheltered growing numbers of orphaned and abandoned children. Following the Russian evacuation, the City Administration inherited basic police, fire, and postal services, not to mention the maintenance of city hospitals, which while they employed tens of thousands and could be considered normal responsibilities of a municipal government in peacetime, proved exceedingly difficult to sustain in a time of total war. From the Russians, the city also inherited payments to pensioners and soldiers' families; the latter alone accounted for almost 9% of all city expenditures by the end of the war. The city spent an equal amount on financing an expanded system of public primary and secondary education, considered a "national" Polish priority after decades of neglect and underfunding during Russian rule.

Something had to give, especially since the Germans refused to subsidize relief and assistance as the Russians had done. In fact, the only significant investment of the occupation administration appears to have been in funding the vaccination of the population against smallpox, cholera, and other diseases. Thus the Russian evacuation of Warsaw had a considerable economic cost beyond the requisitioning, dismantling of industrial plant, and removal of machines and workers and their transport to the east. The Warsaw Citizens Committee and new City Administration lost the main source of funding for the normal social services of peacetime, not to mention the forms of public relief and assistance that had emerged in the war's first year and that, with the exception of refugee relief, would only escalate with each succeeding month. The crisis was, therefore, managed under the Russians, though only barely and with Russian state support. The Russians then left a void that the Germans declined to fill, through this did not amount to autonomy. As we have seen, the range of options for Warsaw's much trumpeted municipal self-government was really quite limited and, in certain respects, more limited than that available to the Warsaw Citizens Committee under the Russians.

No amount of private donations, charity events, fund-raising campaigns abroad, internal taxes and forced loans, and public lotteries could make up for the absence of state support. However, to make bad matters even worse, the Germans not only denied to Warsaw sources of revenue that could have at least made a small difference because they were determined to secure them as their own, but prevented the city from making direct purchases of food and other provisions from outside of the metropolis, purchases that could have reduced the enormous strains of inflation on the city's budget. This tight German control on resources outside of Warsaw was coupled by exploitation of those inside the city by inducing "voluntary" labor registration through planned impoverishment and threats of conscription, and by forcing the municipal administration to bear a significant part of the costs of the city's occupation. No wonder that expenditures exceeded revenues by a factor of four by the end of 1917. That sizable gap would become ever wider in 1918.

Thus, the main responsibility for the failure of the Warsaw City Administration to manage the existential crisis of wartime rests squarely on the German occupation administration, not to mention the imperial German government, which faced its own domestic food and labor shortages and diverted resources from the occupied territories to abate them. This, too, was a losing battle as the Germans essentially lost the war on an exhausted home front. In the meantime, Warsaw was in such critical condition that the city's new status in November 1918 as the capital of an independent Poland with real self-government was hardly a cause for celebration. Faced with a mass demonstration of the unemployed and growing communist agitation, the City Magistrate on 22 December 1918 responded by promising to organize a new employment office, to expand the activities of the public kitchens, and to distribute free dinner coupons to the unemployed.[185] Where the jobs, money, or food would come from was anyone's guess.

POLES AND JEWS

Before the First World War, relations between Poles and Jews, the two major ethno-religious groups in Warsaw, were not good, and they were about to get far worse. As Scott Ury has demonstrated, mass politics in general and electoral politics in particular coming out of the Revolution of 1905 had a most divisive effect on interethnic relations in the city. In part, this was a result of the mushrooming of the mass-circulation press in Polish, Yiddish, and Hebrew, which censorship may have restricted from making direct attacks on the Russian government but hardly affected in terms of the vitriol spilled against rival groups, parties, and personalities on the local scene. The result was a strengthening of nationalist forces on both sides, Jewish Zionists and Polish National Democrats, who came to dominate political discourse in the city through their intense focus on identity politics. Ury sees this as the political outcome of a crisis of modernity and the longing for community by recent migrants in the disorienting atmosphere of a rapidly growing metropolis.[1]

In the aftermath of the revolution, Polish-Jewish relations deteriorated rapidly, marked by increasingly intense economic competition and political conflict and inflamed by largely unrestrained press polemics.[2] A dispute between Poles and Jews over representation in projected but never realized bodies of municipal government, Jews' refusal to support a Polish national candidate in the elections for Warsaw's seat in the Russian State Duma, and a Polish boycott of Jewish commerce and trade were still fresh memories in Warsaw when war broke out in the summer of 1914.[3] The intellectual historian Jerzy Jedlicki has referred to this period immediately before the war in Warsaw as "the end of the dialogue" between Polish and Jewish political elites, which itself was based on flawed nineteenth-century liberal assumptions of Jewish "assimilation" and "integration."[4]

Still, voices on the progressive and socialist Left thought that some kind of accommodation between Poles and Jews was possible, if not in the existing political and economic system then in opposition to it.[5] There were also Poles and Jews in Warsaw, perhaps even majorities, who gave little time or thought to the politics of identity, were not effectively mobilized by political parties or the daily press, and continued to conduct the business of everyday life with one another as they had for centuries. These inhabitants of Warsaw constituted a political missionary field and were scolded, cajoled, and even coerced when they failed to live up to nationalist expectations to vote a certain way (or even to vote at all!) and "to stick to their own kind" in purchasing goods and contracting services, especially when it was to their economic disadvantage. Nevertheless, there is no doubt that both Poles and Jews were "becoming national" at the turn of the last century, a trend that pitted them against one another, especially in Warsaw, the metropolis that they had been destined to share.

The First World War accelerated this downhill slide in Polish-Jewish relations in Warsaw, which is part of a larger central and eastern European story about the deterioration of Christian-Jewish relations at the turn of the twentieth century. During the First World War, the image of the speculating and profiteering Jew became widespread in central Europe, especially during the second half of the war, when food and other shortages became the norm and fed already exaggerated notions of excessive Jewish wealth. That image became prominent in the front-line town of Freiburg and was disseminated through the caricatures of the Munich-based *Simplicissimus*.[6] In Berlin, Jewish middlemen were blamed for profiteering, while the very idea of making a profit became characterized as unpatriotic. Rising antisemitism in wartime Berlin also owed much to an influx of Jewish refugees and labor migrants, some of whom had been recruited in Warsaw.[7] In Vienna, where conditions most closely approximated those in Warsaw, the food profiteer was depicted as stereotypically male and Jewish. In addition, Jews were choice targets for rumors about internal enemies in Vienna, while tens of thousands of Jewish refugees from Galicja fed wartime "expulsion fantasies" that would become law in September 1919.[8] Responsibility for the unprecedented social and economic catastrophe of wartime was rather easily transferred onto Christian Europe's eternal "other." The resulting virulent antisemitism, which came to characterize much of Europe in the interwar years, was, therefore, a direct result of the war, its deprivations, and the long-term damages it afflicted on economies and societies.

Aside from a brief period of tentative and partial unity between Poles and Jews in Warsaw at the very outset of the war, interethnic conflict was renewed soon enough, reshaped and intensified by the ever-increasing hardships brought on by Europe's first total war. This chapter explores themes that mainly transcend the periods of Russian rule and German occupation in Warsaw, despite the dramatically different attitudes of these regimes toward the Jewish population. The actions of the Russian Army, to be sure, were largely responsible for the large Jewish refugee population in the city during the first part of the war, one of the main contributing factors to Polish-Jewish tensions. By contrast, the principal goal of the German occupation regime was to maintain stability, which required a balancing act between Poles and Jews in Warsaw, an approach that many Poles interpreted as serving Jewish interests. The existential crisis of wartime, however, would do more than the presence of either Russians or Germans to define political, socio-economic, and cultural expressions of Polish-Jewish relations, which reached the breaking point on two occasions—at the time of the Russian evacuation in the summer of 1915, and when Polish forces took control of the city from the Germans in November 1918. In fact, it is difficult to find evidence of anything that wasn't contested between Warsaw's Poles and Jews during the war, including spare change. Yet despite these heightened tensions, exceptional intercommunal violence was avoided. The absence of outright rupture, anticlimactic and therefore unexplored, also requires our attention.

Spy Scares and Divided Loyalties

As previously discussed in chapter 1, the first weeks of the war for Warsaw's Jews were already fraught with fears of a pogrom brought on by the attitudes and behaviors of Russian Army commanders who both believed and encouraged rumors of wholesale Jewish espionage on behalf of the Central Powers. Instructions to the Warsaw superintendent of police to suspend the issuing of passports to Warsaw Jews and to provide information about any Jews from Warsaw who were currently abroad reflected the widespread belief that Jews constituted an "unreliable element" that posed a security risk to Russian troops.[9] At approximately the same time, Jewish refugees who began to arrive in Warsaw from Łódź and elsewhere were placed under special police surveillance.[10] In early September, the rumored appearance of an article in the Yiddish-language *Der moment*, which supposedly contained information on how Jews in Warsaw should greet German troops, formed the basis for a police investigation into Jewish attitudes. No such article had been published, but these and similar rumors heightened Jewish fears of impending violence.[11] At times, these rumors of Jewish spying came from far afield. The chief of the Volhynia Provincial Gendarmes, for example, reported receiving information that Jewish spies in Warsaw were providing the Germans with information about Russian troop locations on maps that were sealed in bottles and then allowed to float down the Vistula from where they were retrieved by the enemy.[12]

Meanwhile, panic-buying, immediate price increases, a run on local banks, and the hoarding of coin as a hedge against the inflation of paper banknotes accompanied the outbreak of the war. When combined with the actions of the Russian Army, the association of Jews with coin-hoarding—which would eventually figure in one-fifth of the reports of anti-Jewish violence in the Polish Kingdom during the first year of the war[13]—alarmed even the National Democrats (well known by their collective acronym as Endecja), who shared Jewish fears of major disorders in the city. *Gazeta Poranna 2 grosze*, which had begun publication in 1912 in order to lend explicit support to the Endecja-led anti-Jewish boycott, warned, "All manifestations of physical violence toward Jews we regard as harmful, above all for Polish society, and beneath our national dignity."[14]

Perhaps because the Endecja, the most powerful Polish political organization in Warsaw, was able to moderate its anti-Jewish stance, Poles and Jews were seemingly able to set aside their differences during the immediate emergency caused by the outbreak of the war and the advance of German forces on Warsaw. With mobilization, Polish and Jewish families congregated at mustering points for reservists in Warsaw, where they shared their common concerns.[15] The mass-circulation press in Warsaw, whether Polish- or Yiddish-language, received with enthusiasm the 14 August proclamation of Grand Duke Nikolai Nikolaevich, Russian commander-in-chief and uncle of the tsar, which promised to reunite Poland under the scepter of the Romanovs.[16] Once permitted and accepted by the Russian authorities, Jewish day laborers joined Poles for paid work on field fortifications as the front moved closer to Warsaw in September.[17] As the first groups of refugees began to arrive in Warsaw from the western provinces of the Polish Kingdom, particularly from the area around Kalisz, little public heed was paid to their religion or ethnicity, although half of them were Jewish.[18] In October, as Russian defensive lines held against the German assault, thanksgiving prayer services were held in both St. John's Cathedral and the Great Synagogue on Tłomackie Street, the two main symbolic reference points for the Roman Catholic and Jewish communities in Warsaw.[19]

Even in this period of relative calm, however, tensions lurked not far below the surface. Although the pro-Russian Endecja, recalling the urban violence of the 1905 revolution, may have feared mass disorders in Warsaw, it nevertheless considered Jewish claims of loyalty to the tsarist authorities to be "two-faced."[20] There had always been a certain instrumentality to the Endecja's anti-Jewish politics, and the divided loyalties among Poles—less so in the Polish Kingdom than throughout partitioned Poland—were at least of the same magnitude as those of traditionally state-supporting Polish Jews who had suddenly come under attack by their own state. Moreover, choosing to interpret Russian gestures as promises of autonomy and self-government, the Endecja sought to make sure that "Poles," as it defined them, would not have to share the political and other benefits with "Jews" and with rival parties that didn't accept the Endecja's vision of "Polish interests."

Thus the Endecja, if anything, gave credence to rumors of Jewish disloyalty and spying, already rife within the Russian Army and its officer corps, which then spread throughout the city. When S. Ansky arrived in Warsaw later in the year, he found that "no matter where I went, I kept hearing rumors about Jewish espionage." At the Hotel Europejski, "filled mostly with high-level Russian officers," a Polish chambermaid told Ansky that Jews had sent the Germans signals over the telephone "when the flying machines came over" in order to inform them to drop their bombs where the "biggest generals" were located.[21] Such views were not confined to chambermaids. The diary of Princess Maria Lubomirska is full of references to Jewish spying, "tricks," and "money" in support of the German cause and to the detriment of Russia and its Polish supporters.[22]

For that very reason, Warsaw Jews, as reported by the city's more sober-minded superintendent of police, did everything they possibly could to deflect the suspicion or impression that they were siding with the German enemy. Members of the Jewish community, like Poles, participated in the creation of infirmaries for the wounded returning from the front and encouraged its youth to volunteer for the ambulance service and as nurses. Warsaw's top Russian police official also noted that while the socialist Bund had taken an antiwar stance, the majority of Warsaw's Jewish population did not share its position, nor were they sympathetic to the Central Powers.[23] Many Warsaw Jews, as previously noted, even sought to prove their loyalty by changing their German-sounding names to Slavic ones.[24]

Such measures, some of them undoubtedly desperate, were not enough to remove the stain of guilt by association, as Jews joined ethnic Germans as "enemy aliens" as far as the Russian state was concerned. Suspicion was enough to justify the expulsion of entire populations from a broadly defined zone of military operations following the October "Battle of Warsaw," beginning with a handful of communities before January 1915, which was then followed by coordinated mass expulsions over the next several months.[25] As noted in chapter 1, tens of thousands—and perhaps as many as two hundred thousand in all—most of them Jews, sought temporary or permanent refuge in Warsaw. Within the city, Jewish leaders became justifiably alarmed when the Russian state began to confiscate property from Warsaw's ethnic Germans, since the violation of property rights on the basis of ethnicity was a slippery slope that could easily extend to the city's Jewish community, as had the mass expulsions.[26]

In time, the association of Jews with the German enemy and the ill-treatment of Jews on Warsaw's periphery by the Russian Army would become a self-fulfilling prophecy, as stories of the experiences of the refugees generated negative attitudes within Warsaw's Jewish community toward the cause of Russian arms. As Ansky observed at the end of 1914, "More than any other place, Warsaw bore the evidence of the calamity that had struck the Jews of Poland."[27] At the time, there were more than fifty thousand uprooted Jews in Warsaw, with at least twice that number yet to come in the first months of 1915.[28] The state's repressive measures also began to spread to Warsaw's permanent Jewish residents. In early March, the Warsaw governor-general announced that all letters and correspondence in Yiddish would be destroyed because of the difficulties that language posed for Russian censorship.[29] A couple of weeks before the German takeover of the city in the summer of 1915, the Russian authorities banned the publication of all Yiddish- and Hebrew-language newspapers and periodicals in the Russian Empire, the most important of which were located in Warsaw, including the mass-circulation Yiddish dailies *Hajnt* and *Moment* and the Hebrew-language *Hacifera*.[30]

The final weeks of Russian rule in Warsaw were accompanied by a sharp rise in anti-Jewish pronouncements and actions among the local Polish population, the sources of which went far beyond the issue of loyalty to the tsar—which, after all, was also fading among Warsaw's Polish elites. By the time the Russians began to prepare their evacuation of the city in the summer of 1915, Polish-Jewish relations had deteriorated to the point that the already notorious antisemite Andrzej Niemojewski, whom even *Kurjer Warszawski* criticized for his "one-sidedness" and "demagogic treatment of serious questions," was greeted with "thunderous applause" from an overflowing audience at the Museum of Agriculture and Industry when he spoke of Jewish sins against Polish national dignity.[31] Meanwhile, the Russian retreat from the Warsaw military region coincided with new expulsions that took on the character of outright pogroms in which soldiers and the local Christian population joined in the looting and seizure of Jewish property.[32] In the front zones, the Russian Army tolerated the participation of soldiers in the plundering and rape of Jews, while local Poles gathered outside with carts to haul off their share of the remaining loot. The Warsaw governor-general himself expressed the concern that "especially if soldiers participated," the local population could not be controlled.[33] In Warsaw itself, sudden and steep inflation caused by panic buying, goods shortages, and hoarding of coin reminiscent of the war's first weeks again led to a channeling of Polish popular anger onto Jews.[34] Although acts of collective violence were ultimately avoided inside the city's borders of that time, local Poles did join soldiers in the looting of Jewish stores in the soon-to-be incorporated suburbs of Czyste and Błonie. Even on Warsaw's immediate periphery, however, such incidents were not as widespread as elsewhere in the Polish Kingdom.[35]

Having suffered considerably more from the "various repressions" of the tsarist authorities, as one historian put it, than the Polish population, Warsaw's Jews were bound to express far less anxiety than Poles toward the arriving Germans and the prospect of regime change.[36] Unlike the Poles, who had mixed feelings about the Russian evacuation and the arrival of new occupiers, most Jews greeted the end of Russian rule with open relief, a natural response to the terror they had experienced in the war's first year in Warsaw. According to a German officer's letter published in *Der Lodzer Zeitung* and later quoted in *Gazeta Poranna 2 grosze*, "The Jewish population greeted us by removing their caps and with joyful shouts."[37] Though the republication of such reports of Jewish enthusiasm for the German entrance into Warsaw was meant to bring into question Jewish loyalties, they nevertheless reveal a real division in initial attitudes toward the Germans, a difference that would become an important factor in the intensification of mutual animosities and recriminations in Polish-Jewish relations.

This brings us to an important discussion in German and Holocaust historiography, namely, the role of the German occupation of Poland and the territories of the "Ober Ost" during the Great War in the radicalization of antisemitism in the Second Reich and the interwar Weimar Republic. Much of the debate, beginning in the 1980s, has focused on the encounter of the German Army and officialdom with living and breathing Yiddish-speaking *Ostjuden*, whether from the approach of intellectual history as typified by Steven Aschheim, or from the social and administrative approach adopted by Jack Wertheimer. Aschheim acknowledged that German policy toward eastern Jews was not primarily a matter of anti-Jewish sentiment, but he was quick to add that "political policy was only one aspect of the meeting" and that daily contacts "forged attitudes critical to the postwar *Judenfrage*."[38] Wertheimer, who notes that the term *Ostjuden* had not even entered the German lexicon before the war, argues that the swelled numbers of East European Jewish labor recruits, forced and voluntary, to work inside Germany provided "the genesis of the so-called *Ostjudenfrage* that agitated Germans during and after World War I."[39] More recently, Annemarie Sammartino, who like Wertheimer focused on wartime labor migration and the permeability of German borders, has found evidence of the development of German plans to deport Polish Jews as early as the spring of 1919.[40]

The problem with this historiography is that the "encounter " of Germans and *Ostjuden,* and in the case of Aschheim of German Jews and East European Jews, is that it has been presented only from the German perspective and not in the context of the occupied east. For the *Ostjuden* themselves, particularly in

Poland, the Germans represented a significant improvement over the Russians and something of a buffer, albeit not always an effective one, against the Poles. One finds little evidence, particularly in Warsaw, of Jews being singled out by the Germans for special restrictions and discrimination, or of Jewish complaints against German maltreatment, which were aimed instead almost entirely at local Polish administrators and police officials. The single exception occurred in the fall of 1916, when Beseler targeted Jewish "shirkers" for forced labor, a policy that in any case was never implemented in Warsaw, in contrast to Łódź where five thousand Jews were sent, not to Germany, but to the German border for railroad construction.[41] From the perspective of many Poles, on the other hand, German and local Jewish interests coincided, a view shared by Princess Lubomirska in her diary following the German takeover of the "Polish capital": "I read in the newspaper that Warsaw is the greatest Jewish community of Europe—it has 39% Jews and is a metropolis of Jewish culture. The commonality of culture and language of German and eastern Jews opens up excellent perspectives for Germandom in Poland. Poor Warsaw."[42]

In any case, the German "road to Auschwitz," whether in terms of policy or behaviors, did not lead through Warsaw during the First World War. At the beginning of their occupation, the Germans made it clear that the public aggravation of ethnic tensions would not be tolerated as it had been under the Russians.[43] In his first meeting with editors of Warsaw's local dailies and weeklies, the new German press director Georg Cleinow called for a complete suspension of Polish-Jewish hostilities in print as well as in social and public spheres.[44] One visible consequence was a change on the masthead of *Gazeta Poranna 2 grosze*, which under the Russians contained the slogan "Don't Buy from Jews." This would disappear and be replaced by a milder message: "We accept advertisements from Christian firms only." While the antisemitic daily was forced to become more circumspect, it found other ways of expressing itself—for example, by gleefully reporting on any and all inter-Jewish disputes and polemics.[45]

The Germans would ultimately discover that calming Polish-Jewish relations in the aftermath of the Russian evacuation was easier said than done. Indeed, within a few months of the establishment of the German occupation zone in the Polish Kingdom, newly appointed Warsaw governor-general Beseler reported to the kaiser that "the political future of the country" required a solution to "the difficult and complicated Jewish question" which in Beseler's posing of the issue did not necessarily imply an anti-Jewish attitude.[46] Instead, once the German occupation authorities established themselves in Warsaw, they seemed determined to perform a balancing act between Poles and Jews as a means of keeping the peace. Perhaps the best evidence of German efforts to maintain a sense of fair play between Warsaw's Poles and Jews occurred on the eve of the Easter and Passover holidays in 1917, at which time they announced a 25% reduction in flour rations. In their announcement, the German authorities were careful to note that the new norms were designed to ensure that in the distribution of flour for the making of matzo, "the Christian population will not find itself in a situation worse than the Jewish population."[47] As the Vilnius memoirist Hirsz Abramowicz later quipped, in a statement that could also be applied to Warsaw, "The German occupation during World War I oppressed everyone more or less equally."[48]

Despite such German attempts to occupy a middle ground, many Poles believed that Jews were served by the "new order," while many Jews were soon disappointed by it. The affinity of Yiddish to German would naturally lead to the employment of Jews as interpreters and to their recruitment as office personnel in the occupation administration, which immediately aroused the ire of Warsaw's Poles as well as Jews whose native language was Polish.[49] According to Alexander Kraushar, himself from an assimilated family unfamiliar with Yiddish, the tax offices in the occupation administration were occupied "mainly by persons of Litvak descent,"[50] second-generation Yiddish-speaking migrants from Imperial Russia's Pale of Settlement. The reliance of the occupation authorities on experienced Jewish merchants to procure grain, livestock, and metals meant that, although state monopolies were universal, contracts for the sale of regulated goods went frequently to Jews.[51]

At the same time, the Germans entrusted Polish-dominated institutions—the Warsaw Citizens Committee, its Presidium, and its sections, as well as their successors in a reorganized City Administration—with the essentials of municipal government, local law enforcement, and the distribution of basic provisions, all of which became arenas of conflict with Jews who felt woefully underrepresented and victims of ongoing discrimination. In fact, all "national" concessions from the Germans favored Poles. In this regard, the populist champions of Yiddish language and culture in Warsaw (later known as the "Folkists")—described by the St. Petersburg-based *Wiadomości Polskie* as "younger, louder and demagogic" Jewish nationalists who sought to use the German occupation to attain autonomous national-cultural rights for Jews in the Polish Kingdom[52]—would be deeply disappointed. Instead, the Germans opted to organize and empower, through the assistance of German rabbis from Frankfurt, the Orthodox Union (Agudas Ho-ortodoksim), the precursor to Agudat Israel, which would come to play an important role in interwar Poland.[53] This development, along with others preceding it—particularly in the area of education, where the Germans refused to grant Yiddish recognized legal status as an instructional language—signified that they would treat Jews as a religious rather than a national minority in Poland, as was the case in Germany itself.

In fact, the mobilization of Orthodox Jews, particularly following the first congress of the Orthodox Union in March 1917 and its rapid growth thereafter, was the single most important political development in Warsaw's Jewish community during the First World War, just as the emergence of Zionism had been during the Revolution of 1905. The popularity of the Folkist movement, by contrast, proved more ephemeral as hopes for building a modern, secularized, and autonomous Yiddish-speaking nation with full rights of citizenship in a democratic Poland faded after the war. Nonetheless, the relative political freedoms of association and assembly under German occupation were utilized by all Jewish political formations, including the assimilationists who, left for dead by Zionists and populists, gained a new lease on life through their alliance with the Orthodox—enough to retain power in Warsaw's Jewish community institutions at the end of the war.[54] Thus, when historians like Ezra Mendelsohn refer to the German occupation as a "new era of political freedom for Polish Jewry," they are referring primarily to the new opportunities afforded for mass political mobilization, which for Warsaw's Jews marked the continuation of the fundamental transformation in the local political culture and institutions that had begun at the beginning of the century.[55] The result was ever greater pluralism within Warsaw's Jewish politics, even if Zionism in its ever-growing number of variations and reactions to it continued to shape the discourse.

Otherwise, aside from a few Jewish merchants who profited from state contracts with the occupation regime, Jews gained little from the German presence. Like most Poles, the vast majority of Jews suffered from the restrictions on normal commerce imposed by the occupation regime and the general economic collapse. In fact, even at the beginning of the occupation the reception of the Germans among Jews was far from uniform, and many Jewish leaders were extremely skeptical and cautious in their approach to the "Jewish" enunciations of the new authorities. Some assimilationists, like Kraushar, were unabashedly hostile toward the Germans. As the occupation wore on, Zionists in particular distanced themselves from the German occupier and, after the Balfour Declaration, began to identify themselves with the British and to express support for an independent Poland that would grant Jews equal political rights.[56] The Folkists, who initially took the German lifting of the ban on Yiddish publishing and financing of a Yiddish-language daily *Dos varshever tageblat* as an endorsement of their autonomist agenda, by the middle of 1916 had come to see the establishment of an independent Poland as the best means for realizing their goals.[57] When looking at the duration of the German occupation rather than simply its first weeks, Jewish political positions can only be characterized as complex and dynamic.

Nevertheless, the entire Jewish population came to be perceived by many on the Polish side as supporters of the Germans, just as they had been seen as supporters of tsarist Russia before the First World War (and of the Soviet Union after it). Some of this thinking was undoubtedly inherited from the first year of the war and the widespread rumors of Jewish espionage on behalf of the Germans. As the war continued and a divided Polish opinion came to view support for the Central Powers with increased hostility, a significant number of the city's Poles would come to see Jews as allies of anti-Polish forces, "enemy aliens" from within, an attitude made worse by the deteriorating economic situation for which Poles held Jews, as much as they did Germans, responsible.

An Immoral Economy

Exaggerated notions of illegitimate Jewish wealth, achieved through usury, swindle, fraud, smuggling, counterfeiting, bribery, and corruption, have a long history in eastern and central Europe. In the lands of partitioned Poland these presumed economic transgressions have their origins in the Jewish role as a "middleman minority" of traders and moneylenders in a manorial agrarian economy and in the confinement of Jews to a separate caste in a social structure of estates that began to break down only at the end of the eighteenth century.[58] Left largely in the role of purveyors of goods and services in the era of capitalist development, Jews were often in the direct line of fire in times of economic downturn, which were all too frequent in the boom-bust cycles of the last decades of nineteenth century and first decades of the twentieth, especially when pressures were put on prices and interest rates. Moreover, small Jewish proprietors, artisans, and traders in large urban areas like Warsaw competed successfully with their Christian counterparts, who both envied and sought to displace them, and were the scourge of Polish nationalists, who claimed that their presence blocked the social and economic advance of ordinary Poles. On the very eve of Europe's Great War, the National Democrats effectively declared economic war by organizing a boycott against Jewish trade and commerce in Warsaw, which was accompanied by the rise of a distinctively modern antisemitism that spawned new images of Jewish criminality and reinforced old ones.[59] The best example can be found in the prewar writings of the "progressive antisemite" Andrzej Niemojewski, editor of the monthly *Myśl Niepodległa*, who argued that Jewish dealings with Gentiles were governed by the depraved moral code of the Talmud, a "simply criminal book" that was in conflict with the penal codes of "all civilized nations," and that contained instructions that "directly and indirectly approve[d] every kind of immoral and criminal behavior."[60]

Warsaw had experienced significant economic crises at the beginning of the 1890s and again ten years later, but nothing on the magnitude of the First World War in which the collapse of industrial and artisanal production and an unprecedented unemployment level were accompanied by the runaway inflation of the prices of goods of the most basic necessity, particularly food. Given the substantial Jewish role in the wholesale and retail trade in those goods, as inflationary pressures mounted in the fall of 1914, the accusation in the Polish nationalist press of Jewish price-gouging would quickly become a constant refrain. There followed demands for the imposition of controls to contain the "exploitation" and "profiteering" of wholesale merchants of soap, candles, soda, and other articles whose prices were deemed "excessive."[61]

These thinly disguised attacks on Jewish commerce became even more transparent once these controls were imposed, and newspapers like *Kurjer Warszawski* published the names and addresses of principally Jewish storeowners who had been fined or jailed for violating price regulations.[62] Rumors of Jewish hoarding became particularly intense in February 1915, when Russian police—as a prelude to future requisitioning—inspected commercial stores and stocks in Warsaw's 4th, 7th, 8th, and 15th precincts, where they reportedly found "an enormous amount of supplies" belonging "mainly to Jews," "speculators" who were holding on to goods and then selling the "last batch" for markups of 300–400%. Meanwhile, advertisements appearing in Jewish newspapers for "Dąbrowski coal"—that is, coal from the mining region that had been taken by the Germans seven months earlier—provided further evidence for Polish nationalists of Jewish profiteering.[63] This would lead to calls from the otherwise "liberal" Polish weekly *Tygodnik Illustrowany* for an intensification of the struggle against speculation, which in its words "should have a prophylactic character, one conducted with severity and ruthlessness by all state and social actors."[64]

As winter turned to spring in 1915, speculative purchasing of flour by Jewish bakers was blamed for the rising price of baked goods, leading to a proposal by the Provisions Section of the Warsaw Citizens Committee for a distribution scheme by which bakers in the city's Jewish community would receive a maximum 35% of the available flour, a percentage based on the Jewish proportion of the city's population.[65] Even so, *Gazeta Poranna 2 grosze* accused the committee of giving away flour to Jewish bakers, a charge that had no basis in fact but nevertheless pressured the committee into making a public denial.[66] From the other end, the liberal Russian paper *Severniia Zapiski* accused the committee of refusing to sell basic goods and commodities to Warsaw's Jews, the first of many claims of discrimination fostered by the segregation of public welfare and social assistance programs in the city on the basis of religious affiliation.[67] In response to this charge, the committee's Provisions Section published a communiqué in which it maintained that there were no restrictions on sales based on religion or nationality, but that there were restrictions against large purchases, the aim of which was to "stockpile goods for the purposes of speculation." Restricting

FIGURE 8.   A scene from the Jewish District. Archiwum Państwowe w Warszawie.

purchases to one-time sales were justified, in its opinion, in order to feed a population already living from hand to mouth.[68]

Jews were also blamed for the high price of meat, starting in the spring of
1915. Although Jews claimed that despite high meat prices, no profits were
being made and that every day someone was going out of business,[69] Polish
newspapers like *Kurjer Warszawski* remained skeptical. In particular, the daily
cited the disappearance of three hundred head of cattle from the stockyards,
not one of which had made its way to local butchers, as evidence of a "conspiracy of speculators," when in fact the Russian Army had requisitioned the
cattle.[70] Against the backdrop of such accusations, the Warsaw Citizens Committee at the end of May met with a delegation of Christian butchers who
presented an eight-point plan for the regulation of meat prices, the final point
of which called for the suspension of kosher slaughtering by means of emergency regulations.[71] For its part, *Kurjer Warszawski* called upon the committee
to serve as the "middleman" between meat producers and consumers, which in
effect would drive Jews from the cattle trade.[72] Indeed, in the first half of June,
the committee decided to purchase one hundred head of cattle on a weekly
basis, justifying its action by claiming that it was designed to curtail the profits
of speculators.[73]

As can be seen in the case of meat, charges of Jewish hoarding, specula-tion, profiteering, and exploitation during the hardship of wartime quickly became an extension of the prewar nationalist agenda of reducing the Jewish presence in commerce and trade, the unfulfilled goal of the prewar boycott. The attack on Jewish commerce in the city took forms other than those already mentioned. Under the pretense of defending Warsaw's seamstresses, who were being "mercilessly exploited" from dawn to dusk for 20–25 kopecks per day, *Kurjer Warszawski* called upon the Warsaw Citizens Committee to eliminate Jewish middlemen and establish its own shops.[74] When the Russians began to evacuate Warsaw at the end of June 1915, and the city again experienced a shortage of coin with which to make change, the conservative daily con-demned the practice of some storekeepers of issuing IOUs instead of spare change as a Jewish "trick" to compel customers to return to their stores for their next purchase. The issuing of IOUs among Polish trolley conductors and sausage-makers, however, failed to elicit such commentary.[75] Then, as the Russians prepared their final departure from the city at the end of July 1915, and presumably with the public interest as the only necessary consideration, Polish nationalists called upon the Warsaw Citizens Committee to confiscate goods in the hands of Jewish merchants who were said to be holding basic pro-visions from the market in order to drive up prices.[76] The committee indeed appropriated requisitioning powers to itself, which were then carried out over the next month with particular relish by its Citizens Guard until the Germans rescinded such powers in early September. Not only did the Germans ban the committee's further requisitioning of food products, they also ordered the return of such products to their owners or the payment of compensation if they could not be returned.[77]

The Germans, of course, wanted to reserve requisitioning for themselves and would not make the kind of just compensation they demanded of the Warsaw Citizens Committee. They also had their own ideas about controlling the supply and sale of meat by establishing a monopoly and contracting it with the Jewish cattle merchant Liman Rozenberg. This led to all kinds of Polish protests and petitions, which argued that the monopoly be entrusted to Chris-tian butchers serving the majority of Warsaw's population and, failing that, be placed in the hands of the Polish-dominated City Administration. Even-tually, a consortium consisting of ten Christian and ten Jewish butchers was formed under the City Administration to serve as an intermediary between Rozenberg, who retained exclusive rights under the Germans to bring cattle into Warsaw, and local butchers. Rozenberg's temporary arrest in January 1916 on fabricated criminal charges would lead to the awarding of the meat monopoly to the Frankowski Brothers firm, a solution that temporarily satisfied both Polish nationalist opinion and commercial interests.[78] That is, until *Kurjer Warszawski* discovered that "our inventive butchers," whose nationality it omitted with an eye to German press censorship, had tried to cheat regulated prices by adding a half pound of horse bone for every pound of meat.[79] The supply and politics of meat would remain a sore point in Polish-Jewish relations for the remainder of the war, as Christian butchers protested the proportional distribution of monopolized meat and Jews decried the purchase by Polish consumers of kosher meat.[80]

As discussed previously, inflation would rapidly accelerate during the German occupation, accompanied by additional charges against Jewish "speculators," while Polish police actions against Jewish merchants resembled a shakedown. In bringing Jewish protests of police abuse before the City Council in the summer of 1917, Noah Prylucki argued that he could document "thousands of cases" in which "thousands of people" had been deprived by the city militia of their cash in acts that were justified as "fighting speculation."[81] The militia arrested Jews for a host of other wartime economic "crimes," including the transport of flour without permission, and various alleged fraudulent practices, for example, the manufacturing and sale of butter containing artificial ingredients.[82] *Moment*, perhaps to counter such attacks, blamed Polish farmers for holding back butter from the market to drive up prices in the hungry winter of 1916–17.[83] As rationing became widespread in the course of 1916, the old anti-Jewish charge of counterfeiting resurfaced, as the Polish press in the city reported the nationality of those arrested for making ration coupons only when they were Jewish.[84] With rations came black markets, which would become rampant in Warsaw by the second half of the year. These "bacilli of speculation" were in almost every instance in the possession of the "skullcaps" and "sidelocks," according to *Gazeta Poranna*, which by this time (August 1917) obviously had little to fear from the German censor.[85]

Thus, as Warsaw's wartime economic crisis grew to unprecedented magnitude, accusations of Jewish violations of the city's moral economy also multiplied, targeted by the Polish press and police alike. By 1917 there was little that the German occupation authorities could do about it, or wanted to do about it, especially since the same thing was happening in Germany itself. Besides, in Warsaw's increasingly dire conditions—which they had done so much to create—the Germans likely came to prefer that Polish anger be directed at purported Jewish profiteering and cheating than at the policies and officials of the occupation regime. Thus, the balancing act that the Germans had hoped to perform in 1915 failed, and their defense of Jews became increasingly feeble as the war wore on and their own exploitation of the city and its inhabitants became increasingly uncompromising.

Too Many Jews? The Refugee Crisis and the Specter of Judeo-Polonia

On the eve of the war, Polish nationalists rang many alarms, not the least of which concerned Jewish overpopulation, particularly in the once and future "Polish capital," and the resulting disproportionate political clout. Particularly after the Revolution of 1905 and the rise of Jewish "separatists" who demanded equal rights, including certain rights for Yiddish, in opposition to "the interests of the Polish nation," the victory of the feared "Judeo-Polonia" on the banks of the Vistula seemed to have occurred when Jewish voters joined the Polish Left in defeating the candidate of the Polish Center-Right, Jan Kucharzewski, for Warsaw's seat in the Duma elections of 1912.[86] This political "disaster" gave rise to two developments within the Polish nationalist Right: the initiation of efforts to contain and (better yet) reduce the Jewish presence in Warsaw on the one hand, and the emergence of the "doctrine of the Polish majority" on the other. The latter proclaimed that Warsaw—and, indeed, Poland—should be governed by the Polish majority of voters who tended to cast their ballots for the National Democrats, whether or not those votes were sufficient to win elections.[87]

Dramatic wartime demographic trends, though temporary, increased nationalist anxieties about the size of the Jewish population in Warsaw, which before the war stood at 38.1% of the total population and would rise to as high as 45% by January 1917. This was due largely to male labor out-migration, which was far more pronounced among Poles than Jews; once Poles began to return to Warsaw in 1918, the Jewish proportion receded to 42% in January 1919, and then substantially to 33.1% according to the 1921 census.[88] Nonetheless, given the already existing anxieties about Jewish overpopulation, one can imagine how the sudden presence of tens of thousands of Jewish refugees in the city became a major bone of contention in Polish-Jewish relations, particularly in 1915 and 1916 while Warsaw still remained under Russian rule and then well into the first year of the German occupation.

While exact numbers are difficult to come by, it would appear that the Jewish refugee population in the city reached eighty to ninety thousand by mid-April 1915, of whom well less than half received public support from Jewish community institutions, which the Warsaw Citizens Committee assisted with limited funding. For example, of the 46,000-ruble income reported by the committee's Jewish Refugee Section from all sources for 1914, the committee provided only 7,000 rubles directly, the rest coming from private donations and the contributions of Jewish philanthropic institutions.[89] Almost immediately, however, the Jewish press found itself refuting claims from its Polish nationalist counterparts, particularly *Gazeta Poranna 2 grosze*, that Jewish refugees in Warsaw had become a burden on institutions supported almost entirely by the Christian population—this at the very beginning of Warsaw's refugee crisis. According to radical Polish nationalists, these Jewish refugees "prefer[red] to wait out the ugly times in Warsaw" at the expense of Poles.[90]

By spring of 1915 and the peak of the Jewish refugee crisis, the Polish press published increasingly dire reports of the "enormous influx" of Jews into Warsaw from the provinces, a situation that *Kurjer Warszawski* described as "alarming," citing an article published in the nationalist *Dzień* that inflated the number of Jewish refugees to two hundred thousand. When added to the prewar figure of three hundred thousand, the purported presence of these additional hundreds of thousands would have meant that Jews constituted a majority of Warsaw's inhabitants.[91] Numbers here are important because they featured most prominently in the discourse. Estimates of Jewish refugees in Warsaw during the First World War have varied widely, but the figure of two hundred thousand would be more accurate if it referred to the total number of refugees who came to and left Warsaw during the first year of the war, rather than to refugees who were there in March 1915. The same rings true for Mendelsohn's figure of one hundred thousand Jewish refugees "by the end of 1914 . . . in Warsaw alone."[92] The eighty thousand Jewish refugees noted by Piotr Wróbel for the spring of 1915 seems far more reliable since it closely coincides with the roughly one hundred thousand Jews expelled by the Russian Army from surrounding communities, starting in February.[93] Marian Marek Drozdowski's estimate of thirty thousand Jewish refugees for the spring of 1915, on the other hand, is far too low and is based solely on those who were recorded as receiving public assistance.[94] Of these, on 1 May 1915, approximately eight thousand were residing in the fifty-five shelters operated by the Jewish Refugee Section, which were located mainly in synagogues and prayer houses and supported almost entirely by Warsaw's Jewish community.[95]

According to the Polish press, these Jews, regardless of their actual numbers, had to go. They had reportedly refused offers to resettle in Vilna or Minsk—to which *Kurjer Warszawski* responded that they should be forced to leave for other cities of the empire "whether they liked it or not," especially since they were "making life difficult for the permanent residents of Warsaw." Worse still, according to oft-repeated warnings of the Polish press, the malnourished and poorly dressed Jewish refugees could "easily provoke numerous epidemics" among the city's population and the Russian Army.[96]

Thus, sanitary conditions among the mainly Jewish refugees and general public-health concerns were cited as reasons for their forcible resettlement. For more radical Polish nationalists, the danger to public health came not only from refugees but more generally from the streets inhabited by the Jewish poor. "Dzika, Franciszkańska, Nalewki and Muranowska," they argued, were "the source of every possible kind of epidemic" and were where "the eyes of all members of sanitary commissions" should turn their gaze. "It is necessary in the general interest to resettle part of this impoverished crowd to other localities," claimed *Gazeta Poranna 2 grosze*. "In addition to the many healthy people in the city, there are hundreds of wounded soldiers who would be most threatened by the outbreak of an epidemic."[97] Small wonder that Stanisław Kempner, the editor of the liberal assimilationist *Nowa Gazeta*, would sarcastically refer to such "public health" demands for the resettlement of Jews, whether refugee or resident, as "airing out Warsaw."[98]

In mid-April 1915, a group of Jewish community leaders and physicians signed a petition directed to Russian city president Müller, arguing that the planned evacuation of tens of thousands of Jewish refugees for "sanitary reasons" was completely unjustifiable because Warsaw was well organized and equipped to deal with the appearance of infectious diseases, whereas far more dangerous sanitary conditions in the provinces were precisely of the kind that could lead to the spread of epidemics.[99] Nonetheless, poor sanitary conditions were cited as the main reason for the closing of eight Jewish refugee shelters in early May and the transfer of several hundreds of their inhabitants to Otwock, Falenica, Józefów, Świder, and Płudy, where they would later be observed "living like wild animals."[100] Others would join the 340,000 Jews of the Polish Kingdom who were forced to leave the country entirely.[101] The Russian-orchestrated resettlement of Jewish refugees, however, targeted those receiving public assistance, easily identifiable by their residence in or receipt of support in shelters, which is one reason why only the most desperate found lodging or assistance there, the majority preferring to rely more on family and acquaintance networks.

In any case, the poorest categories of refugees "evacuated" in May and June were merely replaced by new arrivals in the final month of Russian rule, which brought more human traffic into and out of Warsaw.[102] Many came from the large Jewish shtetls of Piaseczno, Jeziorna, Wyszków, Radzymin, and Nasielsk; this influx forced the Warsaw Citizens Committee to approve the creation of a huge facility at the freight station of the Warsaw-Vienna railroad to shelter some of them.[103] Thus, following the establishment of the German General-Government in Warsaw, one of the first envisioned tasks of the occupation regime was to remove the largely Jewish refugees from the city, and in October Governor-General Beseler announced to the kaiser that they were "already prepared."[104]

Over the following weeks, there were concerted efforts between the German authorities, the Jewish refugee-assistance organization in Warsaw, and provincial committees to return refugees to their homes. By November, the number of "homeless Jews" receiving public assistance in the amount of twenty kopecks per day had been substantially reduced to some seven thousand, although according to *Gazeta Poranna* there were still a "significant number" of Jews from other parts of Poland, whose presence in the city was fueling inflation.[105] Indeed, it is likely that more than sixty thousand Jewish refugees in Warsaw remained at the beginning of 1916.[106] Renewed fighting in early 1916 would lead to the arrival of new groups of Jewish refugees into Warsaw, particularly from the Austrian occupation zone to the east of the city. According to *Gazeta Poranna*, although Warsaw's total population had declined by 100,000 by March 1916, the number of Jews in the city had increased by 200,000–300,000.[107] These much-inflated numbers were again rapidly reduced, so that by the summer of 1916 *Gazeta Poranna* had merely four thousand Jewish refugees to concern itself with as a "burden" on "Polish institutions."[108] As late as October 1917, Polish nationalists were still complaining that only 1,228 persons had been evacuated by the Jewish community from Warsaw over the previous six months.[109]

Obviously, for the Polish radical Right, Warsaw could not rid itself of Jewish refugees fast enough, even if only a few thousand managed to remain in Warsaw by 1918. Nor were Jews welcome to return or migrate to the capital of the new Poland after the war. With the end of the German occupation and by the end of the year, according to Konrad Zieliński, the new Polish authorities began to openly discriminate against Jewish returnees and immigrants.[110] Some of these Warsaw Jews had been evacuated by the Russians, but far more had gone to work in Germany. Once the war was over, the Weimar Republic's plans to deport the Polish Jews who still remained within German borders in the spring of 1919 proved impractical because of Poland's refusal to accept them.[111] By such means, among others, did the proportion of Warsaw's Jewish population actually decline in comparison to 1914. Even as it did, the Polish nationalist specter of Judeo-Polonia, translated by *Tygodnik Illustrowany* as "the extermination of Poland,"[112] remained alive and well.

Access to Public Assistance and Institutions

As funding for refugee relief in the city demonstrates, various forms of discrimination accompanied the segregation of public assistance in the city by ethnicity and religion. As noted in the previous chapter, publicly funded and administered assistance barely existed in Warsaw before the war, but the growth of voluntary organizations in both the Polish and Jewish communities, some of which were engaged in charitable and philanthropic activities as well as mutual aid for their members, established a pattern of separation, if not necessarily inequality. The emergence of the Warsaw Citizens Committee during the first weeks of the war offered an opportunity to establish programs of integrated public assistance, particularly when the committee received an offer of cooperation from representatives of all Jewish philanthropic societies in the city.[113] Despite early mutual expressions of good will, the committee and its sections sought to exclude anything more than token Jewish membership. Three of the original fifteen members of the Warsaw Citizens Committee—Mieczysław Pfeiffer, Henryk Konic, and Józef Natanson—were all from the assimilated Jewish elite—and indeed, the first two were more Jewish by descent than religious identity. This led *Hajnt* to express its dissatisfaction that no Jewish activists "who actually live among Jews" were selected to serve on the committee.[114]

The effective nonrepresentation of Jews among the committee's leadership would eventually result in discrimination in access to public assistance and the institutions providing it, although in the early days the committee sought to maintain at least a façade of separate but equal distribution of aid. Nonetheless, the Warsaw Citizens Committee's decisions would be criticized by both sides— by Poles as excessive relief provided at the expense of the Christian population, by Jews as inadequate in comparison with that provided to Roman Catholics. Accusations of fraud and corruption frequently accompanied these claims, especially from the Polish side. As early as the war's first month, for example, the Polish conservative daily *Kurjer Warszawski* claimed that lists submitted to the committee containing the names of individuals needing assistance in Jewish neighborhoods had been deliberately falsified.[115] A month later, the Polish nationalist press identified Jews as a "real plague" on the stores established by the committee to sell goods to those in need at wholesale prices; Jewish women supposedly brought children to these stores by the "bunches" to haul away "bagsful" of purchased salt.[116] Jews, for their part, complained immediately and directly to the committee about the spread of these and other false rumors.[117]

Access to the Warsaw Citizens Committee's employment agencies became another early source of wartime Polish-Jewish conflict. With unemployment already spreading throughout the city by the war's first month, Christian workers began to expel their Jewish counterparts from the committee's labor offices. To maintain the peace, a separate office for day workers was established in the Jewish community.[118] In another effort to balance the competing claims of Poles and Jews, the Warsaw Citizens Committee decided in October 1914 to distribute coupons to its ever-growing number of public kitchens in proportion to Polish and Jewish shares of the city's population.[119] Later, it voted to subsidize three or four public kitchens run by the "Ezra" Society by paying for 1,500 of a total of 5,500 daily meals.[120] In November, it also voted a subvention to a Commission on Jewish Refugees created by the Jewish community, which operated separately from the committee's own Refugee Section.[121] At approximately the same time,

it determined that 30% of the donated clothing collected in Petrograd for belea-
guered Warsaw in the aftermath of the recently lifted German siege would be distributed to the Jewish poor.[122] However, in all of these instances the proportion
of assistance directed to Jews was less, sometimes substantially, than the growing
proportion of Jews in Warsaw's total population; and in the case of Jewish refugees in the city, the gap between need and support was even higher.

In part, the growing discrepancy in the amounts of aid provided to Poles and
Jews was due to the notion that Jews were materially better off than Poles and,
therefore, less deserving of assistance offered through public institutions, first
through the nongovernmental organization of the Warsaw Citizens Committee, and subsequently through the agencies of the Warsaw City Administration.
Indeed, the fact that Jews comprised a relatively small percentage of the industrial
labor force and were, therefore, largely unaffected by the widespread unemployment and underemployment that immediately struck Warsaw's factories, gave
rise to the belief that Jews were better able to weather the wartime economic
crisis.[123] Moreover, the number of Jewish "businesses" actually multiplied as the
war continued, which in the minds of Poles offered evidence of Jewish "prosper-
ity." In reality, the existence of these "firms" was the result of the ever-worsening
economic situation, the collapse of larger Jewish enterprises, and the resort to
panhandling as a survival strategy.[124] Nonetheless, Poles believed that Jews, as
owners of stores and shops, were better able to adjust to inflation and speculation
by raising prices.[125] Finally, the Polish press, which was quick to publish news of
external assistance to Warsaw's Jewish community, whether from the Petrograd
Committee of Russian Jews or later from the Jewish Joint Distribution Committee in the United States, fostered the belief that Jews were well supported by
philanthropy from abroad.[126]

As the Russians prepared to evacuate Warsaw and the economic crisis deepened, however, even newspapers like *Kurjer Warszawski* were forced to recognize
signs of the Jewish population's impoverishment, while Jewish relief workers
spoke even more dramatically of the "pauperization of the entire Jewish population."[127] Discriminatory practices in the face of this pauperization further
strengthened the Zionist movement in Warsaw—and particularly the young
radicals of the growing Jewish populist movement—though there was little
that they could do about it while the city remained under Russian rule. Nonetheless, the growing visibility of Zionism and populist nationalism in the Jewish community was evident in the last months of Russian rule and was reflected
in demands for the use of Yiddish and Hebrew in providing education to Jewish
refugee children, which in turn led Warsaw assimilationists to warn of the "fatal
consequences" for both Poles and Jews that would accompany the spread of
"separatism" among the Jewish masses.[128] Although the Russians would shut

down the Yiddish- and Hebrew-language press, the Zionists and populists were poised to challenge the assimilationists who had long dominated the Jewish community's administrative board, particularly once they gained the upper hand in the distribution of welfare within the community. This in turn led the administrative board to become more assertive in staking Jewish claims to a greater share in funding for public kitchens and refugee shelters, as well as in demanding equal access to basic provisions.[129]

As the Warsaw Citizens Committee began to take on the functions of a municipal administration during and after the Russian evacuation, demands for access to public assistance and relief were translated into political demands for greater representation. Indeed, ever more open instances of discrimination—and in the case of the committee's Citizens Guard, outright persecution—made such representation an imperative of Jewish self-defense. When Warsaw Governor-General Beseler issued his first report to the kaiser in October 1915, one that highlighted Polish-Jewish relations, he was already privy to disputes over the behavior of the Citizens Guard in the Jewish community. As a militia formed under the Warsaw Citizens Committee to preserve order in the city following the Russian evacuation until it could be transformed into a regular police force, the eight thousand–strong Citizens Guard consisted primarily of young male participants in Polish sporting organizations, which in turn had been strongly influenced by the National Democrats.

It is not hard to imagine the consternation aroused by the appearance of such a force in the Jewish community, where it executed the committee's self-appointed requisitioning powers with particular relish, effectively taking the law into its own hands. On the very day of its official "coming out" during the Russian evacuation, the Citizens Guard was forced to respond to charges of anti-Jewish discrimination.[130] In September, Jewish newspaper editors sent a memorandum to the authorities, citing thirty-five serious incidents of violations of the law and discrimination against Jews by the Citizens Guard in the second half of August alone.[131] A commission subsequently created under the City Administration to investigate these charges determined, after some nine months had passed, that they could not be verified.[132]

By that time the Citizens Guard had been transformed into the City Militia, or what Mieczysław Jankowski, one of its members, called "one of the lowest organs of the German police," reduced in number and functions to that of an unarmed traffic, sanitary, building, and industrial police force.[133] Jewish participation in the Citizens Guard had been practically nonexistent, and Jews were no better represented in the City Militia, which was placed under the supervision of the Warsaw City Administration. At the end of October 1916 there was not a single Jewish deputy police commissar. In Warsaw's 7th precinct, where

Jews constituted two-thirds of the property owners and 75% of the population, there were only three Jewish policemen. Moreover, not a single complaint of police brutality had resulted in action against the offending parties.[134] As late as the summer of 1917, Jews comprised only 5% of the City Militia's force, which meant that Jewish policemen were invisible outside the Jewish district, and that the vast majority of policemen in Jewish residential areas were Poles.[135]

As a sanitary police that enforced regulations introduced by the Germans, the City Militia was particularly overzealous in its inspection of Jewish ritual bathhouses "for reasons of hygiene" and in arresting and "disinfecting" bearded Orthodox and Hasidic males for violating public health codes.[136] Such acts led the otherwise conciliatory Orthodox Union to protest repeatedly to the chief of the city militia, Prince Franciszek Radziwiłł, noting that the militia's rounding up of Jews before or after Saturday prayers, including those with certificates of health signed by physicians and medics, and then taking them to disinfection stations to shave their beards, was both a source of personal embarrassment and an affront to the Jewish religion.[137] The Folkist leader Noah Prylucki, a lawyer by training, read several individual complaints verbatim, all of them left unanswered by Radziwiłł, during the 28 February 1917 budget debates of the Warsaw City Council. They included the complaint of Mordechai Wejnberg:

> On Friday, the 19th of this month at 11:00 a.m. I was stopped by three patrolmen of the 11th precinct who asked where I was going. I said that I was going to buy potatoes. This occurred on Wilcza Street. Requests or persuasion didn't help me [and] I was led to the station and put behind bars.
>
> The captain of the 11th precinct appeared [and] I spoke to him in precise terms about my arrest. **The captain stated that I was clean** and, after returning my passport to me, released me from the jail. At the same time two acquaintances of mine were sitting there, also arrested on the street and placed behind bars. Having heard that they needed their passports and not having them on their persons, they asked me if I would retrieve them from their homes. I agreed to carry out their request. I brought them their passports. When I was returning home, the patrolman Zakrzewski detained me. I stated that I had been certified as completely clean by the captain and had been released. For my declaration I received a strong beating from Zakrzewski and the following words: **"You will go home when you no longer have a beard and only after I shave it off, so that you'll never come back to this precinct. Go to Nalewki, Krochmalna."**

I was taken to the disinfection facility for shaving my beard and cutting my hair, but my hygiene didn't require compulsory shaving and cutting; in addition I declared that I would pay ten rubles for a doctor to examine the state of my cleanliness. If there are regulations that require the preservation of cleanliness and the shaving of dirty beards, it's necessary to screen and verify such candidates. My beard didn't need shaving, which the precinct captain had confirmed when he released me.

I ask therefore: 1) Why did the patrolman Zakrzewski twice place me behind bars? 2) Why did he beat me? 3) Why did he execute the shaving of my beard? 4) Why did he tell me that I should go to Nalewki and Krochmalna? 5) Why is walking in the 11th precinct forbidden? 6) Why at the disinfection facility was my request to call for a doctor to verify the state of my cleanliness denied?

Prylucki then added that he had many other formal complaints about sanitary regulations being used to cleanse "Christian districts" of Jews.[138]

Meanwhile, support from the Jewish Joint Distribution Committee for the distribution of relief and assistance in Warsaw's Jewish community became an excuse for the Warsaw Citizens Committee and the City Administration to further restrict public funding. At the end of 1915, in response to requests to the committee from the "Ezra" Society for additional funding of its public kitchens, *Gazeta Poranna* called for Jewish organizations to turn over all donated funds, "including one million rubles from America," to the Warsaw Citizens Committee.[139] In the summer of 1916, *Gazeta Poranna* complained that even though Jews had important resources from a variety of sources at their disposal, including a recent donation of 186,000 rubles from America, "they never cease to demand and receive large sums for their needs from the city administration," which "proves that the Jewish community is more privileged from a monetary standpoint and that the city administration is too quick to extend credits to the Jewish community, while simultaneously rejecting the necessary and positive requests of Christian institutions—and sentencing them to inactivity as a result of insufficient funds."[140] These were not simply the rantings of the Polish radical Right. In the summer of 1917 Drzewiecki, now the mayor, during a City Council budget debate, said that Jews were receiving financial help "from all over the world" and, therefore, did not need the city's help.[141] Despite being presented with evidence that following the U.S. declaration of war against the Central Powers, the money from American Jewish organizations to assist Warsaw's Jews had come to an end, Drzewiecki restated his position: "We Poles have to take care of ourselves, since the entire world is taking care of Jews."[142] On the basis of such logic, the

City Administration had earlier refused the extension of a 30,000-ruble monthly subvention to Jewish public kitchens, while continuing to support non-Jewish kitchens to the tune of 500,000 rubles per month.

Such facts even caught the attention of the Ministry of Internal Affairs in Berlin. A letter from German police president Glasenapp to City President Prince Zdzisław Lubomirski forwarded the ministry's concerns about a number of issues, not the least of which was the meager support for public kitchens in the Jewish community. The ministry cited the segregation of and discrimination against Jewish merchants in the city's market halls, the forcing of Jewish merchants to observe Sundays as a day of rest, and the suspension of support to wives of Jewish soldiers who had been called to the Russian Army because they didn't possess civil marriage documents not required of their Polish counterparts as evidence of the Warsaw City Administration's anti-Jewish policies.[143] Glasenapp might have added the issue of public employment. Of 13,000 city employees, a mere 731 were Jewish, and not a single Jew worked in the City Administration, waterworks, and fire department, this despite the fact that 60% of the city's tax

FIGURE 9. Caricature of Jewish donations to and assistance from the Warsaw Citizens Committee. "Obrazek z Warszawy," *Mucha* 18 (30 April 1915): 9. Biblioteka Narodowa.

revenues came from Jews.[144] An even smaller fraction of Jews, four hundred of a total of twelve thousand individuals, was employed in public works—which Prylucki, for one, referred to as a "boycott" that had carried over from the former committee.[145] That Jews would seek greater political representation to voice opposition to such policies, and perhaps even to influence and contain them, would create a new arena of conflict between Poles and Jews.

Political Conflicts: The Warsaw City Council and the Jewish Community Board

The contentious issue of Jewish representation in a new Warsaw City Council, once such a possibility materialized in the spring of 1916, would divide not only Poles and Jews but also the Jewish public sphere, which had emerged ten years earlier and had become both radicalized and polarized during the first two years of the war. The previous year had brought with it the Russian promise to establish urban self-governing institutions in the Polish Kingdom, including and especially in Warsaw, which the assimilationist and liberal daily *Nowa Gazeta* conceded "must understandably be Polish" so long as they were "democratic" and "accessible to all."[146] Such promises remained unrealized by the time of the Russian evacuation of the city. However, when the Germans began to consider and then approved the transformation of the Warsaw Citizens Committee into an eighty-member "city representation" in March 1916, entrusting that process of transformation to the committee,[147] the barely visible presence of Jews in that body suddenly became a matter of acute political concern. Although the committee had been expanded to include three additional Jewish members during the course of the Russian evacuation, among them President of the Jewish Community Board Michał Bergson, thus bringing the total number to six, all were assimilated Jews or Poles of Jewish descent.[148] That number had remained unchanged by March 1916, when the committee consisted of sixty members. For that reason, Jewish intellectuals presented a petition to the Community Board, calling for the dramatic expansion of Jewish representation on the committee. According to *Moment* (as reported in *Gazeta Poranna 2 grosze*), Jews were entitled to at least twenty places on the committee, given that they accounted for around 40% of Warsaw's population at that time.[149]

Such representation was not forthcoming, and Jews had little voice in the drafting of an ordinance for the planned municipal elections, which, as noted, the Germans initially entrusted to the Warsaw Citizens Committee. To organize these elections, the committee in turn appointed a special commission, which met in several extraordinary sessions in April. Of these, the most extended and divisive deliberations occurred during the session of 16 April in its consideration of a tabled motion made the previous day to reserve 80% of the seats in the new council for Christians.[150] Piotr Drzewiecki, then the city's vice president, argued for a set quota for Jewish participation, ostensibly to prevent Jews from capturing a majority. Prince Lubomirski, installed as city president by the Germans the previous summer, argued that the "Polish character" of the council had to be preserved by all means, despite whatever bad impression this might leave externally. However, Drzewiecki and Lubomirski were unable to sway those on the commission, who not only were concerned with how their decision would be judged from the outside, but also agreed with arguments in the "jargon press" that Poles, once given a little power (with specific reference to the City Militia), had been unable to refrain from abusing it in relation to Jews. Thus, a final motion to restrict Jewish participation through quota restrictions was defeated by a vote of fifteen to eight with one abstention.[151]

The rejection of Drzewiecki and Lubomirski's quotas is an indication of a growing division between the City Administration and a committee in which National Democratic and Realist influences had been weakened following the Russian evacuation. By employing the "doctrine of the Polish majority," Drzewiecki and Lubomirski had sought to secure a majority for those influences in the new City Council, which their more liberal and democratically minded opponents, both Polish and Jewish, were able to defeat. In any event, the Germans rejected the committee's projected ordinance in May and drafted one of their own based on the Prussian model, which more than halved the size of the committee's proposed electorate and divided it into six curiae based on property, educational, tax, residential, age, and gender qualifications, with voting scheduled for the first half of July.

In the pre-election political maneuvering that followed, the Jewish Election Committee, a Zionist-led coalition that also included neo-assimilationists and the Orthodox Union, negotiated a deal with a similarly broad cross section of Polish parties that provided Jews with fifteen of the seventy-five total seats from the first five curiae. The Jewish Election Committee also agreed that the election pact would not apply to the sixth or general curia of nonpropertied male voters who had resided in Warsaw for at least two years. Warsaw's Zionist leadership accepted this arrangement, which potentially could have left Jews with only 17% of the ninety council seats, to avoid the kind of fallout that the 1912 Duma elections had generated. Within the Jewish community, the political clout of the Zionist organization in Warsaw—led by Yitshak Grünbaum, Apolinary Hartglas, and Moshe Körner—had increased significantly as a result of its role in the distribution of relief, and thus even the National Democrats were willing to sign on to a deal backed by the Zionists. However, the populists—led in Warsaw by Noah Prylucki and Samuel Hirschhorn—rightly feared that in the interest of Polish-Jewish "peace," the parties of the Jewish Election Committee would not advance their favorite cause of secular Yiddish schools subsidized by public monies. Forming what essentially was an opposition party, the newly branded "Folkists" broke with the Jewish Election Committee in order to run their own candidates in the sixth curia, which also pitted them against the Polish Christian Democrats, the Polish socialist parties, and the Jewish Bund, which also went its own way in opposition to the "bourgeois" parties of the Jewish Election Committee.[152]

For those on the Polish Right, the Folkist challenge to the Jewish Election Committee and its mobilization of voters in the sixth curia resurrected their fears of Judeo-Polonia in Warsaw. Bolesław Koskowski, writing on the eve of the elections in *Tygodnik Illustrowany*, argued that Jewish voters, as a relatively large proportion of the electorate, comprised "an element completely different and separate from the autochthonous Polish population." "Our principal concern," Koskowski continued, "should be that the Council have a distinguished and categorically Polish character, that the Poles on it have an unconditional majority," which could only be achieved by a strong Polish turnout and vote for a common list of candidates dominated by the National Democrats and their allies.[153] For its part, *Gazeta Poranna 2 grosze* regretted that there were too few "rational Zionists" willing to build cadres of pioneers who after the war would go to Palestine and work there. "No Pole can have anything against this movement," but unfortunately, "the majority of Jewish nationalists, Zionists and neo-assimilationists"—groups that *Gazeta Poranna* lumped together despite the divergence in their political outlooks—"prefer to build Palestine in Poland."[154]

Thus, when the Folkists won four seats in the sixth curia, which along with the Bund's single seat raised the Jewish total to twenty, *Gazeta Poranna* in particular worked itself into a frenzy, interpreting the voting results as a "victory" of "extreme nationalism" among Jews.[155] The more moderate *Tygodnik Illustrowany* chose to interpret the election results, both within and outside of the sixth curia—where National Democratic, Christian Democratic, and Realist candidates won a plurality of 40% of the vote—as a victory for the "national list" and a guarantee that the council would not only have a Polish "national character" but would also be able to govern.[156] Having earlier anticipated such a result, however, *Tygodnik Illustrowany* warned that radical Polish nationalist rhetoric should be contained to avoid undermining the possibility of compromise with those Jewish "camps" that were not "narrowly nationalist" and "aggressively disposed toward Polish society."[157]

As we shall see, the language of radical Polish nationalism on the Warsaw City Council was not held in check, but were Warsaw's first modern municipal elections actually a victory for "aggressive nationalism," Polish and Jewish? In reality, the Zionists and Folkists competed among the same mass of voters, the Jewish petite bourgeoisie, even if the Folkists could claim a decisive victory over their Zionist rivals in the sixth curia. Moreover, the Folkists—whose "aggressive nationalism" consisted of demands for equal civil rights, an end to public discrimination, and Yiddish-based cultural autonomy—occupied only four of the twenty Jewish seats on the council. Prylucki repeatedly denied charges that the small group of Jewish populists was anti-Polish: "If [anyone] thinks that the defense by Jews of their own interests is something hostile to Polishness, then [they] have a very bad idea of what constitutes Polishness."[158] In any event, most of the Jewish council seats belonged to the Zionist-led bloc in the Jewish Election Committee that had conceded that the future council would have a "Polish character," something even Prylucki didn't contest. Even with the extra mandates from the sixth curia, Jews held only 22% of seats in the new council, thus remaining seriously underrepresented, which is what had partially inspired the Folkist revolt in the first place.

On the other side, the 40% plurality won by the Polish "national list" did not "guarantee" that it would be able to govern. That list was strongly opposed by the Central Democratic Election Committee, which represented the "independence camp" of leftist and centrist parties grouped around the increasingly popular figure of Józef Piłsudski. During the campaign, this coalition vowed to "take up the most intense struggle against the pro-Muscovites," the brush it used to smear the "national list" dominated by the Endecja.[159] In several matters, as we shall see, the Jewish members of the Warsaw City Council could rely on the support of the "independence camp" led by the pro-Piłsudski wing of the PPS, which alone held twenty-three mandates, to defeat many of the anti-Jewish motions of the National Democrats, if not the radical nationalist rhetoric behind them.

Despite invoking the doctrine of the Polish majority, the National Democrats and their allies didn't even command a majority of eligible Polish voters. In fact, voter turnout in the German-staged municipal elections was low among both Poles and Jews, as only 40% of the eligible electorate, itself reduced to eighty thousand voters, actually cast ballots for any candidates.[160] Even though *Tygodnik Illustrowany* tried to put a positive spin on the 40% turnout, claiming that many otherwise eligible voters, especially in the sixth curia, had been taken into the Russian Army or labored "in emigration," its arithmetic was still not enough to claim a solid Polish majority behind the "national list."[161] On the Jewish side, while Zionist voting strength certainly exceeded that of the

Folkists in all curiae but the sixth, even the Zionists could not claim to have majority support in the Jewish community. In the summer of 1917, Zionist organizations in Warsaw organized a referendum on the creation of a Jewish state in Palestine in which only one-third of the adult Jewish population of Warsaw participated.[162] The Folkists, to be sure, had campaigned against the referendum, claiming that the "living nation" would not allow itself to be "hypnotized" by Palestine, which it referred to as a "Hebrew relic." However, the referendum's poor showing of support had more to do with the attitude of the Orthodox Union, which condemned it as a fraud, one that "every real Jew who strongly adheres to our faith" should avoid.[163] In elections to a "reformed" Jewish community administrative board in 1917, held shortly before the referendum on Palestine, assimilationists managed to remain in control, even with an expanded franchise of Jewish voters, thanks to the support of the Orthodox Union, which was more than sufficient to defeat both the Zionists and the Folkists. In exchange for the Orthodox Union's support, the assimilationists conceded to the Orthodox rabbinate complete autonomy in the supervision of all religious matters in the community.[164] So much for the "victory" of radical nationalism!

In the event, the Warsaw City Council became one of the main arenas where Polish-Jewish conflicts played out for the remainder of the war. As a sign of things to come, the first session of the council was set for a Saturday, causing the Folkists to petition the authorities with a request to move it to the following Monday to preserve the Jewish Sabbath.[165] Though successful in this action, when the council actually met at its first session on 24 July 1916, the four Folkists remained in their seats as the rest of the delegates rose to their feet to hail "Long Live Poland!" *Hajnt*, representing the Zionists, quickly condemned the Folkists' demonstrative political behavior as "scandalous irresponsibility."[166] Indeed, the municipal elections had led to a new eruption of sharp polemical hostilities between *Moment* and *Hajnt*, which among other things mocked the "Yiddishism" of Hirschhorn, who commonly gave his Folkist party speeches in his native Polish.[167] Thereafter the Folkists repeatedly crossed swords with representatives of the Polish "national concentration" over the language of instruction in Jewish schools and the accessibility of Jews to public elementary schools more generally; the introduction of a general Sunday holiday as a day of rest in Warsaw; subsidies for the establishment and maintenance of public kitchens; the ban on entrance to public parks and gardens to individuals not dressed in "proper European attire"; and ongoing complaints by Jews over their treatment at the hands of the city police.[168] Prylucki was particularly meticulous in collecting testimonies of police abuse to justify voting against confirmation of the City Militia's budget. Typical was that of Jankiel Sroka from 21 December 1916:

> On the 15th of this month I went to the city store #117 of the Food Section [a department within the City Administration] on Muranowska Street 24 to purchase a few food items. I was standing in line when the doors opened and several of us waiting on the street entered the store. When the militiaman no. 437 noticed me, he ordered me to leave. I asked him to leave me alone because there was enough room in the store, but instead of answering me he grabbed me by the beard, tore off a handful of hair, and pushed me against the door which led to breaking one of the store windows.
>
> Witnesses were: Josef GUTMAN (Muranowska 29), Szeine Ester KELMAN (Muranowska 30), Golde SZPILSINGER (Muranowska 47), Gitla HITEŁMAN (Wołyńska 15).
>
> I complained to them that the militiaman had no right to tear off my beard, but he could arrest me if I was guilty of anything. Hearing this, the militiaman arrested me and took me to the commissariat. The person writing up the protocol kept me there from 9:30 a.m. to 1:00 p.m., after which he ordered me to leave. When I said that I wanted to file a complaint against the militiaman, he ordered my arrest and placed me in jail in the company of criminals until 6:00 p.m.
>
> Finally, after signing the protocol a young man appeared and demanded a ruble to pay for the damaged glass in the city store. I paid so that they would release me.[169]

By the end of 1916, *Nowa Gazeta* lamented that the "Jewish question" had come to dominate the meetings of the Warsaw City Council and that it, in turn, was dominated by "demagogues on both sides," while voices of the "democratic camps" were not being heard.[170] Shortly thereafter, the Zionists withdrew from the bloc of Jewish councilmen to join and compete with the Folkists in opposition to the remaining factions of assimilationists, Orthodox, and nonparty Jewish representatives. Without the Zionists, the effectiveness of the assimilationists and their ability to act as a "buffer" between more radical Polish and Jewish positions was seriously undermined. There followed the sale of *Nowa Gazeta*, which *Moment* celebrated as "the end of Jewish assimilation in Poland . . . even on paper."[171] Meanwhile, the representatives of Warsaw's Jewish community were repeatedly assaulted by Dr. Konrad Ilski from the Endecja, who on one occasion before the council reportedly said that "the Jewish district is full of fences, thieves, and dealers in human flesh."[172] Earlier, when Prylucki had raised the issue of discrimination in the employment of Jews in municipal institutions, Ilski had

FIGURE 10.   First session of the Warsaw City Council, 24 July 1916. Muzeum Narodowe w Warszawie.

threatened the Folkists with "the most terrible catastrophe" if they continued to press their demands.[173] Ilski would later be nominated to the position of director of the City Provisions Department, which met with the protests of practically all Jewish councilmen, especially after Ilski vowed "to act everywhere against the enemies of Polishness."[174] Such exchanges often paralyzed sessions of the council, causing one delegate to complain: "In the morning, the Jewish question. In the afternoon, the Jewish question. In the evening again the Jewish question."[175]

However, Jews were able to work with Poles from the other parties in the council to fight against certain forms of discrimination. For example, in March 1917 the council voted to restore payments to hundreds of Jewish *rezerwistki* who had been left to their own devices by the Warsaw City Administration on the basis of an August 1916 resolution of the Russian authorities to require only Jewish women to possess civil documents of marriage in order to receive state assistance.[176] Thanks mainly to the organization and lobbying of the Orthodox Union, efforts to pass legislation to ban all commerce in Warsaw on Sundays were defeated.[177] And although it took a walkout from the council that left it without a quorum at its last session of December 1916, followed by several stormy sessions and the suspension of Prylucki from three future council sessions, the council voted to remove the ban on Jews in gabardines entering the grounds of the Łazienki.[178]

Nonetheless, the unelected City Administration, first under Lubomirski before he joined the Regency Council in October 1917 and then under Drze-wiecki, often ignored the council's decisions and, in the case of the lifting of all restrictions on Jewish entrance into the Łazienki, insisted on following Russian-era regulations requiring "proper European attire."[179] In so doing, Prylucki protested, the magistrate had shown it was "Polish in form, but Russian in spirit" when it came to its approach to Warsaw's Jewish community.[180] It was also the City Administration that introduced segregated vending stalls at the Gościnny Dwór public market in response to a petition of Christian tradesmen.[181] In fact, tensions between the magistrate and the council, which as a body was well to the left of a City Administration dominated by National Democrats and their allies, led to Lubomirski's resignation as city president on 19 July 1917. That resignation was withdrawn only after the creation of a three-person commission charged with arbitrating differences between the two institutions.[182]

In the end, there was one matter upon which most Poles of the political class could agree, as expressed in an interview by Jan Kucharzewski, the defeated candidate of the "national list" in the 1912 Duma elections and the first prime minister of the "Polish government" under the German-sponsored Regency Council. After fending off charges of antisemitism, Kucharzewski claimed that no matter the size of their Jewish population, the cities of the Polish Kingdom must remain in Polish hands because "cities are not separate republics . . . but are closely connected to the countryside, where Jews constitute a minority."[183] Kucharzewski was hardly a radical nationalist; even the platform of the "independence camp" in the 1916 municipal elections claimed that candidates supported by the Central Democratic Election Committee would strive to ensure "the Polish character of the city council."[184] This did not necessarily mean the denial of civil and legal rights to Jews, but in their conscious recognition of the perceived need to contain Jewish voting power precisely where Jews lived—in the cities—such arguments could also be used to contain Jews in other areas of "Polish" public life as well.

Meanwhile, the city's economy had reached the point of collapse. Rationing, inflation, and the black market had become the order of the day; hunger was turning into starvation; and fear of epidemics had been replaced by their reality. The Warsaw City Administration was barely able to pay its own workers, let alone provide relief to the mass of the city's poor and unemployed.[185] By the summer of 1918, Warsaw's inhabitants faced a real existential catastrophe, one revealed in the dramatic multiplication of mortality rates.

The city's wartime demographic catastrophe requires further exploration, this time from the perspective of Polish-Jewish relations. More than forty years ago, Warsaw historian Krzysztof Dunin-Wąsowicz argued that during the war Warsaw's

Poles suffered more than its Jews in that the decline in the birth rate was more dramatic among Christians and the increase in the mortality rate was lower among Jews.[186] Although Dunin-Wąsowicz provided little evidence for such a conclusion, data published in *Nowa Gazeta* at least partially bear him out. During the week of 18–24 March 1917, some 462 birth certificates were issued in Warsaw, 288 to Jews. During this same period, there were 405 registered deaths of Christians, compared to 248 deaths of Jews.[187] Data from a few months later, however, reflect a rapidly deteriorating situation among the Jewish population at the height of the typhus epidemic, though they still generally indicate lower birth if not higher mortality rates among Christians. For the week of 8–14 July 1917, there were 124 registered births of Christian children, compared to 146 for Jews, and 338 registered deaths of Christians, compared to 255 for Jews.[188]

Such comparative demographic data of birth and mortality rates among Christians and Jews during the middle of the war cannot be explained in terms of higher living standards, better nutrition, or relative resistance to disease among Warsaw's Jews—especially since Jews, over 25% of them dependent on public assistance, were particularly susceptible to typhus and tuberculosis, the two great catastrophic illnesses of the war. Higher marriage rates among Jews, family structures peculiar to the nonindustrial employment of Jews, different cultures of childcare, and different patterns of out-migration—factors that explain demographic differences among Warsaw's Jewish and Polish populations before the war—are of similar importance in understanding such differences during the war. For example, the death rate for Jews in the Polish Kingdom in 1908 was 14.50 per thousand, compared to 22.20 per thousand among Christians.[189] According to Wróbel, one of the factors influencing Jewish mortality rates was the fact that Jewish women in Warsaw rarely worked in factories far removed from their homes, resulting in better infant and child care.[190] In a speech before the city council on 14 June 1917, Prylucki also attributed lower prewar child mortality rates (by 11.3%) to the practice of breast-feeding by Jewish women.

However, Prylucki brought to the Warsaw City Council alarming data documenting a dramatic rise in Jewish child mortality during the war, which by 1915 had already increased by 70%, not counting refugees. By the beginning of 1916, Jewish children up to five years of age were dying at double the rate of Christian children, and in the first months of 1917 the death rate among all Jewish children up to the age of fifteen had increased by 180% compared to that of 1914. With the cutoff of assistance from the American Jewish Joint Distribution Committee following U.S. entrance into the war and the calamitous impoverishment of the Warsaw Jewish community in the absence of municipal employment and public assistance, Jewish child mortality rates were continuing to rise. By the summer of 1917, the weight of Jewish children had dipped to 60% of the average minimum, which led Prylucki to call for a dramatic increase in municipal support. Of the 738,000 rubles allocated from city funds for child philanthropy and assistance, he claimed, the Jewish community was receiving a mere trickle.[191]

Regardless of the actual situation, the nationalist Polish press was keen to create its own reality around other kinds of statistics. Even though the Jewish population of Warsaw would decline by approximately 10% between 1914 and 1919, the Christian population declined by 23%, the main cause of which was Polish male out-migration.[192] *Gazeta Poranna 2 grosze*, however, attributed the temporarily higher Jewish proportion of the city's population to a general well-being, or *dobrobyt* (which could also be translated as "the good life"), among Jews. More absurdly, the newspaper argued that "a huge percentage of Jews have avoided the army.... And now they are fathering children in *dobrobyt*."[193] In reality, a "huge percentage" of both Poles and Jews had managed to avoid military service in relative proportion to their shares in Warsaw's total population, thanks to the Russian evacuation, which effectively ended conscription in Warsaw after the war's first year.[194]

In June 1918 German occupation authorities began to receive reports of pogrom agitation in Warsaw, where the Endecja—no longer deterred by the German occupation regime's strictures on anti-Jewish propaganda—was openly calling for a boycott of Jewish trade and commerce. By October, Jews—perceived as better off by most Poles—were becoming frequent targets of physical attacks and robberies. Fighting actually broke out between Poles and Jews in one of Warsaw's market areas, as well as at the newly reopened Warsaw University, where Jewish students who had expressed their willingness to work for Polish independence were told to go to Palestine. As the occupation regime melted away in the first weeks of November, there were instances of attacks on Jewish pedestrians by newly minted Polish soldiers who threatened them with weapons and beatings, and shouted at them "traitors" and "collaborators."[195] In its first issue following the transfer of power in Warsaw from the German occupation authorities to Piłsudski, *Tygodnik Illustrowany* was much relieved that the "crowds" had stood firm against "the semitic agitators" of Lenin and Trotsky.[196] For *Tygodnik Illustrowany* and other representatives of "the most serious part of society" that had supported Russia and had imbibed its equation of Jews with the German enemy, the new Jewish bogeyman had already appeared.

Earlier, we noted that the long German "road to Auschwitz," assuming that there was one, did not lead through Warsaw during the German occupation of the city in the Great War. To be sure, Warsaw's Jews were ultimately sacrificed to Germany's *Polenpolitik*, particularly after the Act of 5 November 1916, which left them largely at the mercy of Polish institutions and particularly the City Administration and its agencies, not to mention an intensified and publicly expressed antisemitism in the Polish press that German censors had earlier banned. There is also no question that Germany's wartime economic policies, the requisitioning of resources, and the restrictions on commerce were the main contributing factors to Jewish impoverishment, a condition that Jews shared with the Polish population. Even then, however, Jews did not see the Germans as the cause of their wartime misfortunes in Warsaw, and there is little evidence from Jewish testimonies of German mistreatment and abuse. Instead, it was their negative interactions with Poles that overwhelmingly dominate the documentary evidence. Thus, what did lead through Warsaw was not any road to Auschwitz, but policies of segregation, isolation, discrimination, and persecution of the city's Jewish community by the future Polish authorities—and by the second half of the 1930s, their growing support for plans of forced Jewish emigration.

All of this begs the question—if Polish-Jewish relations in Warsaw had deteriorated to such an extent, why was there no pogrom in November of 1918 as would occur, for example, in Lwów in that month, or in Vilnius in April 1919? After all, Warsaw's economic freefall, its skyrocketing inflation, its crisis of industrial employment, its catastrophic shortages of food and fuels, its inhabitants' acute vulnerability to disease, and its ever-mounting social tensions created an environment no less combustible than that prevailing in Lwów and Vilnius. Yet in Lwów's case, three days of rioting, looting, and mayhem from 22 to 24 November 1918 would lead to the murder of dozens of Jews and the wounding of several hundreds more, not to mention the victimization of several thousands who suffered material losses from the destruction. Similarly, dozens of Jews were killed and huge property damages were reported in Vilnius following the entrance of Polish troops into the city in the spring of 1919.[197] As William Hagen points out, the visceral nature of the pogrom violence in Lwów and the apocalyptic mindset of many of its perpetrators were unprecedented, at least until the Second World War, when such scenes were played out on a larger scale in places like Jedwabne.[198]

Certainly, the struggle for hegemony in Lwów between Poles and Ukrainians in the vacuum left by the final collapse of Austrian authority, and the failed attempt of Jews to have both sides respect their neutrality in the conflict, created a situation quite unlike that prevailing in Warsaw, where a third party never contested Polish hegemony. However, a more fundamental difference is that unlike Lwów, which had been the scene of actual military conflict during the war as control of the city passed back and forth between the Austrian and Russian Armies and then between Polish and Ukrainian forces, Warsaw never experienced such fighting within its borders. Similarly, control of Vilnius had changed hands from Imperial Russia to Imperial Germany, and then in rapid fashion to Bolshevik, briefly to Lithuanian, and finally to Polish forces, whereupon Jews were accused of collaboration with the previous and short-lived Soviet occupation. Certainly, control of Warsaw had passed from Russian to German hands in August 1915, and between German and Polish hands in the second week of November 1918, but the transfer of authority had occurred in both instances almost peacefully, accompanied far more by negotiation than by military action. Prior to November 1918, exceptional violence against Lwów and Vilnius Jews during the war had already occurred, courtesy of the Russian Army, which in a sense legitimized and encouraged future acts of brutality against the Jewish community.[199] The Russian Army in the Polish Kingdom, as we have seen, behaved similarly, but outside rather than inside the city limits of Warsaw.

The inhabitants of Lwów and Vilnius, in other words, had become desensitized toward a kind of brutalizing violence in a way that Warsaw's residents had not. Though tensions ran high in Warsaw and Polish-Jewish relations had likely never been so distressed, assaults on Jews remained individual rather than collective acts. Piłsudski's ability to establish his authority without challenge in Warsaw in November 1918 and to negotiate the peaceful evacuation of German forces from the city, in other words, may have spared the city considerable interethnic violence. It basically meant that the majority of Poles and Jews, who despite everything had remained largely indifferent to efforts to mobilize them around the politics of identity, could remain indifferent to one another at this critical juncture. Had German forces put up resistance to a Polish takeover or to their own disarmament, which was not inconceivable, Warsaw's Jews may well have experienced a Lwów-style pogrom. Fortunately, both Poles and Jews in Warsaw were spared the test.

WOMEN AND THE WARSAW HOME FRONT

The unique features of Warsaw's wartime experience discussed in previous chapters did much to set and reset the "home front" as a stage for its female actors. Of particular importance was Warsaw's chronic economic crisis, which began immediately at the outbreak of the war and was subsequently exacerbated by the exactions of Russian evacuation and German occupation. The city's demographic feminization resembled that of other major European cities, although the increasing preponderance of women over men in Warsaw's population—which reached 32% by January 1917[1]—owed less to military conscription than it did to voluntary and involuntary male labor out-migration. By my count, approximately twenty-one thousand male reservists, conscripts, and volunteers from Warsaw were taken into the Russian Army and other military formations between the summer of 1914 and the autumn of 1918, while as many as five times that number left the city for work outside of it.

Elsewhere in Europe, as well as in the United States, the war promoted both the quantitative and qualitative growth of women's participation in the labor force. This was the case in the capital of practically every belligerent state—more so in Berlin and Petrograd perhaps than in London or Paris—but proportionally significant regardless. The value of this labor, moreover, was the main source of women's social power in these cities during the war years.[2] In Great Britain and the United States, women's work in the munitions industry served as a basis for claiming and achieving political rights after the war. In this regard, Warsaw was dramatically different, as female participation in the industrial labor force declined precipitously in terms of numbers employed and remained unchanged in proportion to male participation as a consequence of the collapse of industrial production in the city. Before the war, 18,420 women—23.9% out of a total of 77,809 industrial workers—were employed in Warsaw's factories. By early 1916, that number had dropped to only 3,650 women out of a total industrial labor force of 14,632, or 24.9% of all workers.[3] As we have seen, women employed as domestic servants and sales clerks also lost their jobs in large numbers as the economic crisis deepened, while employment outside of the city and temporary employment in public-works projects were options largely restricted to men.

Indeed, thousands of unemployed working-age males remained in the city, as Stanisław Kutrzeba remarked following his visit to Warsaw in May 1916: "One doesn't see here the absence of adult males, as it is with us [in Krakow]." Instead, many of them had been reduced to begging, the ubiquity of which made a lasting impression on Kutrzeba: "It was possible to see beggars in Warsaw in the past, but now they are everywhere."[4] Thus, despite the city's marked feminization as a consequence of massive male labor out-migration, the presence and availability of unemployed men to compete with women for the few jobs that were to be had in Warsaw effectively prevented the feminization of the labor force. Whatever social power Warsaw's women acquired during the war in support of economic and political demands would have to be derived from other sources.

In other words, women in the city were not without options altogether, although they varied widely depending on women's circumstances. Broadly speaking, Warsaw's women can be divided into two categories. The first, to use Davis's term in reference to wartime Berlin, were the "women of lesser means,"[5] who in Warsaw as well as Berlin comprised the vast majority of women, though in Warsaw's case the means at their disposal were lesser still. Such women included the laboring poor but, more significantly, the female unemployed, particularly former domestic servants who before the war comprised the largest number of employed women in Warsaw and whose jobs were lost due to the evacuation of Russian officials and the growing impoverishment of middle-class and intelligentsia households. Joining these "women of lesser means" were single mothers and wives left temporarily or permanently without male partners due to military conscription and male labor out-migration. Among the most publicly and politically visible women in this category were the *rezerwistki*, soldiers' wives whose sense of entitlement was publicly acknowledged—that is, until it came to be perceived as a threat to the existing social order in their respective communities. Finally, there were the "women of loose morality," as they were sometimes referred to in the press, prostitutes whose numbers increased significantly in the midst of the city's economic destitution.

The second kind of women in Warsaw were similar to those identified by Healy in her study of wartime Vienna, defined as a vocal minority among women of affluence who spoke on behalf of "women" in general, including "women of lesser means."[6] Although the numbers of women of affluence declined in Warsaw during the war years as economic misery traveled up the social hierarchy, the size of the minority speaking on behalf of women grew noticeably as a small number of prewar feminists of conviction were joined by a much larger group of feminists of wartime circumstance. The latter can be defined as the female members of prewar social and cultural elites whose perspectives and, ultimately, demands were shaped by their wartime experience in philanthropy, social work, and public assistance. In fact, receipt and distribution of relief and assistance brought these two groups of women face to face, often for the first time. Both would make their voices heard, often forcefully, in the social and political arena.

For that very reason, virtually every Warsaw daily and periodical regardless of its political profile and allegiances took up the "woman question" during the war, interpreting it from a unique perspective. Given the rapid rise of female participation in the broadly defined public sphere occasioned by the war, the press had little choice. Thus, the following discussion will not address the policies and pronouncements of imperial regimes and their representatives in Warsaw, whether Russian or German, which when it came to the issue of women left the field open to local actors. Instead, in its examination of women on Warsaw's home front, this chapter will identify stereotypes, images, messages, prescriptions, and proscriptions promoted by various interest groups and their publicists in a Warsaw press that itself was far from uniform in its political outlooks but by war's end belonged largely to the same chorus in its approach to women.

Gender and the Politics of Social Work

As we have noted, at the beginning of the war, Polish "society" in Warsaw mobilized in support of the Russian military cause and in cooperation with the Russian government. The Warsaw Citizens Committee led this effort, and among its original eight sections was the Women's Section, located on 32 Jasna Street and headed by Helena Weychert.[7] Before the emergence of the Warsaw Citizens Committee, the Christian Society for the Protection of Women had already set up seven sections, which practically ran parallel to those eventually created by the new nongovernmental organization in the city.[8] Chaired by Weychert, this conservative organization of affluent Catholic women concentrated its efforts before the war almost entirely on fighting prostitution and pornography. Joined by other upper-class women involved in the charitable work of the Warsaw Philan-thropic Society, the Women's Section under Weychert's direction clearly expected to move beyond the traditional activities of its constituent organizations in serv-ing the Warsaw home front, even when its newly conceived roles overlapped and collided with those assigned to other sections of the Warsaw Citizens Commit-tee by its male leadership. Thus, from the very outset of the war, the definition of women's roles in the public sphere, a sphere expanded by the demands of Europe's first total war, led to controversy and conflict.

The Women's Section quickly found itself under attack for overstepping juris-dictional and gender boundaries. An early dispute revolved around its involve-ment in fundraising activities, which led to conflict with the committee's Dona-tions Section.[9] Despite the General Section's intervention in favor of the latter, the Women's Section stubbornly continued its practice of door-to-door solicitations to fund its own activities.[10] The Women's Section would also be reprimanded for sending announcements directly to the press rather than vetting them through the committee's Press and Information Section.[11] Such conflicts would lead in mid-September to the resignation of Weychert and other leaders of Women's Section, followed by the dissolution of the section itself and its replacement with a revealingly labeled "Commission for Women's Work under the Citizens Com-mittee."[12]

The dissolution of the Women's Section coincided with accusations in the Warsaw press that identified women as the main sources of rumor and panic as the front closed in on Warsaw that fall. Responding to such attacks in *Bluszcz*, the era's leading women's periodical with close ties to the leadership of the Women's Section, Julia Kisielewska reminded her readers, "Rumor-mongering is not, as the Greeks would have it, a monopoly of women" but also characteristic of men who had not gone to the front.[13] This denigration of "left-at-home men," who actually comprised the majority of men in Warsaw, was an early if timid challenge to the gendered division of the war into masculine and feminine realms.

Several weeks before its demise, the Women's Section received permission directly from the Russian authorities to organize nursing courses.[14] Hundreds of women from all social classes but especially the Polish intelligentsia would sub-sequently respond to the section's appeal toward the end of August 1914 to serve as nurses and nurses' aides in treating wounded soldiers after attending lectures on emergency care.[15] *Kurjer Warszawski*, however, found fault with many of the young nurses' aides who supposedly treated their work as "fashionable sport," and the conservative daily called upon them to be "tactful, modestly attired and severe toward their colleagues who are interrupting their work."[16] *Bluszcz* took such criticism seriously. Treating the wounded was "not something to be taken lightly," confirmed Julia Kisielewska in its pages.[17]

Nonetheless, during the October 1914 "Battle of Warsaw," a *Bluszcz* editorial noted that women alone were organizing care of the wounded in Warsaw's hospitals and that this constituted additional proof of women's expanding roles in the organization of the home front. In response to the committee's efforts to curtail those roles by dissolving the Women's Section, *Bluszcz* argued that women should not surrender their newfound positions voluntarily, especially in those areas where they had been successful.[18] In any case, the restrictions that the committee's leadership sought to impose on its female social activists proved impossible to maintain as the numbers of those in need of public assistance and the types of public assistance that they needed continued to expand, as did the numbers of women involved in rendering such assistance. Consequently, the conflicts that the Warsaw Citizens Committee had thought it had laid to rest with the dissolution of its Women's Section reemerged quickly enough with the female leadership of the Commission for Women's Work.[19]

Originally set up to organize and provide direct assistance to women and children whose lives had been disrupted by the war, the commission's activities rapidly expanded, leading to a division of labor and the establishment of seven subcommissions—again according to the model earlier established by the Christian Society for the Protection of Women. By February 1915, *Bluszcz* could report with pride and satisfaction, "Women's energies, grouped in this commission, worked miracles of labor and industry, creating in a matter of days shelters for refugees, hostels for the intelligentsia, tearooms, Sunday centers, a shelter for soldiers' children, etc."[20] To be sure, the welfare of mothers and especially children would remain at the heart of the commission's activities during the first year of war, and by February 1915 it had registered more than nineteen thousand children who qualified for assistance in Warsaw, while feeding and clothing seven thousand directly.[21] The commission also operated four refugee shelters, provided significant assistance to an increasingly impoverished and unemployed intelligentsia, and found work for some 3,500 women through its employment office,[22] though this paled by comparison to the tens of thousands of placements offered to unemployed males by the Warsaw Citizens Committee's Labor Section.

The fact of the matter, as later noted by committee activist Franciszek Herbst, was that women carried out almost all of the direct distribution of public assistance during the committee's existence (to the middle of 1916).[23] Moreover, the Commission for Women's Work was largely dependent on its own resources derived from charitable giving. During the winter of 1914–15, for example, 1,070 women participated in a fundraising campaign for the commission, selling "gold stars" that raised thousands of rubles in support of its assistance to children.[24] These and other achievements marking their baptism under the fire of war, *Bluszcz* proclaimed in February 1915, were already sufficient evidence that "Polish women are good material for social work," not just as rank-and-file participants but as those directing it.[25]

Such confidence, boosted by the organizational and financial autonomy of women's organizations both before and during the war, was demonstrated in the commission's refusal to subordinate its subcommission on assistance to the intelligentsia to a national commission created in conjunction with the Central Citizens Committee, despite the demands of the leadership of the Warsaw Citizens Committee.[26] In March 1915, the Commission for Women's Work vigorously defended its position in *Kurjer Warszawski* by contesting as erroneous published information that had belittled the commission's long-standing aid to the intelligentsia, work that it had absolutely no intention of ending.[27] The following month the Union for the Equal Rights of Women, a feminist organization, hosted a meeting of representatives of women's associations and of women in mixed associations to discuss matters connected to social work on the Warsaw home front. From the speeches given at the meeting, one could easily have received the impression that all institutions created to deal with the difficult conditions of wartime had functioned effectively only because of the involvement of women in them. Indeed, cafeterias, hostels, shelters, recreation halls, and schools were being run almost exclusively by women.[28]

For some of these women of affluence, involvement in public philanthropy and assistance was clearly a social calling; for others, it was a source of political empowerment; for yet others, it was simply fashionable, especially in the war's first year. Such motivations were not necessarily incompatible. *Bluszcz* described the situation in the following terms in July 1915: "Here at present there is perhaps not a single young woman who has not devoted her time to social work. The fashion today is that each and every woman does something—we could do with more such fashion. A beautiful fashion, let it last as long as possible."[29] The political dimensions of this "fashion" were clearly emerging before the Russian evacuation. Emboldened by its resistance to both the Warsaw and the Central Citizens Committees on the matter of assistance to the intelligentsia, the Commission for Women's Work began to take up the issue of women's rights in a projected Warsaw municipal government, to the extent that existing Russian legislation recognized those rights at all.[30] Jan Czempiński, for one, clearly hoped to turn back the clock and redirect the growing ambitions of elite women. Harkening back to the days when Weychert and her colleagues contented themselves with rescuing young women from the evils of the sex trade, Czempiński called upon the female readership of *Bluszcz* to join him in a crusade against prostitution in wartime, a crusade that should include the fight against "prostitution literature" and "prostitution of the brain."[31]

The social and political conservatives who comprised Warsaw's Polish elite, however, were already too dependent on the efficacy of women's wartime social work to risk direct confrontation with the female activists behind that work—often enough their wives, sisters, and daughters—even as they sought to preserve traditional gender roles. Unlike the situation in September 1914 when the Warsaw Citizens Committee's General Section forced female activists into a defensive stance when it voted to dissolve the Women's Section, in the summer of 1915 nine women's organizations went on the offensive to demand greater representation of women in the work of the Warsaw Citizens Committee.[32] By the time the Russians began their weeks-long evacuation of the city in early July 1915, this consortium created what was essentially a political action committee to guide a small but otherwise eligible minority of female voters to participate in elections that were never held.[33] In early 1916, with Warsaw now under German occupation, these groups merged to form and legally register as the Union of Polish Women's Associations.[34] The following June the union issued an appeal that made its position clear. Since the burden of social work had fallen on women's shoulders, it argued, "simple justice and rational understanding of the public interest" should give women a greater voice in the organization and leadership of those very social, philanthropic, and public institutions that they were serving. In short, the union demanded "equal rights with men in every sphere where her work is needed."[35]

Soldiers' Wives

Among Warsaw's women of lesser means, soldiers' wives, popularly known as *rezerwistki*, were also successful in making their voices heard, though their tools for doing so were far different from those used by the affluent women engaged in social work. Within days of the outbreak of the war in 1914, a number of *rezerwistki* sought to hire themselves out as domestic servants in an effort to make ends meet, even as employer demand for such labor had already begun its steep decline.[36] With that option effectively closed, a substantial number of soldiers' wives, together with family members, left Warsaw for the surrounding countryside, where they joined other men and women, unemployed as a consequence of factory closings and slowdowns, to seek work as seasonal farm laborers. They were often paid in kind, which they brought back with them to Warsaw every couple of days.[37] As a consequence of well-publicized scenes of their desperation in the first weeks of the war, soldiers' wives and families became immediate objects of considerable public empathy, as evidenced in the Warsaw Citizens Committee's intention to provide them with direct assistance—that is, until the Russian government came to their aid.

In fact, the sympathy of elite opinion for the wives and families of soldiers serving at the front was sufficiently widespread that professional beggars, with children in tow, successfully posed as *rezerwistki* in asking for handouts.[38] Not only did *rezerwistki* receive social payments from the Russian government to support themselves and their families in the absence of husbands and fathers taken into military service, they were also the beneficiaries of special regulations enacted by the Russian government that protected them from eviction for failing to pay rents, a protection strongly endorsed in the Warsaw press.[39] While many of the disputes over rent involved Jewish landlords, which may have influenced support for *rezerwistki* in the Polish press and inside the Warsaw Citizens Committee, those same landlords also rented to Jewish *rezerwistki*, who too were emboldened by their ability to sway public opinion.[40] When Warsaw's refugee shelters were forcibly evacuated of their Jewish residents in June 1915, only the *rezerwistki* among them were able to offer effective resistance, forcing the city authorities to retreat from the use of coercive methods against them.[41]

With few alternative means to feed themselves and their families, widows of soldiers were reportedly afraid to talk about the deaths of their husbands for fear of losing payments from the state, though in reality such assistance was meant to continue to the end of their husband's terms of service, even if wounded or killed in the line of duty.[42] In Warsaw, as elsewhere in Europe, by providing subsidies and protection, the state had become a "surrogate husband" for soldiers' wives, as Maureen Healy put it in her study of Vienna.[43] With such a degree of dependence on Russian transfer payments as well as on Russian regulations that granted them relative immunity from eviction, *rezerwistki* were left in a particularly vulnerable position with the departure of the "surrogate husband," the tsarist state, from Warsaw in early August 1915. At the same time, *rezerwistki*, with a sense of entitlement that had been publicly acknowledged and effectively tested, had reason to expect that organized protest against their circumstances would be successful in finding a new "surrogate husband."[44]

Thus, on 14 August, a crowd of *rezerwistki*, bereft of Russian support and to whom the new German occupation authorities felt no obligation, appeared before the offices housing the Warsaw Magistrate, which had just been taken over by the recently appointed City Administration headed by Prince Lubomirski. There they demanded bread for themselves and their families.[45] The City Administration's immediate response was a promise to treat *rezerwistki* like others among Warsaw's poor who were eligible for public support from the Warsaw Citizens Committee.[46] This promise, however, was not enough to mollify the *rezerwistki*, who demanded nothing less than the assumption by Warsaw's municipal institutions of the obligations of the recently departed Russian state. The prominence of *rezerwistki* in demonstrations throughout the city on 13 September and ongoing public sympathy for their plight would lead wealthier Polish farmers and landowners to feed and shelter thousands of soldiers' children in response to an appeal by Warsaw archbishop Aleksander Kakowski.[47] At the same time, the Warsaw Citizens Committee made an additional seven hundred free dinners available to *rezerwistki* at one of the public kitchens, as the City Administration negotiated a major loan to cover the Russian government's obligations.[48] By such means, transfer payments to *rezerwistki* and their children were restored by mid-October to the exact level provided earlier by the Russian state. In the meantime, about one thousand *rezerwistki* had received limited support since the Russian evacuation from the Jewish Community Administrative Board, with which they had deposited documents proving their eligibility. With the City Administration taking over financial responsibility for the Russian-era "Curatorium" to provide support to all soldiers' wives irrespective of religion or ethnicity, a tumult ensued at the board's headquarters when at the end of September the demand by Jewish *rezerwistki* for the return of their documents was not satisfied immediately.[49]

For the next eleven months, Jewish *rezerwistki* would receive payments on a par with their Polish counterparts, though in mid-December 1915 the Warsaw Citizens Committee decided to reduce the total amount of subsidies by one-third by eliminating those paid to families with other sources of income—a decision that affected Jews more than it did Poles.[50] Nonetheless, the reductions led to angry protests among both groups in March 2016, which for Princess Lubomirska contained the seeds of potential revolution: "Already in front of the Ratusz [city hall] there have been gatherings of soldiers' wives which had to be dispersed. The enraged women fell upon Zdziś and tore off the button on his fur coat. So it begins. . . ."[51] A new opportunity for reducing payments to *rezerwistki* availed itself to the City Administration on 28 August 1916, when the Russian government decided to accept only civil documents as proof of marriage from the wives of Jewish soldiers. This action was clearly discriminatory since the wives of Christian soldiers could still receive benefits on the basis of religious certificates of marriage. As noted in the previous chapter, even with the Russians now more than a year removed from Warsaw, in things Jewish the Warsaw City Administration often chose to adhere to imperial Russian regulations, claiming they were still legally binding.[52] As a consequence, hundreds of Jewish *rezerwistki* were effectively disenfranchised for several months until the Warsaw City Council finally voted in March 1917 to restore payments to the affected women.[53] From that time until the end of the war, all *rezerwistki* in Warsaw retained their subsidies, which had become pittances as a consequence of inflation but nonetheless ate up a significant portion of the City Administration's revenues.

By then the City Administration had tried, unsuccessfully, to transfer the burden of its financial support of Warsaw's *rezerwistki* to the "Polish government" established under the Regency Council.[54] However, the fact that payments to *rezerwistki* continued while all other public services were deeply cut or eliminated attests to the power of these seemingly powerless women. The pro-German *Godzina Polski*, relatively "progressive" in matters related to women's political rights and education, was the only daily in Warsaw that took on the "privileges" of *rezerwistki* and attempted to challenge their moral claims to public assistance. Indeed, *Godzina Polski* even took the unpopular side of landlords in their attempts to gather rent from *rezerwistki*.

In the first half of September 1915, Warsaw's Property-Owners Association, claiming that landlords had lost 1.7 million rubles in income from *rezerwistki* living in rent-free apartments, petitioned the Warsaw Citizens Committee to create public housing from unoccupied buildings and to transfer soldiers' wives and families to them.[55] Unsuccessful in this effort, building-owners turned to the courts to pursue evictions of Warsaw's unemployed, particularly women, who had also stopped paying rents. The multiplication of these lawsuits led various labor organizations in the city to seek the same kind of moratorium for the unemployed that *rezerwistki* had enjoyed since the beginning of the war. The Warsaw Citizens Committee withheld its support for such a moratorium but appealed to landlords as "citizens" to refrain from taking legal action to evict their tenants, setting up offices to arbitrate the disputes. This was basically the same position the committee had occupied in the fall of 1914, prior to the Russian government's declaration of a moratorium on rent payments from soldiers' families.[56]

The committee's lack of sympathy for the position of landlords was in line with the "opinion" of "Polish society" more generally, which "stridently condemned evictions," as Kutrzeba noted during his visit to Warsaw in the spring of 1916. Even so, the tide of "Polish opinion" against landlords began to shift when one of them, facing bankruptcy, jumped four floors to his death on the pavement below during Kutrzeba's stay in Warsaw.[57] It was that event that brought *Godzina Polski* out in support of the landlords, though it was still not ready to attack the privileges of *rezerwistki* head on. Instead, it attacked the wives of workers who, like *rezerwistki*, had been separated from their husbands by the circumstances of war and were taking advantage of Article 182 of the civil code, according to which they could not appear in court without the permission of their husbands. Using this strategy, these women had managed to avoid legal action against them by landlords seeking rent payments and arrears.[58]

To be sure, *Godzina Polski*, like the German occupation regime it supported, had little patience for the unemployed poor in general and little respect for the laws and regulations of the deposed Russian state, which it abhorred. By April 1918, with city finances in dire straits, *Godzina Polski* called upon the magistrate to seek the services of a neutral government to approach the new Soviet regime about taking over payments to *rezerwistki* in German-occupied Poland. Since it was always understood that the Russian government would be held responsible for these payments after the war (in the books of the Warsaw City Administration, payments to *rezerwistki* were assigned to "the account of the Russian government"), and since Russia was now at peace with its enemies following the recently signed Treaty of Brest-Litovsk, it should now resume its obligations—or, at least, such was the reasoning. However, if the Soviet government refused, as *Godzina Polski* clearly expected, the tsarist regulations of 1914 could be declared inoperative, thus relieving the City Administration of a major burden and bringing an end to the rent moratorium. The latter had become insufferable to landlords, the newspaper argued, especially those who "had twenty, even forty apartments" occupied rent-free by *rezerwistki*.[59]

Two months later, the Warsaw City Council, in assigning yet another monthly sum of 500,000 marks to support *rezerwistki*, also defeated a motion by a vote of twenty-one to eighteen to make it the last such allocation. *Godzina Polski* was outraged that the city would continue to make payments to *rezerwistki* that it could not afford, payments roughly equal in amount to allocations for public kitchens and public works—which, in truth, the city also could ill afford.[60] Clearly, elite sympathy for *rezerwistki* had eroded, as it had for the varied plights of all women of lesser means, but it had not evaporated. Gone, however, were the idealized portraits of lower-class women that had appeared in the Warsaw press earlier in the war, such as the one published in March 1915 in *Tygodnik Illustrowany*, whose anonymous reporter proclaimed that each day he passed by a public grocery store operated by the Warsaw Citizens Committee, its doors still closed, "a long line of poorly dressed women waits for the happy moment of its opening." "No one is maintaining order here," he continued. "Not a trace of the police."[61]

The police would have to be called soon enough to maintain order in such lines. While still under Russian rule, however, the mainstream press perceived little danger posed to the social order by women of lesser means, be they *rezerwistki* or other consumers of basic goods, so long as they remained calmly in line with elite expectations of their proper social place and behavior. If Warsaw's women of lesser means remained relatively passive in the face of periodic shortages of basic commodities during the first year of the war, under German occupation, rising anger caused by food deprivation became ever more visible and was directed first and foremost at those institutions providing public assistance. Women of lesser means played a prominent role in Warsaw's food riots of June 1916, which resulted in the ransacking and looting of twenty-three grocery stores operating

FIGURE 11. Purchasing rationed bread and sugar. Despite this staged scene of order and availability of goods, note the barbed wire above the counter. Author's personal collection.

under the supervision of the City Administration—the very same stores where order had been maintained without police presence fifteen months earlier.[62] When these riots were reprised in May 1917 following similar disturbances in Petrograd that culminated in the overthrow of the tsarist regime, the threat to the existing social order posed by lower-class women became palpable to Warsaw's local elites.[63] Consequently, women of lesser means became less objects of sympathy and more of criticism and even condemnation, beginning with the most vulnerable women, those on the social margin, also known as the women of "easy morals."

Prostytutki and Matki Polki

During the war, the number of prostitutes in the city increased exponentially as a result of two main factors, the presence of large numbers of troops on the one hand, and extraordinarily high female unemployment on the other, particularly among domestic servants who before the war constituted the single most significant category of recruitment into the "profession." On the demand side, one-third of the entire Russian Army had been stationed in the Polish Kingdom on the eve of the war, and a substantial number of officers and enlisted men had been posted to the Warsaw military region and resided in barracks scattered throughout the city's adjacent suburbs and at the Warsaw Citadel. They were replaced by some twelve thousand German occupation troops in the summer of 1915, who were accompanied by some eighteen thousand civilians brought in from Germany to serve in the occupation administration of the General-Government headquartered in Warsaw. On the supply side, tens of thousands of domestic servants and factory women were thrown out of work by various evacuations of Russian officials and their families, the ever-growing impoverishment of the middle class and intelligentsia, and the almost total collapse of industrial production. As time went on, prostitution became the only possible alternative to starvation for many of them.

Before the war, as shown by Keely Stauter-Halsted in her groundbreaking study of commercial sex in partitioned Poland, public perceptions and discourse on prostitution evolved from depictions of "fallen women" shaped by the moral panic that accompanied the migration of single women from the post-emancipation countryside to the rapidly growing cities in the last decades of the nineteenth century, to more sensitive treatments of prostitutes as social actors, and, finally, to portrayals as medical subjects requiring the supervision and control of physicians and police.[64] During the war years, as sexually transmitted diseases spread from the cities to the countryside as a result of the migrations of soldiers and civilians alike, the issue of police-medical control of commercial sex became even more prominent, while the sheer scale of wartime prostitution reignited the moral panic of earlier decades. At the same time, moral condemnations of prostitution and its female practitioners became a stick to contain change and the aspirations of women more generally, whether expressed in rapidly evolving fashion or demands for the right to vote, and the threat they posed to the existing patriarchal order.

Early in the war, the growth in the number of prostitutes in Warsaw coincided with the call-up into the Russian armed forces of half of the personnel in the Medical-Police Commission, whose task it was to supervise regulated prostitution and arrest and examine those women who escaped the system of police regulation. Unregistered prostitutes, mainly consisting of those who moved in and out of the commercial sex trade as economic circumstance warranted, had long exceeded registered prostitutes working in public brothels. As the number of unregistered prostitutes grew and the regime of detection, arrest, and disease-control weakened, the Russian state in November 1914 sought to beef up the city's medical-police force through an allocation of 250,000 rubles to the Medical Council under the Warsaw Magistrate.[65] While the city hired additional personnel, corruption among those assigned to control vice abetted its spread, particularly as Russian soldiers and officers constituted the vast majority of consumers of commercial sex. In January 1915 a number of arrests of policemen and agents of the Medical-Police Commission were carried out in Warsaw's Eighth Precinct and elsewhere in the city where they had tolerated the existence of illegal "houses of debauchery," as the Warsaw press put it; however, sentences of three days in jail for the offenders may well have been worth it.[66] The emphasis of Russian authorities clearly remained on independent sex workers rather than corruption among their own, as the magistrate received funding for two more "inspection points" in April 1915 while the numbers of prostitutes in the city continued to multiply.[67]

Such were the trends that led Jan Czempiński, whose appeal to Polish women was mentioned earlier in this chapter, to proclaim the need for a new crusade: "With war and its monstrous logic have come hunger, unemployment, and the most terrible curse of human culture, namely, prostitution." Calling upon Polish women to join this moral cause "in defense of their own rights and the health of future generations," Czempiński connected the crusade against prostitution to the fight against pornography, or what he termed "prostitution literature," though in the minds of conservative moralists pornography also embraced many different aspects of popular culture.[68] Czempiński also may have had in mind the spread of "illusions," or photographs of partially naked women that were available for viewing at peepshows in various locations throughout the city. The growing popularity of "illusions" during the war drew an open letter of protest from a group of Polish women who claimed that the demoralization of society by pornography, a disease to which peasant and refugee youth were particularly suspect, was "worse than any epidemic."[69]

Not surprisingly, many of the Russian officers arrested after 5 August 1915 by arriving German forces were retrieved from brothels, where they had sought to find one last evening of pleasure before being evacuated.[70] They would be replaced soon enough by their German counterparts, who also brought prostitutes directly to their quarters. General Erich von Etzdorf, the German governor of Warsaw, in a government order addressing the behavior of officers barely a month into the occupation, reprimanded them for such relationships, which "affect the good name of the army and its officers corps among the general population."[71] The main concern, however, soon turned to the health of German occupation troops. By October, six hundred hospital beds had been set up for German soldiers suffering from venereal disease, and of the 1,011 prostitutes examined by German physicians in the first two months of the occupation, more than half were found to be infected.[72]

Germans working in the civilian administration also did little to hide their sex purchases and at times openly flaunted them. According to Aleksander

Kraushar, the appearance of German "dignitaries" with "strongly suspect women in public places and restaurants" aroused more than a few condemnations from polite society. Several of these women were dancers in the Warsaw ballet who in exchange for "special favors," as Kraushar called them, took advantage of their relationships with the "most privileged" among the Germans. While officials availed themselves of ballerinas, soldiers made their sex purchases in the streets, which they took over in the evening. Overall, Kraushar judged the behavior of these "representatives of this God-fearing and well-mannered nation" worse than that of the Russians and "one hundred times more harmful."[73]

Meanwhile, many prostitutes took up residence in abandoned Russian military barracks and the Russian summer camp in the Pole Mokotowskie, locations adjacent to where they had earlier plied their trade. There they were joined by other local "riffraff," who reportedly slept there, had "orgies," and were demolishing wood floors and fences for heating materials. The Warsaw Citizens Committee asked for and received permission from the Germans to take over these structures in November 1915.[74] While the presence of prostitutes in city-owned property could be eliminated, their larger presence throughout the city could not be reduced without a substantial turn in wartime economic conditions; at best, they could only be contained. The availability of new recruits to the sex trade in Warsaw, the *rezerwistki* abandoned by the Russian state, indeed may have been a factor in the City Administration's decision to take over responsibility for payments to soldiers' families, which in any case helped to limit further swelling in the ranks of prostitutes by not leaving additional thousands of women to the whims of war and occupation for more than a couple of months.[75]

Available statistical data about the wartime practitioners of prostitution, though limited only to women on the registry, reveal that those who had newly entered the legal trade in the first months of 1917 were far more likely to be Catholic than Jewish, by a ratio of slightly less than five to one.[76] The majority had been born outside of Warsaw, and most were literate, though this likely meant that they were not completely illiterate. The largest single professional category among new prostitutes, as among those already in the sex trade, was that of domestic servants (approximately one-third), followed by seamstresses (one-fifth). The trade's practitioners ranged from fifteen to forty-seven years in age. While some of these women may have also been *rezerwistki*, they do not figure in the data as a separate category.[77] In his analysis of the more than two thousand new registrants to Warsaw's police rolls in 1915–16, Dr. Alfred Sokołowski, an expert in infectious diseases, found that 90% had been infected with a sexually transmitted disease at the time they had been registered.[78]

The undeniable growth in the number of prostitutes, both registered and unregistered, along with the escalating prevalence of venereal disease, created

FIGURE 12.   Józef Rapacki, "In the Service of Love," lithograph from Series *Pro Memoria: Prusak w Polsce 1915-1918* (Warsaw: Wydawnictwo "Tygodniku Ilustrowanego," 1918). Muzeum Narodowy w Warszawie.

conditions for a new moral panic, which like its predecessor targeted the ethnic "other" as the prime generator of the "plague." Polish opinion had long held Jews responsible for the "trade in human flesh," along with the entrapment of women, the spread of pornography, and the demoralization of society. During the war years, *Gazeta Poranna 2 grosze* led the antisemitic charge in this as well as other matters. Thus, among the many Jewish violations of the moral order, *Gazeta Poranna* was pleased to report the arrest of five Jews in the city's 6th police precinct by the self-empowered Citizens Guard. This "ring of criminals" had reportedly kidnapped and sold fifteen-year-old Rifka Hoffman into white slavery for six rubles.[79] Elsewhere, *Gazeta Poranna* claimed that prostitution in the Jewish community was a result of not simply the wartime economic crisis but also the "bad upbringing" of Jewish girls, presumably neglected by parents who devoted all of their attention to boys.[80] The image of prostitution as a Jewish vice had a long history, but as noted already, the Jewish proportion of newly registered prostitutes during the war was about half of its share in the population as a whole. This scapegoating of Jews marked a continuation of prewar trends that I have discussed elsewhere.[81] By the summer of 1918, the Folkists' Polish-language newspaper, *Głos Żydowski,* had had enough of *Gazeta Poranna*'s "prostitution antisemitism." After noting that "the new antisemitism of *2 grosze* is directed . . . against the Jewish prostitute," it called on the Polish nationalist daily to "stick to your own kind": prostitutes of Slavic descent on Marszałkowska Street.[82]

By that time, prostitutes of both kinds, Polish and Jewish, had become a common presence in the city's hospitals, infected with both venereal and other diseases, especially typhus and tuberculosis. Their high number led the German authorities to demand the removal of prostitutes from the hospitals, which also provided care for German soldiers and officials often suffering from the same diseases. The opening of two shelters by the Christian and Jewish societies for the protection of women could accommodate only 150 girls affected by the German ban, while the rest were left to the whims of fate.[83] Such callousness on the part of the German authorities may have led Dr. Henryk Nusbaum to connect prostitution directly with the German occupation and its personnel. "We hope that sometime in the future, a free and independent Poland will not display the orgy of prostitution that we are witnessing today, under foreign rule," Nusbaum wrote. For Nusbaum, a healthy and moral sex life, one that "serves the nation," would be possible only once the city's main sex purchasers had left Warsaw.[84]

Given the gender and sexual turbulence characteristic of these years of war and occupation, it should hardly be surprising that the image of the *Matka Polka,* the iconic Polish mother, was elevated to new heights, in part as an antidote to the "disease" of prostitution. On the eve of the war, examples were taken from the Middle Ages to urge women to be "propagators of life," "Piast worker bees," and "Piast women," nurturers in the tradition of the first Polish dynasty.[85] For guardians of the patriarchal order, the war's reduction of the male presence, the greater visibility of women in the public sphere, and the disordering of gender roles required renewed emphasis on traditional models. For example, after assessing various occupational risks to women's health, *Godzina Polski* concluded, "The statistics show in the end that the 'natural' occupations for women are the healthiest ones, in other words of mother and housewife."[86] "A woman might be able to combine the roles of wife, housewife, and organizer of the household with work in a salaried occupation, though truth be told, it would frequently cost her hours of sleep and rest," *Bluszcz* reckoned. "On the other hand, the calling of motherhood . . . cannot easily coexist with [the] role of working professionally in the labor force."[87] Instead, young women should "model themselves on the virtues of their great grandmothers . . . our ancient mothers of knights, who for the good of the fatherland could rely completely on themselves as they sent their sons off to battle."[88]

The roles of wife and mother thus remained fundamental. A "good mother" was one who enriched and developed her child's soul, taught devotion to the fatherland, and above all raised the child in the likeness of God.[89] "A woman must understand that the fate of the nation rests in her hands," pronounced *Bluszcz* at the time of the Russian evacuation.[90] In *Godzina Polski* the *Matka Polka* rose to the rank of an allegorical figure who, in appealing for the preservation of values and tradition in the education of young women, could not understand why the "teaching [of] girls how to cook and order a household is often considered demeaning"; to the contrary, the formation of habits of a "good housewife" remained essential to the nation.[91] Those women who transgressed the boundaries of proper womanhood as defined by the *Matka Polka*—for example, by revealing a different notion of femininity through fashion—were often compared in the Warsaw press to prostitutes. As one reader pontificated in a letter to *Bluszcz*, young women "need to understand that the store, cashier's desk, office and editorial room is not a salon . . . and that clothing that is simple, modest and dark is more appropriate than some kind of dainty white shirt that is partially fastened." Otherwise, such women could be mistaken "for belonging to the category of women of loose moral standards."[92]

In this way the external appearance of working women could "indict them for vanity, frivolity, coquettishness; it says ugly, shallow things about them, flays them in the eyes of important and intelligent people."[93] This morally questionable choice of style was said to be typical of female office workers, who also displayed a lack of professionalism in their work and "behave as if they were at name-day parties of their friends."[94] As changing fashion spread beyond young working women, the image of the ballerina—which as mentioned was associated with the kept women of German dignitaries—was also used to shame offending women.

The liberal *Nowa Gazeta* doubted that "the independent existence of the nation" had anything to do with the length of women's skirts, but this was a minority opinion expressed in the Warsaw press.[95] More common were images like the following caricature of the female student, described by one publicist as follows: "An unkempt, unwashed frump, a product of the fin-de-siècle's decadence and buffoonery, a man in a skirt, separated from the properties of her sex while not possessing those of the other sex. . . . God, take pity! The female student . . . one leg on top of the other, the essential cigarette in her mouth, hair short and closely cut. . . . In behavior—triviality, in her soul the absence of 'healthy' values; from her lips—perverse statements; in general—an arsenal of all kinds of anachronisms."[96] Models drawn from the historical past were far more comforting. "A Polish woman is brave, proud, full of dignity, feverishly devoted to the public good, active and prudent—with a helpful hand and good advice. We honor this ideal, for which we should strive," *Bluszcz* reminded its readers at the beginning of the war.[97]

Emphasis on the demands of Polish motherhood in wartime coincided with the battering of traditional models of Polish masculinity. Simply put, Warsaw's experience of war was not conducive to spreading ideas of martial masculinity to a broader segment of the population. First, as we have already noted, five times as many Warsaw males left the city for work than for military service as conscription came to an end with the Russian evacuation, while the Germans were able to recruit only a few hundred more men among those who remained in the city to serve in Polish units under German command. Consequently, as I have argued elsewhere, only 2.5% of Warsaw's total prewar population went to war, compared to 8% for Berlin, 15% for London, and 20% for Paris.[98] The men Kutrzeba had observed in May 1916, unemployed and reduced to begging, were hard-pressed to live up to masculine ideals. As for the legendary Polish legions, they were not even allowed by the Germans to enter the city until December 1916, while Piłsudski's Second Brigade was held off even longer. By the summer of 1917, the majority of these men followed Piłsudski's lead and, having refused to subordinate themselves to the Germans, were arrested and interned in prison camps outside of Warsaw. In the meantime, the Polish legions garnered little respect during the few months they were in the city: "Discordant, disobedient, politicized, they wandered around the city like children in uniform" is how Princess Lubomirska characterized them. However, she also predicted sarcastically that "history will create a halo around the idea for which they served, and from our side it will be necessary to recognize their misery and martyrdom."[99]

The Great War thus both challenged and reinforced the *Matka Polka* in Warsaw. On the one hand, the vast majority of Polish women, many of whom had no choice but to resort to prostitution or rely on public support to make ends meet, could not possibly meet this ideal. This clearly alarmed Stanisław Dzikowski, who feared that as a consequence of the ongoing war, "the charms of the patriarchal Polish home . . . the only bastion of national life is disappearing."[100] Yet some citizens reinforced this image, particularly women of the city's elites, who used an established discourse of gender roles to translate their wartime social work and activism, much of it directed at women of lesser means, into political action. As *Bluszcz* put it, "Such active women, shoulder to shoulder with men in common work, have gained by their own labors, by their own service—like medieval squires—the spurs of modern knighthood, namely equal civil rights."[101]

New Educational Opportunities

During the war years, the teaching profession was proclaimed as the vocation outside the household to which women by nature were predisposed, one in which they could continue to uphold the *Matka Polka* model of the nurturer of future generations. "We need fewer doctors, lawyers, and directors of financial institutions than we do women prepared to fulfill the dignity of tutors of children," proclaimed *Godzina Polski*.[102] Before 1914, women already dominated the teaching ranks in elementary schools, and during the war years, some came to believe that only women should be hired at the primary level. More controversial was the employment of women as teachers in secondary schools, where the issue of their influence on boys was raised. "K.Z.," who wrote on educational matters for the "Women's Department" of *Godzina Polski*, brushed aside such concerns, arguing that the "feminization of boys" under female instruction was just as likely as the "masculinization" of girls under the guidance of male teachers.[103] In the event, high demand for secondary school teachers as a result of the growth in enrollments following the Russian evacuation as well as the relative lack of men able to meet that demand created an opening for women, who by the end of the war comprised 56% of all teachers in Warsaw's secondary schools.[104]

The wartime urgency to employ more women in the system of secondary education also served to justify the opening of higher education to women. Before the war, not a single woman was enrolled in Warsaw's two institutions of higher education, the Imperial Russian Warsaw University and the Warsaw Polytechnic Institute. Studies at both schools were suspended during the first year of the war due to the fighting. When they reopened as "Polish" institutions under German occupation in the fall of 1915, 10% of the students enrolled at Warsaw University were women. Two years later, the proportion of women studying at Warsaw University had increased to 18.2% of the 2,200 enrolled students, while the student body at the Polytechnic Institute now contained 58 women, or 4.42% of the 1,310 total enrolled.[105] Though the admission of women to university studies was not without its challenges, one can only imagine the obstacles faced by young women seeking training as technicians and engineers.

Some men clearly considered female enrollment at the university as dangerous proof of women's liberation and gender rivalry.[106] Maria Eiger (later Kamińska), who came from a wealthy assimilated Jewish family and was the daughter of a city councilman, was among the first group of fifty women students who attended the reopened university. "Girls had a multitude of difficulties with their living conditions in the dormitory," she recalled. "And not a single representative in 'Bratniak' [the student fraternity]! It made me angry. The cause of women's equality was for me a canon. Raised among boys, I considered it a point of honor from childhood not to be outdone by them. . . . I decided to go to the meeting [of 'Bratniak'] and demand the inclusion of women on the list of candidates." While Kamińska failed to convince her male colleagues, who claimed that "they themselves could look after the needs of female students," she was pleased that she had overcome her fears of speaking before large meetings and had persevered despite interruptions from those who opposed her.[107]

Despite various justifications for ongoing exclusion and discrimination, even social and cultural conservatives like Zofia Reuttówna were prepared to admit that the higher education of women was no longer socially dangerous and that "real knowledge" was necessary to women, "which they could also use to manage their households."[108] This does not mean that conservatives supported the notion of equal access, even if they agreed to opening up higher education to women. "I am a proponent of women's higher education," maintained Reuttówna in *Bluszcz*, "but I do not want to encourage in any way the general population of women to take up university studies."[109] A few years later Apolinary Krupiński, a proponent of women in higher education, regretted that "thus far, a woman, as a student, feels constrained and uncertain in her role" and that a "typical" female student thinks mainly about marriage.[110] Given such motivations, according to *Godzina Polski*, it would be "sufficient for society" if annually "a hundred or two hundred girls were able to matriculate."[111]

Even less encouragement was offered to those women seeking a technical education. To be sure, the Union of Equal Rights of Polish Women, a feminist organization, organized a special course for future female factory inspectors,[112] as well as a conference titled "Women's Work in Technical Vocations."[113] However, the "technical vocations" promoted by the Congress of Technicians in Warsaw included such occupations as "home economics innovator" and instructors in the use of water closets.[114] Thus, the notion of women's vocational education was closely tied to teaching practical skills in trades like clock-making, shoemaking, and haberdashery, with the first courses offered in August 1915.[115] A year later, practical training became available in "two-year women's courses in gardening, home economics, and commerce," which were advertised as valuable "for the future physician, and the future professor, for the director of a school or a hospital, for the craftswoman and factory worker alike."[116] According to *Bluszcz* contributor Julia Kisielewska, the opening of Warsaw University and the Polytechnic to women may have been an expression of equal rights, but she bemoaned the "senseless" lack of alternatives in vocational education.[117] For its part, *Kurjer Warszawski* called the creation of vocational education opportunities for women one of the most urgent tasks in the reconstruction of a future Polish state.[118]

Among those charged with creating those opportunities for women of lesser means were the women of landed wealth. Given their rural connections (though many resided in the city), landed women were called upon to take responsibility for "the intellectual development of the people through the systematic accustoming of their younger sisters from the village to the virtues of learning." They were to teach small crafts, which would enable village women to earn a living. Thanks to such social work, the landed woman could also "shed the reputation of a salon doll, thoughtlessly vegetating from day to day."[119] At the same time, the landed woman was expected to advance her own education while managing a rural estate. "The theory that an intelligent woman with higher education is unable to occupy herself with different parts of a farmstead is simply mistaken and appears completely without basis," opined *Godzina Polski*, "because education makes practical work easier and ennobles it, simply stripping it of all vulgarity. Work disgraces no one, to the contrary it brings honor to all."[120]

Thus, the public discourse on women's access to education reflected a great deal of ambivalence during the war years, often in the same newspapers and periodicals. Divisions did not run exclusively along gender lines but also along those of class and social origin. The "apolitical" nature of the issue favored its discussion in the legal Warsaw press, and the occupation regime refrained from sending special directives that would otherwise limit debate. Instead, the absence of formal censorship promoted a presentation of views that were limited primarily by prevailing cultural values. Most, however, would agree that vocational education for women needed to be expanded substantially, that women's secondary education needed to be reformed to meet the demands of a new era,[121] that the study of engineering and other highly technical fields was not a realistic option for women, and that while women might attain a higher education, most were ill-prepared to do so. And regardless of a woman's aspirations, a principal benefit of her education was its expected positive impact on household management. Thus, tradition accompanied change, which is not to deny that opportunities for women, or at least for some women, to acquire knowledge and expertise expanded considerably. The question was whether that knowledge and expertise would be able to erode and challenge the masculinity of certain professions, as it had for teachers in the city's secondary schools.

The Victory of the Suffrage Movement

In Warsaw's increasingly radicalized social environment, the political demands of affluent women, expressed not by wild-eyed feminists but women involved in conservative Catholic organizations, gradually appeared in a more positive light. In early 1916, as previously mentioned, nine of these women's organizations merged to form and legally register as the Union of Polish Women's Associations.[122] Almost immediately, the union began to lobby the Warsaw Citizens Committee, which had appointed a commission to draft an ordinance for new city council elections. "The fulfillment of obligations bestows rights," the union maintained in an appeal published in the larger Warsaw newspapers,[123] basing its demands for complete political rights on women's fulfillment of the duties of citizenship both inside and outside the social organizations operating under the committee's auspices.

On 14 April 1916 Prince Lubomirski met with representatives from one of the associations, the Union of Equal Rights of Polish Women, and heard their demand for equal suffrage.[124] That demand would be denied, as women had to meet higher educational and property qualifications, but Article 2 of the committee's electoral ordinance did extend voting rights to women who met the same minimum age qualifications (twenty-five years) and residential requirements (three years) as men. Interestingly, Article 4 explicitly excluded from voting those who operated houses of ill repute or rented to those who established brothels on their property. In Article 5 of the committee's ordinance, only men over the age of thirty who met voting qualifications could stand for election to city council.[125]

Although what the committee had to offer fell short of equal political rights, the electoral ordinance subsequently imposed by the Germans that actually governed Warsaw's first City Council elections denied women the vote almost entirely, save for a few single women who met its stringent property qualifications. Even these women had to cast their ballots through a male plenipotentiary. Undeterred by this defeat, the Union of Polish Women's Associations published an appeal to those very few women who could exercise their limited rights: "We can and must nurture the hope that future citizenship will bring us changes." Nonetheless, even if done through plenipotentiaries, voting was the responsibility of citizenship: "Let no woman have on her conscience the sin of neglect."[126] At the same time, a women's meeting was organized in the middle of July to promote their claims to citizenship. Librarian Jadwiga Borsteinowa expressed the frustration of these women, declaring that in the area of developing Warsaw's urban economy, "women are capable of doing more in two months than are men in ten years."[127] Similarly, the women's magazine *Bluszcz* no longer remained timid in its call for equal political rights and condemned all Polish state-building projects "that leave no place for half of the Polish nation." It was a "laughable absurdity," its editors continued, "that an alcoholic day laborer might have the right to vote, but not a woman who owns her own business, or is a teacher, a guide to young souls, or a worker who maintains her family on her own."[128]

By the time of the Polish Women's Congress of 8–9 September 1917, the Union of Polish Women's Associations counted fifteen different organizations, including the Association of United Female Landowners, the Catholic Polish

FIGURE 13.   Union of Polish Women marching in 3 May 1916 procession.
Muzeum Narodowe w Warszawie.

Women's Union, the Christian Society for the Protection of Women, and the
Society of Young Christian Women, groups that hardly would have been considered radical or feminist in any other circumstances.[129] On the eve of the congress,
the magazine *Rozwaga* reprinted the petition of the famous novelist and writer
Eliza Orzeszkowa and others to Poles from Lithuania who had been elected
to the First Russian State Duma in 1906, calling upon them to support equal
political rights.[130] Presiding over the congress was one of the movement's most
respected representatives, Dr. Justyna Budzińska-Tylicka.[131] The main items on
the agenda were the war's impact on the women's movement and the progress
that had been made in these trying conditions. Addressing the congress were the
most important women's activists from the prewar period, and delegates heard
reports on the role of women in municipal government, on political equality
and civil rights, and on women's involvement in social organizations. The congress passed a number of resolutions, the most important of which included the
demand for equal political rights. Particularly in regard to institutions of self-
government like the Warsaw City Council, it called for the immediate realization
of those rights, which were not to be limited to passive voting rights but should
also include active rights so that women could stand for election and begin to
participate directly in representative assemblies. The congress also resolved to
create a political organization to advocate for women's issues on an active and

ongoing basis and to call a National Women's Council, which would participate in future meetings of the International Committee for Women's Rights.[132]

The executive committee of the Polish Women's Congress, acting in the spirit of its resolutions calling for the immediate realization of equal political rights, twice petitioned the Warsaw City Council and Magistrate in November 1917 to reform the electoral ordinance of the previous year.[133] In December, the congress organized another women's meeting, which overflowed the theater on Śniadecki Street where it was held. At this assembly, speaker after speaker noted the persecution of women and the systematic rejection by men of their efforts to assume leadership positions, regardless of the extent of their participation and involvement in public life.[134]

Shortly after the Polish Women's Congress, *Nowa Gazeta* stated the obvious: "This small women's parliament, which took place in the last couple of days, has proven that Polish women have managed to strengthen their forces in recent years."[135] Consequently, men indeed began to listen and to accept what had previously been unacceptable, part of a redefinition in the political discourse over what exactly constituted "radical women" in the public sphere. In this regard, the threat to the social order posed in the streets of Warsaw by *rezerwistki* and other women of lesser means helped to legitimize the demands of affluent women in conservative Catholic organizations for political rights. Consequently, many of Warsaw's important male public figures, conservative and Catholic themselves, began to voice their support for the equal rights of women in self-governing institutions. Following a meeting with the women's delegation led by Budzińska-Tylicka, City Council vice president Józef Zawadzki declared his support for equal political rights for women in future electoral ordinances, while Mayor Piotr Drzewiecki promised that service in city administrative posts would become open to women after 1 January 1918.[136] Strategic male backing also came from Franciszek Nowodworski, the president of the penal division of the Supreme Court under the Regency Council, who came out publicly in favor of women's suffrage and their right to stand for election to a future Polish parliament.[137]

In making the final push to achieve their goals, female activists decided to campaign actively for the inclusion of women's rights in the planned constitution of the quasi-independent Polish state that the German occupation regime sought to establish during the second half of the war. The Polish Women's Congress of September 1917 directly confronted politicians with the question "Will you support in the future constitution the cause of equal political rights for women?"[138] "If a woman has the right to go to the scaffold," *Bluszcz* wrote in reference to the French Jacobin Convention of 1793, "she also has the right to mount the podium."[139] In anticipation of an unfavorable decision of the German-sponsored State Council in this regard in the summer of 1918, activists intensified their press campaign: "They will refuse women voting rights. Therefore they will refuse women the rights of citizenship. The largest Polish democratic circles should be reminded of this injustice and insult."[140] It was precisely the moderate political milieu that feared women would vote for extremist groups—clericalist, socialist, radical populist—and, therefore, looked unfavorably on women's suffrage. Indeed, conservative Catholic politicians no longer opposed women's political participation and actually came out in favor of equal rights. Such support was even more forthcoming from socialist and democratic left-wing organizations.[141]

The limited Polish historiography on women's experiences during the First World War has focused almost exclusively on the auxiliary organizations that supported the military activity of the Polish legions initially formed under Austrian command. According to Sylwia Kuźma-Markowska, these organizations played "the most significant role" in the political mobilization of Polish women during the war.[142] It was their successful effort, Joanna Dufrat argues, to merge women's participation in the struggle for independence with emancipatory aspirations that culminated in the granting of women's suffrage by the new Polish government in December 1918.[143] These organizations, which had an estimated combined membership of sixteen thousand in the middle of 1916 and perhaps twice that many members by the end of the war, seemed to have had little presence in Warsaw, tied as they were to the Supreme National Committee in Krakow, to which the Polish legions were politically subordinate. To be sure, they formed departments of equal rights, but they were divided over the tactical issue of when that political agenda should be pushed. The Women's Military Ambulance League, the stronger of the auxiliary organizations in Warsaw, studiously avoided political demands. Toward the end of the war and on the eve of German withdrawal from the city, the press published its "Call to all Polish Women" to provide material and moral support for a new Polish Army, regardless of age or social position: "Let every Polish woman, taking as her example the women of France, state her preparedness to bring one or two Polish soldiers under her care; let her strengthen them with her moral influence, and provide them material help according to her abilities, possibilities and good will."[144]

In Warsaw, however, what counted among male political elites were the abilities and the organizational skills women had demonstrated on the home front, rather than in support of the Polish legions, which drew only a few hundred soldiers from the city in any case. Indeed, as we have seen, social work constituted the main tool affluent women used for exerting political leverage. What is indisputable is that by the end of the war and the emergence of a Polish state, the case for women's suffrage and equal political rights had essentially been won. In this regard, the wartime experience of Warsaw women forms part of a larger European story, with the notable exception of France, even if similar ends were reached by different means. Similar as well was the subsequent defusing of the women's movement in Poland, whose success in achieving both active and passive political rights was in part due to the threat to the social order posed by women of lesser means who themselves did not participate in campaigns for rights and representation. Moreover, Warsaw's wartime suffragettes were not primarily feminists of conviction but feminists of circumstance, and thus were not prepared or willing to sustain the momentum of the war years.

Voter turnout was high in Warsaw for the parliamentary elections held on 26 January 1919, the first in independent interwar Poland. With approximately 70% of the eligible electorate casting ballots in the city,[145] it is safe to say that the majority of adult women age twenty-one and older participated in voting. First and foremost, these were women of lesser means, who comprised the vast majority of Warsaw's women. Having been awarded active political rights, women also stood for election to the Sejm in 1919. The National Election Organization of Polish Women was founded to acquaint women with the electoral process.[146] At the same time, the Central Committee of Equal Political Rights of Polish Women called upon all women to prepare for the obligations of citizenship resulting from the achievement of suffrage.[147] Zofia Staniszewska, writing in the pages of *Bluszcz*, made the following proposition: "Men can get along without us. There are enough women that we should be able to put together our own list of male and female candidates. Let there be people of 'good will' on this list. Let the most noble of individuals meet there, the most idealistic in spirit, the most pure of sentiment and effort. Let apostles of honest selflessness come together there."[148] Not all were so confident about the potential results, particularly for women candidates. Kazimiera Neronowiczowa admitted less than a month before the elections, "We have to say clearly to ourselves that the majority of us are poorly prepared to assume these responsibilities."[149] In the event only five women were elected throughout the territories of the former Polish Kingdom and Galicja, thus constituting a mere 1.7% of the new members of Parliament from those electoral districts.[150]

Women may not have voted for women, but gender boundaries were transgressed during the war years—in politics, education, and cultural norms, the latter expressed most visibly in forms of dress in which "women liberated themselves from prewar styles faster than men," according to Irena Krzywicka.[151] These transgressions, however, were driven more by necessity than ideology, primarily by conservative middle-aged women from the city's elites, and, in fashion, by their daughters working in offices and (like Krzywicka) studying at the university. Voting rights, greater access to educational opportunities, and shorter skirts may have trickled down to women of lesser means, but these were not their concerns during the war years. Instead of demanding the right to vote, they demanded from male elites the right to food and the right to housing, for themselves and for their children. They found what they had in common with women from the upper classes and the intelligentsia through philanthropy and public assistance, and when the delivery of aid became disrupted or threatened, one can imagine the heated exchanges between and among women in those public spaces where they encountered one another.

These two groups of women also shared primary roles as wives and mothers in the family and in a patriarchal home setting. The *Matka Polka* model, as Anna Żarnowska has shown, had broken its class confines before the war, extending beyond the nobility and intelligentsia into the working class.[152] Thus, both groups justified their political demands in terms of their nurturing roles in the public as well as private spheres and, for women of lesser means in particular, in the relative absence of men. For Roman Catholic if not Jewish women, an imagined, mythical female figure whose sacrifices are made for others—faith, fatherland, and family—and never for herself buttressed those roles. Thus, when *rezerwistki* and others demonstrated in front of the municipal administrative offices, they engaged in political action on behalf of their hungry families. When affluent women demanded the right of citizenship or access to higher education, it was never meant to conflict with their traditional roles in the household, but to aid and abet them. Thus the boundaries of gender were reset, the traditional and modern roles of women were reconciled, and the vast majority of women from all walks of life chose overwhelmingly to entrust their fates and those of their children with men, just as they had in the past. These developments, too, are part of a larger European and Western story, despite the different kind of home front that served as the generator of both change and retrenchment in Warsaw.

WARSAW'S WARTIME CULTURE WARS

The exigencies of the Great War in Warsaw, as we have seen, produced or exacerbated conflicts along and across boundaries defined by class, ethnicity, gender, and politics. However, these demands also had cultural impacts, evident as early as the war's first weeks. What follows is an attempt to link metropolitan cultural life in Warsaw to the everyday social and economic realities of the First World War. For Warsaw in particular and for east-central Europe more generally, the existing historiography offers little assistance. A recent conference devoted to "cultures at war" in the Austro-Hungarian territories, to take but one example, failed for the most part to connect cultural issues to the material factors that determined the substance of daily lives in wartime.[1] However, I found some guidance for my efforts in the studies of the wartime cultural histories of Paris, London, and Berlin contained in the second volume of the major collaborative project *Capital Cities at War*, edited by Jay Winter and Jean-Louis Robert.[2] Particularly useful is Winter's general observation that "the first fully industrialized war in history precipitated a deluge of traditional forms of language, perception and signifying practices."[3] This "nostalgic turn" was one vector of metropolitan cultural life, according to Winter, while the other moved in the opposite direction—that is, in anticipation of the future.

By "cultural life" in the following pages I refer mainly to different modes and sites of cultural expression, which were in turn challenged, reshaped, or created by various disruptions to prewar routines. Since the war affected practically everything, including and especially the food supply but also transportation, street illumination, alcohol consumption, the availability of clothing and footwear, home and family life, not to mention the city's demography, anxious debates over entertainments, fashion, and appropriate cultural practices and behaviors in wartime reverberated in public discourse. Left relatively unchecked by military censorship, these debates reflected more often than not preexisting social, ethnic, and gender-based tensions that, as highlighted in previous chapters, were sharpened by the exactions of the Great War.

However, there was one rather large group in Warsaw, the military and civilian personnel of the German occupation force, that from 1915 to 1918 effectively isolated itself from its surroundings by creating a culture of privilege and abundance, which when contrasted to the culture of poverty that constituted the everyday experience of the vast majority of Varsovians and came largely at their expense, appears as obscene today as it did to those participating in the May 1917 "sweet-shop riots" angered by conspicuous German consumption. This culture of the occupier, too, constituted a "culture at war," one that those who witnessed it deeply resented. Thus, we begin with a diversion into another world of food and material culture, and of entertainments, peculiar to Warsaw's wartime German visitors.

Deutschtum in Warschau

The German officials and troops who resided in Warsaw from 1915 to 1918 inhabited a world of their own, materially and culturally. Their numbers peaked at twelve thousand soldiers and eighteen thousand officials[4] but were obviously much larger for the entire course of the occupation when one takes into account transfers and reinforcements. Moreover, they were joined by German merchants who provided special goods and services to the occupation regime, as well as the occasional tourist. According to Aleksander Kraushar, the presence of German firms in Warsaw's midtown business district was ubiquitous: "In one hundred years following the Russian invasion and their living among us, they never managed to post as many Muscovite specimens of an exotic eastern character in stores and on signboards, in as many commercial establishments of different kinds, as the Germans did in barely the first few months of their economy," thus giving "the capital city of Poland the character of a Berlin branch."[5] A rare glimpse into this world is contained in a guidebook that the German state publishing house in Warsaw published in at least four editions. In its fourth "revised" edition from 1917 (and likely its predecessors as well), this *Weg-Weiser durch Warschau* advertised its "special attention to everything that the German soldier, official and traveler must know" about the city.[6] The price of the 1917 version of the *Weg-Weiser* was thirty pfennig at the time of printing but had risen to forty pfennig once it became available for sale, a sign of the era's rapid inflation.

WARSAW'S WARTIME CULTURE WARS

Before a reader began to explore the "Warsaw for Germans" in the *Weg-Weiser*, he (this German world was almost entirely a male one) was treated to advertisements aimed at this market, beginning with the banking services offered by the Warsaw branch of the Ostbank for Commerce and Trade, the "paying agent" of the Imperial German Civil Administration in the General-Government, which had taken over the former Russian State Bank building on Bielańska Street. Headquartered in Königsberg with subsidiaries throughout Germany and the occupied territories of the Russian Empire, and capitalized at 32 million marks, the Ostbank apparently faced no competition in Warsaw from other German banks. Not so the variety of firms that competed to equip the army and officials in uniforms, leather garments and goods, footwear, "military effects," and tailoring services. The Berlin merchant S. Adam, with his convenient Warsaw location on 11 Krakowskie Przedmieście Street, offered "custom-made" garments and articles to officers and officials, while S. Zan aimed at a larger market, offering both furs and rubber covers in addition to leather garments. As "tailor to the army," Zan also promised to fill orders for alterations and repairs in eight hours at cheap prices, faster than the twenty-four–hour tailoring services offered by D. Karp, also at "discount prices" for the army.

Others vied for purchases from the army commissariat and military hospitals; the "Proviant" Dairy Products Company on 44 Chmielna Street offered itself as the "cheapest source" of butter, eggs, cheeses, and honey, while the Wachler Brothers "National" on 39 Jerozolimskie Boulevard stood out for its variety of goods, ranging from alcohol and tobacco products, to dairy products and condiments, and finally soap, candles, suspenders, and shoe polish. J. H. Nisenkern, by contrast, focused its business on selling soap, candles, starch, bleach, brushes, and writing materials to officials; the Cukierman Brothers offered drugs, dyes, perfumes, and cosmetics; and the Wertheim firm specialized in the sale of chocolates, bonbons, and marmalades, including products from the "G.G. Lardelli" factory. "Trier" sold Mosel, Saar, and Rhein wines along with other "war supplies," including cigars, cigarettes, and other tobacco products, to the army commissariat. "Salvator," a brewery on 108 Marszałkowska Street, sold its products "only to military canteen and casino purchasers," and its pub on 65 Grzybowska Street offered special discounts to members of the army. Some of these merchants sought to highlight their convenient location. G. Rosen, who sold goods to military canteens from its location on 21 Królewska Street, was only "3 minutes from the Command headquarters," while Józef Rosenberg, supplier of foodstuffs to the Warsaw Citadel, military hospitals, soldiers' homes, and canteens, was a mere "three steps from the Vienna Station" on 28 Jerozolimskie Boulevard.

The German traveler to the city, meanwhile, was invited to stay at the luxurious 250-room Hotel de l'Europe (known to Varsovians as the Hotel Europejski), with

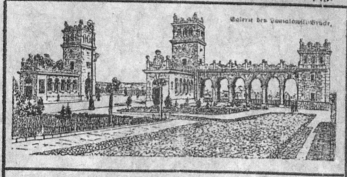

Preis 40 Pfg.
Preis 30 Pfg.

Galerie des Poniatowski-Grabes.

Weg-
Weiser
durch
Warschau

Kurzgefaßter Führer durch die Stadt Warschau mit
besonderer Berücksichtigung alles dessen, was der
deutsche Soldat, Beamte und Reisende wissen muß.

Vierte verbesserte Auflage.

1917
Verlag der Deutschen Staatsdruckerei Warschau.

FIGURE 14. Front cover of *Weg-Weiser durch Warschau* (1917). Biblioteka
Narodowa.

its "comfortable location in the city center," and to dine at its restaurant offering "exquisite cuisine" and "a large stock of vintage wines." The Hotel Europejski, despite its advertised "affordable prices," at four marks per night tied the Hotel Polonia on Jerozolimskie Boulevard near the Vienna train station as the most expensive of the seven Warsaw hotels recommended by the *Weg-Weiser*. Lodging at the Hotel Bristol, built at the end of the nineteenth century and today the most expensive of the city's hotels, was then a comparative bargain at a mere three marks per night.[7]

Our German traveler, if staying at the Europejski or Bristol, would have had an easy walk to 8 Krakowskie Przedmieście Street and the restaurant of J. Lijewski and Company, which had received "multiple awards," or from the Polonia and the Vienna Station to the "Ermitage" Wine Bar and First-Class Restaurant. The Korona Brewery on 40 Grzybowska to the north of the Vienna Station served both light and dark beers. For those strolling in the Saxon Garden, butter and coffee cakes could be purchased from the Kotlicki sweetshop at the Gate 3 entrance, and fine pastries from B. Semadeni at the Opera House. For guests returning to the Europejski, such delicacies were available from L. Lourse and Company. Soldiers, officials, and travelers alike—visitors all—could choose to purchase postcards "of all kinds" from A. D. Pacanowski on 25 Bielańska Street or from the "great selection" offered by his competitor Borstein and Richter on 3 Bielańska, which may have included one titled "Ring around Warsaw" formed from the images of German and Austro-Hungarian Army commanders and generals, headed by Hindenburg and Ludendorff.[8] "Volkskunst" on the corner of Świętokrzyska and Mazowiecka competed with the "Haus Lowitsch" adjacent to the Europejski in the sale of "typical" Polish folk art and souvenirs, though the "Haus Lowitsch" sought to distinguish itself by its "German" customer service and its "presents for children."

The actual narrative of the *Weg-Weiser* began with a brief three-page history of Warsaw, ending with German "conquest" of the city on 5 August 1915. It was followed by a list of German military and civilian authorities and institutions, the location of German post and telegraph offices, registration obligations for both resident and nonresident civilians, and information on the control of goods and foodstuffs coming into or leaving Warsaw. Otherwise, one would hardly know from the *Weg-Weiser* that Warsaw was a city under wartime occupation. There was information on train stations and schedules, Warsaw's trolley system and fares (with map), steamboats and their schedules to and from Płock and Włocławek, prevailing exchange rates between the ruble and the mark, and recommended hotels, wine bars, cafes, pastry and sweet shops, dining halls, and bathhouses. Of the military dining halls listed, officers and officials enjoyed exclusive access to that located at the General German Casino on Nowy Świat Street, while the rank-and-file could dine at any of Warsaw's three Soldiers' Homes. The Soldiers' Homes, in addition to dinner, offered coffee and supper, games, lectures, newspapers, books, motion pictures, interdenominational pastoral care, and—most recently—instruction in the Polish language.

Recommended entertainment included the city's theaters but "above all the opera" and the "especially remarkable" Warsaw ballet, whose female dancers, as noted in the previous chapter, appealed to Germans of higher rank.[9] According to Kraushar, the only place that Germans "behaved themselves, relatively beyond reproach" during the occupation was at the Grand Theater (*Teatr Wielki*) during opera performances. Otherwise, "their cynically lascivious groups insulted all notions of propriety."[10] Basic theater entrance fees, as well as those for the Philharmonic, were sixty pfennig, but soldiers could receive discounts for more expensive seats. Also recommended was the Museum of Industry and Agriculture. For sightseeing, Zygmunt III's column in Castle Square topped the list of monuments, which also included reminders of the recently deposed Russian Empire, one to Ivan Paskevich, the Russian general who suppressed the 1830 insurrection, and another to Alexander I at the Warsaw Citadel. St. John's Cathedral in the Old Town headed a long list of churches, which concluded with a paragraph on two Protestant churches, the recently constructed Orthodox Cathedral on Saxon Square, "with the highest tower in Warsaw,"[11] and the Great Synagogue on Tłomackie Street. Of the city's libraries, only the Krasiński and Warsaw University libraries were worth mentioning, while today's tourists would be familiar with the recommended list of official and historic buildings, including the Royal Castle, the university, the Namiestnikowski Palace (today's presidential palace), the Krasiński Palace, and various sites in Old Town, including the site of today's Fukier Restaurant, then the residence of the Fukier (Fugger) family. Parks and gardens, beginning with the Łazienki, also beckoned the German visitor, and in the surrounding area, Praga, Wilanów, Natolin, and Modlin were said to be of special interest.

This wonderful world awaiting the soldiers and employees of the German occupation regime as well as German travelers to the city on official business and visiting family members was one that intersected only in a few places with that of Varsovians. The city's elites would have shared in German officialdom's praises of theater and opera, and lower-ranking German personnel and their civilian contacts would have shared in fueling black markets and in spreading venereal disease, but not much else. German separateness extended to public transportation, as soldiers had exclusive riding and seating priority over civilians in specially designated cars on the city's functioning trolleys and, moreover, were absolved from paying fares for their use.[12] Such practices, not to mention the food and material culture enjoyed by the occupying Germans, were bound to breed envy and disgust among ordinary Varsovians whose everyday lives were characterized by scarcity and privation and whose coerced sacrifices enabled Germans in the city to live in this separate land of abundance, discounts, and cheap prices.

Warsaw's elites may not have been residents in much of this land known only to the German occupiers, but their economic and social advantages created a sphere of common cultural interest with German officialdom (as in devotion to opera or dining at the Hotel Europejski) while simultaneously separating them from ordinary Varsovians, who themselves were divided along lines of religion, ethnicity, class, generation, and gender. One glance at the menu prepared by Princess Lubomirska for her guests (including Beseler, as well as other German, Austro-Hungarian, and Polish dignitaries) following the proclamation of the Regency Council is symbolic of the sizable gap between the elite and popular classes:

> *Potage à la Reine*
> *Petits patés*
> *Selle de lievre*
> *Salade assortie*
> *Choux-fleurs polonaise*
> *Bombe au chocolat*
> *Petits gateaux*
> Modest as befits wartime.
> *Dessert*
> Salted Italian walnuts
> White and Red wine—ending with a sweet old Hungarian.[13]

These divisions also extended to cultural preferences and to cultural policy, as elites sought to define "national" norms of propriety in wartime and their cultural forms when and where they had the opportunity. In the process, they waged battles in the press and through political institutions against already existing and emerging forms of popular culture, often connecting their "alien" with their "depraved" nature, though ultimate victory proved elusive. Opera survived the war, but so too did cabaret.

The Show Must Go On

A year before the German "conquest" of Warsaw, the imposition of martial law in the city accompanied the outbreak of the war. By Russian government order, state monopoly stores were closed and existing supplies of vodka destroyed. For a time all restaurants in the city were closed, save for those in the Europejski, Polonia, and

Bristol hotels, which themselves were initially forbidden to sell "even a single glass" containing alcohol. Meanwhile, new traffic restrictions included a ban on private automobiles from entering the Warsaw military region as well as the cancellation of a planned pilgrimage from Warsaw to the shrine of the Black Madonna in Częstochowa.[14] The Russian Army's requisitioning of horses led to a decline in vehicular traffic in the city and delays in waste removal.[15] These were the first signs of cultural disruption, and they would not be the last. Two weeks into the war, the Russian military authorities banned photography in public spaces, though Warsaw photographers would maintain a brisk business well into 1915 as Russian officers and soldiers posed for individual and group photos in private spaces to send to their families.[16] As summer vacations came to an abrupt end, the Russian government, acting on the initiative of the Warsaw Citizens Committee, decided on an early reopening of the city's primary schools, but then postponed the opening of the academic year in secondary and higher schools until mid-November.[17]

The decision to reopen the city's primary schools was part of a calculated strategy to calm public opinion through a "business as usual" approach following the initial panic that accompanied the outbreak of the war. In this regard, the city's pro-Russian elites were relatively successful, which Stanisław Dzikowski attributed to "the liquidation of all hopes for free national development" after the Revolution of 1905, as well as to the elites' purported worship of theater. Railing against this "deity," Dzikowski condemned *Kurjer Warszawski* for continuing to devote major print space to Lucyna Messal, then "the prima donna of the Warsaw operetta," as German forces marched on the city in October 1914.[18] Well before that, *Kurjer Warszawski* cited strong theater attendance, along with its own advertising revenues, a thriving café and sweetshop business, and the frequency of religious observance as visible signs that life was returning to "normal" despite the restrictions of martial law.[19] Soon the cinemas reopened, revitalized by the showing of motion pictures depicting war themes, to packed houses.[20] The daily even applauded the decision to open the fall horseracing season as planned, "insofar as it helps maintain a sense of normal life." Though it acknowledged the receipt of letters expressing "that life in the city should be more serious" under the wartime circumstances, *Kurjer Warszawski* defended "amusements," whether at the theater, cafés, cinemas, or racetrack, which continued to employ "thousands" at a time when many other Varsovians were losing their jobs.[21] As we shall see, the conservative daily soon changed its tune on some of these "amusements" once they were determined to be in violation of acceptable cultural norms.

Maintaining business as usual was difficult under any circumstances but nearly impossible in moments of acute crisis, beginning with the German offensive targeted at Warsaw in October. In his diary entries beginning at the end of September, Walenty Miklaszewski recorded the paralyzing impact of the fighting on social and cultural life in the city and its reduction of philosophers into bar-barians at the sight of bread and lard.[22] The Russian authorities now imposed a total ban on the sale of all drinks containing alcohol in the city, including beer and wine, which led to the closing of many of the first-class restaurants that had still been allowed to serve them.[23] As the fighting continued around Warsaw in mid-October, private telephone use was also suspended for several days by order of the Russian military authorities.[24] However, as Miklaszewski noted, the show went on in the city's theaters and cinemas, particularly when their repertoires served the objectives of Russian "government agitation" against the enemy. There was also a genuine loosening of the state's cultural policy. For Miklaszewski, the variety of plays from which to choose was "unbelievable" compared to the recent past and included *Dziady* (*Forefathers' Eve*) by Adam Mickiewicz and *Wesele* (*The Wedding Party*) by Stanisław Wyspiański, both of which had been banned from the Warsaw stage before the war.[25]

Early November brought news of the Russian declaration of war against the Ottoman Empire following the attack of the Turkish fleet on Odessa, which cre-ated a panic among Turks in Warsaw who feared arrest and deportation. Dozens of Turkish bakeries and sweetshops in Warsaw closed as a result, further reducing the diversity of the city's existing food culture.[26] At the same time, private and commercial riverboat traffic ceased as a consequence of the military requisition-ing of ships and boats. By the end of the month, Russian military and civilian dig-nitaries had largely taken over Warsaw's first-class hotels, while the city's smaller hotels and pensions were "overflowing" with provincial landowners and "almost the entire provincial intelligentsia," especially from the legal profession because of the suspension of courts in areas occupied by the Germans.[27] Nonetheless, as the war's first winter approached, there was still sufficient optimism in a prospec-tive Russian victory in the aftermath of the German retreat from Warsaw that the Museum of Industry and Agriculture struck upon the idea of creating a war museum based on artifacts and trophies collected from the present conflict, in a combination of propaganda and entertainment that anticipated the Vienna War Exhibition of 1916–17 and that of London's Imperial War Museum.[28]

Hopes for an early end of the war and a return to prewar conditions were dashed in early 1915 with renewed German air raids on the city. Warsaw's print culture now began to experience a serious crisis as a combined consequence of increased censorship of the press and an increasingly acute paper shortage. Pre-ventive censorship had been established as early as 30 July 1914 but seemed to have little visible impact on publishing, except during the height of the October "Battle of Warsaw." While the paper shortage was felt almost immediately, special supplements and *jednodniówki* (one-day leaflets promoting a certain cause) were published in five thousand– to ten thousand–copy print runs. However, after the

New Year, as both the paper shortage and censorship became more severe, the leaflets and special supplements practically disappeared, and ever larger blank spots began to take over newspaper and magazine column space.[29] Many publications were subsequently driven out of business as a result. Particularly hard hit were weeklies and monthlies, among them Warsaw's only prewar commercially successful women's periodical, *Bluszcz* (*Ivy*), which began the war as a weekly and struggled against the paper shortage to continue as a monthly, before ceasing publication entirely in the middle of 1915.[30] Before the war, some 169 Polish-language periodical press titles were published in Warsaw. By the time of the Russian evacuation in August 1915, that number had dropped to fifty-six.[31] Polish-language dailies, however, fared better than their Yiddish- and Hebrew-language counterparts, which the Russian authorities suspended entirely in July 1915.

As the façade of normality crumbled in 1915, the city's conservative nationalist and Catholic elite, their main organ *Kurjer Warszawski*, and the Warsaw Citizens Committee on which they were strongly represented sought to preserve what they perceived as the cultural foundations of "Polish civilization." This meant above all the preservation of the prewar entertainments enjoyed by the elite as well as their cultural norms. Thus, *Kurjer Warszawski* highlighted that even during the course of the Russian evacuation, the city's theaters and cafés remained full of patrons, who also continued to take their afternoon and evening strolls in the city's parks.[32]

Among the first buildings taken over by the Warsaw Citizens Committee during the Russian evacuation were those housing state-managed and financed theaters, which were claimed as municipal property days before the committee established itself as the new City Administration.[33] Basically, the committee's decision applied to the complex on Theater Square, hosting then as it does now plays, opera, and ballet on separate stages in the Grand Theater. In effect, this takeover amounted to a nationalization of the Russian state theaters, and their maintenance as "Polish theaters" became one of the City Administration's top priorities. Even the otherwise parsimonious Germans proposed to help by renting the Grand Theater every two weeks for three afternoon shows to entertain the troops.[34] At the same time, the Warsaw Citizens Committee raised no objections to the establishment of Yiddish theaters when queried by the German authorities, so long as the city was absolved of any financial responsibility for them.[35] Because of the rough similarity between Yiddish and German and the lack of affinity between German and Polish, entertainment-starved German officers unable to communicate in Polish flocked to the Yiddish theater.[36]

The City Administration maintained its support of elite entertainments until February 1917, at which point in an effort to gain relief from the pressures on its budget by German exactions and other "unreasonable obligations," it declared that its financial difficulties would force the closing of the opera, the cancellation of all contracts, and the limiting of future funding of all of its theaters to building maintenance.[37] In response, the Germans proposed major cuts in the city's existing expenditures on the police, public works, welfare and public philanthropy, hospitals, and public kitchens—that is, everything but the city's theaters.[38] Somehow in this game of bluff, funds were found for the shows to go on. Dzikowski, who had associated Warsaw's "passivity" and "lethargy" at the beginning of the war with the cultivation of theater by its elites, was still amazed at the end of March 1917 that theater was the only thing that seemed to animate the city, though "judging by the lesser talent appearing there, it too belongs to another epoch." Alas, the great soprano Lucyna Messal, whose praises in the Warsaw press during the first year of the war Dzikowski had then criticized as evidence of the city's nonchalance, had fled with the Russians. Fearing that Warsaw with its now "dull and colorless streets" was losing "its old character," what concerned Dzikowski even more was the disappearance of "its frivolities and escapes . . . its customs and peculiarities . . . its humor with its special language."[39]

Frivolity, escapes, and humor, however, had only disappeared from those public spaces and cultural sites frequented by Warsaw's upper classes and, for a time, from restaurants and taverns during the period of wartime prohibition under the Russians. Indeed, the combination of prohibition, the curfews that accompanied martial law, and an energy crunch that led to severe cutbacks in transportation and street illumination seemed to snuff out what had been a thriving night life before the war. Prohibition was gradually repealed under the Germans, but getting around a city that remained in the dark became ever more difficult and dangerous. Entertainments, some of them underground, still abounded in the dark, but their associated "frivolities" and "escapes" were defined as "inappropriate" and "immoral" by Warsaw's elites, who fought hard to control and even suppress the spaces where they occurred. In contrast to theater, opera, and ballet, these were definitely shows that violated elite norms and, therefore, should not be allowed to go on.

Prohibition, Curfews, and Their Discontents

The Russian government's decision to ban sales of alcohol, to close all state monopoly stores in the city, which had employed some eight hundred people, and to destroy all existing supplies of vodka was met with approval by prewar temperance advocates like Princess Lubomirska, who attributed the city's calm demeanor at the outbreak of the war to the absence of vodka.[40] The destruction of vodka at one store on Zimna Street, however, was not treated calmly by a large crowd that had to be dispersed by shots fired into the air.[41] In time, the Russian authorities relaxed restrictions enough to permit first-class restaurants to serve drinks before an officially mandated closing time of 11:00 p.m. For some of these restaurants, the restricted hours were enough to keep them from reopening, while a police ban on sales of beer, wine, and mead at second- and third-class restaurants drove many of the latter completely out of business.[42] Thus, by early September 1914, the only way to get a legal drink in Warsaw was in a few establishments that catered to the wealthy and to high-ranking officials and officers.

As a result of the curfew as well as the coal shortage, Warsaw's trolleys stopped running at 11:30 p.m., an hour earlier than before the war.[43] By 1:00 a.m., large parts of the city turned dark, as two-thirds of its street lamps were taken out of service due to reductions in the use of gas and electricity.[44] Consequently, the night life of the city, where restaurants of all sorts had once stayed open until 3:00 a.m. and cabarets until 5:00 in the morning, died completely. Lamented one *Kurjer Warszawski* beat reporter, "Now one can walk on Nowy Świat after midnight and not meet a single pedestrian."[45] When in early October the Russian authorities imposed a total empire-wide ban on the sale of all alcoholic beverages, including beer and wine, the few first-class restaurants in Warsaw that had still been allowed to serve them also closed.[46] The social discrimination that had characterized the prohibition of alcohol up to that point now came to an official end as the manufacture, sale, and consumption of alcohol became criminalized.

First, the Russians had to police themselves. As noted by Andrzej Chwalba, the very people empowered to enforce the prohibition regulations were often the ones to violate them, thus encouraging the population to do so as well.[47] For example, in the wee hours of the morning of 13 December 1914, city police raided the headquarters of the "Russian Corner" club on 73 Marszałkowska Street where some fifty people—state officials, military officers, their wives, as well as some professional gamblers—were found with spirits, vodka, and cognac. The manager of the club's buffet was subsequently fined 1,000 rubles for the illegal sale of alcohol, and the club was closed for the duration of the war.[48] A few weeks later, a number of Warsaw hotels were fined for serving alcohol on New Year's Eve, including the Hotel Bristol, which had been largely occupied by Russians of high rank; the Bristol was also levied a 1,000-ruble penalty for violating the October prohibition decree.[49] Meanwhile, a thriving bootleg trade developed, contributing to rising crime rates in the city and creating a fertile field for police and administrative corruption. The arrests of several "well-known" purveyors and producers of prohibited vodka, cognacs, and wine in late February 1915 created something of a "sensation" in the local press, especially since the arrested had acquired hospital vouchers permitting the legal use of alcohol for medicinal purposes, most of which was then sold illegally on the side.[50] As discussed previously, the rising number of deaths caused by alcohol poisoning following the total prohibition decree reveals the quality of some of the illegal spirits that were being manufactured and sold in Warsaw.

While the imperial Russian authorities never wavered in maintaining prohibition throughout the empire despite a major loss in state revenues, in Warsaw they slightly loosened existing curfews in the city in early 1915 so that first-class restaurants were allowed to expand their hours and remain open until 12:30 a.m., cabarets until 11:15 p.m., second-class restaurants to 11:00 p.m., and third-class restaurants until 9:00 p.m., with theatrical and other performances allowed until 11:00 p.m.[51] While the main purpose appears to have been to create incentives for the reopening of restaurants and other places of entertainment, this adjusted hierarchy of restrictions again favored Warsaw's elites and Russian officialdom. With no legal possibility to serve even beer, however, the restaurants continued to struggle. That this aspect of Warsaw's war was far from over was perhaps best reflected by the dumping in May 1915 of brewed beer from the previous year into the sewers, representing the abandonment of all hope that the ban on sales would be lifted any time soon.[52] Ongoing restrictions on trolley traffic due to the energy shortfall, lack of trained personnel as a consequence of military conscription, and the inability to repair and replace streetcar wheels also acted as a disincentive to the city's restaurant business, as can be noted in petitions and complaints addressed to the Warsaw Citizens Committee.[53]

The emphasis on sobriety, the reconfiguration of street life, the retreat of urban civilization to an earlier, less mechanized, and less illuminated period, and the significant reduction of vehicular traffic was common in the capitals of the main belligerent powers during the Great War, according to Emmanuelle Cronier.[54] The widely perceived need for moral and material austerity on the London, Berlin, and Paris home fronts during the bloodbath was also shared by the leadership of the Warsaw Citizens Committee, which strongly supported the Russian government's decision to prohibit the sale and consumption of alcohol. Many Polish conservatives and nationalists had long perceived alcohol as the ruin of the lower classes of both city and countryside, and the tavern as an instrument of Jewish profit and exploitation. Thus, as the Warsaw Citizens Committee took over as the City Administration during the course of the Russian evacuation, its decision to maintain the Russian-imposed ban on the public consumption of alcohol hardly came as a surprise.[55]

The Germans, however, had other ideas. To be sure, Warsaw came under martial law, and a much stricter curfew of 9:30 p.m. was imposed at the beginning of the occupation, but these were temporary measures that the Germans subsequently relaxed.[56] In any case, these restrictions on nightlife were not allowed to interfere with the Germans' demand for beer and the opening of beer cellars to serve them, a decision that undermined the committee's attempt to maintain the ban on lighter alcoholic beverages, even as it remained determined to prohibit the sale and consumption of vodka.[57] Nonetheless, one concession followed after another, beginning with the permitted sale of beer and wine in first-class restaurants, "so long as such sales served the philanthropic aims of the committee."[58] Then, at the beginning of December 1915, the Germans announced their intention to reintroduce the sale of vodka, even if they were prepared to turn over licensing to the Warsaw Citizens Committee.[59] By the Christmas holidays, prohibition had effectively come to an end, thanks to German demands and initiatives. To the great alarm of the committee, the reintroduction of the vodka monopoly resulted in one-day sales of 87,000 rubles on 23 December, an indication of the negligible impact of seventeen months of prohibition on popular drinking habits.[60] Indeed, for many Varsovians, libation was synonymous with liberation.

The Warsaw City Administration, however, had not given up and revisited the issue with the Germans in October 1916 as Warsaw stood on the verge of famine. With potatoes the only accessible food for the wider population of the city, President Zdzisław Lubomirski deemed the established ration of eighteen pounds per person over a two-week period insufficient to prevent calamity. In a memorandum to German police chief Glasenapp, Lubomirski accused the occupation authorities of bad faith when they claimed that the low ration was due to a bad harvest, when in reality significant quantities of potatoes were being diverted from the countryside to make vodka and other spirits. Lubomirski called on the authorities to close the distilleries, reintroduce prohibition on all sales of alcohol, and designate potato harvests solely to satisfying the population's nutritional needs.[61] The occupation regime remained unmoved, however, despite the fact that drunkenness, whether on- or off-duty, was the single most punished offense among German troops in Warsaw.[62]

Nevertheless, except perhaps for the Germans, getting to establishments that served alcohol proved difficult. Motor vehicles had more or less disappeared from Warsaw's streets during the Russian evacuation when the Warsaw superintendent of police announced that the city would requisition all means of hauling freight, including private automobiles, belonging to persons who had not already taken these possessions to the right bank of the Vistula by 21 July 1915. By 1 August, the harvest included forty-three cars, sixty-three trucks, and thirty-six motorcycles.[63] The new occupation authorities subsequently requisitioned what horses, wagons, and other means of hauling persons and freight the Russians had not confiscated, essentially reducing vehicular traffic on Warsaw's streets to the privilege of German officers.[64] This left the trolleys, which had been placed under German military administration at the beginning of the occupation; that administration in turn severely limited civilian access. The energy shortfall subsequently led to a reduction of lines and stops until streetcar traffic ceased altogether in the spring and summer of 1916 as a result of a weeks-long strike of trolley employees, which turned even the city's busiest prewar streets into safe havens for children's play.[65]

Stanisław Kutrzeba, the historian from Krakow's Jagiellonian University who visited Warsaw in May 1916, noted how quiet Krakowskie Przedmieście had become in comparison with the street's loud prewar rumble of horses' hooves, carriages, wagons, and trolleys:

> [Formerly] this commotion began in the early morning, continual, unbroken, monotonous, it interrupted dreams and didn't allow one to sleep until 2 in the morning. It's possible to say that only then was Warsaw able to get a bit of rest for a bare two or three hours in the middle of the night. . . . The silence [at the time of his March visit—RB] struck me already at the hotel and on the street even more so.[66]

Admittedly, Kutrzeba's visit coincided with the strike of trolley workers, "but where are the carriages?" Before the war, carriages were cheap and plentiful, enabling rides of thirty minutes for twenty kopecks: "The affordability of carriages explains why no self-respecting Varsovian could get used to taking the trolley" and why "only recently did the electric trolley make its appearance on [Warsaw's] streets, later than in Krakow." Kutrzeba finally found a carriage, but the horse was too exhausted to take him because the driver couldn't afford to feed it oats at 40 rubles per pud. Unable to find a means to reach his destinations other than on foot, he noted that the war had forced Warsaw, the prewar "city in a hurry," to take lessons in "the Krakow slow step."[67]

Streetcar traffic would eventually be restored, but only until 13 April 1917 when an explosion at the power station on Leszczyńska Street that supplied electricity to Warsaw's trolley system destroyed one generator and severely damaged two others.[68] Despite official promises to the contrary, weeks and then months passed without the restoration of electric power to the trolley system. Finally, on 13 August 1917, the authorities allowed four horse-drawn trolleys to move through and to the edges of the city.[69] A couple of months later, the German authorities announced draconian energy-savings measures, including a ban on the lighting of exhibits and punishment of violations of rationed norms of electricity, gas, and coal with six-month prison sentences and fines of 10,000 marks.[70]

Nostalgia for the city's hustle and bustle appeared frequently in the Warsaw press, most notably in the boulevard weekly *Tygodnik Illustrowany*. Early into the German occupation, columnist Zdzisław Dębicki lamented that Warsaw had become "unrecognizable," its streets grey, silent, and serious, where life "now ends at a time when formerly it was just beginning."[71] This was before the reduction, disruption, and finally suspension of streetcar traffic, which turned an already quiet city into a deafeningly silent one. Signs of life on the streets reappeared from time to time—for example, when the Act of 5 November 1916, which proclaimed the reestablishment of an autonomous Polish Kingdom as a constitutional monarchy under the sponsorship of the Central Powers, temporarily animated café conversations.[72] Another such moment occurred at the beginning of the new school year in late August 1917 when wagons and buggies carrying children and parents "from even the farthest reaches of the old Commonwealth" punctured the now customary metropolitan silence "if only for a few days."[73] After such episodes, Warsaw would again retreat into the dull, colorless, lifeless void described by Dzikowski, Kutrzeba, and Dębicki. Even social communication seemingly returned to that of an earlier period, before the advent of the telephone, since the Germans banned all private use of the device. The printed word at times also seemed to disappear as long strikes of journalists and printers along with periodic shortages of paper and ink created month-long interruptions in the runs of the already heavily censored legal Warsaw press.[74]

However, Warsaw's street life and especially its night life had not disappeared entirely but had found other sites of expression and performance, often times after the legally permitted hours. These expressions and performances were far from dull and colorless. In fact, to Warsaw's cultural conservatives, their color, excitement, and growing popularity were the very problem. Those like Dzikowski who mourned the passing of Warsaw's "frivolities," "escapes," "humor," and "special language" were simply looking for them in the wrong places and failed to recognize their appearance in new forms, blinded as they were by an adherence to prewar cultural norms and sites. This was an oversight they shared with Warsaw's conservative Catholic elites. Unlike those elites, however, they didn't feel threatened by what they had failed to perceive.

Wartime Morality and Popular Culture: Gambling, Cinema, Cabaret, and Other "Amusements"

In Paris, the war interrupted the tradition of horseracing, which before 1914 had been a major pursuit of high society in the French capital.[75] At the same time, betting on the horses was an activity that crossed social boundaries, whether in Paris or in Warsaw where, as we have seen, the decision to open the fall 1914 racing season was justified as part of a strategy to maintain a veneer of normality on the home front. However, like other forms of urban entertainment throughout Europe, horseracing in Warsaw had to justify its moral legitimacy at a time of death, suffering, and destruction. While racing itself posed little challenge, gambling on the horses was another matter. Thus, *Kurjer Warszawski*, which often reflected the views of the leadership of the Warsaw Citizens Committee, referred to the decision to open the fall racing season as a "good idea" but also called for a ban on betting so that the money could be better spent on treating wounded soldiers and feeding the poor.[76] The problem, of course, was that horseracing was also a business whose vitality was dependent on gambling, which in wartime conditions transformed it into an arena of conflict.

In the fall, business won out over "morality," but the issue resurfaced in 1915 when it was announced that the spring racing season would be cancelled unless the war ended by 15 April.[77] That decision was rescinded at the end of March, when the Horseracing Association, a powerful lobby that had the ear of the Russian authorities, announced that there would indeed be a spring season, though in a nod to conservative "public opinion," one without betting.[78] When, however, there was a new announcement at the end of April that the season would open on 2 May with betting, *Kurjer Warszawski* went on the offensive, denouncing the decision "because it offends the material and moral interests of society ... when the country is engulfed in a war without parallel, when each day there is growing poverty and spreading sorrow."[79] Joining in the "general protest" was Warsaw archbishop Kakowski, who appealed to the Racing Association not to permit legalized gambling. The issue then was seemingly put to rest when the Racing Association received a telegram from the Russian military authorities banning racetrack betting for the season.[80]

However, this was not the Russians' last word on the subject. As Princess Lubomirska recorded in her diary on 5 May, no doubt expressing the position of her husband, "Thanks to the efforts of the Racing President Juriewicz, and despite public opinion, racetrack gambling has returned by permission of the supreme commander [Grand Duke Nikolai Nikolaevich]."[81] The Racing Association made one last effort at compromise, offering to donate a day of admission ticket proceeds to the Great Fundraising Campaign for Student Tuitions co-sponsored by the Central Citizens Committee and the Warsaw Citizens Committee to support student enrollment in private Polish secondary schools. Lubomirska, who chaired the campaign committee, was opposed to taking any racetrack money tied to gambling, and on 10 May this committee rejected the offered donation.[82]

The spring racing season of 1915 was the last that Warsaw would see until 1919, as the war and its demands on horsepower made it practically impossible to breed, train, and feed Polish thoroughbreds for racing. However, a fairly substantial part of the city's valuable racing stock was evacuated to Odessa, where the horses survived and would return to revive the Warsaw racetrack once the

Great War was over.[83] Meanwhile, with the Germans now in Warsaw, the Warsaw Citizens Committee hardened its attitude against legalized gambling of any sort and preferred to contract large loans and issue bonds covered by future taxes than to receive proceeds from the organization of a public lottery, an idea the committee first rejected in September 1915 and refused to consider again during the remainder of its existence.[84] The City Administration that emerged out of the committee's Presidium continued to seek other—even draconian—means to meet demands that were far outpacing its revenues. Only in March 1918 did the Warsaw City Council, in the face of bankruptcy and having exhausted all other options, finally vote to approve a one-time lottery designed to raise half a million marks to support the work of child-welfare institutions in the city.[85] For many of the intended recipients, this last resort to an untapped source of revenue obviously came too late. In any case, there is no evidence in the documentary record that it was repeated, as elite notions of propriety were upheld despite the consequences for the city's finances and the benefit to those who may have received additional, lifesaving support.

Just as *Kurjer Warszawski* and the Warsaw Citizens Committee turned against the racetrack after initially supporting it, they would also find themselves at odds with the owners of Warsaw's cinemas, after originally expressing concern for their ongoing operation and then praise for their showing of films with patriotic war themes. The outbreak of the war temporarily disrupted Warsaw's movie business as owners of the cinemas needed to adjust their repertoires to new conditions. The showing of war-related films in the blush of imperial patriotism helped to bring back audiences, as did the relatively low cost of admission and the ban on alcohol purchase and consumption. As Hubertus Jahn noted in his study of Russian wartime patriotic culture, "Instead of going to the tavern, people now went to the movies."[86] As the war continued, the film industry boomed throughout Europe, and Warsaw's cinemas, which numbered twenty-five in 1915, shared in both the growing popularity as well as profitability of motion pictures.[87] However, to do so they could not afford to stand still. Within a short time, the viewing public in Warsaw quickly tired of essentially propaganda films, particularly after the realities of war began to strike home in October 1914. To replace these films and to retain audiences, the owners of the movie houses turned to Russian-made productions from the erotic and crime genres whose transgressive nature scandalized conservative opinion.

According to Jahn, the themes of the Russian films during the war emphasized psychological drama resulting from unhappy love, treason, seduction, espionage, crime, and the pursuit of wealth. Some were explicitly pornographic. Their unifying feature, however, was the depiction of violent murder scenes.[88] By the middle of May 1915, films about bandits had become wildly popular in Warsaw as well as objects of condemnation in the conservative Catholic press. Not surprisingly, *Kurjer Warszawski* led the charge against the "hideous" films, which, as "schools of banditism and crime," were spreading "demoralization." Made by "special factories" in Petrograd and Moscow, the Russian films were spreading "an unambiguous cult of criminal refinement," leading to "an unbelievable confusion of moral concepts" in their upholding of villains as heroes.[89]

The newspaper soon stepped up its "struggle against the cinematographic contagion" of crime genre films, this time emphasizing their demoralization of refugees, youth, and rural inhabitants who found themselves in Warsaw on the eve of the Russian evacuation. With its close ties to the leadership of the Warsaw Citizens Committee, *Kurjer Warszawski* reported the committee's intentions to exert pressure and perhaps demand repressive measures against movie houses showing such films on the one hand, and to create a production company for good "Polish" films on the other.[90] Thus, the content of the Russian-made films was not the only matter of grave concern to the guardians of Christian morality in Warsaw, but also their ethnic derivation, not necessarily as "Russian" but as one identified with the Jewish owners of the majority of Warsaw's movie houses.

This became clear in the attacks on the "shrill jargon [i.e., Yiddish] press" as well as the "more serious" Hebrew-language *Hacefira*, which had protested proposals to place controls on the cinemas "as an attack on Jewish property." "As is well known, the cinemas have become hotbeds of moral depravity," claimed *Kurjer Warszawski*. In response to "Polish" protests against "the systematic poisoning of society by the cinemas," the Jewish press was accused of coming to the defense of profit over probity. "Hands off!" is how *Kurjer Warszawski* described the Jewish position: "This is our business and nobody is allowed to touch it!"[91] However, the Warsaw Citizens Committee did "touch" this Jewish "business" as soon as it had the opportunity, once the Russians evacuated Warsaw and before the Germans had established their authority, by imposing a heavy tax on the cinemas as its first revenue-generating measure.[92]

With the German takeover of the city, the supply of Russian-made films that had so scandalized the city's conservative elite came to a halt, and the issue of censoring this form of popular entertainment temporarily receded into the background. It would resurface in the spring of 1917, when City Councilman Bolesław Koskowski, a long-time contributor to *Kurjer Warszawski* and a prewar Catholic warrior against "alien" cultural and economic influences, introduced a motion to create a special commission to review and eliminate images and performances of a "sensational-criminal" nature, not only from Warsaw's cinemas but also in its growing number of cabarets and variety shows. Koskowski's motion passed, accompanied by an appeal to the "residents of Warsaw" to shun these venues.[93] Shortly thereafter, the City Administration requested from the German occupation authorities the power to censor the programs of the cinemas and the variety performances being held in "small theaters" as a consequence of their presumed "demoralizing effects" on audiences.[94] Thus cinema, an entertainment that had existed before the war, was now joined by new popular amusements that had mainly emerged during the war and whose moral legitimacy also came under attack.

As Krzysztof Dunin-Wąsowicz has noted, the beginnings of "an authentic Warsaw cabaret" can be traced back to the first year of the war, when Warsaw was still under Russian rule.[95] Almost immediately, however, the cabarets ran afoul of the official culture of sobriety then enforced by police regulations when two of them, "Oasis" and "Renaissance," were shut down in mid-December 1914 for violating curfew and serving alcoholic beverages.[96] Though curfew restrictions similar to those under the Russians remained in place, the steady erosion of the prohibition regime in the first several months of the German occupation, along with a decrease in the barriers to cultural expression, helped turn Warsaw into the new center of Polish cabaret culture, replacing Krakow where it had originated. That shift had already begun on the eve of the war with the creation of the "Momus" cabaret. "Momus" had disappeared by the outbreak of hostilities, but its locale on 9 Wierzbowa Street housed the "Bi-Ba-Bo" variety show, the most successful in wartime Warsaw.[97] Under the direction of future interwar cabaret star Andrzej Włast, "Bi-Ba-Bo" opened on 22 May 1916 with a program featuring "humor, song and dance."[98] At approximately the same time, the "Sfinks" cabaret opened on 116 Marszałkowska in quarters shared with the cinema bearing the same name, which a year earlier had created a sensation by both its size—then the largest in Warsaw—as well as its silver screen.[99] "Miraż," where Pola Negri began her career on her way to becoming an international film star for her roles as a vamp, opened in April 1915 on 63 Nowy Świat. "Sfinks," with whose production company she signed and later broke a contract to star in motion pictures, also proved an important way-station in Negri's career, which would take off in Berlin in 1916.[100]

Thus, the association in the conservative mind during the war between cinema, cabaret, and variety shows had a certain basis in fact, as they often shared the same locales, writers, actors, and directors and were in close proximity to one another. For example, "Czarny Kot" ("The Black Cat"), the most famous of Warsaw's wartime cabarets, featuring among other entertainments the witty poetry of the young Julian Tuwim, opened in 1917 on 125 Marszałkowska Street, just a few doors down from "Sfinks."[101] Jan Stanisław Mar (Marian Lewin), the first director of "Czarny Kot" who also wrote screenplays during the war, moved within a year to found "Argus," the last of the four notable wartime Warsaw cabarets. The locations of the "small theaters," cinemas, and cabarets on Warsaw's main streets, the Jewish presence in them, and their enormous popularity were bound to draw the attention of conservative critics, particularly after "Miraż" and "Czarny Kot" began to draw huge crowds in March 1917.[102] Even Prylucki, a staunch defender of Warsaw's Yiddish theaters against discriminatory legislation introduced to the Warsaw City Council, supported steep tax increases on the variety shows with the following justification: "We all know the character of the programs of these varieties. Unfortunately, the small theaters deprave the young people who predominantly attend them."[103] Not surprisingly given such universal condemnation, the City Council and municipal administration began to move against the variety shows shortly thereafter.

Popular entertainment, however, like those involved in it, proved to be a moving target. The curfew, which forced early closing hours on restaurants and cafés along with places of popular entertainment, eventually encouraged the development of an underground night life that peaked at the end of 1917. An early hint of this life "after hours" appeared as a result of a police sting on 20 March 1916, which led to the arrest of card sharks who were in league with the well-paid owners of sweetshops and cafés on Bielańska and Długa streets for dispossessing unsuspecting players of their cash at games of *"dziewiąty wał"* ("Ninth Shaft") and *"kiszka"* ("Guts").[104] By the end of 1917, there were reportedly a hundred of these secret locales, many of them in cafés and milk bars but also in private apartments. According to *Godzina Polski*, these equivalents of the American "speakeasy" played host not only to gambling and card games but also to "drunken orgies and debauchery."[105] They also caught the attention of the Warsaw City Council, which called upon the magistrate to empower the militia to shut them down, punish their proprietors with severity, and thus "remove this stain from the life of Warsaw."[106]

The speakeasies represented everything that Warsaw's conservative elites detested in popular culture—drinking, gambling, lewd entertainment, sexual transgression, ethnic mixing, profitability—all of which they failed to control, though not for lack of trying. The death of the great Polish actor Bolesław Leszczyński on 23 June 1918 at age eighty serves as an example of the inability of these elites to preserve the cultural norms that they held so dear. Leszczyński, whose performances on the Warsaw classical stage included roles as Othello, Macbeth, and King Lear, ended his career as a popular film actor. Thus, cultural conservatives had to share Leszczyński's passing with the Warsaw cinemas, whose transgressions they had denounced and had labored to suppress. Six hours after Leszczyński's funeral, the "Polonia" movie house set a new record for attendance by showing the procession of mourners on its silver screen.[107] Like Leszczyński, who adapted his acting to remain culturally relevant, the Warsaw cinemas repeatedly adapted to meet popular demand, whether through changes of repertoire or spectacular demonstrations of new filmmaking technology. As if a cinema's capitalizing on Leszczyński's death were not enough for Catholic conservatives, they could also imagine that some of those who had attended the filmed funeral procession at the "Polonia" that evening later committed the ultimate sacrilege—namely, attending or participating in another kind of performance at one of the "secret" locales that had come to define Warsaw's night life and would continue to do so for the remainder of the war.

Barefoot in the Big City

Many of the cultural conflicts discussed in the previous pages found expression in the so-called Barefoot Movement, which emerged in the last two years of the war. Initiated by students from Warsaw's institutions of higher education as a means of symbolic protest against collapsed living standards, the practice of "going barefoot" (*chodzenie boso* in Polish) would quickly spread to other groups. As it did it generated a discourse that also revealed existing political, ethnic, social, and gender-based tensions among an urban population made destitute by the exactions of the Great War.

The Barefoot Movement, which peaked in the summer months of 1917 and again in 1918, was said (with some exaggeration) to have embraced half of the city's population.[108] However, even the movement's most avid supporters in the Polish press were forced to admit that this percentage had been swelled by a population impoverished by the collapse of Warsaw's economy in the last two years of the war. Warsaw's poor, in other words, simply could not afford and did not wear leather shoes and boots, which were in acute shortage. The wearing of wooden shoes had become a "fashion born of necessity" as early as the summer of 1916, as leather prices had increased by a factor of twenty since the beginning of the war.[109] As crushing wartime poverty traveled up the social ladder, many people were indeed fortunate to wear wooden clogs, which like practically every good and commodity in the local economy had become considerably if not prohibitively expensive. German requisitioning of up to 70% of existing stands of forest created an acute shortage of wood products as well. At the same time, the use of wood to supplement or replace coal as a source of energy also drove up prices of the former, making less wood available for the production of clogs, the cost of which reached fifteen marks—the prewar price of leather shoes—by the spring of 1918.[110] These shortages in footwear and of leather shoes in particular reduced one of the existing differences in attire between workers and intelligentsia, which before the war had been far more pronounced.[111]

During the First World War, belligerent states and armies commonly requisitioned leather. For example, the French government not only requisitioned

FIGURE 15. Warsaw's barefoot children. Archiwum Państwowe w Warszawie.

leather but also leatherworkers. This made it difficult for French families to find boots for sons fighting at the front, let alone shoes for themselves.[112] In Warsaw, leather was already reported to be in short supply in the winter of 1914–15 due to requisitioning in localities to the west of the city that had come under German occupation. Thus, plans for relieving local unemployment by filling Russian Army orders for a million pairs of boots came to naught.[113] While inflation was relatively contained during the first year of the war when Warsaw remained under Russian rule, prices increased on practically a daily basis a few months following German takeover of the city in August 1915. As a consequence of the requisitioning of supplies from outside the city that were normally transported to Warsaw, long lines began to form at grocery stores, the number of beggars multiplied, and with them, as Kraushar recalled, the visible presence of people completely without footwear regardless of the weather conditions. At the same time, many who had been relatively well off before the war were now reduced to wearing wooden clogs.[114]

As leather and then wooden footwear came into ever shorter supply, like other essential goods they became targets of speculation that further fueled inflation. At the beginning of 1917, the average price of a pair of leather shoes was twenty-five rubles. This was before the Polish mark replaced the Russian currency at an admittedly artificial rate of one to one, which led to the new currency's almost immediate loss of 25% of its value. With that in mind, the price of a normal pair of shoes in January would have been between thirty and thirty-five marks, at least double the prewar price. On 22 July 1917, the reported price of a pair of shoes was 110 Polish marks, and two weeks later it had reached 120 Polish marks, placing shoes well beyond the reach of not only workers but also the lower ranks of the intelligentsia.[115] A shoe factory operated by the city and employing 150 workers was opened at the end of 1917 with the intention of selling shoes at eighty marks, but production experienced considerable difficulties due to the existing energy and raw material shortages.[116] In any event, municipal intervention had little visible impact on the market despite the issuing of ration cards for the footwear produced by this factory. Shortly thereafter, its prices too increased by twenty to thirty marks.[117] By August 1918, the black-market price for shoes reportedly ranged between 220 and 240 marks.[118]

Although anger toward the German occupation ran high in Warsaw over every imaginable shortage, particularly of food, scarcity was not the only cause of conflicts in the city that pitted elements of the population against the German authorities on the eve of and during the emergence of the Barefoot Movement in the spring and summer of 1917. Police beatings of demonstrating students on 1 and 3 May had led to strikes and expulsions at Warsaw University and the Polytechnic Institute, which were temporarily closed after students refused to pay tuition.[119] Declining real wages and layoffs had resulted in strikes and mass arrests in Warsaw's militarized metal and machine-building factories in April and again in July, the latter followed by street skirmishes and the erection of barricades.[120] Finally, the arrest of Józef Piłsudski by the German authorities in July 1917 was accompanied by demonstrations on the major midtown thoroughfares of Krakowskie Przedmieście and Nowy Świat, and by the breaking of windows in the offices of *Goniec*, *Godzina Polski*, and *Głos*, Polish press organs perceived as outlets favored by the occupation regime.[121]

It was in this context, dominated above all by the critical food shortage, that the Barefoot Movement came to life. Like food, shoes and footwear had become increasingly inaccessible. Like food, shoes had become an object of thieves as children fortunate enough to have them were reportedly kidnapped and stripped of their belongings.[122] However, unlike food, one could survive at least part of the year without shoes. It was this existential reality that created an opportunity to transform dire necessity into a patriotic virtue, to engage in protest without provoking yet another confrontation with the authorities, and to gain publicity for a "Polish" cause in a heavily censored daily press seeking any means to express itself freely.

Warsaw was not the only central European city to have experienced a barefoot movement during the war. Although Catholic sources subsequently attributed the initiation of the Warsaw movement to one Father Czeczot, who supposedly set the example and began to call for going barefoot as early as the summer of

1916,[123] the movement did not take root until a year later. By then the Polish student organization *Bratnia Pomoc* at Warsaw's institutions of higher education had become the main source of the movement's activists, citing as its inspiration "the examples of Würzburg, Vienna, and several provincial Polish cities as well as the voice of public opinion as expressed in numerous articles [about the shortage and high price of shoes] in the Warsaw press."[124] In particular, the German movement called upon youth in institutions of secondary and higher education to sacrifice their feet for the fatherland so that soldiers at the front had a sufficient supply of boots. The Warsaw press noted the establishment of "barefoot leagues" in cities like Cologne, Strasbourg, and Breslau in the spring of 1917, which had helped to spread the movement's growing popularity in Germany.[125]

By citing German cities as their model, the students and their supporters in an otherwise muzzled press clearly sought to divert the attention of the occupation authorities. As already mentioned, students in Warsaw's institutions of higher education had already drawn their fair share of such attention. The initial enthusiasm over the reopening of Warsaw University and the Polytechnic Institute as "Polish" institutions of higher education in November 1915 soon turned to disappointment in their lack of autonomy under German supervision. Following the dissolution of the Education Department of the Warsaw Citizens Committee, which resulted from the assumption by the German civil administration of control over supervisory personnel, textbooks, and curricula in the city's schools in February 1916, a strike was narrowly averted as faculty senates were able to convince students to remain in their classes.[126] The following year, however, the faculty and rectors could not persuade students to relent from their demands for complete autonomy of Warsaw's two institutions of higher education, and following their refusal to pay fees by a 21 June deadline, activities at the two schools were suspended indefinitely.[127] Student organizations were then dislodged from their locale at Warsaw University, and students whose permanent residence was outside of Warsaw were ordered to leave the city.[128]

Thus, those students from the *Bratnia Pomoc* organization who remained in Warsaw safely cited German inspiration for their "barefoot action." This strategy apparently proved successful, as the German authorities paid little heed to the Barefoot Movement and to its promotion in the daily press. However, in Warsaw's case the idea of home-front sacrifice for soldiers fighting on behalf of the Central Powers was an obvious nonstarter if the movement were to gain support. Instead, the real motivations for joining the movement and going barefoot were mixed. One of the strongest was that it provided an apolitical vehicle to protest against a collapsed standard of living. An afternoon march of barefoot Varsovians down Aleje Ujazdowskie on 22 July 1917, designed to publicize the movement, was preceded by visits of its young male and female activists to the editorial offices of *Kurjer Warszawski*, the largest mass-circulation daily in the city, to gain support for their cause.[129] The students' subsequently published appeal cited "the unimaginable inflation of prices of footwear as well as woolen and cotton goods which, along with the actual absence of stockings on the market, threatens catastrophe with the approach of winter" as one of the main reasons to go barefoot in the summer months and to affect both private and social savings.[130] *Nowa Gazeta*, which was initially critical of the movement, nevertheless concurred that its main goal was to bring down the prices of footwear and hosiery.[131] In restarting the movement in the spring of 1918, appeals distributed at Warsaw University again emphasized its "purely economic" motive.[132]

However, the question of who or what was considered responsible for these shortages and high prices reveals another of the movement's motivations, namely, an opportunity to express growing Polish hostility toward Jews by means of a partial and thinly disguised boycott rather than an open and full-scale one, which the German occupation authorities would not have tolerated. Jews had traditionally dominated the production and sale of shoes and hosiery in Warsaw, even if the increasingly mechanized industry itself had employed large numbers of Christians before the war.[133] In comparison with 1899, when the city was considerably smaller, the number of shoemakers in the spring of 1917 had declined by 25%, the number of journeymen by 40%, and the number of apprentices by nearly 90%.[134] With German requisitioning of leather, the city's shoemaking industry struggled to stay afloat, a situation to which the Barefoot Movement and its supporters in the press appeared to be oblivious.[135] *Godzina Polski*, for instance, referred to shoemakers' arguments that requisitioning of leather had caused the rapid inflation of shoe prices as simply "the lies of speculators."[136] Or to cite another example, *Kurjer Warszawski*, in its rejection of legitimate public health concerns related to exposing one's bare feet to Warsaw's less-than-pristine streets, attacked the "pseudo-hygienists" whose opinion "not accidentally" served the interests of "profiteers."[137] Such code words for Jews, whether in the medical or shoemaking professions, may still have been necessary to avoid German censorship in the summer of 1917, as calls for the city to take action against "speculators" of leather and shoes referred to "secret bands" rather than Jews.[138] Shortly thereafter, Polish nationalists would no longer find such circumvention necessary. In responding to its own question "Why are shoes so expensive?" *Gazeta Poranna 2 grosze* left no doubt as it reported on the raid conducted by the city police, a force that was overwhelmingly Polish, which uncovered "vast supplies of hoarded shoes" in the hands of "Jewish speculators" who had withheld the product from the market "in order to drive up prices."[139]

Finally, it should be noted that Polish nationalist youth dominated the *Bratnia Pomoc* student organization and that hostility against Jews ran particularly high among Polish university students. Irena Krzywicka, who began her university studies in 1919, recalled that "Bratniak" was declared off limits to her as a student of Jewish ancestry.[140] Indeed, antisemitic speeches accompanied meetings to elect representatives to *Bratnia Pomoc* as early as May 1917, immediately before the emergence of the Barefoot Movement, while at the same time the Polish nationalist press complained about the percentage of Jewish medical students at Warsaw University.[141] Jewish students found virtually no support from the university's academic authorities, who refused to recognize a Jewish student association, which they referred to as an "alien national organization of separatist tendencies" in a "Polish institution of higher education."[142] Compared to Łódź, which lacked institutions of higher education and where Polish youth joined a march of the barefoot initiated by Jewish workers,[143] the student-led Barefoot Movement in Warsaw separated Poles from Jews. Indeed, tensions at Warsaw University would reach a boiling point in November 1918 when fighting broke out between Polish and Jewish students.[144]

Thus, if the movement was an expression of economic and social protest against substantially higher costs of living and substantially lower living standards, it was also part and parcel of an economic antisemitism aimed at Jewish commerce in the city, which had long been accompanied by notions of reducing the presence of Jews in the free professions and, by extension, in institutions of higher education. "Going barefoot," in other words, could also mean depriving Jewish shoe- and stocking makers, cast in the role of "speculators" and "profiteers," of their livelihoods and striking a blow against Jewish tradesmen. Of course, the Jewish poor suffered from the same dire economic conditions and likewise had to make do with recycled and repaired footwear or go without entirely, but this was of no relevance to those of an antisemitic mindset. Since the main cause for the high prices and acute shortage of footwear, German requisitioning, could not be addressed publicly, Jews remained the only available target. That the German occupation regime tolerated the Barefoot Movement and its public manifestations, as well as other expressions of antisemitism toward the end of the war, is an indication of how politically convenient, and perhaps even necessary, the Jewish target had become.

With its Jewish-dominated garment industry and apparel trades, Warsaw before the war imagined itself (and was imagined by others, particularly Russian officials) as a Paris of the east, a cosmopolitan center of fashion known for its elegantly dressed women and coach traffic comparable to those of the largest of European cities. As mentioned earlier, daily movement around the city became largely pedestrian by the spring of 1917 as Warsaw indeed became a "city on foot."[145] In this forced return to a less-mechanized past, the wearing down of already expensive footwear reinforced an existing atmosphere of austerity, which also took on moral dimensions. Thus, in remarking on a similarly dramatic change in women's attire that Kutrzeba discovered during his visit, one of his female interlocutors explained, "Today in Warsaw, the fashion of the moment is not to dress fashionably."[146] The Barefoot Movement, in its promotion of a "healthy" and "natural" simplicity, placed itself in opposition to "cosmopolitan" culture and "big city" convention, in favor of styles based on presumed Polish popular custom. The movement's antimodern critique, one should note, also contained an anti-Jewish tone.

The liberal Polish-Jewish daily *Nowa Gazeta*, which had promoted Warsaw's development as an international cultural metropolis before the war, found itself practically alone in its early opposition to the "false and primitive road" of the Barefoot Movement as it emerged in the summer of 1917. "Do we really now need to be compelled to return to nature by attiring ourselves poorly, no longer as civilized people or even as people in general? Is it really necessary that by our appearance we resemble barbarians?" asked one correspondent, a certain "Pani Drozdowska," in response to the young female enthusiasts of the movement. "Maybe it will come to that, that all of us will begin to go barefoot but at the moment there is no such compulsion. And perhaps we Polish women should be the first to make a complete break with fashion, but not to the point of idiocy. Let our women who are working and wearing 40-ruble shoes on 30-ruble salaries be logical and begin to wear clogs and thick stockings. Certainly this will be much more effective and intelligent, and much healthier, than going barefoot." Drozdowska's letter concluded that the appearance and demands of the Barefoot Movement were "yet another marker of a descent into stupidity of a part of the population which is already stupid enough."[147]

Stanisław Fornalski, who emerged as the movement's leading spokesman during its first year, quickly struck back in a letter to the editors of *Nowa Gazeta*, which was simultaneously published in *Kurjer Warszawski*. Before the "march of the barefoot" on 22 July 1917, Fornalski had paraded alone as a young "gentleman," with white gloves and necktie but without shoes, among strolling crowds on Aleje Ujazdowskie. In the beginning, he purposefully targeted "the fair sex" for membership in his proposed Barefoot Union, assuming correctly that young males would follow suit.[148] In his exchange with *Nowa Gazeta*, Fornalski argued that going barefoot was popular in other countries (namely, Germany) and thus "has passed the test of modern culture." If women were concerned with protecting their feet, "instead of elegant ballroom slippers" they could begin to wear sandals, "which would give women's attire a note of unforced simplicity, remove it from the sham and pretense of the big city and bring it closer to the customs of the Polish peasant, who goes barefoot even in winter." "We want to break with big city convention," he concluded, "which is based on a falsely conceived prudery, but we have no intention nor are we introducing a new element of 'exhibition-ism,' 'coquetry,' or 'debauchery,'" as insinuated by the movement's detractors.[149]

Shortly thereafter the movement's student leaders published an appeal in *Kur-jer Warszawski*, which called upon male and female citizens, and especially the city's white-collar workers, to cast away their shoes for the rest of the summer. By then, the movement had already spread from university to middle-school youth, particularly those involved in Polish scouting organizations.[150] After reciting For-nalski's arguments against the cosmopolitan conventions of the big city and his populist message of getting culturally closer to the Polish peasant, the students added a new one of solidarity with Warsaw's "population of lesser means which suffers the most from the shortages and high prices of footwear on the market and will not be properly equipped for winter."[151]

Thus Warsaw's wartime culture wars, of which the Barefoot Movement was but one example, also highlighted growing class divisions in the city. *Godzina Polski*, in particular, noted in May 1918 that even though the movement was acquiring widespread support as it headed into its second summer, the wealthy classes were the most reluctant to become involved.[152] A month later, even though the move-ment had reportedly spread "to one of every two Varsovians," the daily lamented "the indifference of the most important representatives of society" toward the Barefoot Movement and praised the "great civic courage" of Fornalski himself who had recently created a League for the Simplification and Nationalization of Dress. Fornalski and his acolytes, according to *Godzina Polski*, were carrying out "reforms more profound and important than they themselves had imagined by breaking with existing convention and at the same time creating in its place a new style based on Polish rural custom, one that meets the requirements of both ther-apeutic and moral hygiene." The Barefoot Movement, in the version promoted by *Godzina Polski*, had become synonymous with Polish society—minus the Jews, of course, but also minus Warsaw's traditional social, cultural, and political elites. This society "which has been able in such an impressive way to remove itself from international style and convention, from centuries of prudish exaggerations, can be proud of itself because this is its accomplishment alone."[153]

Meanwhile, the high visibility of student female activists in the Barefoot Movement reinforced fears of gender and sexual disorder in the same newspa-pers that applauded Fornalski's populism. The main sources of these fears were Warsaw's demographic feminization during the war and women's increasingly vocal demands for political representation. Secondly, as Warsaw's institutions of higher education reopened in the autumn of 1915, women were allowed to enroll for the first time, and their numbers and percentages increased as the war con-tinued. Moreover, these new female students were not content simply to attend lectures but also sought participation, however unsuccessfully, in the leadership of the *Bratnia Pomoc* student self-help organization, which provided the shock troops for the Barefoot Movement.[154]

Thus when these female students also proposed, in addition to going barefoot, the wearing of short skirts because of the high cost of materials, *Nowa Gazeta* accused them of calling upon women to wear "loincloths" and "to parade in Warsaw in the style of Eve."[155] Although such fears were obviously exaggerated, it is clear that the female students were pursuing their own agenda rather than the Polish version of central European agrarian romanticism that Fornalski and his supporters in the press had taken to heart. The women in the Barefoot Movement, it can be argued, represented the culmination of a fundamental challenge to more traditional aesthetic notions governing female appearance and behavior during the war years. As early as 1915, the external appearance of young women working in clerical positions came under attack and led to comparisons with prostitutes. "Where are the feelings of embarrassment among Warsaw's women," *Kurjer Warszawski* demanded a year later, "when the eyes of Europe have turned on us, eyes that are both friendly and unfriendly? . . . At this moment our obligation is to uphold national dignity and solemnity everywhere and in everything."[156] By the end of the war the situation had reached the point in Warsaw, according to *Godzina Polski*, that "fifty-year-old women have begun to dress like teenagers, wearing skirts to the knees. . . . And as a result, Warsaw has taken on the appearance of a ballet, which is incompatible with the weight of the crucial times in which we are living."[157]

Ironically, both *Kurjer Warszawski* and *Godzina Polski* supported the Barefoot Movement in its nationalist, populist, and—one might argue—male forms. In these dailies, "simple" and "natural" attire meant one thing for men—a return to hallowed national tradition—and another thing for women—a challenge to conventional morality. None of their contributors, in other words, questioned the propriety of the bare male foot or leg. By contrast, the alarms sounded in the Warsaw press about the involvement of young women in the Barefoot Movement reflected larger concerns about the unprecedented presence of women in the public sphere, while questions of whether and what women should be allowed to lay bare—and about women's appearance more generally—expressed anxieties about a patriarchal order that had come partially unraveled during the war years.

The Barefoot Movement in Warsaw was a wartime phenomenon that ended with the war and left little trace, except perhaps in the area of women's fashion. Confined to a specific time and setting, "going barefoot" meant different things to different people. It offered a means to speak out against the war's acute economic hardships, to strike a blow against Jewish commerce in the city, to promote a populist agenda against the "cosmopolitanism" of the big city and its elites, to express empathy with Warsaw's increasingly desperate urban poor, and to participate in the rapidly (and, for some, alarmingly) changing world of women's fashion.

In specifically cultural terms, by examining the Barefoot Movement we can find evidence of the previously mentioned two vectors of wartime metropolitan life highlighted by Winter, a "nostalgic turn" of moving back in time as part of a conservative project of national reconstruction, in this case Polish, and a future-oriented cultural iconoclasm that challenged convention. In Warsaw as elsewhere, the turn toward tradition was accompanied by an emphasis on sobriety and modesty, which was apparent before the German takeover of the city from the Russians, whether in support for state-imposed prohibition of the sale and consumption of alcohol or in calls for a ban on racetrack betting. Cinemas and cabarets also drew the attention of Warsaw's cultural warriors, as venues of relatively cheap popular urban entertainment whose legitimacy, morality, and transgressive nature came under attack both before and after the German occupation. And as we have seen, in a heightened atmosphere of moral austerity, targeting women and their fashion as provocative or frivolous was shared alike by both critics and supporters of the Barefoot Movement in the Warsaw press. This was because women's participation in the Barefoot Movement did indeed challenge tradition, in a sense by wrapping itself in it. Less clothing and bare legs, even if cast in terms of a return to a simple and more natural past, were threatening to a social and cultural order that viewed these developments in women's fashion as a loosening of constraints, and to the "sobriety" and "modesty" they were designed to uphold.

In his discussion of metropolitan wartime culture, Winter makes reference to Svetlana Boym's distinction between "restorative" and "reflective" nostalgia. The former consists largely of elites who invoked tradition to justify their power and policies, while the latter, with a "wistful smile," "build imaginary cathedrals in the air, cathedrals that may never have existed in the first place."[158] "Restorative" nostalgia can be said to characterize the cultural politics of the Polish conservative, Catholic, and nationalist elites represented on the Warsaw Citizens Committee and in the city's "self-governing" institutions, whose voice found expression in dailies like *Kurjer Warszawski*. In their support of the classical performing arts and their opposition to popular culture and its assorted "vulgarities," which seemed to multiply during the war years, Warsaw's political and social elites fought in vain to preserve and then restore an immediate prewar past.

According to Boym, "reflective nostalgia," aware of the impossibility of a full return to the imagined past, is instead a form of "deep mourning that performs a labor of grief both through pondering pain and through play that points to the future."[159] The Barefoot Movement, I would argue, was largely if not entirely "reflective" in its nostalgia. One cannot imagine that it took very seriously its invocation of the traditional Polish peasant "who goes barefoot even in winter" as something worthy of imitation, even if participants in the movement were genuinely moved by visible evidence of unprecedented misery among Warsaw's lower-class inhabitants, who faced precisely that prospect. At the same time, the movement's playfulness, beginning with Fornalski's performances as a barefoot dandy on Aleje Ujazdowskie and culminating in the morally "outrageous" challenges to existing conventions on the part of its young female activists, pointed to the future—as a new form of protest on the one hand,[160] and as a real revolution in women's attire that was hardly confined to Warsaw on the other.

There also remains a more hidden agenda, if one can even call it an agenda, because it was never explicitly stated and cannot be confirmed by any direct evidence. In the face of the existential catastrophe that in one way or another affected practically every resident of Warsaw—where incredible hunger and foul-tasting "bread" would dominate the collective memory of the war, where marriage and birth rates would decline by half by the end of 1916, where the death rate would more than double by the end of 1917 as a consequence of starvation and disease—"going barefoot" in warm weather months may just have offered a means of psychological escape from these conditions. The movement's youthful enthusiasm and its expression in farcical street performance appeared, if not exactly to laugh in the face of death, at least to smile in the face of conditions that had brought about a rapidly increasing mortality. The same could easily be said of the humor that characterized the cabaret and variety shows, whose growing popularity ran parallel with increasing misery and in opposition to the elite emphasis on sobriety and moral probity. In other words, "going barefoot" may have offered one of the few available coping mechanisms—along with the crime and sex films, cabaret performances, and gambling at cards in speakeasies—to deal with the nightmare of everyday life in Warsaw during the First World War. If this is so, then perhaps we may have discovered a final key to the Barefoot Movement's general popularity as it quickly spread from students to other social groups.

Conclusion

A MINOR APOCALYPSE

> **"Warsaw . . . Anyone who remembers its big city, capricious, carefree nature before the war would not recognize it today. Something here has been extinguished, suffocated."**
>
> —Zdzisław Dębicki, "Przez łzy (Through the Tears)," *Tygodnik Illustrowany* (1 January 1916)

> **"Many generations have thought the world was dying. But it was only their world which was dying."**
>
> —Tadeusz Konwicki, *Mała apokalipsa* (1979)

In 2014 Joshua A. Sanborn published his long-awaited study of the Russian experience during the First World War, which he encapsulated with the title *Imperial Apocalypse*. Beginning with the outbreak of the war in the borderlands of Imperial Russia and the shifting front, through chapters on massive population displacements and military and social mobilizations, and ending with revolution and decolonization, Sanborn's history is one that interprets the causes, course, and consequences of the collapse of one of Europe's great empires. Of course, the Russian Empire would have a second life under a new name, which too would collapse, and a third incarnation may now be in the making. By comparison, Warsaw's apocalypse during the Great War was a minor one. Though connected to the collapse of empires, it did not cause them, and the existential challenges and suffering experienced by Varsovians in the years 1914–18 and immediately beyond would subsequently be dwarfed by the physical and human destruction that characterized the city's major apocalypse a generation later.

Warsaw's apocalypse during the Great War may have been minor in the grand scale of things, of collapsing empires and a second, even greater war as the ugliest offspring of the first, but it was an apocalypse nonetheless, one shared in the main with other central and east European cities, particularly those caught between the armies of the Russian Empire and the Central Powers and occupied by them in turn. These were not yet "bloodlands," as Timothy Snyder would refer to them for the next war,[1] but they were "war lands" as described by Gabriel Vejas Liulevicius, of death, starvation, and disease among noncombatants on an unprecedented scale. And they were bloody enough. Warsaw was fortunate to have avoided major military combat in the first year of the war as a frontline city. Not so the city's suburban reaches or the surrounding countryside. As Brian Porter-Szűcs has noted, the population of the territory that would become the Second Polish Republic declined by almost 12% between 1914 and 1918, compared to more than a 16% loss during the Second World War, with the deliberate genocide of the Jews appearing to account for the main difference.[2]

When we confine this comparison between the two wars to Warsaw, it appears that only Jews in the metropolis ate worse during the Second World War, if they managed to eat at all. In both wars, of course, hardship was not shared equally, and some ate better, even substantially better, than others, which means that many did not receive even the official allotments, with the result being starvation. Warsaw's Poles, for their part, appear to have been better fed during the second war, with little evidence of starvation, compared to the first. The same has been said of Czechs during the years of the German Protectorate of Bohemia and Moravia, who ate better than they had in the same territories under the Habsburgs during the First World War.[3]

For its part, Warsaw's population declined by nearly 161,000, or slightly more than 18%, between January 1914 and January 1919.[4] Warsaw's proportional population loss during the Great War appears to have been much greater than for German cities, with the possible exception of Berlin,[5] and was more than double that of Vienna's 7.9% decline between 1910 and 1923. These percentages are admittedly problematic, since the timeframes for analysis do not correspond exactly to the years of the Great War, and the factors that figured into the population losses have to be weighed differently. For example, military conscription was not nearly as significant in Warsaw's population loss as was voluntary and forced male labor out-migration to Russia and Germany. Refugee populations must also be accounted for in any analysis of urban wartime demographics, and by 1918 Warsaw had largely been cleared of refugees, only to return again as a refuge for massive numbers once the Great War had ended and its successor wars had begun. Nonetheless, the increase in Warsaw's mortality rate from 1914 to 1918 appears to have been considerably higher than in other Central European cities, more than doubling that of Leipzig, for example, and the decline in the birth rate was steeper, though marginally so in the case of Vienna, which experienced a 42% decline in live births compared to Warsaw's approximately 50%.[6]

By every measure, Warsaw's experience of the Great War was catastrophic, though a city still inhabited by more than seven hundred thousand people remained on 11 November 1918, the day of the armistice ending the Great War and the beginning of a restored Poland in its old-new capital. Thirty-six years later, following the Warsaw Uprising, that city was totally destroyed and emptied of its population. The major apocalypse is remembered and enshrined in monuments depicting martyrdom and victimization, the minor one largely forgotten, though it too had its fair share of victims, only of a different kind. And instead of martyrs, it had heroes, especially one who has come to dominate whatever Polish memory there is of the war years.

November 1918 in the Metropolis

The disarmament of occupying German soldiers by young irregulars belonging to the Polska Organizacja Wojskowa (POW) is perhaps the most enduring image associated with Warsaw and the recovery of Polish state independence on 11 November 1918. It is one of the more triumphal images in the Polish national narrative, certainly one for an organization that three years earlier had counted barely three hundred members when the Germans entered the city in August 1915, and for its guiding spirit and nominal commander, Józef Piłsudski, recently arrived after months of confinement in the Magdeburg Fortress. With Piłsudski's assistance, a depressed and disoriented Hans von Beseler, the governor-general of the German occupation regime, was dressed in civilian clothes and hustled from the Belweder Palace to the Royal Castle and eventually out of the city, while his principal assistants burned official documents and secret papers.[7] In Maria Kamińska's account, which is corroborated by others, the city was decked out in revolutionary red:

> Today I still have before my eyes the young boys wearing legionnaire caps running up to German soldiers on the street and, just like that, disarming them. I see officers with large red ribbons tied to German uniforms. I see the rank and file with red armbands. Red is everywhere: in the windows of homes, in the lapels of shirts. A large red banner is hanging at the Radziwiłł palace on Krakowskie Przedmieście. This is the seat of the "Soldatenrat." Its main concern is the quickest possible departure to Germany of troops stationed in the Kingdom. Trains with troops withdrawing from Ukraine pass through Warsaw constantly. In Warsaw, they give up their arms at the demand of Polish soldiers. . . . There is unbelievable motion, the mood is unusually joyful—we are getting rid of the occupier, the partitioning power has accepted defeat. Everyone is feverish. Everyone is wearing red armbands and ribbons. It looks as if the revolution has been victorious. . . . Maybe it really is revolution?[8]

Revolution, however, was not to be. The German Soldiers' Council would negotiate with Piłsudski a peaceful evacuation and a bloodless transfer of power. By 16 November, most officers and officials of the German General-Government had left Warsaw, and three days later the evacuation of some twelve thousand troops and eighteen thousand officials had been completed. For Piłsudski, whose authority had been accepted by all parties that counted, these days in mid-November 1918 marked his finest hour, if for no other reason than that an outbreak of violence in the city had been successfully avoided, largely due to his timely and commanding presence on the scene.

Meanwhile, the mainstream Warsaw press scrambled to line up behind the new political reality, none more so than *Tygodnik Illustrowany*, which back in November 1914 had trumpeted a new dawn of Polish-Russian brotherhood.[9] Four years later, *Tygodnik Illustrowany* claimed that at the beginning of the war "the most serious part of society" supported the cause of Russian arms because behind Russia stood the Entente. God then "rewarded" the Poles with the collapse of the Russian Empire, "after which time our road became clear." That road, however, was not clearly delineated in any of the weekly's wartime articles, but then again the muzzle of German censorship had supposedly prevented *Tygodnik Illustrowany* from speaking openly, or so it claimed. Now that the censor's shackles were off, *Tygodnik Illustrowany* and "the most serious part of society" could rejoice that the Warsaw crowds had stood firm against the "Bolshevik contagion" in support of the orderly transition from German to Polish authority represented by Piłsudski.[10]

The sophistry and antisemitism of *Tygodnik Illustrowany* aside, the purpose here is not to challenge this image of the man of the great November hour, one perhaps best memorialized in the statue of a uniformed Piłsudski from this era that greets today's visitors to the Belweder Palace. Instead, it is to add some other, more disturbing images that one would have encountered on Warsaw's streets in November 1918 but that have largely disappeared from a national narrative and historiography dominated by the story of recovered state sovereignty and independence.[11] These images are tragic rather than triumphal and were longer in formation, the result of Warsaw's experience of more than four years of deprivation and desperation in Europe's first total war.

The image that comes most immediately to mind in the context of the Warsaw street is one of incredible hunger. The main concern of most ordinary Varsovians in November 1918 was not about independence or revolution but about food, and it had been for some time. At the time of the evacuation of Russian forces in the summer of 1915, the reduction of supplies to a trickle threatened Varsovians with the prospect of starvation. Following a brief respite, the Germans introduced rationing in September 1915, beginning with bread. Food products of all types were eventually regulated through ration cards, accompanied by a ban on sales of food on the free market and on shipments of food from the countryside to Warsaw, much of which was requisitioned. Such restrictions, ever more

severe, were accompanied in rapid succession by queuing at food stores and public kitchens, smuggling, the counterfeiting of ration cards, and the registration of
dead souls. Dozens had died of starvation on the streets of Warsaw by the spring
of 1916. Food and hunger riots broke out in June 1916 and again in May 1917, as
the collapse of people in the streets from hunger-related illness had become an
everyday occurrence.

Returning from food lines and public kitchens on which roughly 25% of Warsaw's population had become completely dependent for their meager sustenance,
the vast majority of Warsaw's inhabitants also would have been suffering from
the cold in November 1918. During the war's first year, the shipment of coal to
Warsaw had been disrupted by the German occupation of the Dąbrowskie Basin,
the city's traditional supplier, creating shortfalls that were only partially and temporarily alleviated by transports from the distant Don Basin in eastern Ukraine.
Indeed, as pressures were put on other fuels, particularly firewood and kerosene,
the city teetered on the brink of an energy catastrophe during the winter of 1914–
15. The situation eased somewhat following the German capture of the city and
the restoration of traditional supplies from the coalfields to Warsaw's southwest.
However, signs of renewed shortages of fuels, particularly coal, were evident in
the summer of 1916 as electric power was reduced and the City Administration
confronted corruption within its own distribution network. In October 1917 the
rationing system spread from food products to coal and other fuels, reflecting a
larger energy shortfall whose main effect on the noncombatant population was
reflected in severe shortages of heating materials.

The city's gas supplies were also reduced due to the lack of coal. Most of the
city before the war had been illuminated by gas lanterns, which were now extinguished in the evening hours, well before the midnight curfew, to affect savings.
By the fall of 1918, the city's gas and kerosene supplies had declined so dramatically that Warsaw in November 1918 was not only a cold place but also a
dark, almost completely unlit place in both its public and private spaces, spaces
reached only on foot as there was barely any trolley or vehicular traffic due to
the lack of electricity and the requisitioning of practically all automobiles and
horses. As a combined consequence of curfews and the energy shortfall, Warsaw's
once vibrant nightlife retreated to "secret locales," which in the imagination of
"the serious part of society" and its press functioned as dens of depravity and
debauchery, even more so than the morally suspect cinemas and cabarets.

Warsaw was also a place that in November 1918 had been visited by disease,
most recently by the first signs of the great "Spanish" influenza. Though the
city had already had to brace itself against epidemics while still under Russian
rule, the provision of medical care to the population during the war's first two
years was effective enough to prevent major outbreaks. Cholera, for example,

was limited to some thirty cases. As the war entered its third year, however, the situation deteriorated rapidly, resulting in an unusually threatening typhus epidemic in the spring of 1917. However, the main killer in Warsaw was tuberculosis, which by 1917 accounted for nearly 30% of all deaths in the city.

As elsewhere in European capitals and major cities, tuberculosis mortality increased above all among young women, particularly those who managed to find employment in those of Warsaw's factories and sweatshops that remained operational. Nonetheless, the city's population during the war years had become increasingly feminized as a result of military mobilization in the war's first year and by male labor out-migration. An immediate and precipitous decline in industrial production within the war's first year to 25% of the prewar level had led to mass unemployment, which was only partially alleviated by the migration of thousands of males, first to Russia and then to Germany. By January 1917, there were 32% more females than males in Warsaw's total population. Two years later, in January 1919, females still held a 23% advantage over males, the reduction due mainly to the return of workers from the Soviet Union following the Treaty of Brest-Litovsk of March 1918, and from Germany following the armistice. In the meantime, women not only dominated in the queues for food, coal, and other rationed items, but also in the distribution of a variety of social services to an increasingly impoverished urban population, which became the winning argument of women's associations for suffrage under the new Polish authorities.

Indeed, over the course of the war, Warsaw had become a city in which many of its residents relied partially or completely on public support as the local economy collapsed under the pressure of total war. As early as the war's first year, the Warsaw Citizens Committee, a nongovernmental organization under the City Magistrate created with Russian state approval and subventions to provide emergency assistance to the population, was forced to expand its social welfare activities dramatically. Originally set up to oversee the general provisioning of the city, to assist those affected by the outbreak of the war, especially soldiers' families and the unemployed, through state and private funding, the committee quickly found itself involved in a host of other activities. These included the supplying of coal to industry as well as to the general population, the operation of public kitchens, the management of public wholesale and retail outlets for the distribution of basic goods in short supply, the implementation and enforcement of price controls, the care of wounded soldiers returning from the front, the establishment of public health organizations, the maintenance or improvement of sanitary conditions, the feeding and sheltering of refugees, the protection and education of the city's children, and the provision of low-interest loans to struggling artisans. In October 1914 and again in the summer of 1915, during the partial and then complete evacuations of the city by the Russian authorities, the committee created and then made operational surrogate fire and police departments, which expanded the numbers of Varsovians already employed in the city's public sector, including the twelve thousand then enrolled in the city's public works program.

The Russian evacuation left the Warsaw Citizens Committee financially strapped, and it would become increasingly so under German occupation, despite its transformation into a new City Administration whose main activities focused on public health, education, and welfare. The City Administration would also employ thousands of new workers, many of them in what was initially a makeshift postal service created during the Russian evacuation. In 1917 the city's expenditures exceeded its income by a factor of four, and by the end of the war, it had accumulated a debt more than ten times its annual income. To meet this level of its obligations, the Warsaw City Council approved a forced loan, introduced new taxes on income and property, amortized its debt, and overcame its principled opposition to gambling of any sort to sponsor a lottery. Despite these efforts—not the least of which included the feeding of up to two hundred thousand people in its public kitchens and the maintenance of schools that enrolled up to thirty-eight thousand children—an essentially bankrupted Warsaw City Administration could not hope to meet the escalating needs of the city's residents in the face of ever-mounting wartime hardship.

Under the German occupation regime, although there were political and cultural concessions to a national Polish agenda that focused on Warsaw and included municipal elections and the Polonization of the city's higher educational institutions, there would be no state subsidies as under the Russians. There would, however, be door-to-door requisitioning of food and other supplies in excess of established norms that was carried out by an occupation regime with which the Warsaw municipal authorities had inevitably become associated. Earlier, the occupation regime's introduction of a rapidly inflating Polish mark to replace the still comparatively stable Russian ruble not only served to increase the city's budgetary shortfall but wiped out whatever savings many of Warsaw's residents may have had left.

Among the more interesting documents in the papers of Piotr Drzewiecki, the mayor of Warsaw during the second half of the war, are a couple of undated and anonymous underground leaflets that played on religious themes in their condemnation of the German occupation. The first is "The Ten German Commandments," which begins "I am your German, who has divided you into three parts and submitted you unto slavery." The "German commandments" include the following: 1) "Thou shall not have enemies greater than me"; 5) "Thou shall not kill me, for you shall hang"; 7) "Thou shall not steal, for I am doing so already"; 8) "Say to me what you wish, but pay what I will fine you." Then there is the leaflet based on the Apostles' Creed, which opens with the following: "I believe in Wilhelm the father and his only begotten son, the Warsaw Beseler, who was conceived from a lack of ammunition and was born of requisitioning. . . ."[12]

We should, therefore, not be surprised that Warsaw was a place of acute political and social tensions in November 1918, their expression aimed as much at a hapless and vulnerable City Administration that had become responsible for the delivery of virtually all social services as at the Germans who starved that administration of even a minimal amount of funding. As early as the war's first year and the city's crisis of industrial employment, the Warsaw Citizens Committee, no doubt recalling violent labor unrest during the Revolution of 1905, worried about social peace in the city. Many of its programs—particularly those connected to finding work for those idled by the economic crisis—were certainly designed with its preservation in mind. Early conflicts nonetheless revolved around issues of workers' representation, whether on the committee itself or in its various sections and agencies. However, as state subventions dried up under the German occupation, those who had received support from the Russian government—particularly soldiers' wives and families—found themselves temporarily cut adrift. With a strong sense of entitlement, soldiers' wives were, therefore, the first to express their discontent in crowd and street demonstrations in August and September 1915. Women were also intimately involved in Warsaw's major food riots of June 1916 and May 1917. The former resulted in the partial or complete ransacking of dozens of stores operating under the supervision of the City Administration, many of which were looted a second time the following spring.

Meanwhile, for those who remained employed, the increase in food prices alone was double whatever increase there was in nominal earnings, leading to a decline in real wages by 25% by September 1916. While strikes had been largely avoided before the German occupation, the spring of 1916 brought labor stoppages among Warsaw's bakers, shoemakers, and millers in March and among the city's water, sewer, and trolley workers in May, many of whom had earlier refused to accept payment in marks instead of rubles. With the February 1917 revolution in Russia, social and class issues came even more to the forefront. In the spring of 1917, a strike in Warsaw's militarized metal factories involving thousands of workers led to mass arrests, street skirmishes, and the erection of makeshift barricades. Although there was a mild upturn in the local economy at the end of 1917 and the beginning of 1918, the failure of wages to keep pace with prices led to the city's only general strike during the war years in January 1918, one that began among workers employed by the City Administration and was sparked by the arrest of workers' delegates by the German occupation authorities. Despite attempts by the Warsaw City Council to secure their release as well as the release of other workers arrested for their involvement in the strike, the German response was characterized by repressive measures that would leave the city in an even darker mood and would lead to popular acquiescence in, if not support for, a series of retaliatory assassinations of German police officials carried out by the PPS.[13]

The city's harsh wartime experiences, particularly the severe food shortage, the decline in social services, and the fundamental existential crisis of its inhabitants, were bound to be played out as well in Polish-Jewish relations, an arena of ethnic conflict already well established before the war. As a consequence, the downhill slide in Polish-Jewish relations in Warsaw that began at the end of the nineteenth century not only continued, but accelerated. Shaped and intensified by the ever-increasing hardships brought on by the war, the conflict between Poles and Jews had reached a breaking point by the summer of 1918, when the German occupation authorities began to receive reports of pogrom agitation in Warsaw, where the Polish National Democrats were openly calling for a boycott of Jewish trade and commerce. By October, Jews—perceived as relatively better off by most Poles—were becoming frequent targets of physical attacks and robberies. At the now "Polish" Warsaw University, Jewish students who had expressed their willingness to join the fight for Polish independence were told to go to Palestine. It is a wonder, given the extent of the deterioration of Polish-Jewish relations in the city, that a pogrom was avoided. No doubt the peaceful transfer of authority from the Germans to Piłsudski and his supporters was partially responsible for sparing Warsaw such a nightmare.

So, what would we have seen in Warsaw in November of 1918 in addition to the coming-out party of the POW and the transfer of power in the capital city to Piłsudski? In addition to disarmed German soldiers preparing to evacuate, we just as likely would have encountered common street scenes of begging, long ration lines, perhaps a minor riot accompanied by looting, petty theft and organized banditry, and any number of women reduced to prostitution, some of whom had taken up residence in abandoned military barracks near to which they had plied their trade. We may have heard gunshots from skirmishes in the western reaches of the city and the Jewish quarter, where communists had already mounted demonstrations and where the PPS had created a "People's Militia." We would have seen Princess Lubomirska afraid to leave the family palace on elegant Frascati Street:

> How times have changed. Zdziś's popularity used to accompany us like a halo. When the president's car stopped on the street, unknown people with friendly smiles would rush to open or close the doors, etc. Today, driving on the street, I think that more than one of these people would gladly launch a bomb against "the traitors who have cut a deal with the Germans."[14]

In a word, Warsaw was fortunate to have Piłsudski, its man on horseback, at a time when the city was confronting an invasion of the Four Horsemen of the Apocalypse. Only then can we appreciate his genuine "Miracle on the Vistula," the prevention of a major outbreak of violence in Warsaw, if not elsewhere in a reborn Poland, in November 1918.

The Old-New Warsaw

At the outset of the First World War in 1914, Warsaw had not been the capital of a nominally sovereign state since the Third Partition of Poland in 1795, or the capital of any kind of political/territorial entity since the formal abolition of the Congress Kingdom of Poland, whose autonomy itself had become a legal fiction long before its vestiges disappeared following the suppression of the January Insurrection of 1863. From 1874 on, the city served as the administrative center of ten Russian *gubernii,* which together comprised something known officially as "Vistulaland." By the end of the nineteenth century Warsaw had become the "Third City" of the Russian Empire after St. Petersburg and Moscow, and although it would host Russian imperial institutions—for example, of higher education—the city was denied any institutions of local self-government comparable to the city dumas established in major Russian urban centers. Instead, Warsaw was administered, rather than governed, by a Magistrate whose office oversaw capital construction and infrastructural development that accelerated in the last decade of Russian imperial rule but was ill-equipped to provide modern social services. These were left to a host of charitable and philanthropic organizations, both Polish and Jewish. Moreover, since the end of 1905 and in the aftermath of revolution, Warsaw had been under martial law and other, lesser forms of emergency rule, which further reduced the authority of the Russian civilian administration and, given the city's strategic location in a future war with the Central Powers, added to an already considerable Russian military presence. At best, Warsaw before the war was the imagined capital of a nonexistent state. At worst, it resembled a city under military occupation.

Warsaw's rebirth as a capital city at the end of 1918 was no more preordained than the resurrection of a reunified Polish state, and in fact, the former was not necessarily tied to the latter. Instead, the exigencies of Europe's first total war were the most important factors in Warsaw's transformation from the Third City of the Russian Empire to the status of a capital city, a process already completed in twists and turns before the reestablishment of an independent Poland. This story, an unusual one at that, can be traced to the creation of what was essentially a voluntary nongovernmental organization at the beginning of the war, namely the Warsaw Citizens Committee.

At the committee's core was a group of notables led by Prince Zdzisław Lubomirski, a proponent of the idea of Russian-Polish conciliation that had long found favor in elite circles and experienced something of a revival in the war's first year. Though officially the committee was a nonpartisan organization, almost all of its Polish members could be defined as conservatives (also known as Realists) and National Democrats, who had combined forces in previous elections to the Russian State Duma. They were joined by a sprinkling of Polish "progressives" who sympathized with parts of the nationalist program, especially when it came to reducing the economic influence of Warsaw's Jews. The committee, however, did include a couple of members drawn from Warsaw's assimilated Jewish elite, although they were hardly representative of the Jewish community as a whole. The committee welcomed women's participation, but only in the front lines of social work where they comprised an overwhelming majority of committee volunteers. Definitely men on the right and center of Warsaw's political spectrum, Lubomirski and his male colleagues on the Warsaw Citizens Committee would work hand-in-glove, first with the Russians and then with the Germans, to provide a range of social services, to expand the city's administrative limits, to create a new City Administration and City Council, and in the process to restore Warsaw to the status of a capital city.

When in early August 1915 Prince Lubomirski took over authority from Russian president of the city Müller, he headed what was essentially an already functioning executive institution and skeletal administration, while the committee itself had begun to function as a de facto city council. Faced with this situation and anxious to secure the army's rear, the incoming German military authorities immediately recognized Lubomirski as president of the city, his deputy Piotr Drzewiecki as vice president, and the committee's Citizens Guard as a police force entrusted with maintaining public safety. Soon thereafter, in September 1915, the new City Administration now headed by Lubomirski reclaimed for Warsaw the title of capital city, or *miasto stołeczne*, although at this point Warsaw was little more than the central location of the German occupation regime in a former Polish Kingdom that also included an Austrian zone with its center in Lublin.

Yet in relatively short order, this fiction would be transformed into a reality. Before its dissolution in May 1916, representatives of the Warsaw Citizens Committee met in extraordinary session to write and vote on a municipal electoral ordinance. A year earlier, the Russian government had promised to permit the establishment of urban self-governing institutions in the empire's Polish provinces, including and especially in Warsaw. Elections were indeed subsequently scheduled, though never held. Although the Germans ultimately rejected the committee's April 1916 draft of an electoral ordinance and implemented a less democratic one of their own based on the Prussian system of separate and

unequal curiae, Warsaw's first modern municipal elections were held in the summer of 1916. The elected City Council predictably became one of the main arenas
where Polish-Jewish conflicts were played out for the remainder of the war and
beyond.

In addition to the transformation of its parts into a municipal administration
and City Council, the Warsaw Citizens Committee oversaw the process by which
Warsaw became a true modern metropolis through a dramatic expansion of the
area under the city's jurisdiction. Prior to the war, Warsaw's jurisdictional boundaries were limited to Old Town, New Town, Śródmieście, Powiśle, and Praga. On
the Vistula's east bank, Praga retained certain features of a separate administrative unit and was not originally represented in the Warsaw Citizens Committee. Though many had long advocated the annexation of the suburbs of Wola,
Mokotów, Bródno, and Ochota, it was the war itself that created the necessity for
that action. During the war's fourth week, citizens committees were formed in
Praga and Bródno on the model of the Warsaw Citizens Committee, upon which
they became increasingly dependent as the war continued. In mid-December
1914 the Warsaw County Citizens' Committee appealed to its city counterpart to
take charge of public assistance in Wola, Ochota, and Mokotów. By April 1915,
citizens of Wola and Mokotów were openly lobbying for annexation by Warsaw
in order to better manage the war's increasingly difficult demands and to meet a
very real need for improved sanitation in the suburbs.

As with the development of self-governing institutions and of plans for
municipal elections, what began under the Russians was completed under the
Germans. As a consequence of Beseler's decree of 8 April 1916, Warsaw's city
limits were expanded from 32.7 to 114.8 square kilometers, adding an additional
230,000 residents to the city's total population.[15] Although the expansion of the
city was to have long-term benefits, the Germans' short-term goal was likely to
rid themselves of responsibility for administering and provisioning the suburbs.
Even more so than the Russians before them, the Germans were also concerned
about the health of their army. The suburbs surrounding Warsaw, with the poor
quality of their drinking water and the absence of sewers for waste disposal, were
believed to harbor ideal conditions for the spread of infectious diseases. The rising incidence of typhoid fever and the approaching danger of a major typhus
epidemic in Warsaw in the first months of 1916 certainly played a factor in the
German decision to approve the annexation of the suburbs and the expansion of
Warsaw's sanitation and public health services to them.[16]

Warsaw's rejuvenation as a political capital was accompanied by a cultural
component that was also assisted by the German occupier, whose willingness
to tolerate and even support the relative freedom of cultural expression was
meant, in Beseler's words, "to contain or deflect political propaganda."[17] In this
atmosphere, an authentic Warsaw cabaret emerged, whose artistic content was

contested far more by the city's cultural conservatives than by the censors of the occupation regime. The periodical press, which had been reduced from 169 to 56 titles by the time of the Russian evacuation, also experienced a partial revival, reaching 87 titles by the end of 1916.[18] Greater freedoms were particularly noteworthy in the area of education. The Polska Macierz Szkolna, a network of private Polish schools suspended by the tsarist authorities in 1907, was permitted to renew its activities, only now in public education. A network of private and secular Yiddish-language schools, which had been banned under Russian rule, was also able to emerge after the occupation regime of the General-Government gave up on the idea of Germanizing Ostjuden in October 1916.[19] More symbolically significant, particularly for the revival of Warsaw as a cultural capital, was the reopening of Warsaw University and the Polytechnic Institute as Polish institutions of higher education in November 1915. Though curators of these educational institutions consisted mainly of Poles in German uniform, beginning with Count Bogdan Hutten-Czapski, they generally sought to maintain a low profile until striking students unsuccessfully demanded their removal in 1917.

Not only were the Germans quick to approve the replacement of Russian-language signs with their Polish equivalents, they were also supportive of all public manifestations of anti-Russian sentiment, particularly in national observances and anniversaries—such as those of the November and January insurrections. The most significant national celebration in Warsaw during the First World War was the 3 May anniversary celebration in 1916, which may have involved twice as many spectators in the streets as those who marched in the three-hour procession. The participants included but were not limited to some 3,000 marchers representing 19 sporting organizations and clubs, some 1,200 scouts marching in 75 rows, and another 76 nonsporting organizations, including some 1,500 participants representing the Society for the Development of Industry, Crafts and Commerce.[20] Historian Stanisław Kutrzeba, who had come to Warsaw from Krakow to witness the spectacle, later recalled that in his conversations with local citizens his interlocutors expressed feelings of tremendous satisfaction and pride in the national public display, and in the "model of order" overseen by members of the City Militia in their new and handsome uniforms.[21]

As the war continued, however, such gestures to Polish national sentiments, intended to neutralize potential opposition to the German occupation, became increasingly ineffective. On 5 November 1916, having concluded definitively that Imperial Russia would not sue for a separate peace, the Central Powers announced the creation of an "independent" Kingdom of Poland, a quasi-state that merged their two occupation zones with Warsaw as its capital and in alliance with the Kaiserreich and the Austro-Hungarian Empire. This and other "state-building" measures—including first the creation of a Provisional Council of State and then a Regency Council that presided over a cabinet of nine ministers—may have further raised the status of Warsaw but otherwise ran afoul of the rising political expectations that the occupiers themselves had generated, not to mention the rapid decline in living standards as a consequence of German requisitioning. Consequently, the "model of order" that characterized Warsaw in May 1916 quickly gave way to street riots and looting, theft and banditry, a visible increase in prostitution, and, by the autumn of 1918, political assassinations.

By this time, Warsaw's first modern municipal government, the proud creation of the Warsaw Citizens Committee, had become financially starved, unable to provide relief to the population and struggling to pay its own employees. Ironically, in the immediate aftermath of the armistice and the proclamation of an independent and reunified Poland with Warsaw as its capital, the Warsaw City Council at its session of 22 November 1918 called upon the City Administration to make sure that the sanitary units of each police precinct were provided with the appropriate number of caskets to remove the dead from Warsaw's impoverished, diseased, and starving population.[22] However, with expenditures exceeding revenues by at least 400%, and an accumulated debt of more than 100 million Polish marks by war's end, it was difficult to imagine how the City Administration would be able to afford this last service to Warsaw's poor.

The story of Warsaw during the First World War, and of its transformation from the third city of the Russian Empire to the capital city of an independent Poland, is certainly one of triumph. It is also one of considerable tragedy. Without the war, neither would have occurred. There would not have been a Warsaw Citizens Committee, but then again, there would not have been the need for such an organization created by the wartime economic crisis and the unimaginably high unemployment. There would not have been a Russian evacuation, creating a vacuum that enabled this nongovernmental organization to assume important police and administrative functions. There would not have been a German occupation regime prepared to recognize Warsaw as a capital city in September 1915 and to allow its acquisition of cultural, spatial, and finally political content, part of a misguided policy to win the hearts and minds of Poles while simultaneously stripping the city and its recently annexed suburbs bare. Without wartime deprivations, the city may not have developed the institutional infrastructure for a modern urban welfare system that would survive the war, even as the city treasury faced bankruptcy. Thus, Warsaw had indeed been transformed into a *miasto stołeczne* by war's end, one that for a moment could celebrate its centrality in the emergence of a new and independent Poland. Yet it was also a cold, dark, diseased, and starving capital whose immediate future anticipated the onslaught of the Great Influenza and three more years of rationing and acute hunger.

Notes

ARCHIVES

AAN	**Archiwum Akt Nowych (Archive of New Documents)**
AD	Akta Drzewickich
ASD	Akta Stanisława Dzierzbickiego
TRS	Tymczasowy Rada Stanu w Warszawie
AGAD	**Archiwum Głowny Akt Dawnych (Main Archives of Old Documents)**
CNGGW	Cesarsko-Niemieckie Generał-Gubernatorstwo w Warszawie
CNPPW	Cesarsko-Niemieckie Prezydium Policji w Warszawie
SAGGW	Szef Administracji przy Generał-Gubernatorstwie w Warszawie
APW	**Archiwum Państwowe m.st. Warszawy (State Archive of the Capital City of Warsaw)**
KOMW	Komitet Obywatelski Miasta Warszawy, 1914–1916
KR	Komisja Rekwizyjna IV Rejonu Miasta Warszawy
RNG	Redakcja "Nowej Gazety"
ZMW	Zarząd Miejski m. st. Warszawy, 1915–1919
ZOW	Zarząd Oberpolicmajstra Warszawskiego

INTRODUCTION

1. The reference here is to the fin-de-siécle Polish novelist and 1905 Nobel Prize winner Henryk Sienkiewicz, who is best known for his patriotic trilogy set in the second half of the seventeenth century.

2. Stanisław Dzikowski, *Rok wojny w Warszawie: Notatki* (Cracow: Nakładem Centralnego Biura Wydawnictwo N.K.N., 1916), 9–18.

3. Archiwum Państwowe m.st. Warszawy (APW), Zarząd Oberpolicmajstra Warszawskiego (ZOW), 1107.

4. "Wiadomości bieżące. Dowóz żywności," *Kurjer Warszawski* 209 (31 July 1914): 1.

5. "Nastrój w mieście," *Kurjer Warszawski* 207 (29 July 1914): 4; "Z miasta," *Kurjer Warszawski* 210 (1 August 1914, morn. ed.): 1; Czesław Jankowski, "Pierwsze dni wojny-ostatnie dni rosjan w Warszawie," in *Warszawa w pamiętnikach pierwszej wojny światowej*, ed. Krzysztof Dunin-Wąsowicz (Warsaw: Państwowy Instytut Wydawniczy, 1971), 39–43.

6. For more on prewar Warsaw, see Stephen D. Corrsin, *Warsaw before the First World War: Poles and Jews in the Third City of the Russian Empire, 1880–1914* (Boulder, CO, and Columbia: East European Monographs, 1989). On the imposition of martial law in Warsaw and other cities of the former Polish Kingdom, see Robert E. Blobaum, *Rewolucja: Russian Poland, 1904–1907* (Ithaca, NY: Cornell University Press, 1995), 260–91. On the impact of the Russian Revolution of 1905 on Jewish political culture and Polish-Jewish relations, see Scott Ury, *Barricades and Banners: The Revolution of 1905 and the Transformation of Warsaw Jewry* (Stanford, CA: Stanford University Press, 2012).

7. The elastic and unsettled nature of Germany's eastern border, both during and immediately after the war, and the large-scale population movements across it, is the subject of Annemarie H. Sammartino, *The Impossible Border: Germany and the East, 1914–1922* (Ithaca, NY: Cornell University Press, 2012).

8. See Jesse Kauffman, *Elusive Alliance: The German Occupation of Poland in World War I* (Cambridge, MA: Harvard University Press, 2015); Robert M. Spät, "Für eine gemeinsame deutsch-polnische Zukunft? Hans Hartwig von Beseler als Generalgouverneur in Polen, 1915–1918," *Zeitschrift für Ostmitteleuropa-Forschung* 58, no. 4 (2009): 469–500; and Marta Polsakiewicz, "Spezifika deutscher Besatzungspolitik in Warschau 1914–1916," *Zeitschrift für Ostmitteleuropa-Forschung* 58, no. 4 (2009): 501–37. Polsakiewicz's recently published dissertation, *Warschau im ersten Weltkrieg: Deutsche Besatzungspolitik zwischen kultereller Autonomie und wirtschaftlicher Ausbeutung* (Marburg: Verlag Herder Institut, 2015) appeared after this book went into production.

9. See Lech Królikowski and Krzysztof Oktabiński, *Warszawa 1914–1920: Warszawa i okolice w latach walk o niepodległość i granice Rzeczypospolitej* (Warsaw: Wydawnictwo Akademickie i Profesjonalne, 2008); and Lech Wyszczelski, *Warszawa Listopad 1918* (Warsaw: Bellona, 2008).

10. An exception here is Katarzyna Sierakowska's recent study of wartime death, displacement, and hunger from the perspective of ego-documents, *Śmierć-wygnanie-głód: Ziemia polskie w latach Wielkiej Wojny 1914–1918* (Warsaw: Neriton, 2015).

11. See the works of Kauffman and Polsakiewicz cited earlier in this chapter.

12. Krzysztof Dunin-Wąsowcicz, *Warszawa w czasie pierwszej wojny światowej* (Warsaw: Państwowe Instytut Naukowej, 1974).

13. Krzysztof Dunin-Wąsowicz, "Przedmowa," in *Warszawa w pamiętnikach*, 26, 35. The number for the Second World War comes from Dunin-Wąsowicz, *Warszawa w latach 1939–1945* (Warsaw: Państwowe Wydawnictwo Naukowe, 1984), 12.

14. Ministerstwo Obrony Narodowy, "Grób Nieznanego Żołnierza," accessed 9 July 2013, http://wojsko-polskie.pl/articles/view/3109.

15. A similar process of conflation can be seen in Riga where, according to Mark Hatlie, "the entire six years are fused into a coherent whole in which the multiple experiences, loyalties, and coalitions among the Latvians and the complicated roles of other groups are made invisible" by the 1919 Latvian war of liberation. Mark R. Hatlie, "Riga und der Erste Weltkrieg: Eine Exkursion," in *Über den Weltkrieg hinaus: Kriegserfahrungen in Ostmitteleuropa*, ed. Joachim Tauber, Nordost-Archiv Zeitschrift für Regionalgeschichte, Neue Folge Band XVII/2008 (Lüneberg: Nordost-Institut, 2009), 32.

16. Roman Wapiński, "Władysław Sikorkski," *Polski Słownik Biograficzny* 37, 3, zeszyt 154 (1997): 471.

17. For a discussion of Russia's "forgotten war," see Dietrich Beyrau and Pavel P. Shcherbinin, "Alles für die Front: Russland in Krieg 1914–1922," in *Durchhalten! Krieg und Gesellschaft in Vergleich 1914–1918*, ed. Arnd Bauerkämper and Elise Julien (Göttingen: Vandenhoeck and Ruprecht, 2010), 151–77. Karen Petrone, however, argues that the war was "decentered" rather than forgotten; see her *The Great War in Russian Memory* (Bloomington, IN: Indiana University Press, 2011).

18. Michel-Rolph Trouillot, *Silencing the Past: Power and the Production of History* (Boston: Beacon Press, 1995), 118.

19. Katrin Van Cant, "Historical Memory in Post-Communist Poland: Warsaw's Monuments after 1989," *Studies in Slavic Cultures* 8 (2009): 90–119. Interested primarily in the "street scene," Van Cant's study deliberately excludes cemeteries.

20. Ibid., 98–99.

21. Ibid., 113.

22. Ibid., 112.

23. Tomasz Szarota, *Okupowaniej Warszawy dzień powszedni: Studium historyczny* (Warsaw: Czytelnik, 1973), 181–89; Dunin-Wąsowicz, *Warszawa w latach 1939–1945*, 113.

24. Szarota, 192. Szarota estimates that 50% of all deaths in the Warsaw ghetto resulted from starvation.

25. Ibid., 193; Dunin-Wąsowicz, *Warszawa w latach 1939–1945*, 113, 143; Jan Tomasz Gross, *Polish Society under German Occupation: The Generalgouvernement 1939–1944* (Princeton: Princeton University Press, 1979), 109.

26. Erica L. Tucker, *Remembering Occupied Warsaw: Polish Narratives of World War II* (Dekalb, IL: Northern Illinois University Press, 2011).

27. Szarota, 201.

28. Gross, 45, 112, 145.

29. Szarota, 139–45; Gross, 98; Dunin-Wąsowicz, *Warszawa w latach 1939–1945*, 133–35.

30. Dunin-Wąsowicz, *Warszawa w latach 1939–1945*, 67.

31. For a far more detailed exploration of Warsaw's changing demographics during the Great War, see Robert Blobaum, "A City in Flux: Warsaw's Transient Populations during the First World War," *The Polish Review* 59, no. 4 (2014): 21–43.

32. Szarota, 75; Dunin-Wąsowcicz, *Warszawa w czasie pierwszej wojny światowej*, 88–89.

33. Szarota, 76, 79; Dunin-Wąsowicz, *Warszawa w czasie pierwszej wojny światowej*, 180; Jerzy Holzer and Jan Molenda, *Polska w pierwszej wojnie światowej* (Warsaw: Wiedza Powszechna, 1963), 123.

34. Szarota, 79–80; Dunin-Wąsowicz, *Warszawa w latach 1939–1945*, 85. For tuberculosis in Warsaw during the Great War, see chapter 2 of this book.

35. Reports of the Polish underground noted a 10% annual death rate in the Warsaw ghetto in the first ten months of 1941; see Joshua D. Zimmerman, *The Polish Underground and the Jews, 1939–1945* (New York: Cambridge University Press, 2015), 99, 109, 138.

36. Szarota, 269–77.

37. Ibid., 254–68.

38. Dunin-Wąsowicz, *Warszawa w czasie pierwszej wojny światowej*, 78–79.

39. Jan Assmann, *Cultural Memory and Early Civilization: Writing, Remembrance, and Political Imagination* (Cambridge: Cambridge University Press, 2011), 9.

40. Trouillot, 48, 51.

41. Ibid., xix, 29.

42. APW, Komisja Rekwizyjna IV Rejonu Miasta Warszawy (KR).

43. Bogdan Hutten-Czapski, "Ostatnie dni okupacji niemieckiej w Warszawie," in *Warszawa w pamiętnikach*, 478–79.

44. These are available in three collections: Cesarsko-Niemieckie Generał-Gubernatorstwo w Warszawie (CNGGW), Szef Administracji przy Generał-Gubernatorstwie w Warszawie (SAGGW), and Cesarsko-Niemieckie Prezydium Policji w Warszawie (CNPPW).

45. AGAD CNGGW 1, Beseler to the Kaiser, 23 October 1915.

46. Archiwum Akt Nowych (AAN), Tymczasowy Rada Stanu w Warszawie (TRS), from the archive's description of the collection; Tucker, 91.

47. APW, Komitet Obywatelski Miasta Warszawy 1914–1916 (KOMW).

48. APW, Zarząd Miejski m. st. Warszawy 1915–1919 (ZMW).

49. Konrad Zieliński, *Stosunki polsko-żydowskie na ziemiach Królestwa Polskiego w czasie pierwszej wojny światowej* (Lublin: Wydawnictwo Uniwersytetu Marii Curie-Skłodowskiej, 2005), 116.

50. According to Jewish journalist Bernard Singer, *Kurjer Warszawski* was "the newspaper of every solid home. It wasn't sold just anywhere, but in finely arranged special kiosks or from merchants of imported goods." It was read not only by Poles but also by Jews, "of course, solid ones . . . the assimilated doctors, engineers, bankers; also the Orthodox . . . the richest ones." Its obituaries were especially noteworthy: "Every self-respecting person died in *Kurjer Warszawski*"; Bernard Singer, *Moje Nalewki* (Warsaw: Czytelnik, 1959), 117–19.

248   NOTES TO PAGES 15–26

51. APW, Redakcja "Nowej Gazety" (RNG) 1, Circular #12 of the Press Department of the Chief of Administration under the Warsaw Governor-General, 6 October 1915. This collection of documents from the editorial board of *Nowa Gazeta* contains communications and announcements from the German occupation authorities and offers a rare perspective on how one Warsaw daily dealt with German censorship.

52. See "Rozruchy żywnościowe wybuchły w Warszawie," *Komunikat Informacyjny* 1 (9–11 May 1917): 4. The same could be said for *Rząd i Wojsko*, an "independent" press organ published by Piłsudski's supporters; see "Głód i polityka" and "Rozruchy w Warszawie," *Rząd i Wojsko* 18 (20 May 1917): 7, 8.

53. For discussions of these polemics before the war, see Jerzy Jedlicki, "The End of the Dialogue: Warsaw, 1907–1912," in *The Jews in Poland* 2, ed. Sławomir Kapralski (Krakow: Judaica Foundation, 1999): 111–23; and Theodore R. Weeks, "Fanning the Flames: Jews in the Warsaw Press, 1905–1912," *East European Jewish Affairs* 28, no. 2 (Winter 1998–1999): 63–81.

54. According to Joshua Zimmerman, even the unfolding genocide in the spring of 1942 remained confined to the back pages of the Polish underground press, which only changed with the great deportations from the Warsaw Ghetto from July to September of that year; Zimmerman, 143, 156–60.

55. Dunin-Wąsowicz, "Przedmowa," 27.

56. Nojach Pryłucki, *Mowy wygłoszone w pierwszej Radzie Miejskiej st. m. Warszawy, w b. Radzie Stanu Król. Polsk., w Sejmie Ustawodawczym Rzeczypospolitej Polskiej* 1 (Warsaw: Nakładem Rady Centralnej Żydowskiego Stronnictwa Ludowego w Polsce, 1920).

57. Van Cant, 109.

58. Stanisław Dzierzbicki, *Pamiętnik z lat wojny 1915–1918* (Warsaw: Państwowy Instytut Wydawniczy, 1983).

59. Maria Lubomirska, *Pamiętnik księżnej Marii Zdzisławowej Lubomirskiej, 1914–1918*, ed. Jerzy Pajewski (Poznań: Wydawnictwo Poznańskie, 1997).

60. Dunin-Wąsowicz excerpted various fragments from Kutrzeba's "impressions" of his visit to Warsaw from the latter's *Królestwo i Galicya: Uwagi z czasu wojny* (Warsaw-Krakow: Towarzystwo Wydawnicze w Warszawie, 1917), 44–61.

61. S. Ansky, *The Enemy at His Pleasure: A Journey Through the Jewish Pale of Settlement During World War I*, ed. and trans. Joachim Neugroschel (New York: Metropolitan Books, 2002), 12.

62. As Pierre Nora reminds us, historiography is little more than "the scholarly construction of memory"; *Rethinking France: Les Lieux de Mémoire* 1, ed. Pierre Nora (Chicago: The University of Chicago Press, 2001), xx. Trouillot, for his part, argues that "the value of a historical product cannot be debated without taking into account the context of its production and the context of its consumption"; Trouillot, 146.

63. That the Warsaw "Yiddish press" published Polish titles is not as surprising as it may seem, considering the bilingual capabilities of Warsaw's Jews. Bernard Singer speaks of Jewish couples taking Saturday afternoon strolls on the eve of the war who "spoke exclusively Yiddish on Muranowska, Miła and Nalewki. On Bielańska the same strollers mixed Polish with Yiddish, but in the Saxon Garden and on Marszałkowska they spoke only Polish. They returned before evening to their district. And again on Bielańska Polish was mixed with Yiddish and as soon as they reached Nalewki, Yiddish ruled"; Singer, 127.

1. THE FRONTLINE CITY

1. "Wiadomości bieżące. Z miasta," *Kurjer Warszawski* 211 (2 August 1914, aft. ed.): 4; "Bezrobocia pod miastem," *Nowa Gazeta* 350 (2 August 1914): 4.

2. "Kronika. Z miasta," *Nowa Gazeta* 351 (3 August 1914): 4; "Wiadomości bieżące. Nastrój w mieście," *Kurjer Warszawski* 210 (1 August 1914, aft. ed.): 2.

3. Thanks to the support of the Russian State Bank, Warsaw's commercial banks survived this initial run on their funds; Peter Gatrell, *Russia's First World War: A Social and Economic History* (Harlow, UK: Pearson, 2005), 27.

4. Warsaw's reopened banks announced on 4 August that they would begin to issue coupons in 1-, 3-, and 5-ruble denominations. A few days later, some of Warsaw's larger cafés began to issue vouchers in lieu of change, and shortly thereafter the City Administration authorized trolley conductors to accept newly printed stamps; "Z miasta," *Kurjer Warszawski* 213 (4 August 1914, morn. ed.): 3–4; "Bony," *Nowa Gazeta* 361 (8 August 1914, aft. ed.): 2; APW KOMW 1, protocol no. 16 of 12 August 1914.

5. "Wiadomości bieżące. Z miasta. Nastrój w mieście," *Kurjer Warszawski* 215 (6 August 1914, morn. ed.): 3.

6. Meanwhile, London and Berlin would experience near boom conditions by mid-1915; see Jon Lawrence, "The Transition to War in 1914," in *Capital Cities at War: Paris, London, Berlin 1914–1919* 1, ed. Jay Winter and Jean-Louis Robert (Cambridge, UK: Cambridge University Press, 1997), 135–63.

7. C. Jankowski, "Pierwszy dni wojny—ostatni dnia rosjan w Warszawie," in *Warszawa w pamiętnikach*, 45.

8. Dzikowski, *Rok wojny*, 20.

9. Lubomirska, 14–15, 17.

10. "Wiadomości bieżące. Z miasta," *Kurjer Warszawski* 210 (1 August 1914, aft. ed.): 2.

11. "Po mobilizacji," *Kurjer Warszawski* 221 (12 August 1914, aft. ed.): 2. The success of mobilization reflected imperial-wide trends as 96% of all reservists responded to the call of the Russian government; Joshua Sanborn, *Imperial Apocalypse: The Great War and the Destruction of the Russian Empire* (Oxford: Oxford University Press, 2014), 23.

12. Dzikowski, *Rok wojny*, 21. For less-charged depictions of these scenes, see "Wiadomości bieżące. Nastrój w mieście," *Kurjer Warszawski* 210 (1 August 1914, aft. ed.): 2; and "Kronika. Z miasta," *Nowa Gazeta* 351 (3 August 1914): 4.

13. "Zapomogi dla rodzin rezerwistów," *Kurjer Warszawski* 242 (2 September 1914, morn. ed.): 3.

14. "O mieszkania rezerwistów," *Kurjer Warszawski* 233 (24 August 1914, aft. ed.): 3.

15. Dzikowski, *Rok wojny*, 21. Warsaw and Krakow have shared a long history of not-so-friendly rivalry; for the early twentieth century see Hanna Kozińska-Witt, *Krakau in Warschaus langem Schatten: Konkurrenzkämpfe in der polnischen Städtelandschaft 1900–1939* (Stuttgart: Franz Steiner Verlag, 2008).

16. "Ochotnicy wojenni," *Nowa Gazeta* 358 (7 August 1914, morn. ed.): 2; "Ochotnicy," *Nowa Gazeta* 366 (11 August 1914, morn. ed.): 2; "Ochotnicy," *Nowa Gazeta* 367 (12 August 1914, morn. ed.): 1; "Ochotnicy," *Kurjer Warszawski* 217 (8 August 1914, aft. ed.): 2. These volunteers were soon joined by dozens of Czechs, Austrian citizens, who simultaneously petitioned to be accepted as Russian subjects; APW ZOW 1114.

17. Dzikowski, *Rok wojny*, 22.

18. Walenty Miklaszewski, "Memorabilia," in *Warszawa w pamiętnikach*, 62–63.

19. The exact number from the September 1914 draft is unavailable but probably ranged between 2,000 and 2,100. This estimate is based on precise data from subsequent call-ups in November 1914 and January, February/March, May, and June 1915, which each led to the enlistment of between 2,000 and 2,070 soldiers in Warsaw; "O powołaniu do spełnienia powinności wojskowej w m. Warszawie w r. 1914," *Nowa Gazeta* 535 (14 November 1914, aft. ed.): 3; "Pobór 1915 r.," *Nowa Gazeta* 32 (21 January 1915, aft. ed.): 2; *Kurjer Warszawski* 58 (27 February 1915, aft. ed.): 3–4.

20. "Poszukiwanie popisowych," *Nowa Gazeta* 175 (18 April 1915, morn. ed.): 3.

21. APW KOMW 1, protocol no. 11 of 9 August 1914.

22. "Pomoc sanitarna," *Nowa Gazeta* 378 (18 August 1914, aft. ed.): 2.

23. "Sanitarjuszki warszawskie," *Kurjer Warszawski* 235 (26 August 1914, aft. ed.): 2.

24. W. Perzyński, "Z tygodnia," *Tygodnik Illustrowany* 36 (5 September 1914): 656–57.
25. "Przyjęcie rannych," *Kurjer Warszawski* 237 (28 August 1914, aft. ed.): 3; "Na ulicach Warszawy" and "Ze szpitali," *Kurjer Warszawski* 239 (30 August 1914, Sunday ed.): 4, 5.
26. Lubomirska, 18.
27. APW KOMW 1, protocol no. 16 of 12 August 1914; "Statystyki kriminalne," *Nowa Gazeta* 371 (14 August 1914, morn. ed.): 1.
28. "Spokój w mieście," *Nowa Gazeta* 4 (4 August 1914, aft. ed.): 2; and "Z przedmieść," *Nowa Gazeta* 384 (21 August 1914, aft. ed.): 2.
29. Holzer and Molenda, 63.
30. "Kronika wydarzeń w Warszawie w latach 1914–1918," in *Warszawa w pamiętnikach*, 494.
31. APW ZOW 1116.
32. Laura Engelstein, "'A Belgium of Our Own': The Sack of Russian Kalisz, August 1914," *Kritika: Explorations in Russian and Eurasian History* 10, no. 3 (Summer 2009): 441–73.
33. "Kronika," 495; Lubomirska, 26.
34. Ignacy Grabowski, "Nie przeskadzajcie," *Kurjer Warszawski* 265 (25 September 1914, aft. ed.): 2.
35. "Zeppelin nad Warszawą," *Kurjer Warszawski* 266 (27 September 1914, Sunday ed.): 5; and "Zeppelin nad Warszawą," *Nowa Gazeta* 451 (27 September 1914, morn. ed.): 5.
36. "Wyzysk," *Kurjer Warszawski* 266 (27 September 1914, Sunday ed.): 5.
37. Miklaszewski, 66.
38. Dunin-Wąsowicz, *Warszawa w czasie pierwszej wojny światowej*, 82.
39. That capacity was estimated in a police document at slightly more than twelve thousand beds, less than half of them operated by the Russian Army; APW ZOW 1109.
40. Sanborn, *Imperial Apocalypse*, 155.
41. Lubomirska, 63–65.
42. Ibid., 67.
43. C. Jankowski, 46.
44. Irena Krzywicka, *Wyznania gorszycielki*, ed. Agata Tuszyńska (Warsaw: Czytelnik, 1992), 51.
45. Dzikowski, 24.
46. Z. D. [Zdzisław Dębicki], "Warszawa," *Tygodnik Illustrowany* 44 (31 October 1914): 730–31.
47. "Zmiana," *Kurjer Warszawski* 289 (19 October 1914, aft. ed.): 2.
48. [Pal.], "Dobre miasto," *Kurjer Warszawski* 288 (18 October 1914, Sunday ed.): 2.
49. "Z dnia wczorajszego," *Nowa Gazeta* 480 (14 October 1914, morn. ed.): 2.
50. Dębicki, "Warszawa," 730.
51. "Odparcie i odwrót niemców," *Kurjer Warszawski* 292 (22 October 1914, morn. ed.): 1.
52. "Nabożeństwo dziękczynne," *Kurjer Warszawski* 292 (22 October 1914, aft. ed.): 3; "Komitet Synogogi na Tłomackiem," *Nowa Gazeta* 501 (25 October 1915, morn. ed.): 4.
53. Lubomirska, 76; see also "Armaty niemieckie w Warszawie" and "Jeńcy," *Kurjer Warszawski* 299 (29 October 1914, morn. ed.): 4.
54. Dębicki, "Warszawa," 730.
55. C. Jankowski, 47.
56. Dzikowski, 31.
57. Ibid.
58. APW KOMW 1, protocols nos. 15, 16, 19, and 20 of 11, 12, and 14 August 1914, respectively.
59. Franciszek Herbst, "Działalność społeczna i samorządowa," in *Warszawa w pamiętnikach*, 287.

60. "Narada kaliszan," *Kurjer Warszawski* 247 (7 September 1914, morn. ed.): 3.

61. These estimates came from the Central Citizens Committee, which operated throughout the Polish Kingdom and was dominated by the Polish National Democrats, and from the Central Jewish Committee formed in Petrograd. Since the vast majority of refugees in Warsaw at the time were Jewish, it is possible that a lower proportion of Jews seeking refuge in the city were lodged in public shelters; Jan Lutosławski, "W sprawie opieki nad bezdomymi," *Kurjer Warszawski* 35 (4 February 1915, aft. ed.): 1–2; and "Centralny komitet żydowski," *Kurjer Warszawski* 38 (7 February 1915): 5.

62. Herbst, 287–90.

63. David Rechter, *The Jews of Vienna and the First World War* (London and Portland, OR: The Littman Library of Jewish Civilization, 2001), 72, 78. See also Christoph Mick, *Kriegersfahrungen in einer multiethnicshen Stadt: Lemberg 1914–1947* (Wiesbaden: Harrassowitz Verlag, 2010), 79; according to Mick, by the time the Russian Army had entered Lwów at the end of August 1914, 100,000 out of 800,000 Galician Jews had already fled to the interior of the Habsburg Empire, mainly to Vienna.

64. Peter Gatrell, *A Whole Empire Walking: Refugees in Russia during World War I* (Bloomington and Indianapolis, IN: Indiana University Press, 1999), 17. At the end of January 1915, the Polish daily *Kurjer Warszawski* was calling for the resettlement of a reported one hundred thousand refugees from Warsaw to the east of the Vistula River; "Nadmiar ludności," *Kurjer Warszawski* 29 (29 January 1915, morn. ed.): 3.

65. "65 tysięcy bezdomnych," *Kurjer Warszawski* 287 (17 October 1914, aft. ed.): 2.

66. APW KOMW 1, protocol no. 65 of 10 October 1914.

67. "Wsród bezdomnych," *Kurjer Warszawski* 291 (21 October 1914, aft. ed.): 3; and "Usuwanie bezdomnych," *Kurjer Warszawski* 315 (14 November 1914): 2.

68. Wincenty Kosiakiewicz, "Ewakuacja bezdomnych," *Kurjer Warszawski* 327 (16 November 1914, aft. ed.): 1–2.

69. "Z sekcji bezdomych," *Kurjer Warszawski* 52 (21 February 1915): 5.

70. Herbst, 287.

71. Ansky, 13.

72. Ibid., 33–35; "Żydzi bezdomni," *Nowa Gazeta* 509 (30 October 1914, aft. ed.): 2.

73. Ansky, 14. Similar scenes of Cossack plundering and robbery of Jews were reported in Lwów, which ultimately culminated in a pogrom on 27 September 1914 and resulted in dozens of deaths; Mick, 105.

74. Daniel Graf, "Military Rule behind the Russian Front, 1914–1917," *Jahrbücher für Geschichte Osteuropas* 22 (1974): 398; Joshua A. Sanborn, "Unsettling the Empire: Violent Migrations and Social Disaster in Russia during World War I," *The Journal of Modern History* 77, no. 5 (June 2005): 306.

75. Eric Lohr, "The Russian Army and the Jews: Mass Deportation, Hostages and Violence during World War I," *The Russian Review* 60 (July 2001): 409–10.

76. APW KOMW 2, protocol no. 150 of 17 April 1915 and Presidium protocol no. 69 of 23 April 1915.

77. APW KOMW 2, protocol no. 159 of 20 May 1915.

78. APW KOMW 2, Presidium protocol no. 92 of 26 June 1915; "Bezdomi" and "W hotelach," *Kurjer Warszawski* 167 (19 June 1915, morn. ed.): 4.

79. "Zbiegowie," *Kurjer Warszawski* 140 (22 May 1915, aft. ed.): 4; "Napływ zbiegów," *Nowa Gazeta* 234 (26 May 1915, morn. ed.): 2.

80. "Z chwili," *Nowa Gazeta* 340 (29 July 1915): 1; APW KOMW 2, protocols no. 178 of 25 July 1915 and no. 182 of 29 July 1915.

81. Dzikowski, *Rok wojny*, 46.

82. Eric Lohr, *Nationalizing the Russian Empire: The Campaign Against Enemy Aliens during World War I* (Cambridge, MA: Harvard University Press, 2003), 1.

83. Charges of treason, originally targeted at Jews, spread throughout wartime Russia's imperial political culture and continued beyond the empire's downfall; see William C. Fuller, Jr., *The Foe Within: Fantasies of Treason and the End of Imperial Russia* (Ithaca, NY: Cornell University Press, 2006).

84. "O zmianę nazwiska," in *Nowa Gazeta* 576 (10 December 1914, morn. ed.): 2.

85. In November 1914 the state began to entertain the idea of confiscating the city's "German" gasworks, with its assets of approximately 1 million rubles in cash, certificates, and bonds, which were then indeed sequestered before the winter holidays; "Konfiskaty," *Nowa Gazeta* 541(18 November 1914, aft. ed.): 2; "Sekwester Zakładów Gazowych," *Nowa Gazeta* 600 (24 December 1914, morn. ed.): 2.

86. "Zamknięcie zrzeszeń niemieckich w Warszawie," *Nowa Gazeta* 31 (21 January 1915, morn. ed.): 2.

87. Lohr, *Nationalizing the Russian Empire*, 124.

88. "Wydalenie poddanych zagranicznych," *Kurjer Warszawski* 42 (11 February 1915, morn. ed.): 3.

89. "Wysiedlanie jeńców cywilnych," *Nowa Gazeta* 64 (10 February 1915, aft. ed.): 3.

90. "Wydalania poddanych zagranicznych," *Kurjer Warszawski* 43 (12 February 1915): 3.

91. "Wyjazd niemców," *Kurjer Warszawski* 55 (24 February 1915, morn. ed.): 2; "Wydalanie obcych poddanych," *Nowa Gazeta* 87 (24 February 1915, morn. ed.): 2.

92. "Dla wydalonych poddanych obcych," *Kurjer Warszawski* 56 (25 February 1915, morn. ed.): 3.

93. "Dla poddanych zagranicznych," *Kurjer Warszawski* 44 (13 February 1915, morn. ed.): 2–3.

94. "Echa wydalania obcych poddanych," *Nowa Gazeta* 95 (28 February 1915, morn. ed.): 3; "Usuwanie obcych poddanych," *Kurjer Warszawski* 60 (1 March 1915, aft. ed.): 2.

95. "Poddani zagraniczne," *Kurjer Warszawski* 45 (14 February 1915): 3.

96. Lohr, *Nationalizing the Russian Empire*, 127.

97. On Germanophobia in the Russian imperial capital, see Ivan G. Sobolev, *Borba s "nemetskim zasilem" v Rossii v gody pervoi mirovoi voiny* (St. Petersburg State University dissertation, 1998).

98. Lohr, *Nationalizing the Russian Empire*, 130.

99. Gatrell, *A Whole Empire Walking*, 23–24.

100. "Wysiedleni z Żyrardowa," *Nowa Gazeta* 106 (6 March 1915, morn. ed.): 3.

101. According to figures published in *Kurjer Warszawski*, 75,000 people arrived in Warsaw in the first half of November and another 125,000 in the second half. Although an estimated 50,000 of these arrivals consisted of refugees, the remaining 150,000 were returnees. Those who did not return, however, were the main contributing factor to the city's population decline, which at the end of December stood at 80,000–100,000 fewer inhabitants than at the beginning of the war; "Bezdomi w Warszawie," *Kurjer Warszawski* 357 (28 December 1914, spec. ed.): 2.

102. APW KOMW 1, protocol no. 28 of 23 August 1914.

103. Lars Lih, *Bread and Authority in Russia, 1914–1917* (Berkeley: University of California Press, 1990), 9. Although Lih was primarily interested in the movement of grain, Russia's railways had never served coal producers well, according to Peter Gatrell. Wartime disruptions made things worse, and by October 1915, 1.1 million tons of coal awaited dispatch from the pit head; Gatrell, *Russia's First World War*, 110.

104. "W sprawie opału," *Kurjer Warszawski* 264 (24 September 1914, morn. ed.): 3.

105. "Węgiel dla Warszawy," *Kurjer Warszawski* 270 (30 September 1914, aft. ed.): 2.

106. "Gaz i elektryczność wobec wojny," *Nowa Gazeta* 442 (22 September 1914, aft. ed.): 2; "K.O.m.W," *Nowa Gazeta* 465 (5 October 1914, aft. ed.): 2.

107. Archiwum Głowne Akt Dawnych (AGAD), Szef Administracji przy Generał-Gubernatorstwie w Warszawie (SAGGW) 5, Vierteljahrschaftsbericht des Verwaltungschefs bei dem General-Gouvernement Warschau fur die Zeit vom 1. Januar 1916 bis zum 31 März 1916, appendix III.

108. APW KOMW 1, protocols nos. 4, 8, and 17 of 6, 8, and 13 August 1914, respectively; "Giełda pracy," *Kurjer Warszawski* 229 (20 August 1914, aft. ed.): 3.

109. "Z giełdy pracy rolnej," *Kurjer Warszawski* 263 (23 September 1914, morn. ed.): 3; "Giełda rolna," *Kurjer Warszawski* 272 (2 October 1914): 2.

110. "Z giełdy pracy," *Kurjer Warszawski* 274 (4 October 1914): 5.

111. "Nowe roboty miejskie," *Nowa Gazeta* 397 (28 August 1914, aft. ed.): 2.

112. Herbst, 311–12.

113. "Giełdy pracy," *Kurjer Warszawski* 256 (16 September 1914, aft. ed.): 3.

114. "K.O.m.W," *Nowa Gazeta* 465 (5 October 1914, aft. ed.): 2; Herbst, 296–97.

115. "Działalność giełd pracy," *Kurjer Warszawski* 319 (18 November 1914, aft. ed.): 3; "O pracę," *Kurjer Warszawski* 9 (9 January 1915, aft. ed.): 2; "Giełdy pracy," *Kurjer Warszawski* 54 (23 February 1915, morn. ed.): 2; "Dla poszukujących pracy," *Kurjer Warszawski* 77 (18 March 1915, aft. ed.): 3.

116. Herbst, 292.

117. Dunin-Wąsowicz, *Warszawa w latach pierwszej wojny światowej*, 104–5.

118. Lubomirska, 83.

119. APW ZOW 11.

120. "W sprawie szkół polskich," *Kurjer Warszawski* 323 (22 November 1914, Sunday ed.): 2.

121. Adam Grzymała Siedlecki, "Rosya a Polacy. Słowo wstępne, I," *Tygodnik Illustrowany* 48 (28 November 1914): 768.

122. Holzer and Molenda, 51; APW ZOW, sygn. 14. According to lists later prepared by the City Magistrate's office, the electorate as determined by various tax qualifications and rents would have comprised slightly more than twenty thousand voters; "Przed wprowadzeniem samorządu," *Kurjer Warszawski* 146 (29 May 1915, morn. ed.): 3; and "Przed wprowadzeniem samorządu," *Kurjer Warszawski* (8 June 1915): 3. However, by the time these lists of eligible voters in the city had been compiled, the Russians were already in headlong retreat from the Polish Kingdom and preparing their evacuation from Warsaw.

123. On the deteriorating situation in Warsaw, see "Sprawy żywnościowe i opałowe," *Kurjer Warszawski* 336 (5 December 1914, aft. ed.): 1.

124. In fact, on 23 and 24 December 1914, police arrested some 158 soldiers who had left their barracks without authorization; APW ZOW 1120. Ten days earlier, police conducted a raid on the club "Russian Corner" located on 73 Marszałkowska Street, where some fifty people—state officials, military officers, their wives, and "professional gamblers"—were found with illegal spirits. The manager of the buffet was subsequently fined 1,000 rubles, and the club closed for the duration of the war; APW ZOW 1064.

125. For more on the committee's efforts to receive Russian legal recognition of a citizens militia operating under its auspices, see APW KOMW 1, protocol no. 71 of 15 October 1914; "Z komitetu obywatelskiego Warszawy," *Kurjer Warszawski* 346 (15 December 1914, aft. ed.): 3. The establishment of a "Warsaw Honor Guard" was accompanied by the publication of an official denial issued by the Warsaw Superintendent of Police that permission had been granted to the committee to create a militia; "Zaprzeczenie," *Kurjer Warszawski* 347 (16 December 1914, aft. ed.): 2.

126. APW KOMW 2, Presidium protocol no. 73 of 3 May 1915. Thereafter, the legalization of other committee-established schools and educational institutions would be suspended indefinitely once the Russians began to step up their evacuation of Warsaw in July 1915; APW KOMW 2, protocol no. 170 of 8 July 1915.

127. The committee's proposal in February 1915 to monitor adherence to price ceilings by its own appointed controllers encountered opposition from Russian police authorities; APW KOMW 2, protocol no. 126 of 11 February 1915.

128. Graf, "Military Rule," 395.

129. "Komisja rekwizycyjna," *Kurjer Warszawski* 1 (1 January 1915): 4.

130. "Kontrola nad zapasami produktów," *Kurjer Warszawski* 40 (9 February 1915, morn. ed.): 2.

131. APW KOMW 2, protocol no. 153 of 24 April 1915.

132. "Ostatne wybuchy," *Nowa Gazeta* 95 (28 February 1915, morn. ed.): 3; "Bomby," *Kurjer Warszawski* 60 (1 March 1915, aft. ed.): 3; "Bomby," *Kurjer Warszawski* 61 (2 March 1915, morn. ed.): 3; "Aeroplan niemiecki," *Nowa Gazeta* 134 (23 March 1915, aft. ed.): 2; and "Wybuchy," *Nowa Gazeta* 143 (30 March 1915, morn. ed.): 3.

133. "Manifestacja," *Kurjer Warszawski* 82 (23 March 1915, morn. ed.): 3.

134. Censored items were easily distinguished by blank spots, and large excerpts were deleted by censors, even from the otherwise compliant *Kurjer Warszawski* in its issues of 17, 19, and 20 April 1915.

135. "Prawda o pokładach węgla," *Kurjer Warszawski* 143 (26 May 1915, special ed.): 5; and "Bezsensowne pogłoski," *Nowa Gazeta* 242 (30 May 1915, morn. ed.): 4.

136. Dzikowski, *Rok wojny*, 40–41, 44.

137. APW KOMW 2, protocol no. 165 of 27 June 1915.

138. APW KOMW 2, protocols nos. 167 of 30 June 1915 and 168 of 1 July 1915.

139. APW Komisja Rekwizycyjna IV Rejonu Miasta Warszawy (KR), 1–3.

140. APW ZOW 1067.

141. "Dla poszukujących pracy," *Kurjer Warszawski* 40 (9 February 1915, morn. ed.): 4.

142. Herbst, 296–302.

143. APW KOMW 2, protocols nos. 170 of 8 July 1915 and 174 of 19 July 1915.

144. APW ZOW 1099.

145. APW ZOW 1094.

146. "Panika," *Tygodnik Illustrowany* 27 (3 July 1915), 420.

147. APW ZOW 1049 and 1058.

148. "Nieusprawiedliwiona panika," *Nowa Gazeta* 323 (19 July 1915, aft. ed.): 2.

149. "Zawieszenie wyborów do samorządu," *Nowa Gazeta* 323 (19 July 1915, aft. ed.), 2.

150. "Zaprzeczenie pogłoskom," *Kurjer Warszawski* 199 (21 July 1915, morn. ed.): 2.

151. "Wieść o cudzie," *Kurjer Warszawski* 198 (20 July 1915, morn. ed.): 2.

152. "Z chwili," *Nowa Gazeta* 324 (20 July 1915): 2; "Z chwili," *Kurjer Warszawski* 198 (20 July 1915, morn. ed.): 2. Military authorities subsequently offered to purchase the livestock if they were transported across the Vistula to Mińsk Mazowiecki; "Dla właścicieli krów," *Kurjer Warszawski* 201 (23 July 1915, morn. ed.): 2. Of the 9,000 horses from Warsaw eventually examined by the requisitioning commissions, only 563 were actually deemed fit for service with the army. The harvest of motor vehicles was likewise disappointing and was limited to forty-three automobiles, sixty-three trucks, and thirty-six motorcycles; APW ZOW 1058 and 1067.

153. *Kurjer Warszawski* 200 (22 July 1915, morn. ed.): 2.

154. "Ofiary bomb," *Kurjer Warszawski* 202 (24 July 1915, morn. ed.): 2; "Nastrój w mieście," *Kurjer Warszawski* 202 (24 July 1915, aft. ed.): 2.

155. "W sprawie zakładów przemysłowych i fabryk," *Nowa Gazeta* 330 (23 July 1915, morn. ed.): 1.

156. "Z powodu rozkazu Wodza Naczelnego," *Nowa Gazeta* 250 (5 June 1915): 2; "Rozkaz do policji," *Kurjer Warszawski* 163 (15 June 1915, morn. ed.): 3. "Wyludnienie Warszawy," *Nowa Gazeta* 294 (2 July 1915, morn. ed): 2.

157. "Wysyłanie więźniów," *Kurjer Warszawski* 177 (29 June 1915, aft. ed.): 3.

158. Dunin-Wąsowicz, *Warszawa w czasie pierwszej wojny światowej*, 17; APW ZOW 147; "Los zesłanców z Warszawy," *Nowa Gazeta* 458 (7 October 1915, aft. ed.): 2.

159. "Z kontroli służących," *Kurjer Warszawski* 178 (30 June 1915, aft. ed.): 2.

160. APW ZOW 1065.

161. APW ZOW 1066.

162. APW ZOW 1067.

163. APW ZOW 1068.

164. APW ZOW 1067a.

165. APW ZOW 1068.

166. APW ZOW 1067a. Here is an example of the costs associated with the evacuation of individual factories contained in this file: on 29 July 1915 the Michał Zeleński Steel Factory, which employed 210 individuals, presented a bill of 77,420 rubles to cover workers' wages and administrative salaries for three months, the dismantling and transportation of machines and materials, and additional transfer payments for the families of 100 married workers.

167. APW ZOW 1067.

168. Dunin-Wąsowicz, *Warszawa w czasie pierwszej wojny światowej*,19–20. According to the liberal nationalist Aleksander de Rosset, the factory machinery and metals taken by the Russians often failed to reach their destination and were abandoned on rail lines in territory soon to be occupied by the Central Powers; Aleksander de Rosset, "Warszawa w dniach przełomu," in *Warszawa w pamiętnikach*, 87.

169. APW KOMW 2, protocol no. 178 of 25 July 1914; Herbst, 303. Indeed, the budgets of all committee sections were reduced as the evacuation continued. Consequently, the committee, through short edited statements in the daily press, informed the public of its meager and dwindling resources and called for patience; APW KOMW 2, Presidium protocol of 31 July 1915 and protocol no. 183 of 30 July 1915.

170. Dzikowski, 45.

171. Stanisław Thugutt, "Początek wojny—Niemcy w Warszawie," in *Warszawa w pamiętnikach*, 77.

172. Dzikowski, 46. According to Rosset, those who came to Warsaw in the summer of 1915 were poor and powerless while those who hastily departed with the Russians were richer and stronger, a repetition of the situation from the previous fall; Rosset, "Warszawa," 87.

173. Rosset, "Warszawa," 87; Thugutt, "Początek wojny," 77.

174. APW KOMW 2, Presidium protocol no. 103 of 4 August 1915.

175. Herbst, 302.

176. In the case of Russia's western borderlands, one of the first efforts to do so was by Theodore R. Weeks, *Nation and State in Late Imperial Russia: Nationalism and Russification on the Western Frontier, 1863–1914* (Dekalb, IL: Northern Illinois University Press, 1996). For the period following the partitions of Poland to the mid-nineteenth century, see the recent book by Jörg Ganzenmüller, *Russische Staatsgewalt und polnischer Adel: Elitenintegration und Staatsausbau im Westen des Zarenreiches (1772–1850)* (Cologne: Böhlau Verlag, 2012). For the nineteenth-century Polish Kingdom, see Andrzej Chwalba, *Polacy w służbie Moskali* (Warsaw and Krakow: Wydawn. Nauk. PWN, 1999); and Katya Vladimirov, *The World of Provincial Bureaucracy in Late 19th and 20th Century Russian Poland* (Lewiston, NY: Edwin Mellen Press, 2004). For a more focused discussion on the period immediately preceding the Great War, see Robert Blobaum, "Królestwo Polskie między rewolucją i wojną: Może nie było aż tak źle?" *Historyka: Studia metodologiczne* 28 (1998): 139–46.

177. A strikingly similar plan would inform the strategic thinking of the Polish underground in the Second World War in anticipation of German retreat and the arrival of Soviet forces. Needless to say, it met with far less success.

178. APW KOMW 2, protocols nos. 174 of 19 July 1915, 179 of 26 July 1915, and 182 of 29 July 1915.

179. APW KOMW 2, Presidium protocol no. 99 of 21 July 1915.

180. APW KOMW 2, protocols nos. 177 of 24 July 1915 and 179 of 26 July 1915. The committee immediately created the Section for the Protection of Prisoners whose representatives visited the facility, met with its inmates, and took measures to ensure that they were fed and received medical care. Physicians would soon find sanitary conditions at the prison to be poor and many of the prisoners ill. The majority of the prison's inmates were comprised of political prisoners, and forty of them were released immediately after the Russians had completed their evacuation of the city; see also the account of M. Jankowski, "Pierwsze dni okupacji niemieckiej," in Warszawa pamiętnikach, 129–44.

181. APW KOMW 2, protocols nos. 184 of 31 July 1915 and 187 of 4 August 1915.

182. On 27 July the Citizens Guard issued an appeal that called upon the population to surrender all weapons, horses, and bicycles and, in general, to cooperate with the emerging volunteer force. The appeal was printed in ten thousand copies; APW KOMW 2, protocol no. 180 of 27 July 1915.

183. M. Jankowski, "Pierwsze dni," 137.

184. APW KOMW 2, presidium protocols nos. 97 and 102 of 14 July 1915 and 3 August 1915, respectively; protocol nos. 185 of 2 August 1915 and 187 of 4 August 1915; "Z sądów," Nowa Gazeta 325 (21 July 1914, aft. ed.): 2.

185. APW KOMW 2, protocol no. 186 of 3 August 1915, and protocol no. 103 of KO Presidium of 4 August 1915.

186. Rosset, "Warszawa," 87.

187. APW ZOW 1067.

188. "Życie nie może stanąć," Tygodnik Illustrowany 31 (31 July 1915): 483–84.

189. "Wyludnienie Warszawy," Nowa Gazeta 294 (2 July 1915, morn. ed.): 2. Among those who remained were eleven thousand Russians—mainly women, children, and the elderly—who would share the tribulations of Warsaw's Polish and Jewish residents for the rest of the war and seek assistance from the City Administration; see "Ubodzy rosjanie," Kurjer Warszawski 184 (5 June 1916, morn. ed.): 2.

190. Dzikowski, Rok wojny, 44–45.

191. M. Jankowski, "Pierwsze dni," 129–44.

192. Czesław Jankowski, 52–53.

193. Hutten-Czapski, "Zdobycie Warszawy w 1915 roku," in Warszawa w pamiętnikach, 120.

194. "Usunięcie śladów panowania rosyjskiego w Warszawie," Kurjer Warszawski 291 (20 October 1916, aft. ed.): 2.

195. Andrzej Chwalba, Imperium korupcji w Rosji i w Królestwie Polskim w latach 1861–1917 (Krakow: Universitas, 1995), 137.

196. Holzer and Molenda, 60.

197. "Nastrój w mieście," Kurjer Warszawski 202 (24 July 1915, aft. ed.): 2.

2. LIVING ON THE EDGE

1. Thugutt, "Początek wojny," 78.

2. "Tramwaje," Kurjer Warszawski 214 (5 August 1915, morn. ed.): 2.

3. Aleksander Kraushar, Warszawa podczas okupacji niemieckiej 1915–1918: Notatki naocznego świadka (Lwów-Warsaw-Kraków: Wydawnictwo Zakładu Narodowego im. Ossolińskich, 1921), 7.

4. Herbst, 302–3.

5. "Zakładnicy," *Kurjer Warszawski* 214 (5 August 1915, aft. ed.): 2.

6. Kraushar, 8–9.

7. "Prezydent miasta," "Milicja," and "Komunikacja telefoniczna," *Kurjer Warszawski* 214 (5 August 1915, aft. ed.): 2–3.

8. Vejas Gabriel Liulevicius, *War Land on the Eastern Front: Culture, National Identity and German Occupation in World War I* (Cambridge: Cambridge University Press, 2000), 54.

9. AGAD CNGGW 1, Report of General Hans von Bessler, 23 October 1915.

10. Mieczysław Jankowski, "Życie polityczne w Warszawie pod okupacją niemiecką," in *Warszawa w pamiętnikach*, 164–66.

11. Hutten-Czapski, "Otwarcie Uniwerstytetu Warszawskiego i Politechniki," in *Warszawa w pamiętnikach*, 387.

12. Polsakiewicz, "Spezifika," 517, 529–31.

13. Kraushar, 60–61.

14. Christian Westerhoff, *Zwangsarbeit im Ersten Weltkrieg: Deutsche Arbeitskräftepolitik in besetzen Poland und Litauen 1914–1918* (Paderborn: Ferdinand Schöningh, 2012).

15. See, for example, Liulevicius, 195.

16. Kauffman, 64–105.

17. Thierry Bonzon, "The Labor Market and Industrial Mobilization," in *Capital Cities at War* I, 164–95; see also Maureen Healy, *Vienna and the Fall of the Habsburg Empire: Total War and Everyday Life in World War I* (Cambridge: Cambridge University Press, 2004), 276.

18. See Jonathan Manning, "Wages and Purchasing Power," and Jean-Louis Robert and Jay Winter, "Conclusions: Towards a Social History of Capital Cities at War," in *Capital Cities at War* I, 255–85 and 527–44, respectively.

19. Roger Chickering, *The Great War and Urban Life in Germany: Freiburg, 1914–1918* (Cambridge: Cambridge University Press, 2007), 447.

20. Sean Dobson, *Authority and Upheaval in Leipzig, 1910–1920* (New York: Columbia University Press, 2001), 158–59.

21. Gatrell, *Russia's First World War*, 26.

22. Barbara Alpern Engel, "Not by Bread Alone: Subsistence Riots in Russia during World War I," *The Journal of Modern History* 96, no. 4 (December 1997): 697–98, 715.

23. Healy, *Vienna*, 46.

24. Dunin-Wąsowicz, *Warszawa w czasie pierwszej wojny światowej*, 139, 170–73.

25. AGAD CNGGW 1, Report of General Hans von Beseler, 23 October 1915.

26. "Mydło tualetowe," *Kurjer Warszawski* 189 (14 July 1915, Sunday ed.): 4.

27. Kutrzeba, 50.

28. Dunin-Wąsowicz, *Warszawa w czasie pierwszej wojny światowej*, 172.

29. M. Jankowski, "Życie polityczne," 167.

30. Jan Hupka, "Pobyt w Warszawie, kwiecień-maj 1917 roku," in *Warszawa w pamiętnikach*, 220–21.

31. Kraushar, 250–52.

32. "Przemysł w Warszawie," *Kurjer Warszawski* 64 (5 March 1915, aft. ed.): 3.

33. "Straty przemysłu," *Nowa Gazeta* 569 (4 December 1914, aft. ed.): 1.

34. M. Jankowski, "Życie polityczne," 164–65.

35. Holzer and Molenda, 119–21.

36. "Co dziesiąty," *Nowa Gazeta* 372 (14 August 1914, aft. ed.): 2.

37. "Z ruchu budowlanego," *Kurjer Warszawski* 226 (17 August 1914, morn. ed.): 3; "Zastój w budownictwie," *Kurjer Warszawski* 306 (5 November 1914): 3.

38. "Rzemiosła a wojna," *Kurjer Warszawski* 40 (9 February 1915): 2.

39. "W sprawie mąki," *Kurjer Warszawski* 27 (27 January 1915, morn. ed.): 2.

40. "Farbiarze a wojna," *Kurjer Warszawski* 41 (10 February 1915, aft. ed.): 4; "Meblarze a wojna," *Kurjer Warszawski* 47 (16 February 1915, aft. ed.): 3.

41. APW KOMW 1, Presidium protocol no. 20 of 21 December 1914.

42. Wincenty Kosiakiewicz, "Życie warszawskie," *Kurjer Warszawski* 330 (29 November 1914, Sunday ed.): 3–4.

43. Dunin-Wąsowicz, *Warszawa w czasie pierwszej wojny światowej*, 209.

44. Ignacy Grabowski, "Komu najgorzej," *Kurjer Warszawski* 279 (7 October 1914, aft. ed.): 1–2.

45. Dunin-Wąsowicz, *Warszawa w czasie pierwszej wojny światowej*, 116; Szarota, 103–6.

46. Stanisław Jarkowski, *Prasa warszawska od d. 5 XI 1916 do d. 1 III 1919* (Warsaw: Szkład Główny w Księgarni Gebethnera i Wolffa, 1921), 3.

47. AGAD SAGGW, Vierteljahrschaftsbericht des Verwaltungschefs bei dem General-Gouvernement Warschau für die Zeit vom 1. Januar 1916 bis zum 31 März 1916, Appendix III.

48. Engel, 713.

49. Dunin-Wąsowicz, *Warszawa w czasie pierwszej wojny światowej*, 191.

50. APW KOMW 2, protocol no. 157 of 7 May 1915.

51. "Z przemysłu i rękodzieł," *Kurjer Warszawski* 26 (26 January 1915, aft. ed.): 2.

52. By December 1914, several thousand women had been hired to work up and down the line of the Warsaw-Vienna Railway at seventy-five kopecks per day; "Kobiety przy robotach kolejowych," *Nowa Gazeta* 571 (5 December 1914, aft. ed.): 2. Weeks before the Russian evacuation, city railroad directors requested from their superiors the authority to hire women with secondary education to work on the city lines. It was agreed that women who possessed a primary education could complete apprenticeships, and if the results were good, hiring requests would then be sent to upper state management; "Zhenschchiny na zheleznych drogach," *Varshavskii Dnevnik* 164 (13 June 1915): 2.

53. For a description of the strike, which also involved male tailors, see Bronisław Fijałek, "Powrót do kraju—walki strajkowe krawców," in *Warszawa w pamiętnikach*, 253–66.

54. Dunin-Wąsowicz, *Warszawa w czasie pierwszej wojny światowej*, 196.

55. See Susanna Magri, "Housing," in *Capital Cities at War* I, 374–417.

56. Dunin-Wąsowicz, *Warszawa w czasie pierwszej wojny światowej*, 78.

57. "Gospodarze i lokatorzy," *Kurjer Warszawski* 256 (16 September 1914, aft. ed.): 2.

58. "O komorne," *Kurjer Warszawski* 267 (26 September 1914): 3.

59. Ibid.

60. APW KOMW 1, protocol no. 49 of 18 September 1914 and protocol no. 54 of 25 September 1914.

61. "Sekcja tanich mieszkań," *Kurjer Warszawski* 22 (22 January 1915, aft. ed.): 3.

62. "Właściciele i lokatorzy," *Kurjer Warszawski* 271 (1 October 1914, morn. ed.): 3.

63. "U właścicieli nieruchomości," *Kurjer Warszawski* 317 (16 November 1914, aft. ed.): 2; "Rezerwistki i sublokatarowie," *Kurjer Warszawski* 72 (13 March 1915, morn. ed.): 4.

64. "Bez mieszkań," *Kurjer Warszawski* 102 (14 April 1915, aft. ed.): 4.

65. Miklaszewski, 63.

66. "Nieobecni," *Nowa Gazeta* 39 (26 January 1915, morn. ed.): 2.

67. "Spadek komornego," *Nowa Gazeta* 306 (9 July 1915, morn. ed.): 2; "Zniżka cen mieszkań," *Kurjer Warszawski* 186 (8 July 1915, aft. ed.): 3.

68. "Podatki," *Kurjer Warszawski* 7 (7 January 1915, spec. ed.): 2.

69. "Podatek od nieruchomości," *Kurjer Warszawski* 15 (15 January 1915, aft. ed.): 3.

70. "Odmowa," *Kurjer Warszawski* 65 (6 March 1915, aft. ed.): 3.

71. "Podatek mieszkanowy," *Kurjer Warszawski* 87 (28 March 1915, Sunday ed.): 5.

72. Dunin-Wąsowicz, *Warszawa w czasie pierwszej wojny światowej*, 78–80, 171.

73. Kutrzeba, 56–57.

74. APW KOMW 1, protocol no. 29 of 24 August 1914.

75. X. X., "Z wędrówki po Warszawie," *Tygodnik Illustrowany* 38 (19 September 1914): 671–72.

76. Stały, "Wrażenie z chwili," *Bluszcz* 37–38 (10 October 1914): 378.

77. "Sprawy opałowe," *Kurjer Warszawski* 270 (30 September 1914, morn. ed.): 2.

78. "Drzewo opałowe," *Kurjer Warszawski* 255 (15 September 1914, morn. ed.): 3; "Sprawa opałowa," *Kurjer Warszawski* 235 (15 September 1914, aft. ed.): 3.

79. "Oświetlenie Warszawy, *Kurjer Warszawski* 274 (4 October 1914, Sunday ed.): 5; APW KOMW 1, protocol no. 88 of 7 November 1914; "Oszczędzanie gazu," *Kurjer Warszawski* 334 (3 December 1914, morn. ed.): 2.

80. "Z ruchu tramwajowego," *Nowa Gazeta* 425 (13 September 1914, morn. ed.): 4.

81. "Gaz i elektryczność wobec wojny," *Nowa Gazeta* 442 (22 September 1914, aft. ed.): 2.

82. APW KOMW 1, protocols no. 57 of 29 September 1914 and no. 77 of 22 October 1914.

83. APW KOMW 1, Presidium protocol no. 12 of 2 December 1914 and protocol no. 101 of 5 December 1914.

84. Ignacy Grabowski, "Opał dla Warszawy," *Kurjer Warszawski* 256 (16 September 1914, aft. ed.): 2.

85. Ignacy Grabowski, "Jeszcze opał dla Warszawy," *Kurjer Warszawski* 271 (1 October 1914, morn. ed.): 1.

86. "W sprawie opału," *Kurjer Warszawski* 259 (19 September 1914, morn. ed.): 3; APW KOMW 1, protocol no. 58 of 1 October 1914.

87. APW KOMW 1, protocol no. 80 of 26 October 1914.

88. APW KOMW 1, protocol no. 82 of 28 October 1914.

89. APW KOMW 1, protocol no. 88 of 7 November 1914.

90. "Urojony brak nafty," *Kurjer Warszawski* 321 (20 November 1914, aft. ed.): 2.

91. APW KOMW 1, protocol no. 44 of 10 September 1914.

92. "Brak nafty," *Kurjer Warszawski* 342 (11 December 1914, morn. ed.): 2.

93. "Nafta," *Kurjer Warszawski* 347 (16 December 1914, aft. ed.): 2.

94. "Po czterech miesiącach," *Kurjer Warszawski* 339 (8 December 1914, morn. ed.): 1–2.

95. "Opal, światło, woda, tramwaje," *Kurjer Warszawski* 341 (10 December 1914, aft. ed.): 1–2.

96. "Nowy typ kradzieży," *Kurjer Warszawski* 261(21 September 1914, aft. ed.): 3.

97. "Węgle," *Kurjer Warszawski* 342 (11 December 1914, morn. ed.): 3.

98. "Sprawy opałowe," *Kurjer Warszawski* 334 (3 December 1914, morn. ed.): 3; "Węgiel z piaskiem," *Kurjer Warszawski* 47 (16 February 1915, morn. ed.): 3.

99. "Sprawa opałowa," *Kurjer Warszawski* 273 (3 October 1914, aft. ed.): 3.

100. APW KOMW 2, protocol no. 110 of 2 January 1915.

101. APW KOMW 2, protocol no. 118 of 21 January 1915. Archiwum Akt Nowych (AAN), Akta Stanisław Dzierzbickiego (ASD) 54 contains an open letter of 10 March 1916 from Tomasz Kociatkiewicz who briefly headed the Fuels Section from November 1914 to January 1915. In this letter, Kociatkiewicz was still attempting to answer charges made against him in *Przegląd Poranny* of tolerating and covering up corruption during his few months in office. *Przegląd Poranny* refused to publish his letter.

102. APW KOMW 2, protocol no. 115 of 14 January 1915; "W sprawie wegla," *Kurjer Warszawski* 17 (17 January 1915, Sunday ed.): 4.

103. APW KOMW 2, protocol no. 130 of 20 February 1915.
104. "Kontrola składów wegla," *Kurjer Warszawski* 72 (13 March 1915, Sunday ed.): 3.
105. "Proba gaszenia światel," *Kurjer Warszawski* 28 (28 January 1915, morn. ed.): 3–4.
106. "Warszawa po ciemku," *Tygodnik Illustrowany*, 6 (6 February 1915): 85.
107. "Komisja węglowa," *Kurjer Warszawski* 80 (21 March 1915, Sunday ed.): 4.
108. "Brak węgli," *Kurjer Warszawski* 82 (23 March 1915, aft. ed.): 2.
109. APW KOMW 2, Presidium protocol no. 61 of 31 March 1915; "Węgiel i drzewo," *Kurjer Warszawski* 98 (10 April 1915, aft. ed.): 1–2.
110. APW KOMW 2, protocol no. 153 of 24 April 1915.
111. "Opał dla Warszawy," *Kurjer Warszawski* 122 (4 May 1915, aft. ed.): 3.
112. "Sprawa opałowa," *Kurjer Warszawski* 140 (22 May 1915, aft. ed.): 4; "Opał," *Kurjer Warszawski* 145 (28 May 1915, aft. ed.): 3.
113. "Nafta," *Kurjer Warszawski* 211 (2 August 1915, aft. ed.): 2.
114. APW ZOW 1067, Report of the Warsaw Superintendent of Police to the Warsaw Governor-General, 23 September 1915.
115. "Drzewe na opał," *Kurjer Warszawski* 214 (5 August 1915, aft. ed.): 3.
116. APW, Zarząd Miejski m. st. Warszawy, 1915–1919 (hereafter ZMW) 19, Circular Regarding Coal for Sections and Stores of the City of Warsaw, 12 July 1916.
117. "Proceder ogonkowy," *Godzina Polski* 226a (28 September 1917): 4.
118. Dunin-Wąsowicz, *Warszawa w czasie pierwszej wojny światowej*, 163–64.
119. Holzer and Molenda, 128.
120. Zdzisław Dębicki, "Polano drzewa," *Tygodnik Illustrowany* 39 (25 September 1915): 574; "Drobne ogłoszenia," *Tygodnik Illustrowany* 43 (9 October 1915): 621.
121. See Armin Triebel, "Coal and the Metropolis," in *Capital Cities at War* I, 342–73.
122. Miklaszewski, 64.
123. For a comparison, see Thierry Bonzon and Belinda Davis, "Feeding the Cities," in *Capital Cities at War* I, 305–41.
124. Belinda J. Davis, *Home Fires Burning: Food, Politics and Everyday Life in World War I Berlin* (Chapel Hill: The University of North Carolina Press, 2000), 21; Healy, *Vienna*, 31.
125. Bonzon and Davis, 321.
126. Liulevicius, 75; on conditions specific to Vilnius, see Theodore R. Weeks, "Vilnius in World War I, 1914–1920," in *Über den Weltkrieg hinaus*, 46–47.
127. Engel, 718–21.
128. Gatrell, *Russia's First World War*, 144.
129. Davis, *Home Fires*, 22, 32–34.
130. "Dowóz żywności," *Kurjer Warszawski* 209 (31 July 1914): 1.
131. Graf, "Military Rule," 410; Lih, 9.
132. Lih, 15; Gatrell, *Russia's First World War*, 160–61.
133. "Z miasta," *Kurjer Warszawski* 210 (1 August 1914, aft. ed.): 4; "Z komitetu obywatelskiego Warszawy," *Kurjer Warszawski* 222 (13 August 1914, morn. ed.): 3.
134. "Tanie produkty," *Kurjer Warszawski* 219 (10 August 1914, aft. ed.): 2; "Fala zwyżki cen," *Kurjer Warszawski* 220 (11 August 1914, morn. ed.): 2.
135. "Drożyna chleba," *Kurjer Warszawski* 226 (17 August 1914, aft. ed.): 3; "Drożyna mąki," *Kurjer Warszawski* 227 (18 August 1914, aft. ed.): 2.
136. "Faktyczny stan rzeczy," *Nowa Gazeta* 391 (25 August 1914, aft. ed.): 3; "Mięso," *Kurjer Warszawski* 253 (13 September 1914, Sunday ed.): 3.
137. APW KOMW 1, protocol no. 38 of 3 September 1914.
138. APW KOMW 1, protocol no. 54 of 25 September 1914.
139. "Oszuści," *Kurjer Warszawski* 264 (24 September 1914, morn. ed.): 2.
140. "Za armiją," *Kurjer Warszawski* 274 (4 October 1914, Sunday ed.): 6; "Walka o chleb," *Kurjer Warszawski* 283 (13 October 1914, morn. ed.): 3.

141. APW KOMW 1, protocol no. 37 of 1 September 1914; "Mleko," *Kurjer Warszawski* 286 (16 October 1914, morn. ed.): 3.

142. "Pieczywo" and "Mąka," *Kurjer Warszawski* 292 (22 October 1914, aft. ed.): 3.

143. "Mleko," *Kurjer Warszawski* 297 (27 October 1914, morn. ed.): 2.

144. APW KOMW 1, protocol no. 80 of 26 October 1914.

145. "Głód," *Kurjer Warszawski* 300 (30 October 1914, aft. ed.): 2–3.

146. "Z targowisk miejskich," *Kurjer Warszawski* 308 (7 November 1914, aft. ed.): 3.

147. "Sprawy żywności i opałowe," *Kurjer Warszawski* 336 (5 December 1914): 1; "Z targów praskich," *Kurjer Warszawski* 337 (6 December 1914, Sunday ed.): 4; "Dowóz produktów," *Kurjer Warszawski* 346 (December 15, 1914, morn. ed.): 2.

148. "W obronie dzieci," *Kurjer Warszawski* 338 (7 December 1914, aft. ed.): 2.

149. APW KOMW 1, Presidium protocol no. 23 of 30 December 1914; "Dowóz do Warszawy," *Kurjer Warszawski* 5 (5 January 1915, morn. ed.): 2.

150. "Sprawy mleczarskie," *Kurjer Warszawski* 8 (8 January 1915): 3.

151. APW KOMW 2, protocols no. 136 of 6 March 1915 and no. 138 of 11 March 1915; "Brak mięsa w mieście," *Kurjer Warszawski* 68 (9 March 1915, morn. ed.): 2; "Warszawa bez mięsa wołowego," *Kurjer Warszawski* 70 (11 March 1915, morn. ed.): 3; "Brak mleka," *Nowa Gazeta* 116 (12 March 1915, aft. ed.): 3.

152. "Z handlu mięsem," *Kurjer Warszawski* 75 (16 March 1915, morn. ed.): 2–3; APW KOMW 2, protocol no. 160 of 27 May 1915.

153. "Sprawa mięsna," *Kurjer Warszawski* 144 (27 May 1915, morn. ed.): 3.

154. "O zniesienie taksy na mięso," *Kurjer Warszawski* 148 (31 May 1915, Sunday ed.): 3–4.

155. "Błedny koło," *Kurjer Warszawski* 149 (1 June 1915, aft. ed.): 2.

156. Lih, 15, 20, 67–68.

157. "Jajko po 18 groszy," *Kurjer Warszawski* 91 (1 April 1915, aft. ed.): 3; "Z ruchu przedświątecznego," *Kurjer Warszawski* 92 (2 April 1915): 3.

158. "Z sekcji żywnościowej," *Kurjer Warszawski* 201 (23 July 1915, aft. ed.): 2.

159. APW KOMW 2, protocol no. 182 of 29 July 1915.

160. "Niedojrzale owoce," *Kurjer Warszawski* 206 (28 July 1915, aft. ed.): 2; "Zdzierstwo drożyźniane," *Kurjer Warszawski* 214 (5 August 1915, morn. ed.): 2.

161. "W sprawie drożyny," *Kurjer Warszawski* 205 (27 July 1915, aft. ed.): 2; "Walka z drożyną," *Kurjer Warszawski* 210 (1 August 1915, Sunday ed.): 3; "Z Sekcyi żywnościowej K.O.m.W," *Nowa Gazeta* 346 (1 August 1915, morn. ed.): 2.

162. "Rekwizycja żywności," *Kurjer Warszawski* 231 (4 August 1915, morn. ed.): 3.

163. "Rekwizycja towarów," *Nowa Gazeta* 352 (5 August 1915, morn. ed.): 1; "Deklaracje o zapasach," *Kurjer Warszawski* 214 (5 August 1915, morn. ed.): 1; "Żywność dla Warszawy," *Kurjer Warszawski* 214 (5 August 1915, aft. ed.): 3.

164. Dunin-Wąsowicz, *Warszawa w czasie pierwszej wojny światowej*, 173; APW RNG 1, Notice of the Warsaw Press Department of 17 January 1916.

165. "Chleba naszego powszedniego…," *Tygodnik Illustrowany* 36 (4 September 1915): 539.

166. AAN ASD 60, Minutes of the 125th Session of the Central Citizens Committee of 16 August 1915.

167. Rosset, "Warszawa," 103. According to Franciszek Herbst, the original 165-gram bread ration, calculated regardless of age, could be met only by allowing local bakeries to add even more surrogates; Herbst, 307.

168. "Jeszcze o kartach na chleb," *Tygodnik Illustrowany* 44 (30 October 1915): 636. Initially, bread rations were set at 75% of those prevailing in Germany, a proportion that was subsequently reduced to two-thirds; Holzer and Molenda, 126.

169. Lubomirska, 276.

170. Zieliński, *Stosunki*, 209.

171. "Zapasy żywności w Warszawie," *Kurjer Warszawski* 50 (19 February 1916): 1.

172. Lubomirska, 321, 327.

173. APW RNG 1, Notice of the Imperial German President of Police of 20 February 1916.

174. APW RNG 1, Police Regulation of 27 February 1916.

175. Herbst, 306.

176. Holzer and Molenda, 128.

177. APW RNG 1, Police Regulation of 27 February 1916.

178. APW RNG 1, Announcement and Explanation of the Provisions Section of 30 March 1916.

179. APW RNG 1, Announcement of the President of Police of 6 April 1916.

180. Z. D., "Z ulicy," *Tygodnik Illustrowany* 13 (25 March 1916): 154–55.

181. "Fałszywe bony na chleb," *Kurjer Warszawski* 18 (18 January 1916, morn. ed.): 3.

182. APW RNG 1, Announcement of the President of Police of 21 March 1916.

183. Dunin-Wąsowicz, *Warszawa w czasie pierwszej wojny światowej*, 174; "Martwe dusze," *Gazeta Poranna 2 grosze* 66 (6 March 1916): 2; "Karty na chleb," *Kurjer Warszawski* 151 (1 June 1916, Sunday ed.): 5.

184. Kutrzeba, 50.

185. "Rabunek," *Kurjer Warszawski* 161 (11 June 1916, Sunday ed.): 7.

186. For a list and locations of the looted stores, see APW RNG 3.

187. AGAD CNGGW 1, Quarterly Report for Period of 1 July to 30 September 1916.

188. "'Exodus' żywnościowy," *Kurjer Warszawski* 208 (29 July 1916, morn. ed.): 2.

189. AAN ASD 61, Ronikier to Wolfgang von Kries, Chief of the Civil Administration, 15 July 1916.

190. "Fałszerze kart chlebowych," *Kurjer Warszawski* 179 (30 June 1916, aft. ed.): 3; "Fałszywe karty chlebowe," *Kurjer Warszawski* 185 (6 July 1916, morn. ed.): 2; "Za nadżycia na wadze cheba," *Nowa Gazeta* 560 (6 December 1916, aft. ed.): 3; "Nadużycia rządców," *Nowa Gazeta* 4 (3 January 1917, aft. ed.): 3; "Zamykanie piekarń," *Nowa Gazeta* 54 (1 February 1917, morn. ed.): 2; "W sprawie pierkarni," *Kurjer Warszawski* 110 (22 April 1917, Sunday ed.): 6; "Za sprzedaż chleba ponad taksę," *Nowa Gazeta* 206 (29 April 1917, morn. ed.): 3; "Procesy przeciw piekarzom," *Godzina Polski* 116 (30 April 1917): 2.

191. "Chleb pszenny," *Nowa Gazeta* 572 (14 December 1916, aft. ed.): 3; "Wydział zaopatrzywania," *Kurjer Polski* 152 (7 June 1917): 1.

192. M. Jankowski, "Życie politczyne," 164–65.

193. Kraushar, 13.

194. Davis, *Home Fires*, 180; for comparative data on bread and potato rations between the two cities, see Polsakiewicz, "Spezifika," 531.

195. "Mąka," *Nowa Gazeta* 127 (16 March 1917, morn. ed.): 2; Dunin-Wąsowicz, *Warszawa w czasie pierwszej wojny światowej*, 174. By comparison, Polish Varsovians received on average 200–300 grams in daily bread rations during the Second World War; Szarota, 183.

196. Władysława Głodowska-Sampolska, "Klub gazeciarzy," in *Warszawa w pamiętnikach*, 340–41.

197. M. Jankowski, "Życie polityczne," 180.

198. AAN, Tymczasowa Rada Stanu (TRS) 113, Appeal of the Warsaw Regional Workers Committee of the PPS of 21 May 1917.

199. "Rozruchy żywosciowe wybuchły w Warszawie," *Komunikat Informacyjny* 1 (9–11 May 1917): 4; "Rozruchy w Warszawie," *Komunikat Informacyjny* 3 (15 May 1917): 1; "Rozruchy w Warszawie," *Rząd i Wojsko* 18 (20 May 1917): 8.

200. Lubomirska, 290.

201. APW, Zarząd Miejski m. st. Warszawy, 1915–1919 (ZMW) 2, protocol no. 18 of special session of 22 May 1917; APW ZM 2, Report to the City Council Session of 31 May 1917 of the Delegation to the Lublin Governor-General.

202. AAN TRS 113, Appeal of the Warsaw Regional Workers Committee of the PPS of 21 May 1917.

203. Kraushar, 45–46.

204. AGAD CNGGW 3, Report on the Activity and Conditions in the Territory of the General Government for 1 July to 25 September 1918.

205. Kraushar, 14.

206. "Rozpozrządzenie policyjne dotyczące cukierni," Kurjer Polski 155 (10 June 1917): 5.

207. APW ZMW 1, protocol of the City Council session of 6 December 1917.

208. Dunin-Wąsowicz, Warszawa w czasie pierwszej wojny światowej, 63.

209. APW ZMW 1, protocol no. 13 of the City Council session of 11 April 1918.

210. "Oszustwa," Chwila Świąteczna 5 (6 May 1917): 4.

211. Dunin-Wąsowicz, Warszawa w czasie pierwszej wojny światowej, 174.

212. Fijałek, 256.

213. AGAD CNGGW 21.

214. For an excellent comparative analysis, see the two chapters by Catherine Rollet, "The 'Other War' I: Protecting Public Health" and "The 'Other War' II: Setbacks in Public Health," in Capital Cities at War I, 421–55 and 456–86, respectively.

215. Lih, 270.

216. Dobson, 160.

217. On the Great or "Spanish" Influenza, see John M. Barry, The Great Influenza: The Epic Story of the Deadliest Plague in History (New York: Penguin, 2004).

218. APW KOMW 1, protocol no. 13 of 10 August 1914.

219. APW KOMW 1, protocol no. 25 of 20 August 1914.

220. "Fala zwyżki cen," Kurjer Warszawski 220 (11 August 1914, morn. ed.): 2.

221. "W obawie epidemii," Kurjer Warszawski 251 (11 September 1914, aft. ed.): 3.

222. "Tyfus," Nowa Gazeta 434 (18 September 1914, morn. ed.): 1.

223. APW KOMW 1, protocol no. 51 of 21 September 1914.

224. APW KOMW 1, protocol no. 73 of 17 October 1914.

225. "Wsród bezdomnych," Kurjer Warszawski 291 (21 October 14, aft. ed.): 3.

226. APW KOMW 1, protocol no. 85 of 2 November 1914; "Szczepienie ospy," Kurjer Warszawski 310 (9 November 1914, aft. ed.): 2.

227. APW KOMW 1, protocol no. 93 of 19 November 1914.

228. "Śmiertelność wsród dzieci," Nowa Gazeta 25a (18 January 1915, special supplement): 2.

229. "Z sekcji bezdomnych," Kurjer Warszawski 9 (9 January 1915, morn. ed.): 3.

230. "Zamknięcie przytułku dla bezdomnych," Kurjer Warszawski 27 (27 January 1915, morn. ed.): 3.

231. Sanborn, Imperial Apocalypse, 164.

232. "Zdrowotność okolic Warszawy," Kurjer Warszawski 9 (9 January 1915, aft. ed.): 2.

233. "Stan zdrowotny przedmieść," Kurjer Warszawski 25 (25 January 1915, aft. ed.): 2.

234. "Zdrowotność na przedmieściach," Kurjer Warszawski 61 (2 March 1915, aft. ed.): 2.

235. "Sprawy sanitarne," Kurjer Warszawski 102 (14 April 1915, morn. ed.): 2–3.

236. "Przyłączenie Mokotowa do miasta," Kurjer Warszawski 77 (18 March 1915, morn. ed.): 3.

237. "O przyłączenie Mokotowa do Warszawy," Kurjer Warszawski 96 (8 April 1915, morn. ed.): 2.

238. "Na przedmieściach Warszawy," *Kurjer Warszawski* 74 (15 March 1915, aft. ed.): 2.
239. "Z okolic Warszawy," *Tygodnik Illustrowany* 14 (3 April 1915): 216.
240. "Brak miejsc dla chorych," *Kurjer Warszawski* 312 (11 November 1914, aft. ed.): 3.
241. "Szkoły rządowe w szkołach prywatnych," *Kurjer Warszawski* 319 (18 November 1914, morn. ed.): 3.
242. "Komitet sanitarny," *Kurjer Warszawski* 326 (25 November 1914, morn. ed.): 2–3. During the Russian evacuation in the summer of 1915, the Warsaw Sanitary Committee was dissolved and a new Medical-Sanitary Section formed under the Warsaw Citizens Committee, effectively merging the former with the committee's Medical Section; APW KOMW 2, protocol no. 181 of 28 July 1915.
243. "Otrucia denaturatem," *Kurjer Warszawski* 328 (27 November 1914, morn. ed.): 2.
244. "60 ofiar," *Kurjer Warszwski* 333 (2 December 1914, morn. ed.): 3; "76 ofiar denaturatu," *Kurjer Warszawski* 4 (4 January 1915, morn. ed.): 2; "100 ofiar denaturatu," *Kurjer Warszawski* 34 (3 February 1915, aft. ed.): 2.
245. "Udoskonalona fabrykacja," *Kurjer Warszwski* 76 (17 March 1915, morn. ed.): 3.
246. APW KOMW 1, protocol no. 103 of 12 December 1914.
247. APW KOMW 2, Presidium protocol no. 89 of 19 June 1915.
248. APW KOMW 2, Presidium protocol no. 42 of 17 February 1915.
249. "Zamknięcie wystawy," *Kurjer Warszawski* 180 (2 July 1915, morn. ed.): 3.
250. Rosset, "Warszawa w dniach przełomu," 107–9.
251. Kraushar, 8.
252. AGAD CNGGW 1, Report of Warsaw Governor-General Hans von Beseler of 23 October 1915. In Warsaw, six hundred hospital beds had already been set up for those in the German Army suffering from venereal disease. Medical examination of more than a thousand local prostitutes revealed that over half of them were infected with sexually transmitted diseases; AGAD SAGGW 3, Vierteljahrsbericht des Verwaltungsschefs bei dem General-Gouvernement Warschau für die Zeit vom 21. Juli 1915 bis zum 1 Oktober 1915, 15.
253. APW RNG, Announcement of the Imperial German President of Police Glasenapp of 21 January 1916.
254. "Szczepienie ospy," *Kurjer Warszawski* 143 (24 May 1916, aft. ed.): 2.
255. Polsakiewicz, 533.
256. Zieliński, *Stosunki*, 246–47; for a typical antisemitic interpretation of the 1917 typhus epidemic, see "Żydzi a tyfus," *Gazeta Poranne 2 grosze* 219 (12 August 1917): 4.
257. Typhoid was popularly referred to as "the Jewish fever" as early as the beginning of 1916, according to a German administrative report; see AGAD SAGGW 5, Vierteljahrschaftsbericht des Verwaltunschefs bei dem General-Gouvernement Warschau für die Zeit vom 1. Januar 1916 bis zum 31 März 1916, 15–17.
258. APW ZMW 1, protocol no. 53 of the Warsaw City Council session of 6 December 1917.
259. APW ZMW 1, protocol no. 4 of the Warsaw City Council session of 31 January 1918.
260. APW ZMW 1, protocol no. 14 of the Warsaw City Council session of 18 April 1918.
261. APW RNG 6, "Mortality from Tuberculosis in Warsaw."
262. "Walka z gruźlicą," *Tygodnik Illustrowany* 27 (7 July 1917): 337.
263. AGAD CNGGW 3, Report on the Activity and Conditions in the Territory of the General-Government for 1 July to 25 September 1918.
264. "Samobójstwa w r. 1915 w Warszawie," *Kurjer Warszawski* 13 (13 January 1916, aft. ed.): 2; Dr. Kamizmierz Nidzielski, "Samobójstwa w Warszawie w r. 1916," *Kurjer Warszawski* 75 (16 March 1917, morn. ed.): 5.
265. Dunin-Wąsowicz, *Warszawa w czasie pierwszej wojny światowej*, 180 ; Holzer and Molenda, 123.

266. Weeks reports that mortality among Jews in Vilnius was three times higher in 1917 than in 1911–1913 and that it had more than doubled among the city's Polish residents between 1915 and 1917; Weeks, "Vilnius," 47.

267. AAN, Akta Drzewieckich (AD) 15, Memorial of the Warsaw City Administration in the Matter of the City Budget to Wolfgang von Kries, Chief of Administration of the Warsaw General-Government, 6 April 1916.

268. "W sprawie wyludnienia kraju," *Godzina Polski* 300a (2 November 1918): 2.

269. Jay Winter, "Surviving the War: Life Expectation, Illness and Mortality Rates in Paris, London, and Berlin, 1914–1919," in *Capital Cities at War* I, 497.

270. Healy, *Vienna*, 41.

271. Chickering, 319–20; Dobson, 186; Winter, "Surviving the War," 488, 497.

272. Healy, *Vienna*, 249.

273. APW KOMW 1, protocol no. 38 of 3 September 1914.

274. AAN TRS 66, President of Warsaw Zdzisław Lubomirski to Warsaw Governor-General Hans von Beseler, 26 April 1917.

3. WARTIME CRISIS MANAGEMENT AND ITS FAILURE

1. Davis, *Home Fires*, 32–34.

2. Thierry Bonzon, "Transfer Payments and Social Policy," in *Capital Cities at War* I, 288.

3. Adele Lindenmeyr, *Poverty Is Not a Vice: Charity, Society, and the State in Late Imperial Russia* (Princeton: Princeton University Press, 1996), 228.

4. Ibid., 230.

5. On voluntary associations in Russian Poland, both before and after 1905, see Blobaum, *Rewolucja*, 67–69, 132, 148, 258, 287–91.

6. Władysław Grabski and Antoni Żabko-Potopowicz, *Ratownictwo społeczne w czasie wojny* (Warsaw: Towarzystwo Badania Zagadnień Międzynarodowych, 1932): 30–31.

7. "Z miasta," *Kurjer Warszawski* 212 (3 August 1914, morn. ed.): 3.

8. APW KOMW 1, protocol no. 1 of 3 August 1914.

9. APW KOMW 1, protocol no. 3 of 5 August 1914.

10. APW KOMW 1, protocol no. 6 of 7 August 1914.

11. APW KOMW 1, protocol no. 27 of 22 August 1914; see also protocol no. 6 of 7 August 1914.

12. APW KOMW 1, protocol no. 56 of 28 September 1914.

13. The committee issued a press release to inform reservist families that the Curatorium, and not the committee, was the competent organization; "Z komitetu obywatelskiego," *Kurjer Warszawski* 230 (21 August 1914, morn. ed.): 3.

14. "Zapomogi dla rodzin rezerwistów," *Kurjer Warszawski* 242 (2 September 1914, morn. ed.): 3; Grabski and Żabko-Potopowicz, 43.

15. "Posiłek dla rodzin rezerwistów," *Kurjer Warszawski* 243 (3 September 1914, aft. ed.): 2.

16. "Zapomogi dla rodzin rezerwistów," *Kurjer Warszawski* 5 (5 January 1915, aft. ed.): 2.

17. "Nowe roboty miejskie," *Nowa Gazeta* 397 (28 August 1914, aft. ed.): 2.

18. Grabski and Żabko-Potopowicz, 34.

19. "Ofiarna Warszawa," *Nowa Gazeta* 406 (2 September 1914, aft. ed.): 3.

20. "Sport na pomoc sanitarną," *Kurjer Warszawski* 279 (9 October 1914, morn. ed.): 3.

21. APW KOMW 1, protocols no. 31 of 26 August 1914 and no. 35 of 30 August 1914.

22. "Bandy żebraków," *Nowa Gazeta* 421 (11 September 1914, morn. ed.): 1.

23. Herbst, 285.

24. Grabski and Żabko-Potopowicz, 33–34.

25. Graf, 396: Lih, 20.
26. Ludwik Krzywicki, "Na czasie," *Nowa Gazeta*, 387 (23 August 1914): 1–2.
27. "Taksa," *Kurjer Warszawski* 249 (9 September 1914, special ed.): 3.
28. "Wyzysk," *Kurjer Warszawski* 266 (27 September 1914, Sunday ed.): 5.
29. "Sprawa opałowa," *Kurjer Warszawski* 271 (1 October 1914, aft. ed.): 2.
30. APW KOMW 1, protocol no. 58 of 1 October 1914; "Ustalenie cen," *Kurjer Warszawski* 274 (4 October 1914, Sunday ed.): 5.
31. "W sprawie taksy," *Kurjer Warszawski* 276 (6 October 1914, aft. ed.): 2; "Taksa," *Kurjer Warszawski* 278 (8 October 1914, aft. ed.): 3.
32. APW KOMW 2, protocol no. 126 of 11 February 1915.
33. APW KOMW 2, Presidium protocol no. 55 of 17 March 1915.
34. "Milicja obywatelska," *Kurjer Warszawski* 282 (12 October 1914, aft. ed.): 2–3.
35. APW KOMW 1, protocol no. 96 of 24 November 1914.
36. APW KOMW 1, protocol no. 103 of 12 December 1914.
37. The establishment of the "Warsaw Honor Guard" was accompanied by the publication of an official denial issued by the Warsaw Superintendent of Police that permission had been granted to the Warsaw Citizens Committee to create a militia; "Zaprzeczenie," *Kurjer Warszawski* 347 (16 December 1914, aft. ed.): 2.
38. APW KOMW 1, Presidium protocol no. 21 of 23 December 1914.
39. APW KOMW 1, protocol no. 67 of 12 October 1914.
40. Grabski and Żabko-Potopowicz, 218–19.
41. APW KOMW 1, protocol no. 88 of 7 November 1914.
42. APW KOMW 1, protocol no. 90 of 12 November 1914. By the time of the Russian evacuation, General Section membership still remained limited to twenty-two individuals; Grabski and Żabko-Potopowicz, 219.
43. APW KOMW 1, Presidium protocol no. 10 of 27 November 1914. The figure of nine thousand comes from a *Bluszcz* editorial summarizing the first three months of the committee's activity; "Trzy miesięce pracy," *Bluszcz* 45–47 (28 November 1914): 400–401.
44. APW KOMW 2, protocol no. 115 of 14 January 1915.
45. On the establishment of both commissions and their early successes, see "Komisya pracy kobiet," *Bluszcz* 3–4 (6 February 1915): 1–3; and "Komisya opieki nad dziećmi," *Bluszcz* 7–8 (20 February 1915): 1–2.
46. "Komisja opieki nad dziećmi," *Kurjer Warszawski* 289 (19 October 1914, morn. ed.): 4; Złota gwiazdka," *Kurjer Warszawski* 339 (8 December 1914, morn. ed.): 5.
47. APW KOMW 2, Presidium protocol no. 25 of 11 January 1915 and General Section protocol no. 120 of 26 January 1915.
48. APW KOMW 2, protocol no. 132 of 25 February 1914.
49. APW KOMW 2, protocol no. 140 of 16 March 1915.
50. "Opieka nad dziećmi," *Kurjer Warszawski* 94 (6 April 1915, spec. ed.): 4.
51. "Ochrony na Bródnie," *Kurjer Warszawski* 34 (3 February 1915, aft. ed.): 2.
52. APW KOMW 1, Presidium protocol no. 12 of 2 December 1914.
53. Representatives of these institutions met and reached agreement on the distribution of the first 300,000 rubles, with the remainder to be determined upon the receipt of requests. By 10 March, seventy such requests had been received, with the largest sum, of 63,000 rubles, earmarked for the Society for the Care of the Mentally Ill; "Dla instytucji dobroczynnych," *Kurjer Warszawski* 67 (8 March 1915, aft. ed.): 4; and "Dla instytucji dobroczynnych," *Kurjer Warszawski* 69 (10 March 1915, aft. ed.): 4.
54. "Praski komitet obywatelski" and "Komitet obywatelski pod Warszawą," *Kurjer Warszawski* 230 (21 August 1914, aft. ed.): 1–2.
55. APW KOMW 1, protocol no. 91 of 14 November 1914.
56. "Z K.O. przedm. Pragi," *Nowa Gazeta* 83 (21 February 1915, morn. ed.): 3.

57. "Przyłączenie przedmieść," *Nowa Gazeta* 181 (22 April 1914, morn. ed.): 2.

58. APW KOMW 1, protocol no. 105 of 17 December 1914; "Z komitetu obywatelskiego m. Warszawy," *Kurjer Warszawski* 353 (22 December 1914, morn. ed.): 2.

59. By mid-December, the chief of the Warsaw Postal-Telegraph Department asked for 300–400 coupons to be used in public kitchens by his employees in critical need; APW KOMW 1, protocol no. 104 of 15 December 1914. For the first four months of 1915, the Loans Section issued 14,226 rubles in small loans to 205 individuals, 69% of whom were artisans and 11% small entrepreneurs. The average amount of the loan was seventy rubles; APW KOMW 2, Presidium protocol no. 78 of 19 May 1915.

60. APW KOMW 2, protocol no. 144 of 27 March 1915; Grabski and Żabko-Potopowicz, 31–32.

61. APW KOMW 2, protocol no. 180 of 27 July 1915.

62. APW KOMW 2, protocols no. 179 of 26 July 1915, no. 184 of 31 July 1915, no. 186 of 3 August 1915, and no. 187 of 4 August 1915.

63. Lubomirska, 200.

64. APW KOMW 3, protocol no. 188 of 5 August 1915.

65. APW KOMW 3, protocols no. 189 of 6 August 1915, no. 192 of 11 August 1915, and no. 196 of 20 August 1915.

66. Polsakiewicz, 523.

67. Grabski and Żabko-Potopowicz, 115, 126; Holzer and Molenda, 137.

68. AAN AD 9, Copy of Press Release of 10 September 1915.

69. APW KOMW 3, protocol no. 222 of 19 October 1915 and no. 227 of 29 October 1915.

70. APW RNG 7, Communiqué from the Press Commission of the K.O.m.W to the Editorial Board of *Nowa Gazeta*, 2 November 1915.

71. APW KOMW 3, protocols no. 193 of 13 August 1915 and no. 199 of 27 August 1915. Later, the department voted to eliminate Russian language study from the elementary schools while maintaining it as a foreign language option in the secondary schools, its motion passing by a narrow margin.

72. APW KOMW 3, protocol no. 203 of 6 September 1915.

73. APW KOMW 4, protocols no. 269 of 15 February 1916 and no. 272 of 24 February 1916; AAN AD 10, copy of press release "Zamknięcie Wydziału Oświecenia."

74. Grabski and Żabko-Potopowicz, 112.

75. APW KOMW 3, protocols no. 193 of 23 August 1915 and no. 199 of 27 August 1915.

76. APW KOMW 3, protocols no. 202 of 3 September 1915 and no. 203 of 6 September 1915.

77. APW KOMW 3, protocol no. 227 of 29 October 1915.

78. APW KOMW 3, protocols no. 240 of 29 November 1915 and no. 242 of 3 December 1915.

79. APW KOMW 4, protocols no. 258 of 14 January 1916 and no. 264 of 30 January 1916; Grabski and Żabko-Potopowicz, 113.

80. AGAD CNGGW 42, Memoranda of General Erich von Etzdorf of 19 January 1916 and 17 February 1916.

81. APW KOMW 4, protocol no. 276 of 9 March 1916.

82. APW KOMW 4, protocol no. 281 of 23 March 1916.

83. APW KOMW 6, protocol no. 298 of 9 May 1916; Grabski and Żabko-Potopowicz, 137.

84. APW KOMW 1, protocols no. 30 of 25 August 1914 and no. 32 of 27 August 1914.

85. Lubomirska, 114.

86. APW KOMW 2, protocol no. 131 of 23 February 1915.

87. APW KOMW 1, protocol no. 31 of 26 August 1914.

88. "Charakterystyczne," *Kurjer Warszawski* 12 (12 January 1915, morn. ed.): 4; and "Giełda pracy," *Kurjer Warszawski* 17 (17 January 1915, Sunday ed.): 3.

89. APW KOMW 1, protocol no. 94 of 21 November 1914.

90. "Kuchnie robotnicze," *Nowa Gazeta* 370 (13 August 1914, aft. ed.): 2; "Kuchnie robotnicze," *Kurjer Warszawski* 222 (13 August 1914, aft. ed.): 3.

91. Viewing itself as the only representation of workers in the economic sphere, the RKG was a semilegal organization that sent official delegations to deal openly with the "bourgeois" Warsaw Citizens Committee, while its own sessions with the participation of the radical socialist parties were conspiratorial.

92. Aleksander Tomaszewski, "Wspomnienie o kuchniach robotniczych i o Robotniczym Komitecie Gospodarczym podczas pierwszej wojny światowej w Warszawie," in *Warszawa w pamiętnikach*, 271.

93. Ibid.

94. APW KOMW 1, protocols no. 98 of 28 November 1914 and no. 99 of 1 December 1914.

95. APW KOMW 1, protocol no. 100 of 3 December 1914.

96. APW KOMW 1, Presidium protocol no. 16 of 11 December 1914.

97. APW KOMW 2, protocol no. 117 of 19 January 1915.

98. "Komitet Obywatelski m. W. a organizacye robotnicze," *Nowa Gazeta* 97 (2 March 1915, morn. ed.): 2.

99. APW KOMW 2, protocol no. 138 of 11 March 1915.

100. APW KOMW 2, protocol no. 145 of 30 March 1915.

101. APW KOMW 2, protocol no. 146 of 8 April 1915 and Presidium protocol no. 52 of 30 April 1915.

102. APW KOMW 2, Presidium protocol no. 82 of 31 May 1915.

103. APW KOMW 2, protocol no. 172 of 15 July 1915.

104. Grabski and Żabko-Potopowicz, 149.

105. Tomaszewski, 272–73.

106. Grabski and Żabko-Potopowicz, 141; Dunin-Wąsowicz, *Warszawa w czasie pierwszej wojny światowej*, 177.

107. APW ZMW 2, Report of Delegation of the Warsaw City Council to the Lublin Governor-General, submitted to City Council Session on 31 May 1917.

108. Szarota, 222.

109. "Obiady dla żydów," *Nowa Gazeta* 485 (23 October 1916, aft. ed.): 2; Grabski and Żabko-Potopowicz, 153–54.

110. APW KOMW 1, protocol no. 30 of 25 August 1914.

111. "Obiady dla inteligencji," *Kurjer Warszawski* 68 (9 March 1915, aft. ed.): 3; "Obiady dla inteligencji," *Kurjer Warszawski* 168 (20 June 1915, Sunday ed.): 5.

112. APW KOMW 3, protocol no. 249 of 22 December 1915.

113. "Sprawozdanie Kuchni Robotniczej przy Stowarzyszeniu spożywczem robotników żydów," *Nowa Gazeta* 312 (13 July 1915, morn. ed.): 1–2.

114. Davis, *Home Fires*, 157–58.

115. APW KOMW 2, Presidium protocol no. 39 of 10 February 1915.

116. APW KOMW 6, circular memorandum no. 7 of 18 January 1916.

117. "Szczepienie ochronne," *Kurjer Warszawski* 31 (31 January 1915): 2.

118. APW KOMW 2, protocol no. 133 of 27 February 1915.

119. APW KOMW 2, protocol no. 151 of 20 April 1915.

120. "Teror," *Kurjer Warszawski* 161 (13 June 1915, Sunday ed.): 5.

121. Dunin-Wąsowicz, *Warszawa w czasie pierwszej wojny światowej*, 105.

122. Rosset, "Warszawa," 105.

123. Westerhoff, 66.

124. AGAD CNGGW 15f, undated announcement of the Labor Central under the Imperial German Presidium of Police.

125. AGAD SAGGW 4, Vierteljarhsbericht des Verwaltungschefs bei dem General-Gouvernement Warschau für die Zeit vom 1. Oktober 1915 bis zum 31. Dezember 1915, 58; "Biuro pośredniczenia robotników," *Kurjer Warszawski* 73 (13 March 1916, aft. ed.): 4.

126. Kazimierz-Władysław Kumaniecki, "Stosunki robotnicze w czasie wojny," in *Polska w czasie wielki wojny (1914–1918). Historja społeczna i ekonomiczna* vol. 2: *Historja społeczna*, ed. Marceli Handelsman (Warsaw: Towarzystwo Badania Zagadnień Międzynarodowych, 1932), 247.

127. Herbst, 310; Holzer and Molenda, 124.

128. APW RNG 1, press notice of the Labor Central of 12 April 1916.

129. Herbst, 310.

130. AGAD CNGGW 34, Warsaw Governor-General to the Society of Industrialists of the Polish Kingdom, 21 December 1915.

131. AAN AD 7, Order of General Headquarters of German Army of 3 October 1916.

132. Holzer and Molenda, 125.

133. Westerhoff, 199–206; "Ogłoszenie," *Nowa Gazeta* 494 (28 October 1916, morn. ed.): 2; and "Ogłoszenie," *Nowa Gazeta* 498 (31 October 1916, morn. ed.): 2.

134. APW KOMW 6, President of the City Administration Zdzisław Lubomirski to the Chief of Administration of the Warsaw General-Government, 6 April 1916.

135. AAN AD 7, Warsaw Governor-General Beseler to the Warsaw City Administration, 6 November 1917.

136. Westerhoff, 221–26.

137. Kumaniecki, 270.

138. The city already employed 13,512 individuals in public-works projects at the end of 1915; Grabski and Żabko-Potopowicz, 140.

139. APW KOMW 6, Imperial German President of Police Glasenapp to the Warsaw Magistrate, 22 March 1917.

140. "Opieka nad ubogimi," *Godzina Polski* 147 (1 June 1917): 3.

141. Holzer and Molenda, 178–79.

142. Lubomirska, 530.

143. Ibid., 214; Tomaszewski, 277–79; Zieliński, *Stosunki*, 332.

144. "Zbrodnia!," *Kiliński* (July 1917): 13.

145. AGAD CNGGW 2, Quarterly Report on the Activity and Conditions in the Territory of the General-Government from 1 July to 30 September 1916, 62; AGAD SAGGW 5, Vierteljahrschaftsbericht des Verwaltungschefs bei dem General-Gouvernement Warschau für die Zeit vom 1. Januar 1916 bis zum 31 März 1916, appendix III, table 3.

146. APW ZMW 12, Correspondence of the Factory Inspector, Antoni Eichhorn, of Warsaw's Second Precinct from 1 April 1916 to 31 July 1917.

147. Rosset, "Warszawa," 106.

148. AAN TRS 113, Odezwa PPS do robotników, 21 May 1917.

149. "Bezrobocie w szpitalach warszwskich," *Tygodnik Illustrowany* 3 (19 January 1918): 33.

150. APW ZMW 1, protocol no. 3 of City Council session of 19 January 1918.

151. For an account of the garment workers strike by one of its union organizers, see Bronisław Fijałek, "Powrót do kraju—Walki strajkowe krawców," in *Warszawa w pamiętnikach*, 253–66.

152. APW KOMW 2, protocol no. 126 of 11 February 1915.

153. APW KOMW 2, protocol no. 135 of 4 March 1915; "Budżet Warszawy," *Kurjer Warszawski* 69 (10 March 1915, Sunday ed.): 4; and "Budżet m. st. Warszawy," *Nowa Gazeta* 109 (9 March 1915, morn. ed.): 2. To be sure, the city had exceeded its budgeted

expenditures in 1914 by 4 million rubles, 3.5 million of which went directly into the purchase of provisions; "Budżet miejski," *Nowa Gazeta* 210 (9 May 1915, morn. ed.): 3.

154. APW KOMW 2, Presidium protocol no. 74 of 5 May 1915 and protocol no. 158 of 14 May 1915.

155. APW KOMW 2, Presidium protocol no. 89 of 19 June 1915; "Pożyczka 3-miljonowa," *Kurjer Warszawski* 185 (7 July 1915): 2.

156. APW KOMW 2, protocols no. 170 of 8 July 1915 and no. 278 of 25 July 1915, and Presidium protocol no. 101 of 31 July 1915; "Magistrat bez pieniędzy," *Kurjer Warszawski* 207 (29 July 1915, morn. ed.): 3; Grabski and Żabko-Potopowicz, 34; Herbst, 303.

157. APW KOMW 3, protocol no. 189 of 6 August 1915.

158. APW KOMW 3, protocols no. 194 of 16 August 1915 and no. 201 of 1 September 1915.

159. Grabski and Żabko-Potopowicz, 136–39.

160. APW KOMW 3, protocol no. 195 of 18 August 1915 and Presidium protocol no. 116 of 14 October 1915. At the same time, the Germans demanded payment for their own soldiers posted on street corners; Presidium protocol no. 113 of 5 October 1915.

161. APW KOMW 3, protocol no. 245 of 13 December 1915.

162. APW KOMW 3, protocols no. 215 of 4 October 1915, no. 216 of 6 October 1915, and no. 220 of 15 October 1915. Beginning in November, payments to soldiers' wives were entered into "the account of the Russian government"; protocol no. 236 of 19 November 1915.

163. As of February 1916, these monthly rates remained unchanged, despite rapid inflation; APW KOMW 4, protocol no. 268 of 10 February 1916.

164. APW KOMW 3, protocol no. 227 of 29 October 1915.

165. APW KOMW 3, protocol no. 252 of 31 December 1915.

166. "Na pomoc dla ludności," *Kurjer Warszawski* 205 (26 July 1916, aft. ed.): 2; "Z wydziału pomocy dla ludności," *Kurjer Warszawski* 220 (10 August 1916, Sunday ed.): 3.

167. APW KOMW 4, protocol no. 261 of 20 January 1916.

168. AAN AD 14, Memorial of the Warsaw City Administration in the Matter of City Budget, addressed to the Chief of Administration of the Warsaw General Government, 6 April 1916.

169. "Budżet st. m. Warszawy," *Nowa Gazeta* 495 (28 October 1916, aft. ed.): 2.

170. For more on Polish American and other relief organizations in the United States and their relationship to the Vevey Committee, see Danuta Płygawko, *Polonia Devastata: Polonia i Amerykanie z pomocą dla Polski (1914–1918)* (Poznań: Wydawnictwo Poznańskie, 2003).

171. Grabski and Żabko-Potopowicz, 153.

172. APW KOMW 6, Imperial German President of Police Glasenapp to the City President Lubomirski, 23 December 1916.

173. "A Joint Effort: JDC's Beginnings, 1914–1921," accessed 8 May 2015, http://archives.jdc.org/exhibits/a-joint-effort/.

174. AAN ASD 62, Zdzisław Lubomirski to Stanisław Dzierzbicki, 4 July 1916 and 18 September 1916.

175. APW KOMW 6, Vice President of the City Administration Piotr Drzewiecki to the Imperial German Presidium of Police, 6 February 1917.

176. APW KOMW 6, Imperial German President of Police Glasenapp to the Office of the Warsaw Magistrate, 22 March 1917.

177. "Z Magistratu m. st. W.," *Nowa Gazeta* 96 (24 February 1917, morn. ed.): 2.

178. "Dochody miasta Warszawy," *Godzina Polski* 186 (10 July 1917, aft. ed.): 2; APW ZMW 2, Estimates of the City Treasurer for the 1917 Year-End Budget, 82–83.

179. Dunin-Wąsowicz, *Warszawa w czasie pierwszej wojny światowej*, 157.

180. APW ZMW 1, protocols no. 12 of City Council session of 22 March and no. 15 of 25 April 1918.

181. "Dobroczynność publiczna w Warszawie," *Godzina Polski* 193 (17 July 1917, aft. ed.): 2; "Rozprawy budżetowe w Radzie miejskiej," *Godzina Polski* 189 (13 July 1917, aft. ed.): 4.

182. "Rząd a rezerwistki," *Godzina Polski* 202 (26 July 1918, morn. ed.): 5; APW ZM 1, protocol no. 4 of City Council session of 31 January 1918.

183. APW ZMW 1, protocol no. 54 of City Council session of 13 December 1917.

184. APW ZMW 1, protocol no. 9 of 4 March 1918.

185. "Kronika wydarzeń w Warszawie w latach 1914–1918," in *Warszawa w pamiętnikach*, 528.

4. POLES AND JEWS

1. Scott Ury, *Barricades and Banners: The Revolution of 1905 and the Transformation of Warsaw Jewry* (Stanford, CA: Stanford University Press, 2013). On the ways and means by which the National Democrats came to dominate Polish identity politics, a key feature of which became a strident antisemitism, see Brian Porter, *When Nationalism Began to Hate: Imagining Politics in Nineteenth-Century Poland* (New York: Oxford University Press, 2000). On the transformation of political culture more generally during the revolution, see Blobaum, *Rewolucja*, 188–233.

2. The transformation of the role of the Yiddish press from informing and educating voters to mobilizing them behind a national agenda is discussed by Ury, 172–213; on the Polish-language press, see Theodore R. Weeks, "Fanning the Flames: Jews in the Warsaw Press, 1905–1912," *East European Jewish Affairs* 28, no. 2 (1998): 63–81.

3. These issues in Polish-Jewish relations in Warsaw on the very eve of the war are dealt with separately by Theodore R. Weeks, "Nationality and Municipality: Reforming City Government in the Kingdom of Poland, 1904–1915," *Russian History* 21, no. 1 (1994): 23–47; Stephen D. Corrsin, "Polish-Jewish Relations before the First World War: The Case of the State Duma Elections in Warsaw," *Gal-Ed: On the History of the Jews in Poland* 11 (1989): 31–53; and Robert Blobaum, "The Politics of Antisemitism in Fin-de-Siècle Warsaw," *The Journal of Modern History* 73, no. 2 (June 2001): 275–306.

4. Jerzy Jedlicki, "The End of Dialogue: 1907–1912," in *The Jews in Poland* 2, ed. Sławomir Kapralski (Kraków: Judaica Foundation, 1999), 111–23. For a longer perspective, see Magdalena Opalski and Israel Bartal, *Poles and Jews: A Failed Brotherhood* (Hanover, NH: Brandeis University Press, 1992); Theodore R. Weeks, *From Assimilation to Antisemitism: The "Jewish Question" in Poland, 1850–1914* (Dekalb, IL: Northern Illinois University Press, 2006); and Frank Golczewski, *Polnische-Jüdische Beziehungen, 1881–1922* (Wiesbaden: Franz Steiner Verlag, 1981).

5. See Jerzy Jedlicki, "Resisting the Wave: Intellectuals against Antisemitism in the Last Years of the 'Polish Kingdom,'" in *Antisemitism and Its Opponents in Modern Poland*, ed. Robert Blobaum (Ithaca, NY: Cornell University Press, 2005): 60–80.

6. Chickering, 498; Jean-Louis Robert, "The Image of the Profiteer," in *Capital Cities at War* I, 131.

7. Davis, *Home Fires*, 73.

8. Healy, *Vienna*, 67, 86, and 306; Rechter, 83–84. About the Jewish experience in central and eastern Europe more generally, see Frank Schuster, *Zwischen allen Fronten: Osteuropäische Juden während des Ersten Weltkrieges (1914–1919)* (Cologne: Böhlau Verlag Köln, 2004). For the Polish Kingdom specifically, see Zieliński, *Stosunki*.

9. APW ZOW 1116, Commander of the Army of the Northwestern Front General Zhilinskii to the Warsaw Superintendent of Police, 9 (22) August 1914.

10. APW ZOW 1116, Chief of the Warsaw Provincial Gendarmes to the Warsaw Superintendent of Police, 12 (25) August 1914.

11. APW ZOW 1116, Military Governor-General of the City of Warsaw to the Warsaw Superintendent of Police, 27 August (9 September) 1914. *Der moment*, along with its chief competitor *Der hajnt*, were the two major Yiddish dailies published in Warsaw before the First World War. During the war, *Moment* and *Hajnt* would become closely associated with rival Folkist and Zionist political factions, respectively; see Michael Steinlauf, "The Polish-Jewish Daily Press," *Polin: A Journal of Polish-Jewish Studies* 2 (1987): 220, 228.

12. APW ZOW 1116, Chief of the Volhynia Provincial Gendarmes to the Staff of the Warsaw Military Region, 9 (22) October 1914.

13. Lohr, *Nationalizing the Russian Empire*, 148.

14. "Szkodliwe odruchy," *Gazeta Poranna 2 grosze* 235 (26 August1914): 1.

15. Zieliński, *Stosunki*, 102.

16. "Żydzi a odezwa do polaków," *Kurjer Warszawski* 227 (18 August 1914, aft. ed.): 2.

17. "Żydzi do fortec," *Nowa Gazeta* 421 (11 September 1914, morn. ed.): 1.

18. Herbst, 287–88.

19. "Niebożeństwo dziękoczynne," *Kurjer Warszawski* 292 (22 October 1914, aft. ed.): 3; "Komitet Synagogi na Tłomackiem," *Nowa Gazeta* 550 (25 October 1914, morn. ed.): 4. At the beginning of the war, the Great Synagogue built in 1878 could still be considered a bastion of Warsaw's assimilated Jewish elite. By the end of the war, however, the synagogue's congregation had changed into a much more inclusive community whose representatives were more democratic and nationally minded; see Alexander Guterman, "The Congregation of the Great Synagogue in Warsaw: Its Changing Social Composition and Ideological Affiliations," *Polin: Studies in Polish Jewry* 13 (1998): 112–26.

20. "Umizgi," *Gazeta Poranna 2 grosze* 229 (20 August 1914): 1.

21. Ansky, 14–15.

22. Lubomirska, 114, 178, and 200.

23. APW ZOW 1116, Warsaw Superintendent of Police to the Military Governor-General of the City of Warsaw, 31 August (13 September) 1914.

24. "O zmianę nazwiska," *Nowa Gazeta* 576 (10 December 1914, morn. ed.): 2.

25. Graf, 398.

26. In November 1914 the state began to entertain the idea of confiscating the city's "German" gasworks, with its assets of approximately 1 million rubles in cash, certificates, and bonds, which were then indeed sequestered before the winter holidays; "Konfiskaty," *Nowa Gazeta* 541(18 November 1914, aft. ed.): 2; "Sekwester Zakładów Gazowych," *Nowa Gazeta* 600 (24 December 1914, morn. ed.): 2.

27. Ansky, 13.

28. Lohr, "The Russian Army," 409–10.

29. "Żydowskie listy," *Gazeta Poranna 2 grosze* 62 (3 March 1915): 3.

30. *Kurjer Warszawski* 197 (19 July 1915, spec. ed.): 3; "Zawieszenie gazet," *Nowa Gazeta* 322a (19 July 1915): 2; Zieliński, *Stosunki*, 116.

31. "Odczyt Niemojewskiego," *Kurjer Warszawski* 160 (12 June 1915): 4–5.

32. Lohr, "The Russian Army," 415.

33. Lohr, *Nationalizing the Russian Empire*, 17.

34. According to Princess Lubomirska, the coin shortage during the Russian evacuation was based on the "same Jewish trick" performed at the beginning of the war; Lubomirska, 200.

35. Zieliński, *Stosunki*, 132.

36. Dunin-Wąsowicz, *Warszawa w czasie pierwszej wojny światowej*, 22.

37. "Niemcy w Warszawie," *Gazeta Poranna 2 grosze* 224 (15 August 1915): 1.

38. Steven E. Aschheim, *Brothers and Strangers: The East European Jews in German and German-Jewish Consciousness, 1800–1923* (Madison, WI: The University of Wisconsin Press, 1982), 179.

39. Jack Wertheimer, *Unwelcome Strangers: East European Jews in Imperial Germany* (New York: Oxford University Press, 1987), 6.

40. Sammartino, 129.

41. Westerhoff, 333; on Beseler's approach to the Jewish question in the General-Government more broadly, see Kauffman, 114–24.

42. Lubomirska, 247.

43. On the wartime policies of the imperial German state toward the Jews in both the Kaiserreich and in the occupied territories, see the classic study of Egmont Zechlin, *Die deutsche Politik und die Juden in Ersten Weltkrieg* (Göttingen: Vandenhoeck u. Ruprecht, 1969).

44. Kraushar, 16–17.

45. To cite but a couple of examples of this kind of reporting, see "O interesy żydowskie," *Gazeta Poranna 2 grosze* 222 (13 August 1915): 1–2; and "O przedstawicielstwo żydów," *Gazeta Poranna 2 grosze* 329 (29 November 1915): 3.

46. AGAD CNGGW 1, Report of Warsaw Governor-General Hans von Beseler to the Kaiser of 23 October 1915.

47. "Mąka," *Nowa Gazeta* 127 (16 March 1917, morn. ed.): 3.

48. Weeks, "Vilnius," 43.

49. Mieczysław Jankowski, "Pierwsze dni okupacji niemieckiej," in *Warszawa w pamiętnikach*, 140; see also Zieliński, *Stosunki*, 229–30.

50. Kraushar, 29.

51. Zieliński, *Stosunki*, 222, 233.

52. "Żydzi w Królestwie Polskim [w 1917 r.] (Zarys informacyjny)," in *Żydowska mozaika politczna w Polsce 1917–1927: Wybór dokumentów*, ed. Czesław Brzoza (Kraków: Księgarnia Akademicka, 2003), 17. The original article on political movements among Warsaw's Jews was published by "Spectator" in *Wiadomości Polskie*, 152, 153, 154, and 155 (1917): 8–10, 5–7, 5–6, and 6–10, respectively. The best scholarly treatment of the Folkist movement is that by Kalman (Keith) Weiser, *Noah Prylucki and the Folkists in Poland* (Toronto: University of Toronto Press, 2011).

53. Guterman, "Congregation," 121–22. The role of German rabbis in the fashioning of modern political formations among the Orthodox community in the Polish Kingdom is emphasized by Matthias Morgernstern, *From Frankfurt to Jerusalem: Isaac Breuer and the History of the Secessionist Dispute in Modern Jewish Orthodoxy* (Leiden: Brill Studies in European Judaism, 2002), 65–74. On the significance of local actors, see François Guesnet, "Thinking Globally, Acting Locally: Joel Wegmeister and Modern Hasidic Politics in Warsaw," *Quest. Issues in Contemporary Jewish History* 2 (October 2011), available online at http://www.quest-cdecjournal.it/focus.php?id=222#e. See also Tobias Grill, "The Politicisation of Traditional Polish Jewry: Orthodox German Rabbis and the Founding of *Agudas Ho-Ortodksim* and *Dos yidishe vort* in Gouvernement-General Warsaw, 1916–1918," *East European Jewish Affairs* 39, no. 2 (August 2009), 227–47; and Aschheim, 165–68. On the larger history of Agudat Israel, see Gershon Bacon, *The Politics of Tradition: Agudat Yisrael in Poland, 1916–1939* (Jerusalem: Magnes Press, 1996).

54. Jechiel Halpern, "Żydowskie partie polityczne w Królestwie Polskim w 1918 r.," in *Żydowska mozaika*, 44; Halpern, a Zionist activist and editor of *Nowy Dziennik*, wrote a series of articles in that newspaper in 1918 and 1919 that sought to inform Jews in the former Austrian Poland of Jewish political movements in the former Russian-ruled Polish Kingdom.

55. Ezra Mendelsohn, *Zionism in Poland: The Formative Years, 1915–1926* (New Haven, CT: Yale University Press, 1981), ix, 37–38, 41–43. According to Mendelsohn, "the German occupation made possible the organization of mass political parties, and the Zionists, like their ideological opponents, took full advantage of this opportunity."

56. Zieliński, *Stosunki*, 199–201.

57. Weiser, 125–26, 153. As Weiser argues, in contrast to the Zionists' "negation of the Diaspora," the Folkists viewed the Diaspora as the "future site of [Jewish] national flourishing." Noah Prylucki, the most visible of the Folkist leaders in Warsaw, explained the party's position in his speech of 19 May 1917 in the Warsaw City Council: "We have the right of national-cultural development on this land just as you do. We are not demanding a Judeo-Poland. We have already said that we recognize the Polish character of this land"; Pryłucki, 87.

58. See Hillel Levine, *Economic Origins of Antisemitism: Poland and Its Jews in the Early Modern Poland* (New Haven, CT: Yale University Press, 1991); and Aleksander Hertz, *The Jews in Polish Culture*, trans. Richard Lourie (Evanston, IL: Northwestern University Press, 1988).

59. For more on this subject, see Robert Blobaum, "Criminalizing the 'Other': Crime, Ethnicity, and Antisemitism in Early Twentieth-Century Poland," in *Antisemitism and Its Opponents in Modern Poland*, 81–102. For a discussion of similar developments in early-twentieth-century Germany, see Michael Berkowitz, *The Crime of My Very Existence: Nazism and the Myth of Jewish Criminality* (Berkeley: University of California Press, 2007).

60. Andrzej Niemojewski, "Kodeks złodziejski a szlachetni," *Myśl Niepodległa* 266 (January 1914): 49–58; on the development of "liberal antisemitism" more generally, see Theodore R. Weeks, "Polish 'Progressive Antisemitism,' 1905–1914," *East European Jewish Affairs* 25, no. 2 (1995): 49–68.

61. "Wyzysk hurtowników," *Kurjer Warszawski* 281 (11 October 1914, Sunday ed.): 5.

62. "Ponad taksa," *Kurjer Warszawski* 313 (12 November 1914, morn. ed.): 3 and 323 (22 November 1914, Sunday ed.): 2.

63. "Rewizje w skladach," *Kurjer Warszawski* 41 (10 February 1915, morn. ed.): 5; and "Spekulacja," *Kurjer Warszawski* 42 (11 February 1915, aft. ed.): 2.

64. "Spekulacya," *Tygodnik Illustrowany* 9 (27 February 1915): 316.

65. APW KOMW 2, Presidium protocol no. 66 of 16 April 1915.

66. APW KOMW 2, protocol no. 82 of 31 May 1915.

67. APW KOMW 2, Presidium protocol no. 86 of 11 June 1915. Jewish assimilationists were particularly frustrated with the segregation of public assistance during wartime and blamed it for the sad state of Polish-Jewish relations; see the discussion of an article published in the renewed weekly *Izraelita* by Józef Wasercug in "Z prasy," *Nowa Gazeta* 142 (29 March 1915, aft. ed.): 2.

68. "Sklepy komitetowe," *Kurjer Warszawski* 168 (19 June 1915, aft. ed.): 4–5. In support of its argument that segregation was not synonymous with discrimination, the section also published statistics that showed that 33.38% of the total value of purchases at committee stores had been made by Jews, who also constituted 31.65% of the stores' clientele.

69. "Drożyzna mięsa," *Kurjer Warszawski* 142 (25 May 1915, spec. ed.): 5.

70. "Sprawa mięsna," in *Kurjer Warszawski* 144 (27 May 1915, morn. ed.): 3. For its part, *Gazeta Poranna 2 grosze* questioned why "only Jews" had the right to transport livestock to Warsaw; "Sprawa mięsna, część I," *Gazeta Poranna 2 grosze* 147 (29 May 1915): 1.

71. "Drożyzna mięsa," *Kurjer Warszawski* 147 (30 May 1915, Sunday ed.): 3.

72. "Błędny koło," *Kurjer Warszawski* 149 (1 June 1915, aft. ed.): 2. According to Bina Garncarska, the development of specific "Jewish trades," including the meat trade, was a late-nineteenth-century development; Bina Garncarska, "The Material and Social Situation

of the Jewish Population of Warsaw between 1862 and 1914," *Gal-Ed: On the History of the Jews of Poland* 1 (1973): xvi.

73. "Mięso dla Warszawy," *Kurjer Warszawski* 158 (10 June 1915, morn. ed.): 3.

74. "Wyzysk szwaczek," *Kurjer Warszawski* 14 (14 January 1915, morn. ed.): 2.

75. "Drobne," *Kurjer Warszawski* 178 (30 June 1915, morn. ed.): 3, "Z powodu brak drobnych," *Kurjer Warszawski* 180 (2 July 1915, morn. ed.): 2; and "'Kombinacyjki' na tle 'drobnych,'" *Kurjer Warszawski* 181 (3 July 1915, aft. ed.): 3.

76. "Z chwili," *Nowa Gazeta* 341 (29 July 1915, aft. ed.): 1.

77. APW KOMW 3, protocol no. 201 of 1 September 1915.

78. The subject of the meat monopoly and the German contract with Rozenberg became a regular feature of *Gazeta Poranna 2 grosze*; for a sampling, see "Monopol na mięso," 324 (24 November 1915): 1; "O monopol na mięso," 326 (26 November 1915): 1; "Monopol mięsny," 328 (28 November 1915): 2; "Monopol mięsny," 338 (8 December 1915): 2; "Sprawa mięsna," 352 (22 December 1915): 1; and "Monopoly mięsny," 4 (4 January 1916): 2. For the award of the monopoly to the Frankowski Brothers, see "Monopol mięsny," *Kurjer Warszawski* 39 (6 February 1916, aft. ed.): 7.

79. "Mięso i słonina," *Kurjer Warszawski* 53 (22 February 1916, morn. ed.): 2.

80. "Zmiany w sprzedaży mięsa," *Kurjer Warszawski* 186 (7 July 1916, aft. ed.): 3; "Co mogą jeść chrześcijanie," *Gazeta Poranna 2 grosze* 287 (19 October 1917): 3.

81. Pryłucki, 160–61.

82. "Konfiskata mąka," *Kurjer Warszawski* 28 (28 January 1916, aft. ed.): 2; "Zafałszowane produkty," *Kurjer Warszawski* 68 (9 March 1917, Sunday ed.): 6.

83. As quoted in the article "Spekulacya masłem," *Nowa Gazeta* 558 (5 December 1916): 2.

84. See, for example, "Fałszywe bony na chleb," *Kurjer Warszawski* 18 (18 January 1916, morn. ed.): 2; and "Fałszerze kart chlebowych," *Kurjer Warszawski* 179 (30 June 1916, aft. ed.): 3.

85. "O bakcyle spekulacji," *Gazeta Poranna 2 grosze* 237 (30 August 1917): 3.

86. Jedlicki, "Resisting the Wave," 61–63; Blobaum, "The Politics of Antisemitism," 294–98.

87. On the "doctrine of the Polish majority" and its role in shaping political discourse in the first years of the Second Polish Republic, see Paul Brykczynski, *Primed for Violence: Murder, Antisemitism, and Democratic Politics in Interwar Poland* (Madison, WI: University of Wisconsin Press, 2016).

88. Dunin-Wąsowicz, *Warszawa w czasie pierwszej wojny światowej*, 80–93.

89. APW KOMW 2, protocol no. 116 of 16 January 1915.

90. "Fałszywe i szkodliwe informacye," *Nowa Gazeta* 507 (29 October 1914, aft. ed.): 2.

91. "Napływ żydów bezdomnych do Warszawy," *Kurjer Warszawski* 67 (8 March 1915): 5.

92. Mendelsohn, 38.

93. Piotr Wróbel, "Przed odzyskaniem niepodległości," in *Najnowsze dzieje Żydów w Polsce w zarysie (do 1950 r.)*, ed. Jerzy Tomaszewski (Warsaw: PWN, 1993), 113.

94. M. M. Drozdowski, *Warszawa w latach 1914–1939* (Warsaw: PWN, 1990), 29–30.

95. Eleonora Bergman, "Żydzi uchodźcy w Warszawie w 1915 r.," in *Parlamentaryzm, konserwatyzm, nacjonalizm. Studia ofiarowane Profesorowi Szymonowi Rudnickiemu*, ed. Jolanta Żyndul (Warsaw: Wydawnictwo Sejmowe, 2010), 171–77.

96. "Bezdomi żydzi," *Kurjer Warszawski* 54 (23 February 1915, aft. ed.): 4; "Napływ żydów bezdomnych do Warszawy," *Kurjer Warszawski* 67 (8 March 1915): 5.

97. "Rozsadnik epidemii," *Gazeta Poranna 2 grosze* 84 (25 March 1915): 2.

98. Kempner's caustic remarks appeared, accompanied by a retort, in the article "Ewakuacja czy 'pogrom,'" *Gazeta Poranna 2 grosze* 85 (26 March 1915): 1.

99. "Warszawska gmina starozakonnych," *Nowa Gazeta* 176 (19 April 1915, aft. ed.): 2. For the Polish perspective on the memorial, see "Bezdomi żydzi," *Kurjer Warszawski* 107 (19 April 1915, aft. ed.): 5.

100. *Kurjer Warszawski* 130 (12 May 1915, aft. ed.): 4. For a description of conditions prevailing among the refugees on the Vistula's east bank a couple months following their evacuation from Warsaw, see Dzikowski, *Rok wojny*, 46.

101. Bergman, 172.

102. "Nowi bezdomni," *Gazeta Poranna 2 grosze* 195 (16 July 1915): 2.

103. "Z chwili," *Nowa Gazeta* 340 (29 July 1915); APW KOMW 2, protocols no. 178 of 25 July 1915 and no. 182 of 29 July 1915.

104. AGAD CNGGW 1, Report of General Hans von Beseler on the Development of Administration of the Warsaw General-Government, 23 October 1915, 5.

105. "Bezdomni żydzi," *Gazeta Poranna 2 grosze* 324 (24 November 1915): 2.

106. Kalman Weiser notes that there were some 400,000 Jews in Warsaw at the beginning of 1916, compared to a prewar population of 337,000; Weiser, 121.

107. "Ewakuacja bezdomnych żydów," *Gazeta Poranna 2 grosze* 62 (2 March 1916): 3.

108. "Ewakuacja bezdomnych," *Nowa Gazeta* 568 (12 December 1916): 4.

109. "Nie chcą wyjeżdżać," *Gazeta Poranna 2 grosze* 288 (20 October 1917): 2.

110. Konrad Zieliński, "Population, Displacement and Citizenship in Poland, 1918–1924," in *Homelands: War, Population and Statehood in Eastern Europe and Russia*, ed. Nick Baron and Peter Gatrell (London: Anthem Press, 2004), 100.

111. Sammartino, 129.

112. "Pan Cukierman i co się nim ukrywa," *Tygodnik Illustrowany* 23 (9 June 1917): 287–88.

113. APW KOMW 1, protocol no. 8 of 8 August 1914.

114. Zieliński, *Stosunki*, 172.

115. "Akcja ratunkowa," *Kurjer Warszawski* 231 (22 August 1914): 2.

116. "Sklepy Komitetu Obywatelskiego," *Gazeta Poranna 2 grosze* 262 (22 September 1914): 1.

117. APW KOMW 1, protocol no. 9 of 8 August 1914.

118. APW KOMW 1, protocol no. 31 of 26 August 1914.

119. APW KOMW 1, protocol no. 78 of 23 October 1914.

120. APW KOMW 1, protocols no. 100 of 3 December 1914 and no. 103 of 12 December 1914; for more on "Ezra," the main philanthropic organization sponsored by the Jewish Community Board, see Guesnet, "Thinking Globally."

121. APW KOMW 1, protocol no. 94 of 21 November 1914.

122. APW KOMW 1, protocol no. 98 of 28 November 1914.

123. See, for example, "Giełdy pracy," *Kurjer Warszawski* 256 (16 September 1914, aft. ed.): 3. According to the 1897 census, the percentage of wage-earners among Jews was 30.6%, compared to 61.3% among Christians; Garncarska, xiii. This considerable difference was reflected in the structure of unemployment already visible in the war's first weeks.

124. Zieliński, *Stosunki*, 223.

125. This view can also be found among Polish historians; see, for example, Dunin-Wąsowicz, *Warszawa w czasie pierwszej wojny światowej*, 119–21.

126. On support from the Jewish "Committee" in Petrograd, for example, see the following articles published in *Gazeta Poranna 2 grosze*: "Pomoc za żydów," 359 (30 December 1914): 3; and "Pieniądze z Rosji za żydów," 152 (6 June 1917): 3.

127. To be sure, the daily found evidence of this impoverishment in the decline of "lavish" spending on Jewish weddings; "Bez wesel," *Kurjer Warszawski* 195 (17 July 1915, aft. ed.): 3.

128. "Listy do Redakcyi," *Nowa Gazeta* 151 (3 April 1915, morn. ed.): 1.

129. Mendelsohn, *Zionism*, 41–43.

130. "Straż Obywatelska," *Nowa Gazeta* 336 (27 July 1915, morn. ed.): 2.

131. Zieliński, *Stosunki*, 228.

132. "Skarga redaktorów żargonowskich," *Gazeta Poranna 2 grosze* 134 (15 May 1916): 3.

133. M. Jankowski, "Pierwsze dni," 141.

134. Pryłucki, 18–19, 21.

135. "Z Rady Miejskiej," *Nowa Gazeta* 339 (13 July 1917, aft. ed.): 1–2.

136. "O hygienę kąpielową," *Nowa Gazeta* 102 (27 February 1917, aft. ed.): 2; "O czystość bród," *Nowa Gazeta* 161 (3 April 1917, aft. ed.): 3.

137. "Milicja a brody żydowskie," *Gazeta Poranna 2 grosze* 91 (3 April 1917): 2–3; "Brody są niezbędne," *Gazeta Poranna 2 grosze* 153 (7 June 1917): 4; "Wymiana listów," *Gazeta Poranna 2 grosze* 268 (25 September 1917): 3.

138. Pryłucki, 69–70.

139. "Memoriał żydowski," *Gazeta Poranna 2 grosze* 344 (14 December 1915): 2.

140. "Na dobie," *Gazeta Poranna 2 grosze* 178 (29 June 1916): 2.

141. "Rozprawy budżetowe w Radzie Miejskiej," *Godzina Polski* 179 (3 July 1917, aft. ed.): 2.

142. Pryłucki, 116.

143. APW KOMW 6, Imperial German President of Police Glasenapp to the President of Warsaw Lubomirski, 23 December 1916.

144. "Z magistratu," *Kurjer Warszawski* 54 (23 February 1917): 4; Pryłucki, 6–7.

145. Pryłucki, 5.

146. "Samorząd," *Nowa Gazeta* 160 (9 April 1915, aft. ed.): 1.

147. APW KOMW 4, protocols no. 280 of 21 March 1916 and no. 281 of 23 March 1916.

148. APW KOMW 2, protocol no. 186 of 3 August 1915.

149. "Przedstawicielstwo żydów," *Gazeta Poranna 2 grosze* 75 (15 March 1916): 2.

150. APW KOMW 6, protocol no. 290a of the Extraordinary Session of the Warsaw Citizens Committee of 15 April 1916.

151. APW KOMW 6, protocol no. 290b of the Extraordinary Session of the Warsaw Citizens Committee of 16 April 1916; see also Zieliński, *Stosunki*, 264–66.

152. Zieliński, *Stosunki*, 268–69; Weiser, 140–47.

153. B. Koskowski, "Samorząd w Warszawie," *Tygodnik Illustrowany* 26 (24 June 1916): 306.

154. "Racyonalny syonizm," *Gazeta Poranna 2 grosze* 174 (25 June 1916): 4.

155. "Zwycięstwo," *Gazeta Poranna 2 grosze* 196 (17 July 1916): 2.

156. "Epilog wyborów do Rady Miejskiej," *Tygodnik Illustrowany* 30 (22 July 1916): 358.

157. "Z chwili," *Tygodnik Illustrowany* 27 (1 July 1917): 319.

158. Pryłucki, 102.

159. AAN AD 14, Platform of the Central Democratic Election Committee.

160. Dunin-Wąsowicz, *Warszawa w czasie pierwszej wojny światowej*, 146.

161. "Z chwili, *Tygodnik Illustrowany* 27 (1 July 1917): 319.

162. "Głosowanie za Palestyną," *Gazeta Poranna 2 grosze* 211 (4 August 1917): 2.

163. "Ludowcy żydowscy o sobie," *Godzina Polski* 203 (27 July 1917, morn. ed.): 4; and "Rabini przeciw syonizmowi," *Godzina Polski* (26 July 1917, morn. ed.): 4.

164. For coverage of the election campaign, see "Wybory do zarządu Gminy Starozakonnych," *Nowa Gazeta* 216 (5 May 1917, morn. ed.): 2; and "Wybory do gminy Starozakonnych," *Nowa Gazeta* 239 (18 May 1917, aft. ed.): 1; see also Halpern, 44.

165. "Zachowanie szabasu," *Gazeta Poranna 2 grosze* 199 (20 July 1916): 3.

166. As reported in the article "Pierwszy krok . . . ," *Kurjer Warszawski* 205 (26 July 1916, aft. ed.): 2.

167. Weiser, 159.

168. Some twenty-five thousand signatures were collected to protest the making of Sundays an obligatory day of rest; see "Przeciw święceniu niedzieli," *Nowa Gazeta* 555a (4 December 1916, special morning supplement): 2. The entrance to the Łazienki Park and Botanical Gardens was marked by a sign that read, "Entrance to the Łazienki Park is permitted only to persons in clean, proper and European attire"; "Ubranie europejskie," *Nowa Gazeta* 559 (6 December 1916, morn. ed.): 2.

169. Pryłucki, 149.

170. "Nastroje w Radzie miejskiej," *Nowa Gazeta* 572 (14 December 1916, aft. ed.): 2.

171. As quoted in the article "Nowa Gazeta," *Gazeta Poranna 2 grosze* 227 (9 October 1917): 2.

172. "Mowa r. Ilskiego w żargonówkach," *Gazeta Poranna 2 grosze* 188 (12 July 1917): 3. In response to Ilski's charges, Prylucki noted that "whenever [Ilski] mentions Jews, there is no longer Judaism, the Bible, Spinoza . . . there is only usury, fraud, and trade in human flesh"; Pryłucki, 139.

173. Pryłucki, 34–35. Prylucki's speeches often took the form of rebuttals to those of his opponents, whose speeches were also included in the collection compiled after the war in 1920.

174. "Ilskowstręt," *Gazeta Poranna 2 grosze* 34 (4 February 1918): 3.

175. "Z Rady Miejskiej," *Nowa Gazeta* 339 (13 July 1917, aft. ed.): 1–2.

176. "O zapomogi dla 'rezerwistek' żydówek," *Kurjer Warszawski* 82 (23 March 1917, aft. ed.): 2

177. "O handel w niedzielę," *Kurjer Warszawski* 64 (5 March 1917, morn. ed.): 2.

178. "Z Rady Miejskiej," *Nowa Gazeta* 594 (29 December 1916, morn. ed.): 2; "Z Rady Miejskiej," *Nowa Gazeta* 140 (23 March 1917, morn. ed.): 1; "Z rady miejskiej," *Kurjer Warszawski* 82 (23 March 1917, morn. ed.): 1–2.

179. "Z Rady Miejskiej," *Nowa Gazeta* 263 (1 June 1917, aft. ed.): 1–2.

180. Pryłucki, 111.

181. "Z Magistratu st. m. Warszawy," *Nowa Gazeta* 482 (21 October 1916): 1–2.

182. "Z rady miejskiej," *Godzina Polski* 197 (21 July 1917, morn. ed.): 5.

183. "Premjer polski o żydach," *Godzina Polski* 323 (24 November 1917): 4.

184. AAN AD 14.

185. For a description of Warsaw's financially starved city government and its struggle to provide assistance to its own employees, see Herbst, 322–25.

186. Dunin-Wąsowicz, *Warszawa w czasie pierwszej wojny światowej*, 88–91.

187. "Miasto w cyfrach," *Nowa Gazeta* 188 (19 April 1917, aft. ed.): 2.

188. "Ze statystyki miejskiej," *Nowa Gazeta* 382 (6 August 1917, morn. ed.): 2.

189. Zieliński, *Stosunki*, 31.

190. Piotr Wróbel, "Jewish Warsaw before the First World War," *Polin: A Journal of Polish-Jewish Studies* 3 (1988): 165.

191. Pryłucki, 103–8.

192. For the effect of migratory movements on Warsaw's ever-changing wartime demography, see Robert Blobaum, "A City in Flux: Warsaw's Transient Populations in the First World War," *The Polish Review* 59, no. 4 (2014): 21–43.

193. "Danina krwi a żydzi," *Gazeta Poranna 2 grosze* 33 (8 February 1918): 2.

194. Blobaum, "A City in Flux," 22–25.

195. Mendelsohn, *Zionism*, 88; Zieliński, *Stosunki*, 404.

196. Jan z Marnowa, "Warszawa, d. 11 Listopada 1918 r.," *Tygodnik Illustrowany* 46 (16 November 1918): 532.

197. Weeks, "Vilnius," 55.
198. William W. Hagen, "The Moral Economy of Popular Violence: The Pogrom in Lwów, November 1918," in *Antisemitism and Its Opponents*, 124–47.
199. For a more general discussion of wartime violence against Jews in and around Lwów, see Alexander Victor Prusin, *Nationalizing a Borderland: War, Ethnicity, and Anti-Jewish Violence in East Galicia, 1914–1920* (Tuscaloosa, AL: University of Alabama Press, 2005).

5. WOMEN AND THE WARSAW HOME FRONT

1. Dunin-Wąsowicz, *Warszawa w czasie pierwszej wojny światowej*, 196.
2. See Bonzon, "The Labor Market and Industrial Mobilization," in *Capital Cities at War* 1, 164–95.
3. AGAD SAGGW 5, Vierteljahrschaftsbericht des Verwaltungchefs bei dem General-Gouvernement Warschau für die Zeit vom 1. Januar 1916 bis zum 31. März 1916, appendix III.
4. Kutrzeba, 48.
5. Davis focuses primarily on "women of lesser means" in her book *Home Fires Burning*; for an elaboration of the term, see her introduction.
6. See Healy, *Vienna*, especially chapter 4 "Sisterhood and Citizenship."
7. "Komitet Obywatelski," *Bluszcz* 32 (15 August 1914): 3; APW KOMW 1, protocol no. 1 of 3 August 1914.
8. "Kobieta polska w Komitecie obywatelskim," *Bluszcz* 32 (15 August 1914, special supplement): 3–4.
9. APW KOMW 1, protocol no. 16 of 12 August 1914.
10. APW KOMW 1, protocol no. 25 of 20 August 1914.
11. APW KOMW 1, protocol no. 37 of 1 September 1914.
12. APW KOMW 1, protocols no. 49 of 18 September 1914 and no. 53 of 24 September 1914.
13. Julia Kisielewska (Oksza), "Do polskich kobiet," *Bluszcz* 34–36 (26 September 1914): 355–57.
14. APW KOMW 1, protocol no. 11 of 9 August 1914.
15. "Sanitarjuszki warszawskie," *Kurjer Warszawski* 235 (26 August 1914, aft. ed.): 2.
16. "W sprawie sanitarjuszek," *Kurjer Warszawski* 250 (9 September 1914, aft. ed.): 2.
17. Kisielewska, "Do polskich kobiet."
18. "Wrażenie z chwili," *Bluszcz* 37–38 (10 October 1914): 378.
19. Eight of eleven members of the commission's administrative board were women, and Helena Weychert returned to become one of its leading figures; "Opieka nad dziećmi," *Kurjer Warszawski* 11 (11 January 1915, aft. ed.): 2.
20. "Komisya pracy kobiet," *Bluszcz* 3–4 (6 February 1915): 1–3.
21. "Komisya opieki nad dziećmi," *Bluszcz* 7–8 (20 February 1915): 1–2.
22. APW KOMW 2, Presidium protocol no. 37 of 5 February 1915, Presidium protocol no. 71 of 28 April 1915, and protocol no. 167 of 7 May 1915.
23. Herbst, 306.
24. "Z opieki nad dziećmi," *Kurjer Warszawski* 8 (8 January 1915, aft. ed.): 3.
25. "Komisya pracy kobiet," *Bluszcz* 3–4 (6 February 1915): 1–3.
26. APW KOMW 2, protocol no. 129 of 18 February 1915.
27. "Komisya pracy kobiet," *Kurjer Warszawski* 66 (7 March 1915): 4.
28. "Ze Związku równouprawnienia kobiet," *Kurjer Warszawski* 105 (17 April 1915): 3.
29. Zofia Morawska, "Moda chwili," *Bluszcz* 29–30 (24 July 1915): 226–27.

30. "Prawa kobiet w samorządzie," *Kurjer Warszawski* 136 (18 May 1915, aft. ed.): 2.

31. Jan Czempliński, "Krucjata. Do polskich kobiet," *Bluszcz* 29–30 (24 July 1915): 225–26.

32. APW KOMW 2, Presidium protocol no. 84 of 7 June 1915.

33. "Do wyborczyń-polek," *Kurjer Warszawski* 182 (4 July 1915, Sunday ed.): 6–7.

34. "Ze Związku stowarzyszeń kobiecych," *Godzina Polski* 64 (3 March 1916): 5.

35. "Dział kobiecy. Odezwa Związku Stowarzyszeń Kobiecych," *Godzina Polski* 175 (25 June 1916): 7.

36. "Kronika: Z miasta," *Nowa Gazeta* 353 (4 August 1915, morn. ed.): 2.

37. "Z przedmieść," *Nowa Gazeta* 384 (21 August 1915, aft. ed.): 2.

38. "Wynajęte dzieci," *Kurjer Warszawski* 253 (13 September 1914, Sunday ed.): 3.

39. "O mieszkania rezerwistów," *Kurjer Warszawski* 233 (24 August 1914, aft. ed.): 3.

40. The committee's concern for and efforts "to calm Polish opinion" are evidence of the ethnic dimension of the conflict; APW KOMW 1, protocol no. 32 of 27 August 1914. Despite the relatively high proportion of Jewish ownership of rental properties, the long-standing impression that Jews dominated the real estate market in Warsaw is a false one. According to Konrad Zieliński, Jews comprised roughly one-third of all owners of real estate in Warsaw before the war, a percentage slightly lower than the Jewish proportion of the city's population; Zieliński, *Stosunki*, 33.

41. APW KOMW 2, Presidium protocol no. 88 of 16 June 1915.

42. "Wdowy po rezerwistkach," *Kurjer Warszawski* 40 (9 February 1915, aft. ed.): 2.

43. Healy, *Vienna*, 194.

44. In Russia as well, as Barbara Engel has noted, *soldatki* were able to exploit a publicly acknowledged sense of entitlement during the war to mobilize in defense of their economic interests and demand that the state meet its obligations; Engel, 710.

45. Rosset, "Warszawa w dniach przełomu," 104.

46. APW KOMW 3, protocol no. 196 of 20 August 1915.

47. Rosset, "Warszawa w dniach przełomu," 105. In December 1915 the Warsaw Citizens Committee learned that a thousand of these children sent to the countryside were in need of clothing and underwear; APW ZOMW 3, protocol no. 243 of 6 December 1915.

48. APW KOMW 3, protocol no. 210 of 22 September 1915.

49. "Zajście z rezerwistkami," *Gazeta Poranna 2 grosze* 270 (30 September 1915): 4.

50. APW KOMW 3, protocol no. 245 of 13 December 1915.

51. Lubomirska, 328.

52. APW KOMW 6, Imperial German President of Police Glasenapp to the President of Warsaw Lubomirski, 23 December 1916.

53. Of the approximately one thousand *rezerwistki* affected by this decision, slightly more than three hundred were able to receive temporary support from the Jewish community board; "Biura okręgowe dobroczynne," *Nowa Gazeta* 97 (24 February 1917, aft. ed.): 4.

54. "Rząd a rezerwistki," *Godzina Polski* 202 (26 July 1918, morn. ed.): 5.

55. APW KOMW 3, Presidium protocol no. 107 of 11 September 1915.

56. APW KOMW 4, protocol no. 266 of 3 February 1916.

57. Kutrzeba, 56–57.

58. "'Nietykalność' mężatek," *Godzina Polski* 133 (13 May 1916): 5.

59. B. F., "Sprawa rezerwistek," *Godzina Polski* 96 (9 April 1918, aft. ed.): 2.

60. "Znowu sprawa rezerwistek," *Godzina Polski* 164 (18 June 1918, morn. ed.): 5.

61. "Z ulicy," *Tygodnik Illustrowany* 10 (6 March 1915): 152.

62. APW RNG 3, list of stores looted in the food riots of 19–20 June 1916.

63. APW RNG 6, Informational Communiqué "Rozruchy w Warszawie," no. 3 (15 May 1917); Holzer and Molenda, 213–14.

64. Keely Stauter-Halsted, *The Devil's Chain: Prostitution and Social Control in Partitioned Poland* (Ithaca, NY: Cornell University Press, 2015).

65. "Walka z prostytucyą," *Nowa Gazeta* 547 (21 November 1914, aft. ed.): 2.

66. "Za tolerowanie rozpusty," *Nowa Gazeta* 49 (31 January 1915, morn. ed.): 2.

67. "Nadzór nad prostytucyą," *Nowa Gazeta* 156 (7 April 1915, aft. ed.): 2.

68. Jan Czempiński, "Krucjata. Do polskich kobiet," *Bluszcz* 29–30 (24 July 1915): 225–26.

69. "Protest," *Kurjer Warszawski* 78 (19 March 1915, aft. ed.): 4.

70. Herbst, 302–3.

71. AGAD CNGGW 42, Government Order of General von Etzdorf of 8 September 1915.

72. AGAD SAGGW 3, Vierteljahrsbericht des Verwaltungschefs beidem General-Gouvernement Warschau für die Zeit von 21. Juli 1915 bis zum 1. Oktober 1915, 15.

73. Kraushar, 23–24, 36.

74. APW KOMW 3, Presidium protocol no. 119 of 4 November 1915, and protocols no. 232 of 10 November 1915 and no. 233 of 12 November 1915.

75. On *rezerwistki* and wartime prostitution, see Stauter-Halsted, 314–17.

76. Aschheim, citing early figures from 1915 and 1916, notes that 25.7% or 457 of 1,778 prostitutes in Warsaw were Jewish; Aschheim, 148.

77. "Polskie Tow. Walki z chorobami wenerycznymi i nierządem," *Nowa Gazeta* 225 (27 May 1917, morn. ed.): 4–5.

78. Stauter-Halsted, 316.

79. "Handel kobietami," *Gazeta Poranna 2 grosze* 221 (12 August 1915): 2.

80. "O wychowaniu żydówek," *Gazeta Poranna 2 grosze* 32 (1 February 1916): 2.

81. Blobaum, "Criminalizing the 'Other,'" 87–88.

82. "Antysemityzm 'prostytucyjny,'" *Głos Żydowski* 32 (77) (16 August 1918): 4–5.

83. "Dobroczynność publiczna w Warszawie," *Godzina Polski* 193 (17 July 1917, aft. ed.): 2.

84. Dr. Henryk Nusbaum, "Prostytucya ze stanowiska etyki społecznej," *Rozwaga* 3–4 (March–April 1917): 65.

85. "Udział kobiet w społecznych zadaniach naszego wieku," *Bluszcz* 12 (21 March 1914): 117.

86. "Szkodliwe zawody kobiece," *Godzina Polski* 217 (10 August 1917, aft. ed): 4.

87. R. Centerszwerowa, "Z zadań doby obecnej," *Bluszcz* 13 (31 March 1917): 91–92.

88. I. Piątkowska, "Dział kobiecy. Kobieta nowoczesna," *Godzina Polski* 233 (22 August 1916): 2; "Dział kobiecy. Kobieta w społeczeństwie," *Godzina Polski* 131 (15 May 1917): 6.

89. "Dział kobiecy. Obowiązki kobiety-matki," *Godzina Polski* 261 (19 September 1917): 6.

90. "Kobieta—domowe ognisko," *Bluszcz* 29–30 (24 July 1915): 228–29.

91. "Reforma wykształcenia kobiecego. Szkoły gospodarstwa domowego," *Godzina Polski* 162 (12 June 1916): 12–13.

92. "Głosy czytelniczek: Strój kobiet pracujących," *Bluszcz* 22 (29 May 1915): 174–75.

93. Ibid.

94. "Praca urzędniczek," *Godzina Polski* 195 (19 July 1918, aft. ed.): 2.

95. "Uwagi," *Nowa Gazeta* 405 (5 September 1916, aft. ed.): 2.

96. Apolinary Krupiński, "Studentka," *Godzina Polski* 85 (27 March 1918, morn. ed.): 1.

97. "Do kobiet polskich," *Bluszcz* 34 (26 September 1914): 355–57.

98. Blobaum, "A City in Flux," 24.

99. Lubomirska, 614.

100. Stanisław Dzikowski, "Warszawa dzisiejsza i wczorajsza," *Tygodnik Illustrowany* 13 (31 March 1917): 153–54.

101. "Czuwajcie," *Bluszcz* 2 (13 January 1917): 11.

102. "Dział kobiecy. Kobiety a wychowanie przedszkolne," *Godzina Polski* 86 (29 March 1917): 6.

103. K. Z., "Dział kobiecy. Reforma wykształcenia kobiecego. Kobieta w szkolnictwie średnim," *Godzina Polski* 189 (9 July 1916): 6–7.

104. Dunin-Wąsowicz, *Warszawa w czasie pierwszej wojny światowej,* 196.

105. "Uniwersytet w cyfrach," *Godzina Polski* 93 (6 April 1918, aft. ed.): 2; "Ze statystyki politechniki," *Godzina Polski* 101 (14 April 1918, morn. ed.): 3–4.

106. Krupiński, "Studentka," *Godzina Polski* 84 (26 March 1918, morn. ed.): 1.

107. Maria Kamińska, *Ścieżkami wspomnien* (Warsaw: Książka i Wiedza, 1960), 128–31.

108. Zofia Ruettówna, "Szkoła przyszłości," *Bluszcz* 15 (10 April 1915):116 and 16 (17 April 1915): 123.

109. Reuttówna, "Szkoła przyszłości," *Bluszcz* 21 (22 May 1915): 164.

110. Krupiński, "Studentka," *Godzina Polski* 85 (27 March 1918, morn. ed.): 1.

111. "Reforma szkół żeńskich," *Godzina Polski* 249 (7 September 1917): 6.

112. "Inspektorki fabryczne," *Kurjer Warszawski* 313 (12 November 1917, aft. ed.): 3.

113. "Do studentek politechniki," *Kurjer Warszawski* 101 (13 April 1917): 2.

114. "Praca kobiet w zawodach technicznych," *Kurjer Warszawski* 105 (17 April 1917, aft. ed.): 3.

115. "Szkoły zawodowe żeńskie," *Kurjer Warszawski* 228 (19 August 1915, morn. ed.): 1–2.

116. J. Oksza, "Reformy w wychowaniu dziewcząt," *Bluszcz* 8 (24 February 1917): 57.

117. J. Oksza, "Reformy w wychowaniu dziewcząt," *Bluszcz* 7 (17 February 1917): 50–51.

118. "Szkoły zawodowe dla dziewcząt," *Kurjer Warszawski* 321 (20 November 1915): 4–5.

119. I. Piątkowska, "Słów kilka o kobietach na wsi," *Godzina Polski* 242 (31 August 1916): 3.

120. "Kilka słów o kobietach na wsi," *Godzina Polski* 242 (31 August 1916): 6.

121. See, for example, "Reforma szkół żeńskich," *Godzina Polski* 249 (7 September 1917): 6.

122. "Ze Związku stowarzyszeń kobiecych," *Godzina Polski* 64 (3 March 1916): 5.

123. "Prawa wyborcze kobiet," *Nowa Gazeta* 151 (1 April 1916, aft. ed.): 2; "Prawa wyborcze kobiet," *Godzina Polski* 94 (2 April 1916): 5; and "Kobiety i rada miejska," *Kurjer Warszawski* 94 (3 April 1916, aft. ed.): 1–2.

124. APW KOMW 4, protocol no. 289 of the extraordinary session of the Warsaw Citizens Committee of 14 April 1916.

125. APW KOMW 6, protocol no. 290a of the extraordinary session of the Warsaw Citizens Committee of 15 April 1915.

126. "Do wyborczyń-polek," *Kurjer Warszawski* 167 (18 July 1916): 7.

127. "Dział kobiecy. Wiec kobiet," *Godzina Polski* 198 (18 July 1916): 6.

128. "W przededniu Sejmu Polskiego," *Bluszcz* 2 (13 January 1917): 9–10.

129. "Zjazd kobiet polskich," *Tygodnik Illustrowany* 37 (15 September 1917): 456–57.

130. "Głos Elizy Orzeszkowej w sprawie równouprawnienia politycznego kobiet polskich," *Rozwaga* 8–9 (August–September 1917): 147–49.

131. "Zjazd kobiet," *Kurjer Warszawski* 247 (7 September 1917, aft. ed.): 1.

132. "Zjazd kobiet polskich," *Tygodnik Illustrowany* 37 (15 September 1917): 456–57.

133. "O prawa wyborcze dla kobiet w samorządzie," *Godzina Polski* 316 (17 November 1917, morn. ed.): 4; and "O udział kobiet w samorządzie," *Godzina Polski* 322 (23 November 1917, morn. ed.): 4.

134. "Wiec kobiet," *Godzina Polski* 322a (3 December 1917): 3.

135. "Po zjeździe kobiet," *Nowa Gazeta* 446 (10 September 1917): 1.

136. "O prawa wyborcze dla kobiet w samorządzie," *Godzina Polski* 316 (17 November 1917, morn. ed.): 4.

137. "Kobiety w sejmie," *Godzina Polski* 293 (26 October 1918, morn. ed.): 4.

138. "Zjazd kobiet," *Nowa Gazeta* 445 (10 September 1917): 2.

139. "W przededniu Sejmu Polskiego," *Bluszcz* 2 (13 January 1917): 9.

140. "Kronika działalności kobiecej," *Bluszcz* 29 (20 July 1918): 219–20.

141. M. Niedziałkowski, "Prawo wyborcze kobiet," *Bluszcz* 35 (31 August 1918): 255.

142. Sylwia Kuźma-Markowska, "Soldiers, Members of Parliament, Social Activists: The Polish Women's Movement after World War I," in *Aftermaths of War: Women's Movements and Female Activists, 1918–1923*, ed. Ingrid Sharp and Matthew Stibbe (Leiden and Boston: Brill, 2011): 265–86.

143. Joanna Dufrat, "Ligi Kobiet Królestwa, Galicji i Śląska. Próba politycznej aktywizacji kobiet w okresie I wojny świątowej," in *Działaczki społeczne, feministki, obywatelki. Samoorganizowanie się kobiet na ziemiach polskich do 1918 roku (na tle porównaczym)* 1, ed. Agnieszka Janiak-Jasińska, Katarzyna Sierakowska, and Andrzej Szwarc (Warsaw: Wydawnictwo Neriton, 2008): 113–30.

144. "Wezwanie do wszystkich polek," *Kurjer Warszawski* 282 (12 October 1918, aft. ed.): 3; "Wezwanie do wszystkich polek," *Bluszcz* 42 (19 October 1918): 316.

145. Kamil Kacperski, *System wyborczy do Sejmu i Senatu w progu Drugiej Rzeczypospolitej* (Warsaw: Wydawnictwo Sejmowe, 2007): 115.

146. "Prawa wyborcze kobiet," *Kurjer Warszawski* 328 (27 November 1918, morn. ed.): 3.

147. "Z centr. kom. równoupr. polit. kobiet," *Kurjer Warszawski* 330 (29 November 1918, aft. ed.): 4.

148. "Głosy czytelniczek. Do kobiet w przeddzień wyborów," *Bluszcz* 52 (28 December 1918): 392.

149. "Nowe prawa—nowe obowiązki," *Bluszcz* 52 (28 December 1918): 391.

150. Kuźma-Markowska, 280. The January elections were held only in the territories comprising the former Polish Kingdom and the Austrian crownland; subsequent elections were held later in the year in the territories of Prussian Poland that were incorporated into the new Polish state, most significantly in June 1919 in the Poznań region.

151. Krzywicka, 72.

152. Anna Żarnowska, "Social Change, Women and the Family in the Era of Industrialization: Recent Polish Research," *Journal of Family History* 22, no. 2 (1997): 191–203.

6. WARSAW'S WARTIME CULTURE WARS

1. See the review of "Cultures at War: Austria-Hungary 1914–1918 (St. Hilda's College, Oxford, 13–15 April 2011)" by Megan Brandow-Faller, published in H-Habsburg, 14 June 2011.

2. *Capital Cities at War: Paris, London, Berlin 1914–1919*, II (*A Cultural History*), ed. Jay Winter and Jean-Louis Robert (New York: Cambridge University Press, 2007).

3. Jay Winter, "The Practices of Metropolitan Life in Wartime," in *Capital Cities at War* II, 10.

4. Dunin-Wąsowicz, *Warszawa w czasie pierwszej wojny światowej*, 67; Hutten-Czapski, "Ostatnie dni okupacji niemieckiej w Warszawie," in *Warszawa w pamiętnikach*, 482.

5. Krashaur, 22.

6. *Weg-Weiser durch Warschau: Kurzgefasster Führer durch die Stadt Warschau mit besonderer Berücksichtigung alles dessen, was der deutsche Soldat, Beamte und Reisende wissen muss*, 4th revised edition (Warsaw: Verlag der Deutschen Staatsdruckerei, 1917).

7. Ibid., 18.

8. Rafał Bielski, *Było takie miasto: Warszawa na starych pocztówkach* (Warsaw: Agencja Wydawnicza Veda, 2008), 141.

9. *Weg-Weiser*, 19.

10. Kraushar, 23–24, 36.

11. *Weg-Weiser*, 23.

12. APW ZMW 1, protocol no. 9 of City Council session of 4 March 1918.

13. Lubomirska, 550.

14. C. Jankowski, "Pierwsze dni wojny," 45; "Wiadomości bieżące. Z miasta," *Kurjer Warszawski* 213 (4 August 1914, aft. ed.): 2.

15. "Zwierzęcość," *Nowa Gazeta* 380 (19 August 1914, aft. ed.): 3; "Do obywateli miejskich," *Kurjer Warszawski* 227 (18 August 1914, aft. ed.): 2.

16. "Ostrożnie z fotografowaniem," *Kurjer Warszawski* 223 (14 August 1914, aft. ed.): 3; "Fotografia podczas wojny," *Kurjer Warszawski* 44 (13 February 1915, aft. ed.): 3.

17. APW KOMW 1, protocol no. 16 of 11 August 1914.

18. Dzikowski, *Rok wojny*, 11.

19. "Powracamy do normy," *Kurjer Warszawski* 227 (18 August 1914, aft. ed.): 2; and "Trzecia niedziela," *Kurjer Warszawski* 233 (24 August 1914): 3.

20. "Z kinomatografów," *Kurjer Warszawski* 251 (11 September 1914, aft. ed.): 3.

21. "Totalizator i chwila obecna," *Kurjer Warszawski* 252 (12 September 1914): 2; and "Z życiu miasta," *Kurjer Warszawski* 258 (18 September 1914, aft. ed.): 1.

22. Miklaszewski, 63–64.

23. "Zakaz sprzedaży wszelkich trunków," *Kurjer Warszawski* 275 (5 October 1914, morn. ed.): 4.

24. "Zawieszenie komunikacji telefonicznej," *Kurjer Warszawski* 287 (17 October 1914, morn. ed.): 3.

25. Miklaszewski, 65.

26. "Turcy w Warszawie," *Kurjer Warszawski* 303 (2 November 1914, special ed.): 4.

27. "Przepełniona Warszawa," *Nowa Gazeta* 555 (26 November 1914, aft. ed.): 2.

28. "Muzeum wojny," *Nowa Gazeta* 568 (4 December 1914, morn. ed.): 2. On the Vienna exhibition, which like its Warsaw counterpart ultimately fell victim to "competing truths," see Healy, *Vienna*, 107–21. On the beginnings of London's Imperial War Museum, see Gaynor Kavanagh, "Museum as Memorial: The Origins of the Imperial War Museum," *Journal of Contemporary History* 23, no. 1 (January 1988): 77–97.

29. Stanisław Jarkowski, *Prasa warszawska od początku sierpnia 1914 do końca grudnia 1915* (Warsaw: Zakł. Graf. B. Wierzbicki i S-ka, 1916): 2–14; "Papier," *Kurjer Warszawski* 63 (4 March 1915, aft. ed.): 4.

30. *Bluszcz* would renew publication only at the beginning of 1917.

31. Dunin-Wąsowicz, *Warszawa w czasie pierwszej wojny światowej*, 209.

32. "Nastrój w mieście," *Kurjer Warszawski* 202 (24 July 1915, aft. ed.): 2.

33. APW KOMW 2, protocol no. 184 of 31 July 1915.

34. APW KOMW 3, protocol no. 219 of 13 October 1915.

35. APW KOMW 3, protocol no. 221 of 18 October 1915.

36. Aschheim, 149–50.

37. "Z Magistratu st. m. W.," *Nowa Gazeta* 96 (24 February 1917, morn. ed.): 2.

38. For these exchanges over the city's budget, see APW KOMW 6, Vice President of the City Administration Piotr Drzewiecki to the Imperial German Presidium of Police, 6 February 1917, and Imperial German President of Police Glasenapp to the Office of the Warsaw Magistrate, 22 March 1917.

39. Staniław Dzikowski, "Warszawa dzisiejsza i wczorajsza," *Tygodnik Illustrowany* 13 (31 March 1917): 153–54.

40. Lubomirska, 19.

41. "Niszczenia zapasów wódki," *Nowa Gazeta* 354 (5 August 1914, morn. ed.): 2.

42. "Sprzedaż trunków," *Nowa Gazeta* 370 (13 August 1914, aft. ed.): 2; "Restauracje," *Kurjer Warszawski* (13 August 1914, aft. ed.): 3; "Zamykanie restauracji," *Kurjer Warszawski* (3 September 1914, aft. ed.): 2–3.

43. "Ruch tramwajowy," *Kurjer Warszawski* 255 (15 September 1914, aft. ed.): 3.

44. APW ZOMW 1, protocol no. 41 of 7 September 1914.

45. "Życie nocne," *Kurjer Warszawski* 223 (14 August 1914, aft. ed.): 3.

46. "Zakaz sprzedaży wszelkich trunków," *Kurjer Warszawski* 275 (5 October 1914, morn. ed.): 4.

47. Chwalba, *Imperium korupcji*, 111.

48. APW ZOW 1064.

49. "Kary administracjne," *Kurjer Warszawski* 5 (5 January 1915, morn. ed.): 2.

50. "Pokątny handel trunkami," *Kurjer Warszawski* 56 (25 February 1915, morn. ed.): 3.

51. "Postanowienie obowiązujące," *Kurjer Warszawski* 21 (21 January 1915, morn. ed.): 3.

52. "Wylewanie piwa do kanałów," *Nowa Gazeta* 222 (18 May 1915, morn. ed.): 2.

53. APW KOMW 2, protocols no. 135 of 4 March 1915 and no. 146 of 8 April 1915.

54. Emmanuelle Cronier, "The Street," in *Capital Cities at War* II, 57–104.

55. APW KOMW 3, protocol no. 189 of 6 August 1915.

56. Dunin-Wąsowicz, *Warszawa w czasie pierwszej wojny światowej*, 23–24; Rosset, "Warszawa," 96–98.

57. APW KOMW 3, protocols no. 192 of 11 August 1915 and no. 193 of 13 August 1915.

58. APW KOMW 3, protocols no. 194 of 16 August 1915 and no. 196 of 20 August 1915.

59. APW KOMW 3, protocol no. 242 of 3 December 1915.

60. APW KOMW 3, protocol no. 251 of 29 December 1915.

61. APW KOMW 6, Copy of Memorandum of the President of Warsaw Zdzisław Lubomirski to the Imperial German Presidium of Police in Warsaw, 9 October 1916.

62. AGAD CNGGW 42, Governor of Warsaw General Ulrich von Etzdorf to the Warsaw Governor-General Hans von Beseler, 28 April 1916.

63. *Kurjer Warszawski* 197 (19 July 2015, spec. ed.): 3; APW ZOW 1058, Temporary Regulation of the Commander of the Warsaw Military Region regarding the Requisitioning of Automobiles, 18 (31) July 1914.

64. Kraushar, 14.

65. "Warszawa bez tramwajów," *Tygodnik Illustrowany* 24 (10 June 1916): 287.

66. Kutrzeba, 47.

67. Kutrzeba, 47–48.

68. "Wypadek i przerwa w komunikacji," *Chwila Świąteczna* 4 (29 April 1917): 4.

69. "Kronika wydarzeń w Warszawie w latach w 1914–1918," in *Warszawa w pamietnikach*, 516.

70. Ibid., 517.

71. Z. D., "Warszawa," *Tygodnik Illustrowany* 38 (18 September 1915): 564.

72. "Z tygodnia na tydzień," *Tygodnik Illustrowany* 47 (18 November 1916): 559–61.

73. "Po wakacyach," *Tygodnik Illustrowany* 35 (1 September 1917): 430.

74. "Telefony," *Tygodnik Illustrowany* 35 (28 August 1915); "Pisma żydowskie," *Gazeta Poranna 2 grosze* 223 (16 August 1916): 2; "Kronika," 516, 522. For more on the condition of the Warsaw press after November 1916, see Jarkowski, *Prasa warszawska od d. 5 XI 1916 do d. 1 III 1919*.

75. Cronier, 64.

76. "Totalizator i chwila obecna," *Kurjer Warszawski* 252 (12 September 1914, aft. ed.): 2.

77. "Czy będą w Warszawie wyścigi?," *Kurjer Warszawski* 40 (9 February 1915): 3.

78. "Z Tow. wyścigów konnych," *Kurjer Warszawski* 87 (28 March 1915, Sunday ed.): 6.
79. "Powszechny protest," *Kurjer Warszawski* 119 (1 May 1915, aft. ed.): 3.
80. "Zakaz totalizatora," *Kurjer Warszawski* 121 (3 May 1915, aft. ed.): 4.
81. Lubomirska, 174.
82. Ibid.; "Nieprzyjęcie ofiary," *Kurjer Warszawski* 128 (10 May 1915, special ed.): 3.
83. "Zanim powstał tor na Służewcu," accessed 8 May 2015, http://torsluzewiec.pl/historia-toru/.
84. APW KOMW 3, protocol no. 203 of 6 September 1915.
85. APW ZMW 1, protocol no. 9 of City Council session of 4 March 1918.
86. Hubertus F. Jahn, *Patriotic Culture in Russia during World War I* (Ithaca, NY: Cornell University Press, 1995), 153.
87. According to Jan Rüger, the war "offered vast opportunities to the entrepreneurs of popular entertainment" and "accelerated the formation of an urban entertainment industry that had begun in the pre-war decades"; Jan Rüger, "Entertainments," in *Capital Cities at War* II, 108. The number of cinemas in Warsaw is taken from Dunin-Wąsowicz, *Warszawa w czasie pierwszej wojny światowej*, 222.
88. Jahn, 154.
89. "Warsztaty demoralizacji," *Kurjer Warszawski* 133 (15 May 1915, aft. ed.): 3.
90. "Walka z zarazą kinematograficzną," *Kurjer Warszawski* 169 (21 June 1915, aft. ed.): 2.
91. "W sprawie kinematografów," *Kurjer Warszawski* 174 (26 June 1915, aft. ed.): 4.
92. APW KOMW 3, protocol no. 189 of 6 August 1915.
93. "Z Rady miejskiej," *Nowa Gazeta* 189 (20 April 1917, morn. ed.): 2.
94. "Gospodarka miejska," *Kurjer Polski* 144 (30 May 1917): 5.
95. Dunin-Wąsowicz, *Warszawa w czasie pierwszej wojny światowej*, 218.
96. "Zamknięcie kabaretów," *Kurjer Warszawski* 346 (15 December 1914, aft. ed.): 4.
97. Harold B. Segel, "Culture in Poland during World War I," in *European Culture in the Great War: The Arts, Entertainment and Propaganda*, ed. Aviel Roshwald and Richard Stites (Cambridge: Cambridge University Press, 2002), 71–72.
98. "Kronika," 506.
99. Ibid., 498; "Kabarety przedwojennej Warszawy (1910–1939)," accessed 22 February 2016, http://culture.pl/pl/artykul/kabarety-przedwojennej-warszawy-1910-1939.
100. Segel, 77.
101. Ibid., 77–79.
102. "Kronika," 513.
103. Pryłucki, 62. According to Kalman Weiser, Prylucki deplored vaudeville, often imported from American Yiddish theater, which violated his notion of a sophisticated Yiddish stage representing high art on a European scale; Weiser, 111–12.
104. "Kronika," 504–5.
105. "Życie nocne Warszawy," *Godzina Polski* 352 (23 December 1917, morn. ed.): 4.
106. APW ZMW 1, protocol no. 57 of 28 December 1917.
107. "Kronika," 523.
108. "Chodzimy boso," *Godzina Polski* 164 (18 June 1918, aft. ed.): 2–3.
109. Stanisław Hiszpański, "Drewniaki," *Kurjer Warszawski* 227 (17 August 1916, aft. ed.): 2.
110. "Boso albo w trepach," *Godzina Polski* 120 (4 May 1918, aft. ed.): 2; "Drewniaki," *Kurjer Warszawski* 93 (4 April 1918, aft. ed.): 2.
111. Irena Krzywicka, during the war a young socialist activist, later recalled that before 1914 the workers' "uniform" included calf-length boots; Krzywicka, 71.
112. Catherine Rollet, "The Home and Family Life," *Capital Cities at War* II, 332.
113. "Brak skór," *Kurjer Warszawski* 12 (12 January 1915, aft. ed.): 2.

114. Kraushar, 11–12.

115. "Na widnokręgu. Przeciw spekulacji," *Nowa Gazeta* 355 (22 July 1917, morn. ed.): 1; and "Obuwie," *Nowa Gazeta* 384 (7 August 1917, morn. ed.): 2.

116. "Miejska fabryka obuwia," *Godzina Polski* 31 (31 January 1918, morn. ed.): 4; "Miejska fabryka obuwia," *Kurjer Warszawski* 113 (25 April 1918, morn. ed.): 2.

117. These cards, however, were issued in small quantities to privilege city workers and student youth; "Obuwie za kartkami," *Kurjer Warszawski* 37 (6 February 1918, aft. ed.): 3.

118. "Napływ obuwia," *Kurjer Warszawski* 215 (6 August 1918, aft. ed.): 3.

119. "Strejk akademicki," *Rząd i Wojsko* 17 (10 May 1917): 8; "Wygnanie akademików z Warszawy," *Kiliński* (July 1917): 16.

120. Tomaszewski, 277; "Zbrodnia!" *Kiliński* (July 1917): 13.

121. "Demonstracje," *Komunikat Informacyjny* 42 (23 July 1917): 2.

122. "Nowa forma rabunku," *Godzina Polski* 74 (16 March 1918, aft. ed.): 2.

123. "Inicjator chodzenia boso," *Kurjer Warszawski* 186 (8 July 1917): 7.

124. "Chodzenie boso," *Kurjer Warszawski* 200 (22 July 1917): 5.

125. "Chodzenie boso," *Kurjer Warszawski* 230 (21 August 1917, morn. ed.): 1.

126. AAN AD 9, "Zamknięcię Wydziału Oświęcenia" (copy of press release announcing the dissolution of the Education Department on 17 February 1916 by decision of the Warsaw Citizens Committee), and 11, Appeal of the Warsaw University Faculty Senate to Students of 20 February 1916. Students at both institutions, having voted against a strike, approved instead the issuing of formal letters of protest.

127. Hutten-Czapski, "Strajk akademicki w 1917 roku," in *Warszawa w pamiętnikach*, 408–18. Hutten-Czapski, as a "Polish" representative of the German civil administration, served in the position of curator and sought unsuccessfully to negotiate with the students through the rectors. According to Hutten-Czapski, even Piłsudski was unable to get the students to change their position.

128. "Wygnanie akademików z Warszawy," 16.

129. "Bosonóżki i bosonodzy," *Kurjer Warszawski* 199 (21 July 1917, morn. ed.): 3.

130. "Chodzenie boso," *Kurjer Warszawski* 200 (22 July 1917): 5.

131. "W kwestii t.zw. bosonóżek," *Nowa Gazeta* 370 (30 July 1917, aft. ed.): 1–2.

132. "Chodzenie boso," *Kurjer Warszawski* 118 (30 April 1918, aft. ed.): 3.

133. For more on professional and employment patterns among Poles and Jews before the First World War, see Corrsin, *Warsaw*, 51–64.

134. "Rzemiosła w Warszawie," *Kurjer Warszawski* 98 (8 April 1917): 3–4.

135. They also ignored the proposal of the Union of Jewish Merchants that the city purchase finished shoes from neutral countries at considerably lower prices in order to fight against inflation and speculation; "O tańsze obuwie," *Kurjer Warszawski* 170 (22 June 1917, morn. ed.): 1.

136. "Drożyna skór a szewcy," *Godzina Polski* 161 (15 August 1917): 5.

137. "Chodzenie boso," *Kurjer Warszawski* 230 (21 August 1917, morn. ed.): 1.

138. "Warszawa bez butów," *Kurjer Warszawski* 230 (21 August 1917, aft. ed.): 2.

139. "Dlaczego buty są drogie," *Gazeta Poranna 2 grosze* 116 (2 April 1918): 3.

140. Krzywicka, 72.

141. Zieliński, *Stosunki*, 311.

142. Ibid., 364.

143. "Pochód bosonogich," *Nowa Gazeta* 410 (21 August 1917, aft. ed.): 2.

144. Zieliński, *Stosunki*, 404.

145. W. Perzyński, "Warszawa na piechotę," *Tygodnik Illustrowany* 30 (28 July 1917): 371.

146. Kutrzeba, 48.

147. "W kwestii t.zw. bosonóżek," *Nowa Gazeta* 370 (30 July 1917, aft. ed.): 1–2. In publishing Drozdowska's letter, the newspaper's editors remarked, "It is difficult to deny that it contains a good deal of truth." Drozdowska's letter also appeared as "W sprawie chodzenia boso," *Kurjer Warszawski* 201 (1 August 1917, morn. ed.): 3.

148. "Związek bosochodów," *Kurjer Warszawski* 197 (18 July 1917, morn. ed.): 2.

149. "Listy do Redakcyi," *Nowa Gazeta* 374 (1 August 1917, aft. ed.): 4. The relationship between Fornalski and Bratnia Pomoc is somewhat murky. He doesn't appear to have been a member, but his solo performances on Aleje Ujazdowskie certainly inspired the students in "Bratniak" to take up the cause. A year later, Fornalski seemed to be marching to a different drummer that went well beyond the issues of shoes in his efforts to create a new aesthetics.

150. "Boso," *Kurjer Warszawski* 204 (26 July 1917): 2.

151. "Chodzenie boso," *Kurjer Warszawski* 217 (8 August 1917, aft. ed.): 3. Despite its early misgivings about the movement, *Nowa Gazeta* also published the appeal; see "Chodźcie boso," *Nowa Gazeta* 390 (10 August 1917, morn. ed.): 2.

152. "Boso albo w trepach," *Gazeta Polski* 120b (4 May 1918, aft. ed.): 2.

153. "Chodzimy boso," *Gazeta Polski* 164b (18 July 1918, aft. ed.): 2–3.

154. The increase in the proportion of women students in various European capitals during the war was seldom welcome, and fears of the feminization of higher education and a decline in intellectual standards were particularly characteristic of Berlin and Paris; see Elizabeth Fordham, "Universities," in *Capital Cities at War* II, 260.

155. "W kwestii t. zw. bosonóżek," *Nowa Gazeta* 370 (30 July 1917, aft. ed.): 1–2.

156. "Gorsząca moda," *Kurjer Warszawski* 244 (3 September 1916, aft. ed.): 4.

157. "Praca urzędniczek," *Godzina Polski* 195b (19 July 1918, aft. ed.): 2.

158. Winter, "The Practices of Metropolitan Life," 12.

159. Svetlana Boym, *The Future of Nostalgia* (New York: Basic Books, 2001), 55.

160. The Barefoot Movement of the First World War, especially in its farcical street performances and avoidance of explicitly political protest, bears a striking resemblance to the social movements of the 1980s in Poland and Central Europe examined by Padraic Kenney, *A Carnival of Revolution: Central Europe 1989* (Princeton: Princeton University Press, 2002).

CONCLUSION: A MINOR APOCALYPSE

1. Timothy Snyder, *Bloodlands: Europe Between Hitler and Stalin* (New York: Basic Books, 2010).

2. Brian Porter-Szűcs, *Poland in the Modern World: Beyond Martyrdom* (Hoboken, NJ: Wiley-Blackwell), 70, 144.

3. Melissa Feinberg, "Dumplings and Domesticity: Women, Collaboration, and Resistance in the Protectorate of Bohemia and Moravia," in *Gender and War*, 104.

4. Dunin-Wąsowicz, *Warszawa w czasie pierwszej wojny światowej*, 82–84.

5. Berlin's population of more than 2 million before the war declined by 389,000, or nearly 19%, by December 1917, with many deaths related to the virtual famine in the city of the winter of 1916–17 as mortality rates among civilians climbed to three to five times higher than those prevailing among military personnel. However, Berlin's population again began to rise in 1918 and by October 1919 had already made up half of its losses, whereas Warsaw's population continued to decline to the end of the war; Das Amt für Statistik Berlin-Brandenburg, accessed 2 November 2011, http://www.statistik-berlin-brandenburg.de/pms/2011/11-02-04.pdf.

6. Dobson, 186; Healy, *Vienna*, 41, 216.

7. The destruction of documents is described by one of its participants, Hutten-Czapski, "Ostatnie dni okupacji niemieckiej w Warszawie," in *Warszawa w pamietnikach*, 478–80.

8. Kamińska, 145–46; see also M. Jankowski, "11 listopada 1918 roku," in *Warszawa w pamiętnikach*, 486.

9. Adam Grzymała Siedliecki, "Rosya a Polacy," *Tygodnik Illustrowany* 48 (28 November 1914): 768.

10. Jan z Marnowa, "Warszawa, d. 11 Listopada 1918 r.," *Tygodnik Illustrowany* 46 (16 November 1914): 532; Lubomirska, 629.

11. Indeed, it is telling that the most recent general history of Poland during the First World War is that by Jerzy Holzer and Jan Molenda, *Polska w pierwszej wojny światowej* (Warsaw: Wiedza Powszechna, 1973), itself a second and expanded edition of the original 1963 publication that focuses primarily on the political and military history of the war—in other words, on the twists and turns of the "Polish question."

12. AAN AD 6.

13. Without a doubt the most spectacular act of retaliatory terror carried out by the PPS was the assassination of the German Political Police Chief Dr. Erich Schultz on 1 October 1918, which was quickly followed by the assassination of two police inspectors. For competing accounts of these assassinations, see Antoni Purtal, "Zamach na naczelnika niemieckiego policji politicznej, Dr. Ericha Schultzego w Warszawie," and Marian Malinowski, "W sprawie zamuchu na Szulcego," both in *Warszawa w pamiętnikach*, 447–56 and 457–62, respectively.

14. Lubomirska, 673, 690.

15. Dunin-Wąsowicz, *Warszawa w czasie pierwszej wojny światowej*, 72.

16. AGAD SAGGW 5, Vierteljahrschaftsbericht des Verwaltungschefts bei dem General-Gouvernement Warschau für die Zeit vom 1. Januar 1916 bis zum 31. März 1916.

17. AGAD CNGGW 1, Report of Beseler of 23 October 1915.

18. Dunin-Wąsowicz, 211.

19. Weiser, 139.

20. APW RGN 2. A partial list of clubs and organizations participating in the 3 May celebration can be found in the files of the editorial board of *Nowa Gazeta*. The list does not account for participants from registered political parties and organizations, as well as academic and youth organizations.

21. Kutrzeba, 52–55.

22. APW ZMW 1, protocol no. 50 of 22 November 1918.

Bibliography

NEWSPAPERS AND PERIODICALS

Bluszcz
Chwila Świąteczna
Gazeta Świąteczna
Gazeta Poranna 2 grosze
Głos Żydowski
Godzina Polski
Kiliński
Komunikat Informacyjny
Kurjer Polski
Kurjer Warszawski
Myśl Niepodległa
Nowa Gazeta
Przegląd Poranny
Rozwaga
Rząd i Wojsko
Słowo Żydowskie
Tygodnik Illustrowany
Varshavskii Dnevnik
Wiadomości Polskie

PUBLISHED PRIMARY SOURCES

Ansky, S. *The Enemy at His Pleasure: A Journey through the Jewish Pale of Settlement during World War I*. Edited and translated by Joachim Neugroschel. New York: Metropolitan Books, 2002.

Bielski, Rafał. *Było takie miasto: Warszawa na starych pocztówkach*. Warsaw: Agencja Wydawnicza Veda, 2008.

Brzoza, Czesław, ed. *Żydowska mozaika polityczna w Polsce 1917–1927: Wybór dokumentów*. Kraków: Księgarnia Akademicka, 2003.

Dunin-Wąsowicz, Krzysztof, ed. *Warszawa w pamiętnikach pierwszej wojny światowej*. Warsaw: Państwowy Instytut Wydawniczy, 1971.

Dzierzbicki, Stanisław. *Pamiętnik z lat wojny 1915–1918*. Warsaw: Państwowy Instytut Wydawniczy, 1983.

Dzikowski, Stanisław. *Rok wojny w Warszawie. Notatki*. Kraków: Nakładem Centralnego Biura Wydawnictw N.K.N., 1916.

Głodowska-Sampolska, Władysława. *Czerwony zorze. Wspomnienia*. Warsaw: Książka i Wiedza, 1965.

Grabski, Władysław, and Antoni Żabko-Potopowicz. *Ratownictwo społeczne w czasie wojny*. Warsaw: Towarzystwo Badania Zagadnień Międzynarodowych, 1932.

Jankowski, Czesław. *Z dnia na dzień. Warszawa 1914–1915 Wilno*. Wilno: Wydawnictwo Kazimierza Rutskiego, 1923.

Jarkowski, Stanisław. *Prasa warszawska od d. 5 XI 1916 do d. 1 III 1919*. Warsaw: Szkład
    Główny w Księgarni Gebethnera i Wolffa, 1921.
——. *Prasa warszawska od początku sierpnia 1914 do końca grudnia 1915*. Warsaw:
    Zakł. Graf. B. Wierzbicki i S-ka, 1916.
Kamińska, Maria. *Ścieżkami wspomnien*. Warsaw: Książka i Wiedza, 1960.
Kumaniecki, Kazimierz-Władysław. "Stosunki robotnicze w czasie wojny." In *Polska
    w czasie wielki wojny (1914–1918). Historja społeczna i ekonomiczna 2: Historja
    społeczna*. Edited by Marceli Handelsman. Warsaw: Towarzystwo Badania
    Zagadnień Międzynarodowych, 1932.
Kraushar, Aleksander. *Warszawa podczas okupacji niemieckiej 1915–1918: Notatki naocznego
    świadka*. Lwów: Wydawnictwo Zakładu Narodowego im. Ossolińskich, 1921.
Kutrzeba, Stanisław. *Królestwo i Galicya: Uwagi z czasu wojny*. Warsaw: Towarzystwo
    Wydawnicze w Warszawie, 1917.
Krzywicka, Irena. *Wyznania gorszycielki*. Edited by Agata Tuszyńska. Warsaw:
    Czytelnik, 1992.
Lubomirska, Maria. *Pamiętnik księżnej Marii Zdzisławowej Lubomirskiej, 1914–1918*.
    Edited by Jerzy Pajewski. Poznań: Wydawnictwo Poznańskie, 1997.
Pryłucki, Nojach. *Mowy wygłoszone w pierwszej Radzie Miejskiej st. m. Warszawy, w b.
    Radzie Stanu Król. Polsk., w Sejmie Ustawodawczym Rzeczypospolitej Polskiej 1*.
    Warsaw: Nakładem Rady Centralnej Żydowskiego Stronnictwa Ludowego w
    Polsce, 1920.
Singer, Bernard. *Moje Nalewki*. Warsaw: Czytelnik, 1959.
*Weg-Weiser durch Warschau: Kurzgefasster Führer durch die Stadt Warschau mit besonderer
    Berücksichtigung alles dessen, was der deutsche Soldat, Beamte und Reisende wissen
    muss*. 4th revised edition. Warsaw: Verlag der Deutschen Staatsdruckerei, 1917.

INTERNET SOURCES

Das Amt für Statistik Berlin-Brandenburg. Accessed 2 November 2011. http://www.
    statistik-berlin-brandenburg.de/pms/2011/11-02-04.pdf.
Brandow-Faller, Megan. "Cultures at War: Austria-Hungary 1914–1918 (St. Hilda's
    College, Oxford, 13–15 April 2011)." Accessed 14 June 2011. https://
    networks.h-net.org/habsburg.
"A Joint Effort: JDC's Beginnings, 1914–1921." Accessed 8 May 2015. http://archives.
    jdc.org/exhibits/a-joint-effort/.
"Kabarety przedwojennej Warszawy (1910–1939)." Accessed 22 February 2016. http://
    culture.pl/artykul/kabarety-przedwojennej-warszawy-1910-1939.
Ministerstwo Obrony Narodowy. "Grób Nieznanego Żołnierza." Accessed 9 July 2013.
    http://wojsko-polskie.pl/articles/view/3109.
"Zanim powstał tor na Służewcu." Accessed 8 May 2015. http://torsluzewiec.pl/
    historia-toru/.

BOOKS AND ARTICLES

Aschheim, Steven E. *Brothers and Strangers: The East European Jews in German and
    German-Jewish Consciousness, 1800–1923*. Madison: The University of Wisconsin
    Press, 1982.
Assmann, Jan. *Cultural Memory and Early Civilization: Writing, Remembrance, and
    Political Imagination*. Cambridge: Cambridge University Press, 2011.
Audoin-Rouzeau, Stéphane, and Annette Becker. *14–18: Understanding the Great War*.
    Translated by Catherine Temerson. New York: Hill and Wang, 2002.
Bacon, Gershon. *The Politics of Tradition: Agudat Yisrael in Poland, 1916–1939*.
    Jerusalem: Magnes Press, 1996.

Baron, Nick, and Peter Gatrell, eds. *Homelands: War, Population and Statehood in Eastern Europe and Russia*. London: Anthem Press, 2004.
Barry, John M. *The Great Influenza: The Epic Story of the Deadliest Plague in History*. New York: Penguin, 2004.
Bauerkämper, Arnd, and Elise Julien, eds. *Durchhalten! Krieg und Gesellschaft in Vergleich 1914–1918*. Göttingen: Vandenhoeck and Ruprecht, 2010.
Bergman, Eleonora. "Żydzi uchodźcy w Warszawie w 1915 r." In *Parlamentaryzm, konserwatyzm, nacjonalizm. Studia ofiarowane Profesorowi Szymonowi Rudnickiemu*, 171–77. Edited by Jolanta Żyndul. Warsaw: Wydawnictwo Sejmowe, 2010.
Berkowitz, Michael. *The Crime of My Very Existence: Nazism and the Myth of Jewish Criminality*. Berkeley: University of California Press, 2007.
Blobaum, Robert, ed. *Antisemitism and Its Opponents in Modern Poland*. Ithaca, NY: Cornell University Press, 2005.
——. "A City in Flux: Warsaw's Transient Populations during the First World War." *The Polish Review* 59, no. 4 (2014): 21–43.
——. "Going Barefoot in Warsaw during the First World War." *East European Politics, Societies and Cultures* 27, no. 2 (May 2013): 187–204.
——. "Królestwo Polskie między rewolucją i wojną: Może nie było aż tak źle?" *Historyka: Studia metodologiczne* 28 (1998): 139–46.
——. "The Politics of Antisemitism in Fin-de-Siècle Warsaw." *The Journal of Modern History*, 73, no. 2 (June 2001): 275–306.
——. *Rewolucja: Russian Poland, 1904–1907*. Ithaca, NY: Cornell University Press, 1995.
——. "A Warsaw Story: Polish-Jewish Relations during the First World War." In *Warsaw. The Jewish Metropolis: Essays in Honor of the 75th Birthday of Professor Antony Polonsky*, 271–96. Edited by Glenn Dynner and François Guesnet. Leiden: Brill, 2015.
——. "Warsaw's Forgotten War." *Remembrance and Solidarity: Studies in 20th-Century European History*, no. 2: *First World War Centenary* (March 2014): 185–207.
Blobaum, Robert, and Donata Blobaum. "A Different Kind of Home Front: War, Gender and Propaganda in Warsaw, 1914–1918." In *Propaganda and World War I*, 249–72. Edited by Troy Paddock. Leiden: Brill, 2014.
Boym, Svetlana. *The Future of Nostalgia*. New York: Basic Books, 2001.
Brykczynski, Paul. *Primed for Violence: Murder, Antisemitism, and Democratic Politics in Interwar Poland*. Madison: University of Wisconsin Press, 2016.
Chickering, Roger. *The Great War and Urban Life in Germany: Freiburg, 1914–1918*. Cambridge: Cambridge University Press, 2007.
Chwalba, Andrzej. *Imperium korupcji w Rosji i w Królestwie Polskiim w latach 1861–1917*. Krakow: Universitas, 1995.
——. *Polacy w służbie Moskali*. Warsaw: Wydawnictwo Naukowe PWN, 1999.
Corrsin, Stephen D. "Polish-Jewish Relations before the First World War: The Case of the State Duma Elections in Warsaw." *Gal-Ed: On the History of the Jews in Poland* 11 (1989): 31–53.
——. *Warsaw before the First World War: Poles and Jews in the Third City of the Russian Empire, 1880–1914*. Boulder, CO: East European Monographs, 1989.
Davis, Belinda J. *Home Fires Burning: Food, Politics and Everyday Life in World War I Berlin*. Chapel Hill: The University of North Carolina Press, 2000.
Dobson, Sean. *Authority and Upheaval in Leipzig, 1910–1920*. New York: Columbia University Press, 2001.
Drozdowski, M. M. *Warszawa w latach 1914–1939*. Warsaw: PWN, 1990.
Dufrat, Joanna. "Ligi Kobiet Królestwa, Galicji i Śląska. Próba politycznej aktywizacji kobiet w okresie I wojny świątowej." In *Działaczki społeczne, feministki, obywatelki. Samo-*

organizowanie się kobiet na ziemiach polskich do 1918 roku (na tle porównaczym) 1, 113–30. Edited by Agnieszka Janiak-Jasińska, Katarzyna Sierakowska, and Andrzej Szwarc. Warsaw: Wydawnictwo Neriton, 2008.

Dunin-Wąsowicz, Krzysztof. *Warszawa w czasie pierwszej wojny światowej.* Warsaw: Państwowe Instytut Naukowej, 1974.

——. *Warszawa w latach 1939–1945.* Warsaw: Państwowe Wydawnictwo Naukowe, 1984.

Engel, Barbara Alpern. "Not by Bread Alone: Subsistence Riots in Russia during World War I." *The Journal of Modern History* 96, no. 4 (December 1997): 696–721.

Engelstein, Laura. "'A Belgium of Our Own': The Sack of Russian Kalisz, August 1914." *Kritika: Explorations in Russian and Eurasian History* 10, no. 3 (Summer 2009): 441–73.

Fuller, William C., Jr. *The Foe Within: Fantasies of Treason and the End of Imperial Russia.* Ithaca, NY: Cornell University Press, 2006.

Ganzenmüller, Jörg. *Russische Staatsgewalt und polnischer Adel: Elitenintegration und Staatsausbau im Westen des Zarenreiches (1772–1850).* Cologne: Böhlau Verlag, 2012.

Garncarska, Bina. "The Material and Social Situation of the Jewish Population of Warsaw between 1862 and 1914." *Gal-Ed: On the History of the Jews of Poland* 1 (1973): xiii–xiv.

Gatrell, Peter. *Russia's First World War: A Social and Economic History.* Harlow, UK: Pearson, 2005.

——. "Tsarist Russia at War: The View from Above, 1914-February, 1917." *Journal of Modern History* 87, no. 3 (September 2015): 688–700.

——. *A Whole Empire Walking: Refugees in Russia during World War I.* Bloomington: Indiana University Press, 1999.

Golczewski, Frank. *Polnische-Jüdische Beziehungen, 1881–1922.* Wiesbaden: Franz Steiner Verlag, 1981.

Graf, Daniel. "Military Rule behind the Russian Front, 1914–1917." *Jahrbücher für Geschichte Osteuropas* 22 (1974): 390–411.

Grill, Tobias. "The Politicisation of Traditional Polish Jewry: Orthodox German Rabbis and the Founding of *Agudas Ho-Ortodksim* and *Dos yidishe vort* in Gouvernement-General Warsaw, 1916–1918." *East European Jewish Affairs* 39, no. 2 (August 2009): 227–47.

Gross, Jan Tomasz. *Polish Society under German Occupation: The Generalgouvernement 1939–1944.* Princeton: Princeton University Press, 1979.

Guesnet, François. "Thinking Globally, Acting Locally: Joel Wegmeister and Modern Hasidic Politics in Warsaw." *Quest. Issues in Contemporary Jewish History* 2 (October 2011).

Guterman, Alexander. "The Congregation of the Great Synagogue in Warsaw: Its Changing Social Composition and Ideological Affiliations." *Polin: Studies in Polish Jewry* 13 (1998): 112–26.

Halbwachs, Maurice. *The Collective Memory.* Translated by Francis J. Ditter and Vida Yazdi Ditter. New York: Harper, 1980.

Healy, Maureen. *Vienna and the Fall of the Habsburg Empire: Total War and Everyday Life in World War I.* Cambridge: Cambridge University Press, 2004.

Hertz, Aleksander. *The Jews in Polish Culture.* Translated by Richard Lourie. Evanston, IL: Northwestern University Press, 1988.

Holzer, Jerzy, and Jan Molenda. *Polska w pierwszej wojnie światowej.* Warsaw: Wiedza Powszechna, 1963.

Jahn, Hubertus F. *Patriotic Culture in Russia during World War I.* Ithaca, NY: Cornell University Press, 1995.

Jedlicki, Jerzy. "The End of the Dialogue: Warsaw, 1907–1912." In *The Jews in Poland 2,* 111–23. Edited by Sławomir Kapralski. Krakow: Judaica Foundation, 1999.

Kacperski, Kamil. *System wyborczy do Sejmu i Senatu w progu Drugiej Rzeczypospolitej.* Warsaw: Wydawnictwo Sejmowe, 2007.

Kauffman, Jesse. *Elusive Alliance: The German Occupation of Poland in World War I.* Cambridge, MA: Harvard University Press, 2015.

Kavanagh, Gaynor. "Museum as Memorial: The Origins of the Imperial War Museum." *Journal of Contemporary History* 23, no. 1 (January, 1988): 77–97.

Kozińska-Witt, Hanna. *Krakau in Warschaus langem Schatten: Konkurrenzkämpfe in der polnischen Städtelandschaft 1900–1939.* Stuttgart: Franz Steiner Verlag, 2008.

Kramer, Alan. *Dynamic of Destruction: Culture and Mass Killing in the First World War.* Oxford: Oxford University Press, 2007.

Kratko, Zalman. "The Jewish Trade Union Movement in Congress Poland in the First World War." *Gal-Ed: On the History of the Jews of Poland* 2 (1975): xii–xiv.

Królikowski, Lech, and Krzysztof Oktabiński. *Warszawa 1914–1920: Warszawa i okolice w latach walk o niepodległość i granice Rzeczypospolitej.* Warsaw: Wydawnictwo Akademickie i Profesjonalne, 2008.

Kuźma-Markowska, Sylvia. "Soldiers, Members of Parliament, Social Activists: The Polish Women's Movement after World War I." In *Aftermaths of War: Women's Movements and Female Activists, 1918–1923,* 265–86. Edited by Ingrid Sharp and Matthew Stibbe. Leiden: Brill, 2011.

Levine, Hillel. *Economic Origins of Antisemitism: Poland and Its Jews in the Early Modern Poland.* New Haven, CT: Yale University Press, 1991.

Lih, Lars. *Bread and Authority in Russia, 1914–1917.* Berkeley: University of California Press, 1990.

Lindenmeyr, Adele. *Poverty Is Not a Vice: Charity, Society, and the State in Late Imperial Russia.* Princeton: Princeton University Press, 1996.

Liulevicius, Vejas Gabriel. *War Land on the Eastern Front: Culture, National Identity and German Occupation in World War I.* Cambridge: Cambridge University Press, 2000.

Lohr, Eric. *Nationalizing the Russian Empire: The Campaign Against Enemy Aliens during World War I.* Cambridge, MA: Harvard University Press, 2003.

——. "The Russian Army and the Jews: Mass Deportation, Hostages and Violence during World War I." *The Russian Review* 60 (July 2001): 404–19.

Mendelsohn, Ezra. *Zionism in Poland: The Formative Years, 1915–1926.* New Haven, CT: Yale University Press, 1981.

Mich, Włodzimierz. *Związek Ziemian w Warszawie (1916–1926). Organizacja i wpływy.* Lublin: Wydawnictwo UMCS, 2007.

Mick, Christoph. *Kriegserfahrungen in einer multiethnicshen Stadt: Lemberg 1914–1947.* Wiesbaden: Harrassowitz Verlag, 2010.

Morgernstern, Matthias. *From Frankfurt to Jerusalem: Isaac Breuer and the History of the Secessionist Dispute in Modern Jewish Orthodoxy.* Leiden: Brill Studies in European Judaism, 2002.

Nora, Pierre. *Rethinking France: Les Lieux de Mémoire.* 2 volumes. Chicago: The University of Chicago Press, 2001, 2006.

Opalski, Magdalena, and Israel Bartal. *Poles and Jews: A Failed Brotherhood.* Hanover, NH: Brandeis University Press, 1992.

Petrone, Karen. *The Great War in Russian Memory.* Bloomington: Indiana University Press, 2011.

Pływawko, Danuta. *Polonia Devastata: Polonia i Amerykanie z pomocą dla Polski (1914–1918).* Poznań: Wydawnictwo Poznańskie, 2003.

Polsakiewicz, Marta. "Spezifika deutscher Besatzungspolitik in Warschau 1914–1916." *Zeitschrift für Ostmitteleuropa-Forschung* 58, no. 4 (2009): 501–37.

——. *Warschau im ersten Weltkrieg: Deutsche Besatzungspolitik zwischen kultereller Autonomie und wirtschaftlicher Ausbeutung.* Marburg: Verlag Herder Institut, 2015.

Porter, Brian. *When Nationalism Began to Hate: Imagining Politics in Nineteenth-Century Poland.* New York: Oxford University Press, 2000.

Porter-Szűcs, Brian. *Poland in the Modern World: Beyond Martyrdom.* Hoboken, NJ: Wiley-Blackwell, 2014.

Prusin, Alexander Victor. *Nationalizing a Borderland: War, Ethnicity, and Anti-Jewish Violence in East Galicia, 1914–1920.* Tuscaloosa: University of Alabama Press, 2005.

Rachaminov, Alon. *POWs and the Great War: Captivity on the Eastern Front.* New York: Berg Publishers, 2002.

Rechter, David. *The Jews of Vienna and the First World War.* London: The Littman Library of Jewish Civilization, 2001.

Sammartino, Annemarie H. *The Impossible Border: Germany and the East, 1914–1922.* Ithaca, NY: Cornell University Press, 2012.

Sanborn, Joshua. *Imperial Apocalypse: The Great War and the Destruction of the Russian Empire.* Oxford: Oxford University Press, 2014.

——. "Unsettling the Empire: Violent Migrations and Social Disaster in Russia during World War I." *The Journal of Modern History* 77, no. 5 (June 2005): 290–324.

Schuster, Frank. *Zwischen allen Fronten: Osteuropäische Juden während des Ersten Weltkrieges (1914–1919).* Cologne: Böhlau Verlag Köln, 2004.

Segel, Harold B. "Culture in Poland during World War I." In *European Culture in the Great War: The Arts, Entertainment and Propaganda,* 58–88. Edited by Aviel Roshwald and Richard Stites. Cambridge: Cambridge University Press, 2002.

Sierakowska, Katarzyna. *Śmierć-wygnanie-głód: Ziemia polskie w latach Wielkiej Wojny 1914–1918.* Warsaw: Neriton, 2015.

Snyder, Timothy. *Bloodlands: Europe Between Hitler and Stalin.* New York: Basic Books, 2010.

Sobolev, Ivan G. *Borba s "nemetskim zasilem" v Rossii v gody pervoi mirovoi voiny.* St. Petersburg University dissertation, 1998.

Spät, Robert M. "Für eine gemeinsame deutsch-polnische Zukunft? Hans Hartwig von Beseler als Generalgouverneur in Polen, 1915–1918." *Zeitschrift für Ostmitteleuropa-Forschung* 58, no. 4 (2009): 501–37.

Stauter-Halsted, Keely. *The Devil's Chain: Prostitution and Social Control in Partitioned Poland.* Ithaca, NY: Cornell University Press, 2015.

Steinlauf, Michael. "The Polish-Jewish Daily Press." *Polin: A Journal of Polish-Jewish Studies* 2 (1987): 219–45.

Sukiennicki, Wiktor. *East-Central Europe during World War I: From Domination to National Independence* 2. Boulder, CO: East European Monographs, 1984.

Szarota, Tomasz. *Okupowaniej Warszawy dzień powszedni. Studium historyczny.* Warsaw: Czytelnik, 1973.

Tauber, Joachim, ed. *Über den Weltkrieg hinaus: Kriegserfahrungen in Ostmitteleuropa,* Nordost-Archiv Zeitschrift für Regionalgeschichte. Neue Folge Band XVII/2008. Lüneberg: Nordost-Institut, 2009.

Tucker, Erica L. *Remembering Occupied Warsaw: Polish Narratives of World War II.* Dekalb: Northern Illinois University Press, 2011.

Trouillot, Michel-Rolph. *Silencing the Past: Power and the Production of History.* Boston: Beacon Press, 1995.

Ury, Scott. *Barricades and Banners: The Revolution of 1905 and the Transformation of Warsaw Jewry*. Stanford, CA: Stanford University Press, 2012.

Van Cant, Katrin. "Historical Memory in Post-Communist Poland: Warsaw's Monuments after 1989." *Studies in Slavic Cultures* 8 (2009): 90–119.

Vladimirov, Katya. *The World of Provincial Bureaucracy in Late 19th and 20th Century Russian Poland*. Lewiston, NY: Edwin Mellen Press, 2004.

Wapiński, Roman. "Władysław Sikorski." *Polski Słownik Biograficzny* 37, 3, no. 154 (1997): 468–78.

Weeks, Theodore R. *From Assimilation to Antisemitism: The "Jewish Question" in Poland, 1850–1914*. Dekalb: Northern Illinois University Press, 2006.

——. "Fanning the Flames: Jews in the Warsaw Press, 1905–1912." *East European Jewish Affairs* 28, no. 2 (Winter 1998–1999): 63–81.

——. *Nation and State in Late Imperial Russia: Nationalism and Russification on the Western Frontier, 1863–1914*. Dekalb: Northern Illinois University Press, 1996.

——. "Nationality and Municipality: Reforming City Government in the Kingdom of Poland, 1904–1915." *Russian History* 21, no. 1 (1994): 23–47.

——. "Polish 'Progressive Antisemitism,' 1905–1914." *East European Jewish Affairs* 25, no. 2 (1995): 49–68.

Weiser, Kalman (Keith). *Noah Prylucki and the Folkists in Poland*. Toronto: University of Toronto Press, 2011.

Wertheimer, Jack. *Unwelcome Strangers: East European Jews in Imperial Germany*. New York: Oxford University Press, 1987.

Westerhoff, Christian. *Zwangsarbeit im Ersten Weltkrieg: Deutsche Arbeitskräftepolitik in besetzen Polen und Litauen 1914–1918*. Paderborn: Ferdinand Schöningh, 2012.

Wingfield, Nancy M., and Maria Bucur, eds. *Gender and War in Twentieth-Century Eastern Europe*. Bloomington: Indiana University Press, 2006.

Winter, Jay, and Jean-Louis Robert, eds. *Capital Cities at War: Paris, London, Berlin 1914–1919*. 2 volumes. Cambridge: Cambridge University Press, 1997 and 2007.

Wróbel, Piotr. "Jewish Warsaw before the First World War." *Polin: A Journal of Polish-Jewish Studies* 3 (1988): 156–87.

——. "Przed odzyskaniem niepodległości." In *Najnowsze dzieje Żydów w Polsce w zarysie (do 1950 r.)*, 11–139. Edited by Jerzy Tomaszewski. Warsaw: PWN, 1993.

Wyszczelski, Lech. *Warszawa Listopad 1918*. Warsaw: Bellona, 2008.

Żarnowska, Anna. "Social Change, Women and the Family in the Era of Industrialization: Recent Polish Research." Translated by Robert Blobaum. *Journal of Family History* 22, no. 2 (1997): 191–203.

Zechlin, Egmont. *Die deutsche Politik und die Juden in Ersten Weltkrieg*. Göttingen: Vandenhoeck u. Ruprecht, 1969.

Zieliński, Konrad. *Stosunki polsko-żydowskie na ziemiach Królestwa Polskiego w czasie pierwszej wojny światowej*. Lublin: Wydawnictwo Uniwersytetu Marii Curie-Skłodowskiej, 2005.

Zimmerman, Joshua D. *The Polish Underground and the Jews, 1939–1945*. New York: Cambridge University Press, 2015.

Index